DATE DUE

FLAGGING PATRIOTISM

FLAGGING PATRIOTISM

Crises of Narcissism and Anti-Americanism

Robert Stam & Ella Shohat

Routledge
Taylor & Francis Group
New York   London

Routledge is an imprint of the
Taylor & Francis Group, an informa business

Routledge
Taylor & Francis Group
270 Madison Avenue
New York, NY 10016

Routledge
Taylor & Francis Group
2 Park Square
Milton Park, Abingdon
Oxon OX14 4RN

© 2007 by Robert Stam & Ella Shohat
Routledge is an imprint of Taylor & Francis Group, an Informa business

Printed in the United States of America on acid-free paper
10 9 8 7 6 5 4 3 2 1

International Standard Book Number-10: 0-415-97922-6 (Softcover) 0-415-97921-8 (Hardcover)
International Standard Book Number-13: 978-0-415-97922-1 (Softcover) 978-0-415-97921-4 (Hardcover)

Visit the Taylor & Francis Web site at
http://www.taylorandfrancis.com

and the Routledge Web site at
http://www.routledge-ny.com

To Stephen Colbert, Janeane Garofalo, Rachel Maddow, Bill Maher, Chris Rock, Jon Stewart, and all the other patriotic clowns who have kept us sane in crazy times

CONTENTS

Acknowledgments

We are grateful to a number of people who contributed to this project in various ways: James H. Stam for his finely tuned and philosophically informed reading of the manuscript; Dana Polan for his witty and knowledgeable commentary; and Jessica Scarlata for her useful suggestions and shrewd analysis of popular culture. Chris Dunn and Richard Porton were also kind enough to read the manuscript, offering insightful and constructive feedback. Patrick Erouart was especially generous in sharing his knowledge of French colonialism and its aftermath, while Daniel Levy, in so many conversations, was thoughtful, sending invaluable materials on Franco-American relations. We are also grateful to Tony Kushner, Alissa Solomon, Moncef Cheikhrouhou, Mark Cohen, Evelyn Alsultany, Shaista Husain, Yigal Nizri, Zillah Eisenstein, and Yvette Raby. We are immensely appreciative of our impeccable and resourceful research assistants Alice Black and Karim Tartoussieh. Finally, we are grateful to all the friends and colleagues—too numerous to mention here—who make New York University an intellectually exciting place to be. It is much easier to keep in touch with intellectual currents in various parts of the world through the fine work being done by diverse programs and centers, including La Maison Française, the Institute of French Studies, Center for Latin American and Caribbean Studies, Hagop Kevorkian Center for Near Eastern Studies, Africa House, Center for European and Mediterranean Studies, Center for Media, Culture and History, Center for Art and Public Policy, The Hemispheric Institute of Performance and Politics, The King Juan Carlos I of Spain Center, Center for the Study of

Gender and Sexuality, and the International Center for Advanced Studies. Finally, we would like to extend our sincerest appreciation to Mary Schmidt Campbell and Randy Martin for their enthusiastic support of this project and for including a portion, titled "Patriotism, Fear, and Artistic Citizenship," in their coedited volume *Artistic Citizenship: A Public Voice for the Arts*.

Preface

Love, Hate, and the Nation-State

*F*lagging Patriotism: Crises of Narcissism and Anti-Americanism
is written at a moment of double crisis for Americans, one external—anti-Americanism—and the other internal—American self-doubt
and division. This book explores the connections between the two crises and the relation of both crises to patriotism. In terms of anti-Americanism, this external crisis has now reached a fever pitch around the
world, leading to the ubiquitous question, "Why do they hate us?" Usually, the question implies, "Why do the Muslims/Arabs hate us?" But
resentment against the United States, due to the Iraq War, has become
virtually universal; it is hardly limited to Arabs/Muslims. Polls show
that majorities in most countries in Europe, Asia, Africa, and Latin
America oppose American foreign policy and the U.S. role as self-
appointed global "leader."[1] Even many Canadians now find the United
States frightening.

This opposition at times takes hyperbolic forms, even in "allied"
spaces like Spain. According to one Spanish writer, Moncho Tamames, anti-Americanism

> is now the principal ideological current in the world. It knows no
> frontiers and is more massive than any social movement in his-
> tory. ... Although Americans, who measure everything through
> the prism of material wealth, like to think it is motivated by envy,
> in fact it is motivated by the atrocities that have accompanied all
> aspects of the emergence of the country and by the cultural colo-
> nialism that they impose on us.[2]

Whether or not one agrees with such judgments, it is important for Americans to know that such things are being said and to weigh the truth or falsity of the claims. The easy, self-flattering answer to the "hate us" question, of course, is that they hate us because they envy our freedom. (Which leaves unexplained why they don't hate other equally free countries such as Canada, Sweden, or Costa Rica.) Indeed, one jocular response to the question was that "they hate us because we are so ignorant that we don't even know *why* they hate us."

In terms of the internal crisis, meanwhile, American self-confidence is quite literally "flagging." Polls show an inchoate sense of disillusionment, with large majorities feeling that "the country is moving in the wrong direction." Americans are less and less convinced that the United States is truly fair or democratic. According to a 1999 poll, only 19 percent believed that the U.S. government served the "interests of all."[3] Two-thirds of respondents in a 2002 Gallup poll believed that "no matter what new laws are passed, special interests will always find a way to maintain their power in Washington."[4] Events such as 9/11, Enron, the Iraq War, and the response to Hurricane Katrina have undermined American self-confidence, leading some Americans to wonder what there is left to love about America. The events of 9/11 posed the question "Why do Islamic fundamentalists hate us?" Then the Iraq War posed the question of whether "preventive war" was legitimate and wise, or a gigantic moral lapse and strategic blunder. Hurricane Katrina, finally, triggered a crisis in self-confidence, as it became clearer and clearer that despite all the bluster about "national security," the government could not, or perhaps would not, protect us in a crisis. The same government that could airlift food to the hungry in Afghanistan, that could mobilize helicopters to rescue downed pilots in Iraq, could not marshal its forces to save the dying in New Orleans.

All the rhetoric about "terror," it turned out, was meant to terrorize *us*. Iraq was not a threat; we invaded Iraq, it became apparent, not because it was strong but because it was weak. In terms of terrorism, meanwhile, almost nothing had been done to make us safe, and in many ways things had gotten worse. While George W. Bush made it a top priority to **talk** about security, he did precious little to actually make us more secure. Katrina posed in the starkest terms the question of the basic contract between a government and its people—the contract to protect citizens. When the levees broke, that basic contract failed. Not only did George W. Bush "not care about black people," as rapper Kanye West put it, but also he did not seem to care about the disaster victims in general. Utterly uncurious, Bush had to be given a DVD of TV reports about the hurricane's impact four days after landfall. While worrying about losing an American city through terrorism, we actually lost a city through neglect and inaction. What, after all, is government for, if not to protect us, and if not during and after a natural disaster, when? And if we cannot collectively protect one another, who are we, and what kind of "us" do we assume or imagine? Shrinking civil liberties, suspect elections results, and the widening inequalities of wealth, meanwhile, led many Americans to wonder about the future of American democracy. The signs of a systemic crisis, in sum, are all around us, and all the flag-waving in the world cannot conjure away that deep crisis of legitimacy.

Flagging Patriotism, then, explores the interconnections between the crisis in American self-love and the crisis in others' attitudes toward us. We go beyond the "hate us" question, however, to also ask other questions, such as "Who are they?" and "Why are they the ones to hate us?" and "What precisely is it that they hate?" and "Why do they love themselves?" and "How is their self-love, or even their self-hatred, connected to their hating us?"

Although many books have been written about anti-Americanism, and many about patriotism, the novelty here is to link the two issues. To our minds, culture and politics in the United States are best understood within an interconnective, transnational framework, involving diverse regions of the world. Knowledge and self-knowledge, in our view, are transcultural. We know ourselves through knowing other people, and we know our own society through knowing other societies. That is why we delve into comparative patriotism and comparative anti-Americanism. Our emphasis is not on simplistic contrasts but rather on interconnectedness both in terms of space—the links between the United States and other regions—and in terms of time—the parallels and connections between various historical moments. Debates in Europe, Latin America, and the Middle East, we will discover, have much to do with debates in the United States, and debates about the past have everything to do with debates about the present.

But the "hate us" question is, in the end, ill posed. The "us" and the "them" division is often unclear, or at least much more complicated than both the American superpatriots and the anti-Americans seem to believe. While the "hate us" discussion has largely involved the Arab/Muslim world, recent times have seen a growing rift between the United States and its allies. Although our discussion will range over many geographies, we will repeatedly draw most of our examples of anti-Americanism from two countries traditionally seen as allies of the United States—France and Brazil. While our choice of countries might seem arbitrary, in fact it is quite plausible. First, apart from the U.S. "mother country" (Great Britain), France and Brazil are the two countries that have elicited the greatest amount of comparative study vis-à-vis the United States. In the case of France, those studies have focused on comparative revolutions, comparative political systems, and comparative social mores, and on anti-Americanism in France and Francophobia in the United States. In the case of Brazil, the comparisons have had to do with the two countries' shared status as settler states in the Americas, whose histories have been marked by European conquest (British and Portuguese), colonialism, slavery, abolition, and immigration. (While most Brazilian intellectuals are aware of the historical parallelism between the two countries, many "United Statesian" intellectuals, regrettably, are not.)

The histories of the three countries have been intermingled for centuries. Some of the first African Americans to arrive in North America came from Africa to New Amsterdam—later New York—via Brazil, just as some of the first Jews came via Portugal and Brazil to found the first synagogue in Manhattan. In terms of the "what ifs" of history, meanwhile, both Brazil and the United States *might have been* French, or at least partly French. France was among the first colonizers in Brazil, but it never managed to expand its tiny sixteenth-century colony ("FrancAntartique") from its base in Rio de Janeiro. And parts of the United States might also have been French. If Napoleon, frightened by the Haitian revolution, had not "sold" the Louisiana Purchase territories (i.e., Native American lands) to the United States, much of what is now the continental United States might have ended up in French hands. Interestingly, Napoleon was also involved in the events that led to Brazilian independence—this time as the frightener rather than as the frightened—in that the trigger for the removal of the Portuguese court to Brazil was the Napoleonic invasion of Iberia. Cultural critic Heloisa Buarque de Holanda speaks of Brazilian independence as a "hilarious episode of a frightened monarch coming to hide from Napoleon on the other side of the Atlantic."[5]

At the same time, France and Brazil signify larger political geographies. They stand in for broader, transnational entities. France in some ways represents broader European tendencies, while Brazil represents Latin America and what used to be called the "Third World" and is now called the "global South." A transnational approach, we will suggest, helps illuminate questions of patriotism and love of country. How do the various social problems, and the responses to those problems, differ from country to country, and how does this bear on both patriotism and anti-Americanism? In what ways does national narcissism blinker the vision of those eager to criticize other nations' bad behavior but who remain blind to their own? When do other nation-states become scapegoats, serving to hide the scapegoating nation's own crimes and dysfunctionalities? The United States, we will discover, is neither uniquely evil nor uniquely perfect.

The "us" in the "why do they hate us" question, meanwhile, is misleading in that it is supposed to mean all Americans, as if the country were unified and as if all Americans were hated. But in fact the United States, like all countries, is not of one mind; it is a conflictual terrain of debates and power struggles. At this point in history, the United States is deeply divided, riven between red states and blue states, between hawks and doves, between the cultural right and the cultural left. Nor are all Americans hated, nor is it necessarily the "American people" who are hated. What "they" tend to hate is the arrogant "preventive war" foreign policy of the "hawks" and what they see as the predatory practices of U.S.-dominated transnational corporations. The attack on Iraq provoked unprecedented massive antiwar demonstrations, usually directed not against the American people but against U.S. foreign policy. But to the extent that Americans showed tacit or explicit approval of the hawks' policies, the resentment is bound to carry over to the American people as a whole.

The hate in the "hate us" question, furthermore, is assumed to be unidirectional—the others hate America—while America never hates. Yet from an Arab/Muslim perspective, U.S. policies regarding Iraq, Israel/ Palestine, and Israel/Lebanon clearly reflect a hatred for **them**. Right-wing American political discourse, moreover, is often a form of hate speech directed not only at "liberal elitists" but also at Arabs, Muslims, the French, and the Third World. Calling entire countries "evildoers" and "axis of evil" is an act of discursive violence; it already constitutes hate speech. Right-wing animosity toward the United Nations, embodied in the angry bluster of John Bolton, reflects a hatred for the world represented, however imperfectly, by the United Nations. Is it not hate speech when Ann Coulter suggests that the United States should invade Muslim countries and convert them to Christianity or when Bill O'Reilly suggests that the FBI put the staff of the liberal radio station Air America in chains because they're "traitors"? Is it not a form of hate speech when "religious" leader Pat Robertson calls publicly for the assassination of Hugo Chavez, who, whatever his faults, is still the elected political leader in Venezuela, one enjoying a much broader mandate than that enjoyed by George W. Bush? In right-wing Christian "rapture" fiction, meanwhile, hatred takes the form of genocidal fantasies, where enemy hordes are exterminated with gleeful abandon, all in the name of God and Nation. And right-wing talk show hosts constantly rant against a whole gallery of ideological and ethnic enemies. (The genocide in Rwanda, we recall, began with "hate radio.")

Thus rather than our asking, "Why do they hate us," we can just as easily ask, "Why do so many of us hate *them*?" or, given Americans' frequent ignorance about the world, "Why do we hate people about whom we know so little?" Comedian George Carlin once took apart the us–them dichotomy through a whimsical proposal for ending war. Because we never bomb people we know personally, he argued, what is needed is a program whereby every person on earth could get to personally meet everyone else. Carlin's scheme had all the world's inhabitants forming two very long and separate lines—let's call them "us" and "them"—moving in opposite directions. Each person would successively greet everyone in the other line, look him or her in the eye, ask his or her name, and say, "How do you do?" Then when politicians would propose bombing any group, masses of people would rise up and protest: "You can't bomb them! We know them!"

The "hate us" question is premised on an unsustainable "clash of cultures" dichotomy that breaks down even in relation to the ultimate "other" of the right wing—Arabs and Muslims. Not only do some of "them" (i.e., Middle Easterners) live among us, some also share, whether they live in the United States or in the Middle East, similar values, aspirations, and tastes. The portrayal of the Arab/Muslim Middle East as fundamentally alien is largely a product of the Orientalist and neo-Orientalist discourse of figures like Bernard Lewis, Samuel Huntington, Richard Perle, and David Frum, all of whom portray an Islamic world inherently incapable of adjusting to globalized, democratic "modernity."[6] At the same time, paradoxically, the neocons—who are not called "cons" for nothing—sold the Iraq War by promising to "democratize" the very same societies they denounced as hopelessly, even congenitally, antidemocratic. And when those societies actually become democratic and vote their will, the neocons often do not like the results, which they then work to overturn.

The point, however, is that even here the "us" and the "them" are hopelessly scrambled. In a very real sense, "we are them" and "they are us." Nor do we mean this in some lovey-dovey, hippy-dippy sense. On 9/11, it is said, "they," that is, the Muslims, attacked "us." Yet before 9/11, hundreds of Muslims had regularly come for Friday prayers to the World Trade Center mosque. In religious terms, some of "us" Americans are indeed Muslims and/or Arabs, just as millions of "them" (i.e., Arabs) are Christians and Jews, since "Arab" is an ethnic and national, not a religious, category and Arab Jews (i.e., people who are Jewish in religion but Arab in culture and language) have lived within Arab and later Islamic civilization for millennia. (Few people in the West know, for example, that Baghdad was a very Jewish city up through the late 1940s.) The fanatics on all sides, meanwhile, resemble each other in a different, almost opposite, sense. Rather like long-separated fraternal twins who are unaware of their kinship, Christian and Muslim fundamentalists hate each other yet look alike. They are brothers under the skin in their shared dogmatism, misogyny, homophobia, and apocalyptic Manicheanism. The border between "us" and "them," in sum, is constantly shifting; it is more a mirage than a wall.[7]

Even the quintessential "them"—the Islamic fundamentalists—were not always a "them." First, "we" Americans helped create "them," in the sense that various U.S. (and Israeli) governments supported Islamic fundamentalist movements as a counterweight to communism, socialism, and secular nationalism.[8] Between 1994 and 1996, the United States even supported the Taliban through its allies Pakistan and Saudi Arabia.[9] The issue is not that "one person's terrorist is another person's freedom fighter" but rather that the same person's "terrorist" today was that very same person's "freedom fighter" yesterday. In the 1980s the mujahideen were embraced by the American right, which encouraged them to train in U.S. camps and to run CIA-supported recruiting centers. Their cause was so popular that the 1980s hero Rambo fought at their side in Sylvester Stallone's *Rambo III,* where the Vietnam vet, lonely cowboy vigilante joined the noble Afghan Muslims against the cruel Russian Communists. Although George W. Bush claims today that the jihadists "hate our freedom," Ronald Reagan, two decades earlier, called those very same jihadists "freedom fighters" and "the moral equivalent of the Founding Fathers." Even Osama bin Laden's family wealth is linked to respectable institutions: Goldman Sachs, Merrill Lynch, and General Electric.[10] Thus the "we" and the "them" have an uncanny way of trading places. Who, within this perspective, after all, could be more "us" than the Founding Fathers, clearly the very quintessence of "us-ness"? What remains in place despite the shifts, then, is the ideology that generates an "us" and a "them."

The word *hate,* in any case, is both accurate and hyperbolic. While protestors burn U.S. flags, Americans are not routinely spat on or even insulted in most parts of Europe, Latin America, or even the Middle East.[11] As individuals, Americans are often treated with great hospitality. The anti-American feeling is much more subtle than that, and the subtleties are sometimes noticeable only to quasi insiders familiar with the host language and culture. As people who are personally and professionally intertwined with Europe, Latin America, and the Middle East, we are constantly prodded to reflect on these issues of transnational affections and hostilities. Living in diverse cultures catalyzes a sense—and it is **only** a sense—of each society's illusions about itself and its misconceptions about others. While hardly scientific, this experience and even all the "hearsay" and anecdotes one hears still have a certain cognitive value, even if only as a register of prejudice.

In our constant shuttle back and forth between Brazil and the United States, for example, we feel, almost viscerally, the decline of American prestige "on the ground." We also notice a hardening of anti-American attitudes over time. It has become a cliché among Brazilian journalists to say that in just a few short years the Bush administration has "completely destroyed the reputation of America." When journalists denounce the United States as the "most hated country on the planet," there are no letters to the editor protesting such claims. After decades of living, teaching, and lecturing in Brazil, we are now, for the first time, occasionally given the "American but" treatment. That is, we are introduced at conferences or festivals in terms of "being American, but OK," because we are perceived as being "almost Brazilian" in that we speak Portuguese, know Brazil, have relatives in Brazil, and so forth. No other nationality, not Canadians, French, Italians, or Argentineans, currently receives the dubious honor of this "yes, but" and "thank God you're not like the others" treatment.

It is also revealing to be in situations where one is the only American or where one is assumed not to be American and where Brazilians do not feel obliged to spare Americans' feelings. At the academic conferences and film festivals that we attend abroad, references to the United States are rarely positive. At a 2005 conference on "Cinema and Politics," in Salvador Bahia, the Greek filmmaker Costa-Gavras was asked two questions about Americans, presumably because he had made critical films in the United States: "Why do the Americans always have to think of themselves as heroes?" and "Why do Americans, in life and on the screen, love to blow things up?" And one picks up interesting morsels in the Brazilian press. Brazilian journalist Sergio Augusto, shortly after the onset of the Iraq War, announced in the countercultural magazine *Pasquim* that he was abandoning his former pro-Americanism. He wrote that although many of his friends and readers knew him as an enthusiast for American society and popular culture, in the light of the Iraq War, he had to admit that it was now time to abandon the United States and reconsider the values of old Europe. When even old pro-Americans are jumping ship, we know that the U.S. image in the world has been gravely damaged.

The "hate us" discourse, whether it rejects or endorses the "haters'" critiques of the United States, remains narcissistic in that it is still "all about us." As in the showbiz maxim "speak ill of me but speak," it concerns only what "they think about us" and not what "they" think about themselves or what "we" might learn both from what they think about us and from what they think about themselves. In fact, it is often less a question of "what they think about us" than of what "we think they think" about us. Our book therefore focuses not only on how Europeans (especially the French) and Latin Americans (Brazilians) see us but also on how that view is related to how they see themselves at this historical juncture. What are *their* concerns, *their* self-images, *their* civic emotions, and *their* points of pride or shame, and how do these concerns intersect with their view of us and ours of them in the in-between of transcultural relations?

While many books about anti-Americanism either endorse or reject the criticisms of the United States, we try to develop a more complex and nuanced approach. We have tried to follow some of the key debates in Europe, Latin America, and the Middle East concerning anti-Americanism. We present, mediate, and sometimes literally translate these debates and thus make them available for English-speaking readers, but we also adjudicate them, trying to sift out the wheat from the chaff. The fact that we are deeply critical of U.S. policies does not mean that we automatically support all criticisms of the United States. We want to reflect on what we can learn, but also on what we cannot learn, from such criticisms, since the anti-Americans, after all, often "get it wrong," whether because of basic misinformation, hasty generalization, or projective hostility. This book thus engages polemically not only with U.S. rightists but also with anti-Americans elsewhere, whether rightists or leftists. Our book, in this sense, is about dumb and smart forms of anti-Americanisms, but where dumb criticisms, in our view, sometimes come out of the mouths of smart people.

Present-day tensions must be seen against the backdrop of the much longer history of various national mythologies. What are the long-term historical sources and current manifestations of love and hate, pride and anger, in patriotic nationalism? How do rival conceptions of patriotism interact and interpenetrate across national boundaries? How did we arrive at this point of crisis? How have the various countries tended to imagine one another, and for what historical reasons, and what has changed in the present? What does the term *anti-Americanism* mean in different contexts? Depending on the site and the moment, we will argue, anti-Americanism has specific historical determinants, psychic configurations, emotional thrusts, and social logics. In some cases anti-Americanism is largely political, in other cases it is largely cultural, and in still others it forms a mélange of the two. At times anti-Americanism is a completely rational response to specific offenses by the U.S. government or by U.S.-led transnational corporations; yet at other times legitimate political critique becomes mingled with blind displacements, paranoid projections, and even defensive guilt.

The "hate us" discourse forgets that hate and love, not only in personal relationships but also in international politics, can become terribly commingled. The very word *hate* leaves little room for contradiction and ambivalence. In the context of 1960s leftism, French New Wave filmmaker Jean-Luc Godard spoke of the French "children of Marx and Coca-Cola"; that is, the young radicals who hated American imperialism but loved America's consumer products. The contemporary grandchildren of Marx and Coca-Cola, similarly, might resent U.S. power, but they do not necessarily hate American popular culture. The same people who resent U.S. actions abroad might also consume American star culture and TV programs. The antiglobalizers, meanwhile, might love Bruce Springsteen and Michael Moore for their adversary stance. In short, not unlike homegrown critics, they are ambivalent. Indeed, contradiction and mixed feelings are the norm, even within the same person. One can hate a country's politics yet love its music, its landscapes, and its culture. One can be proud of a nation's international behavior at one point in history (e.g., U.S. behavior during and immediately after World War II) and be ashamed of it at another (e.g., U.S. behavior in the present). And love and hate between countries are not static; nations that once loved us can come to hate us. Right-wing talk show hosts often claim, for example, that "the Arabs have hated us ever since the Crusades." Yet in fact the hostility to the United States among Arabs is quite recent, and even then it tends to be directed more to policies than to people

Even the term *anti-Americanism* has been defined in contradictory ways. Sociologist Paul Hollander defines *anti-Americanism* as:

a predisposition to hostility toward the United States and American society, a relentless critical impulse toward American social, economic, and political institutions, and values; it entails an aversion to American culture and its influence abroad, often also contempt for the American national character and dislike of American people, manners, behavior, dress; and a firm belief in the malignity of American influence and presence anywhere in the world.[12]

Hollander's vocabulary—*impulse, aversion, contempt*—implies a pathological dimension within anti-Americanism. Without denying a psychological dimension in such phenomena, his definition risks reducing all critique of the United States to a form of pathology. His definition, in short, raises as many questions as answers. Is there *one* American culture and one American character? Are people born with a "predisposition to hostility"? Does any and all criticism imply hostility or merely an honest difference of opinion? Cannot American intellectuals also pursue a "critical impulse toward American social, economic, and political institutions" not out of anti-Americanism but rather out of a patriotic desire to achieve a "more perfect union"? And could it be—and here we approach one of the key themes of this book—that the "superpatriots" who speak so much about patriotism are not really patriots at all?

The critics of anti-Americanism sometimes connect it to anti-Semitism, as if it were a variant example of the same phenomenon. But that connection risks implying that America is a powerless victim, the object of a pathological exterminationist prejudice, analogous to that which victimized Jews during the Holocaust. Indeed, neoconservative writers such as David Frum and Richard Perle abuse exactly that rhetoric when they suggest that the United States is in danger of a "holocaust" due to terrorism: "There is no middle way for Americans: It is victory or holocaust."[13] (We need to think twice when Richard Perle, the man dubbed the "Prince of Darkness," warns us about "evil.") But at this point in history the United States has rarely been physically attacked by others—Pearl Harbor, the 1993 World Trade Center attack, and 9/11 stand out as rare counterexamples—and it has often been on the attack. To begin with, the very formation of the U.S. nation-state—like that of most settler-colonial states—involved tremendous violence toward Native Americans, African Americans, and other communities. And the present-day United States is not a helpless victim but rather an unrivaled power in military, economic, and geopolitical power. And unlike "established" prejudices such as those against minorities such as Jews, blacks, gays, and gypsies—groups traditionally holding little power over the majority populations in the countries where they reside—the "prejudice" in anti-Americanism is not against a powerless minority but against a hyperpowerful state. The term *anti-Americanism* puts all critics of U.S. policies—including those within the United States—on the defensive, obliged to "prove a negative" before advancing their argument.

Patriotism would not normally have been the focus of our work. But we are not living in normal times, and the concept of patriotism is constantly being flogged and abused. We would rather have engaged other issues, but since the right constantly denounces critical intellectuals such as ourselves as "unpatriotic," as "not real Americans," and as "out of the mainstream," we are forced to deal with this ludicrous yet effective charge.

Our discussion will therefore focus on the reigning national mythologies and exceptionalisms and the myriad forms of patriotism, in terms of the following questions: What is the role of narcissism both in American superpatriotism and in anti-Americanism? Can shame and outrage also be forms of patriotism? Why is patriotism so often caught up with feelings of false victimization, in delusions not of grandeur but of *malheur*? Is xenophobia a sign of self-love or perhaps also of disguised self-hatred? Does loving one's country necessarily mean hating other countries? Is patriotism just another word for nationalism? Is it merely jingoism in disguise? Is love of country exclusive and monogamous? Or can one love a number of countries, in a polyandrous fashion, embracing various countries in widening circles of affection? Can one criticize one's own homeland without ceasing to love it? Is a critical patriotism possible, or is patriotism always and everywhere chauvinistic? Love of country, we suggest, is just as fraught as love in general. Our project, then, is to chart the cross-border transactions between these diverse forms of xenophobia and xenophilia, self-love and self-hatred.

What especially interests us here is what happens when one reflects on patriotism and anti-Americanism outside of the narrow self-involved frame of individual nation-states and their national vanities. How are contemporary debates about both issues rooted in much older debates? What are the buried metaphors that structure our thinking about patriotism? Are nations gendered as "fatherlands" or "motherlands," symbolized, for example, by France's "Marianne" or by the "gentle mother" of the Brazilian national anthem? Is the nation seen as fundamentally heterosexual, and is that why the right wants an amendment forbidding gay marriage? Do nations have kinship relations? ("I don't want a fatherland," Brazilian singer Caetano Veloso sings in "Lingua," "I want a brotherland.") Are the settler-states of the Americas the "offspring" of Europe? What is the relation between patriotism and the indigenous peoples of the Americas? Are France and the United States sister republics? Sibling rivals? Are Brazil and the United States cousins? How are the various national stories told? What are the myths of past origins and of future prospects and teleologies?

Flagging Patriotism touches on a number of "hot button" issues and polemics—the debates about Bush-style unilateralism; Franco-American tensions over neoliberal economics and the Iraq War; tensions between the United States and Brazil around globalization, fair trade, and North–South relations; and constitutional crises in the United States. In the course of the discussion, we will certainly poke fun at the "freedom fries" Francophobia of the American right wing, but we will also poke fun at some of the more hysterical strands of French anti-Americanism. Finally, we will point to the ways that U.S. official arrogance also hurts Americans themselves. False notions of patriotism, we will argue, have become obstacles to lucidity and social betterment.

Our book analyzes contemporary political discourses within a broader historical context, alongside more anecdotal reflections having to do with our own cross-national experiences. Although our previous books have been academic, *Flagging Patriotism* is aimed at a broader readership and written in what we hope is a more colloquial, accessible, and at times polemical style. We take seriously and refer repeatedly to the satirical humor of the "patriotic clowns" and truth-tellers such as George Carlin, Chris Rock, Michael Moore, Wanda Sykes, Rachel Maddow, Stephen Colbert, Janeane Garofalo, Bill Maher, and Jon Stewart, those who speak comic truth to the powerful and the pious. An astute Jon Stewart quip, in our view, can carry as much truth as many a social science dissertation. At times, we often incorporate jokes to tease out the national flavor of humor.[14] The tone of our screed ranges from that of sober analysis to whimsical speculation, from comic irreverence to passionate denunciation. Our prose plays on various linguistic registers; a million-dollar polysyllabic term might neighbor with a four-letter obscenity. Indeed, even the "we" is shifting in this book. At times, it means "we Americans," at times "we intellectuals," at times "we on the left," at times "we human beings," and at times "we the authors." The book is at once a serious study, a work of humor, and a rant, and we trust the reader to recognize when we are writing in which mode. In a sense we are most serious when we are laughing the hardest (sometimes to keep from crying).

While the book is defiantly political, it is not partisan. Although the Bush administration comes in for its fair share of abuse—and abuse, as Donald Rumsfeld has pointed out with regard to Abu Ghraib, is "technically not the same thing as torture"—the Democrats are hardly spared, for they too are clearly part of the problem. In fact we worry less about Republicans taking their stands than about Democrats too frightened to stand up. The real conflict for us is not between Republicans and Democrats but between right and left or, as Jim Hightower often puts it, between top and bottom. In our completely "fair and balanced" definition, the right is largely concerned with property and with legitimizing (and strengthening) hierarchies of power, while the left is more concerned with equality and with lessening (and delegitimizing) social, racial, and cultural hierarchies. While the right blames the powerless, the left faults the powerful. But our views, it should become clear, are not easily pigeonholed. They form a mix of radicalism, in that we try to go to the root of social problems; of social democracy or socialism; of liberalism, in our invocation of social and economic "rights"; of populism, in that we have a certain, qualified faith in "the people"; and even of conservativism (if qualified respect for the Constitution and for the Bill of Rights counts as conservatism).

Our engagement in this book is simultaneously personal and scholarly. We (together or separately) have lived and taught in Europe, Latin America, and the Middle East, and we have studied and taught the relevant languages, histories, literatures, and popular cultures. We have tried, perhaps quixotically, to keep up with the cultural and political debates in the three "zones." Thus we hope our experience and knowledge facilitate a transnational perspective that allows us to discern certain trends and patterns and to stage a dialogue between diverse points of view. Our constant back and forth between the three continents, and our position as teachers of European, Latin American, and Middle Eastern cultures in the United States, hopefully open up views and possibilities less available to those constrained by a purely national perspective.

Each chapter explores a specific dimension of our overall project. The first chapter, "On Narcissism and Exceptionalism," sets out the basic framework of our argument. After we provide a general discussion of nationalism and narcissism, we discuss the three cases of exceptionalist nationalism: the United States, France, and Brazil. In what ways do these three nations see themselves as exceptional?

The second chapter, "Variations on an Anti-American Theme," probes the subject of anti-Americanism in Europe and Latin America by looking at the cases of two United States allies—France and Brazil. What do these two anti-Americanisms share, and how do they differ? We conclude with a discussion of the two converse phenomena: that is, Francophilia and Francophobia in the United States.

The third chapter, "Discrepant Histories of Citizenship," detours into the political histories of all three countries in terms of how they have shaped basic notions of citizenship, democracy, and patriotism, all as necessary background for our trilateral comparison.

The fourth chapter, "Political Sense, Cultural Nonsense," returns to the question of American exceptionalism in terms of two classical issues—the influence of the Protestant "work ethic" on the American character, and the alleged lack of socialism in the United States. We then examine specific French critiques of American politics and culture, trying to separate out the sense and nonsense in the critiques.

The fifth chapter, "Contemporary Politics and the Crisis of Democracy," focuses almost exclusively on the United States. Here we discuss the various crises—war, militarism, inequality, the atrophy of democratic processes—generated by the right-wing takeover of the United States over the past few decades.

The final chapter, "None Dare Call It Patriotism," reformulates and reconceptualizes the initial question—"What is patriotism?" Here we argue that the current superpatriots, when tested against any valid criteria for patriotism, are really not patriots at all.

The book's title—*Flagging Patriotism*—alludes, punningly, to our multiple intentions. Apart from the obvious reference to the flag itself, we are "flagging" patriotism in the sense of noting it and analyzing it. On the other hand, we are charting a crisis in the very idea of patriotism—its flagging or decline—in a globalized world where patriotism has become as much a problem as a solution. (When the right wing controlled the National Endowment for the Humanities, it reportedly used a process of "flagging" to disqualify projects dealing with such issues as racism, sexism, and colonialism.) What are the contemporary forms of patriotic discourse? What happens when patriotism is reduced to "showing the flag"? The failure to raise one's voice against mistaken policies in the name of patriotism, we argue, can become a form of disloyalty to the better interests of the nation, and thus is unpatriotic.

One can easily argue that patriotism is an obsolete concept in the era of globalization. As the planet spins toward globalized injustice and ecological destruction, it is perhaps silly to think in terms of single nations. Tsunamis, global warming, acid rain, and globalization do not respect nation-state borders. Yet national policies speed a destructive globalizing process.

We call, finally, for new forms of "tough love" patriotism—for a critical, bottom-up, multicultural, and transnational patriotism, a legitimate love of country untainted by chauvinism. We hope that even those readers who do not share our perspective will be able to enjoy and learn from the book. Our goal, in any case, is not to provide definitive answers but rather to pose productive and stimulating questions. So let the debate begin.

1. On Narcissism and Exceptionalism

Patriotism: Myths That Bind and Blind

One portrait of the patriot goes more or less as follows: patriots wave the flag, literally or figuratively, on all possible occasions. They fly it over the door, glue it to the windshield, and carry it to sports events. They tirelessly repeat that they live in "the greatest country in world." They see their country's history as an endless saga of wondrous deeds and glorious victories. If their leader declares war on another country, they instinctively salute and then go on an automatic pilot of hate toward the so-called enemy, even if they actually know nothing about the country in question. They agree with every presidential policy, because "the president has more information than we do." They do not object to the extraconstitutional abuse of prisoners, since "the prisoners wouldn't have been detained if they hadn't done something." They don't mind warrantless spying on citizens, since only people with "something to hide" would worry about such trivial things as the Bill of Rights. When demagogues speak, the patriots are there in the audience chanting the name of their country above all others.

But is this the portrait of a perfect patriot or of a perfect idiot? Of the perfect citizen or of the perfect hypocrite? Of the perfect democrat or the perfect fascist? The same superpatriots who brag about living in the "greatest country in the world" might know very little about their own country's history, or about the other countries to which they feel so blankly superior, or about the historical relationships between the various countries. The same person who waves the flag might be shirking his or her fair burden of taxes through a tax haven in the Caribbean. For the affluent classes, as journalist Cynthia Tucker puts it, patriotism sometimes amounts to "sticking an American flag decal on the tax-deductible Hummer."[1] The same person who supports all the country's wars might be a "chicken hawk" or might not realize that the war being supported actually hurts both the other country and one's own, even as it benefits the pockets of a few. The same senator who lauds "this great land of ours" might pass antienvironmental legislation that actually damages the land itself. And the same people waving the flag so enthusiastically might not realize that they are being exploited by politicians who abuse the flag to advance their own interests. No one is in a position to declare any country the "greatest in the world," moreover, unless he or she has lived in, speaks the languages of, and knows the cultures of all the countries in the world. Otherwise, the claim is meaningless.

Because so much of the patriotism of politicians is mere show, we propose a new law, which we call the "patriotic law of inverse proportion." This law suggests that those who speak the most about patriotism are often the least patriotic, just as the biblical Pharisees who made a public show of their faith were actually, in the end, the least "faithful." Just as the televangelists, priests, or politicians who obsessively denounce pornography or homosexuality are often those most likely to be closet gays or involved in kinky sex, so those who speak most about patriotism, according to our law of inversion, are often the least patriotic. On the other hand, those who speak least about patriotism—who are even irritated by patriotic talk—might be the most patriotic. It was King Lear's most faithful daughter, Cordelia, after all, who refused to say that she loved her father the most, because she thought her love needed no saying. For Cordelia, those who constantly proclaim their love, like her sisters, were the most despicable of hypocrites.

But we are getting ahead of ourselves. First, we have to place patriotism into a larger and more international frame. Any critical discussion of patriotism and nationalism inevitably bumps up against the question of national pride. The "anti" in relation to one country cannot be separated from the "pro" in relation to another. Much of the anti-American resentment around the world, moreover, focuses on what is perceived as American "self-centeredness." Countless jokes mock American ignorance about the world. One joke has pollsters interrogating various nationalities about their opinion concerning "the problem of hunger in the world," with each nationality perplexed by a different element in the question. The American, in the joke, is perplexed by just one part of the question: "What is ... the world?" Many foreign visitors to the United States return with horror stories about Americans who were absolutely clueless about geography, who thought Belgium was in South America, Brazil in Europe, and so forth. Jon Stewart and Stephen Colbert frequently make fun of this ignorance, as when Stewart asks "correspondent" Samantha Bee, reporting on Canadian politics, "Where's Canada?" or when Colbert, in his mock Bill O'Reilly persona, proudly claims that "patriotic Americans should not know about geography!" Meanwhile, some Americans who could not locate Iraq on a map vigorously applaud bombing it.

Other jokes focus on American reluctance to learn other languages: "What is the definition of a person who speaks three languages?" Answer: trilingual. And a person who speaks two languages? Bilingual. And a person who speaks only one language? An American. Non-Americans complain that Americans abroad often assume that everyone else speaks English and simply repeat their questions with more volume when they are not understood. And here we encounter a paradox. On one hand, the United States is perhaps the most heterogeneous, cosmopolitan, and international of all nations. The whole world has washed up on our shores, to the point that few countries can claim the dazzling linguistic, ethnic, and religious diversity of American cities such as New York, San Francisco, or Los Angeles. Millions of people from all continents have been drawn to the United States as a place of personal and collective realization. Yet for a variety of reasons, the United States, especially in its official incarnations, has become terribly provincial, cut off from debates and perceptions around the world, wrapped in a cocoon of indulgent self-approval and head-in-the-sand denial.

Although the United States, going back to George Washington and Thomas Jefferson, has had many cosmopolitan and polyglot presidents, Americans have also elected presidents who confused Brazil with Bolivia (Ronald Reagan) and who were unaware that Brazil has black people (George W. Bush) and vice presidents who think Latin Americans speak "Latin" (Dan Quayle). George W. Bush, when shown a map of Brazil on his fall 2005 trip, responded, "Wow, it's big." An Internet joke had George W. Bush thinking that "Brazilions" was a number like millions and trillions. Another (post-9/11) Brazilian joke made fun both of Bush's ignorance and of Brazilian attitudes toward one of its closest Latin American neighbors. The joke goes as follows. A few hours after the 9/11 attacks, Brazilian president Lula calls Bush to inform him that Brazilians perpetrated the attack. Shocked, Bush tells Lula that he will have to bomb Brazil to smithereens. "That's all right," Lula responds, "go ahead and bomb." "Which is your capital," Bush asks, "so I can bomb you?" Then comes Lula's sly answer: "Buenos Aires."

On a trip to Europe, President George W. Bush displayed a severe case of linguistic provincialism during a joint press conference with President Jacques Chirac in Paris. When American MSNBC reporter David Gregory addressed a question to Chirac in French, Bush accused him of trying to show off by being "intercontinental." Then Bush indulged in his own display of language skills, putting Gregory down with a derisive Spanishism: "que bueno!" Apparently Bush found it unacceptable for an American journalist to address a French president in French in France. Were he to follow this same logic in the United States itself, no foreign correspondent would ever address a U.S. president in English at the White House: Pakistanis would speak Urdu, Nigerians Yoruba, and so forth.

The United States is hardly alone, of course, in its self-love and self-absorption: most nations, like most individuals, tend to be primarily concerned with themselves. Narcissism, psychoanalysis tells us, is a cultural universal. In the same vein, conventional psychology insists that self-love is basically a very positive thing, that we have to love ourselves before we can love others, and that by extension we have to love our own country before we can love another country. Yet, sometimes the problem is a **lack** of collective national self-love. Colonialism, at times, engendered self-rejection in subject peoples. Some "natives," taught to hate themselves, began to regard the metropolitan nation-state as the real love object. Thus colonized schoolchildren in Asia and Africa, in the time of French colonialism, were taught that their real ancestors were the "Gauls," who "had blond hair and blue eyes." They were made to be ashamed of their culture, history, language, and appearance. Independence, for colonized peoples, was a way of "coming out" into a self-love and pride previously undermined by colonial subjugation.

The idealized "we" of the imagined nation already exists in relation to other countries. The very idea of the nation-state is premised on demarcating a community and a territory vis-à-vis other communities and territories. Nations, like individuals, affirm their identity through a mirrorlike play of national self and foreign other. A well-known aphorism says that "travel broadens the mind," and travel can even potentially put a person's national identity into a state of productive crisis. We have all heard the stories of "United Statesians" who discover their "Americanness" only in Europe, Europeans who discover their "Europeanness" only in the United States, Latin Americans who discover their "Latinidad" only abroad, or Middle Easterners who discover their "Middle Easternness" in the West.

Individuals and nations thus attain self-identity and self-awareness through a comparative process, defining themselves in contradistinction to other individuals and nations. At its best, this process generates individuation and national maturity, a salutary relativizing or decentering of one's place in the world. At its worst, a failed encounter or nonencounter with the "other" undermines all sense of shared humanity; an inability to "translate" produces symptoms of withdrawal and even hostility to those who "don't understand us" and whom we don't understand. Animosity toward others then becomes a unifying glue for a fractured society. For some French people, anti-Americanism functions as a false form of French patriotism, just as Francophobia, for some Americans, constitutes a form of American pseudopatriotism.

Virtually all nations see themselves as qualitatively different from and in partial opposition to other nations; they historically define themselves "with" and "against" and "through" their neighbors and victims and enemies. Official France, for example, has historically defined itself against the Muslim world (Charles Martel, the Crusades, *El Cid*), Great Britain, Germany, and now the United States. The dominant United States has defined itself with and against Native Americans internally and externally against Great Britain (the Revolutionary War), Spain (the Spanish-American War), Germany and Japan (the two world wars), the Soviet Union (the Cold War), and now Islamic fundamentalism (the war on terror). Official Brazil too has successively defined itself against various colonizing or neocolonizing powers—Portugal, France, Spain, Holland, Great Britain, and the United States. Patriotic nationalism in contemporary Brazil—and to some extent in France—is linked to the idea of resisting American influence and domination or at least "U.S.-led globalization," resulting in a kind of negative patriotism.

Hostility, then, can be a catalyst for identity. In recent years, animosity to the United States has become a trigger for European identity, as Europe begins to imagine itself as a "not U.S." In the United States, meanwhile, right-wing "superpatriots" have been trying to define the country in terms of what it is not, whether as anti-Europe, anti-France, anti-Muslim or anti-Arab, or even antiworld. But negative self-definition carries with it a great risk. If all we are is what we are against, for example, if we define ourselves as "the people who oppose terror," in that case, we have become the psychic hostages of the enemy, in that we depend on "them" for our very identity. The obsession turns us into mad Ahab hunting down the Great Whale. When we are told that we cannot leave Iraq because "that is what the terrorists want"—even though it was the U.S. occupation that catalyzed a new era of terror—that formulation begs another question; that is, what if leaving Iraq is also what the American people want? What defines us as a people? Are we the people who created and abide by the Constitution and the Bill of Rights, or are we the people who will do anything, including even suspending the provisions of our own Constitution, to combat terror? When we weave the enemy's assumptions into the very woof and warp of our own desire, do we not become that enemy? The worst "blowback," in this sense, is not what the enemy does to us but rather what we do to ourselves.

Patriotism is a form of relational narcissism, whereby nations exalt themselves (or on occasion demean themselves) vis-à-vis other nations. The actual theme and content of narcissism can vary widely: it might claim that "we" are more civilized than "they" are, or more developed, or more democratic, or more hospitable, or more warm. Narcissism can also take negative, comparative forms, for example, "we are bad, but they are worse" (e.g., we torture from time to time, but they behead; we kill accidentally, but they kill deliberately). With us, there are "a few bad apples," but with them it is the apple itself that is rotten to the core. At times, the claim that "they" are "the worst" implies that we, by implication, are "the best." George W. Bush seems to have the illusion that the undeniable badness of the terrorists somehow produces his own unblemished goodness. Thus patriotism usually assumes the form of an implied "conversation" with "others." It is a question not only of how a nation projects itself but also of how it projects others and what self-flattering functions are served by these projections.

The concept of the nation and the national entails historical and ideological ambiguities—the sliding between the original meaning of *nation* as "racial group" and its later meaning as "politically organized entity," and the oscillation between nationalism's progressive and reactionary poles. Nationalism changes its valence in different historical and geographical contexts. A proactive European nationalism—such as Nazi Germany's ambitions to conquer its neighbors—cannot be equated with the reactive nationalism of countries in Latin America where nationalism is directed not against Latin American neighbors but rather against the colossus to the north. Nor can an atomizing nationalism—such as that which fractured the former Yugoslavia—be equated with the nationalism of diasporic movements such as those of the indigenous peoples of the Americas, who at the same time call both for local autonomy in demarcated territories and for larger interwoven solidarities across deterritorialized continents. At the end of wars, some border peoples, for example, those inhabiting Alsace-Lorraine on the borders of France and Germany, were expected to suddenly shift national allegiance. Racist vigilantes, "minutemen," are now policing the United States–Mexico border, but as Mexican Americans (Chicanos) often say, "We didn't cross over the border; the border crossed over us," a fact that the dominant U.S. media, in their treatment of the issue of "illegal aliens," somehow "forget" to point out.

At its worst, nationalism turns into pathological hatred for irredeemably evil enemies. It was this kind of nationalism—that of fascist and imperialist European states, for example—that triggered the greatest catastrophes of the twentieth century. It is precisely because hypernationalist attitudes and language were abused then that they seem so unappealing and retrograde to many Europeans now. Yet some American hawks adopt today precisely that same archaic language, when they urge the United States to proudly take on its "rightful" imperial role.[2]

National mythologies provide warm and fuzzy fables of unity to "cover over" what are actually extremely conflictual histories. The educational systems of most nation-states relay these myths for the benefit of schoolchildren. Rather than being simply false, these myths are partial and selective attempts to shape national loyalty. But if all nations are narcissistic, each is narcissistic in its own way. The points of pride vary tremendously. Nations can pride themselves on their military power or, like Switzerland or Costa Rica, on their lack of an army. Nations can be proud of their military victories or lick the narcissistic wound of historic defeats, relished as tokens of ontological victimization (and therefore innocence). They can be proud of their economic might and natural resources or their creativity in "making do," despite economic scarcity. Nations can be proud of a noble past or anticipate a glorious future. In this sense, national stories fall into different narrative genres. To speculate, is U.S. national history a comedy, in the sense that it is presumed to have a "happy ending"? Is Mexican history a melodrama, in the sense that it is rooted in a symbolic violation (*la chingada*) of the Mexican woman? Is Brazilian history a tragicomedy? Is French history a philosophical fable?

At times, national narcissism takes the form of ethnocentrism; that is, the view of one's own society's customs and habits and ideas as everywhere normative and universal. Montesquieu mocked this sort of provinciality in his famous satirical question—"How can one possibly be Persian?"—with its implied amazement that any other society might ever choose not to do things exactly as we do them, not to think exactly as we think, or not to speak exactly as we speak. Narcissists, especially empowered narcissists, usually have trouble imagining that their norms are not universal or that everyone else does not find them as vastly lovable as they find themselves.

Yet here too there is no foolproof pattern. The nation is "imprinted" on all its citizens but with widely variant types and fonts. Individual citizens do not speak with the same voice. Some might be proud of their nation's leaders, while others glory in their nation's dissidents and conscientious objectors. Some become "internal émigrés," who are "in but not of" the society. Citizens have widely divergent experiences of the nation-state and therefore widely divergent attitudes toward it. The "owners," feeling that the state is theirs, speak of an "ownership" society. Others feel like "second-class" citizens who have been "disowned" by that same society, denied of their legacy. What was for European Americans a proud "conquest of the West" was for Native Americans a terrible calamity, a dislocation that turned them into refugees on their own land or exiles in a distant region. The loyalty of patriot chiefs such as Hiawatha, Pontiac, Tecumseh, and Chief Joseph was first to their native community, not to the new nation-state that dispossessed them. Others have difficulty loving the society as it is but try hard to reshape it into a more lovable form. The ambivalence of the African American experience is captured in the aphorism that Malcolm X borrowed from a popular song: "We didn't land on Plymouth Rock; it landed on us!" Indeed, African Americans have often been among those who have fought the hardest to change America, who have fought the most valiantly for substantive democracy, for a guaranteed right to vote, and, recently, for the right to contest the abuses that marred the 2000 and 2004 elections. Blacks have fought as if their very survival depended on it, partially because, in fact, it did.

Nations are complex constellations of historical experiences, material interests, and ideological points of view. Every person, and every community, looks at the nation from a specific place in society and history, with specific perspectives deserving of respect. The cheerleading approach to patriotism asks people with very discrepant experiences to love the country in exactly the same way. But how could those who were already here (the Native Americans), those who were forced to come here (enslaved Africans, indentured servants of many colors), and those who chose to come here, all see the nation in the same way? How could those who arrived in slave ships via Gorée Island and those who arrived in immigrant ships via Ellis Island see the Statue of Liberty through exactly the same lens?

Patriotism should not be a masked loyalty to only one segment of the nation, as if that segment represented the totality. The loyalty should be to the national conversation, to all the participants engaged in that conversation, and to the fairness and equality of the dialogue, or better, what we would call a plurilogue. To ask everyone to feel exactly the same way about the nation is a form of saying, "Forget your experience, think like me, and shut up." It is like asking a spouse who has been abused and violated by her husband to regard the institution of marriage exactly the same way as someone enjoying a stable and equal and fulfilling relationship. It is a way of denying that different people and communities have experienced America in very divergent ways.

Nationalism everywhere creates reassuring fictions of national unity. Yet nations are not monoliths; they are always already fissured along lines of race, class, gender, sexuality, region, religion, and ideology. Nations are above all multiple. The American "E pluribus unum" gestures toward that multiplicity, even if at the time the phrase was coined the "pluribus" was terribly restrictive. Nationalism also creates fictions of virtue, yet the very foundations of modern nation-states entail violence, suppression, and mandatory amnesia. Despite the conflictual heterogeneity of the American experience, for example, the official ideology, the educational system, and the dominant media often render that complexity in fairy-tale terms. The endlessly manufactured sense of innocence sometimes leads to the United States' becoming isolated from a larger, more critical world, deprived of a sense of how it is seen by others. Cut off from the tragic complexity of historical experience and critical views of other peoples and often unaware of the violence that has been committed in their name and that has been funded by their tax dollars, some Americans become bewildered about why anyone could hate such an unimpeachably wonderful country.

In line with postcolonial and postnationalist theory, we question the concept of nations as fixed, static, and unitary essences. The idea of nations forever frozen in their traits forgets the unpredictable metamorphoses over time. Who would have imagined, sixty years after the end of the Third Reich, that right-wing American politicians would be complaining that the Germans, of all people, were insufficiently militaristic! During the Nuremberg trials following World War II, American lawyers were interrogating German officials about their crimes against humanity; now it is German officials—and we in no way mean to imply equivalence in the crimes involved—who are interrogating American officials about torture, rendition, and other abuses. Today, the United States is often called "militaristic." Yet at the time of its founding, the United States was radically hostile to "standing armies," seen then as a symptom of Europe's perpetual warmongering. At that point in history, it was the United States that was from Venus and Europe that was from Mars, rather than the reverse as it is now. And in the immediate aftermath of World War II, Europe was more worried about American "isolationism" than it was about American militarism.

Static and originary ideas of nationhood also obscure the presence of what Eric Hobsbawm calls "invented" and "borrowed" traditions.[3] Nations can pride themselves on features that they imagine to be unique but that in fact are widely shared. Right-wing polemicist Dinesh D'Souza speaks of the United States' "unique" capacity to absorb immigrants, yet the same claim can be made for Canada, Mexico, Brazil, and many other "New World" countries.[4] Even the most prized national symbols can be indelibly marked by the foreign. Italians are proud of their pasta, but pasta came from China and the tomato came from the Americas. In the case of Brazil, the prototypically "Brazilian" sport of soccer came from England, typically Brazilian flora such as palm trees came from India, and the national dish "feijoada" came from Africa.

During past decades, scholars have begun to interpret national identity as a kind of consensus fiction, one that is narrated, mediated, constructed, and performed. Any definition of national identity or patriotism, therefore, must see it as constructed through discourse and rhetoric, must allow for cultural and political heterogeneity, and must be dynamic, seeing the nation as an evolving, imaginary construct rather than an originary essence. The idea of the unified national family camouflages the tensions between and within the different families that form the nation. All nations are to some extent heterogeneous, at once urban and rural, male and female, religious and secular, and so forth. The view of the nation as homogeneous muffles the polyphony of voices, shrouding the cornucopia of social and ethnic heterogeneities characteristic of complex nations. Some of "us," in other words, are like "them," and some of "them" are like "us." This is another reason why us–them discourse is inadequate.

The Angels, and Devils, of History

National histories, like individual lives, inevitably mingle good and bad, innocence and guilt. Yet some historians "angelize" their own country's history while demonizing that of other countries. Historians can always cherry-pick their examples so as to cast national history in a completely positive or completely negative light. Painting another country's history in a highly negative light, for example, is rather easy: all one has to do is selectively emphasize all the sore points in that nation's history—and there always are sore points—and then trace the dots between them to form an unending saga of perfidy. Such accounts always contain a grain of truth—the perfidies usually did occur—but they can also convey gross oversimplification.

Historical writing proliferates in examples of tendentious accounts of national history, where the "whitewashing" of one history goes hand in hand with the "blackwashing" of another. For the moment, we will briefly address two recent examples, a hostile American account of Franco-American relations and a hostile Spanish account of American culture and history. John J. Miller and Mark Molesky's 2004 book *Our Oldest Enemy: A History of America's Disastrous Relationship with France,* as its subtitle suggests, provides an excellent example of a selective animus against France. The book writes history backward from the presumed French "betrayal" in opposing the Iraq War and offers a long list of French crimes to undermine the "myth of Franco-American solidarity." (A hypothetical pro-French book titled, for example, *Our Oldest Friend: A History of America's Marvelous Relationship with France* would of course be just as problematic.) Miller and Molesky apply a double standard throughout: when the Americans use duplicity, for example, it is a sign of their diplomatic or military genius but with the French it is a symptom of their essential mendacity. Everything French is seen with suspicion, as in the following sentence: "In France, Lafayette's grave is said to be on American soil—a symbolic gesture that cost the French nothing but reaped an enormous windfall of American goodwill."[5]

Our Oldest Enemy opportunistically sides with any declared enemy of France, with the eighteenth-century Haitian revolutionaries, for example, not out of any principled anticolonialism but out of hostility to the French. The book sides with the Mexicans, but only insofar as they opposed the French, not insofar as they opposed Americans.

Everything is grist for the Francophobic mill. The authors treat the great protosurrealist writer Alfred Jarry, for example, not only as being "obnoxious" in real life but also as having "created one of the most offensive characters in literature in his play *Ubu Roi*" ("King Ubu," a title that evokes the classical tragedy *Oedipus Rex* but that the authors mistranslate as "King Turd") (p. 143). By this logic, they would condemn Shakespeare for creating an Iago or a Richard III and all the great American writers who created "offensive characters"—Melville's Captain Ahab comes to mind—or who were "obnoxious in real life."

Miller and Molesky write what might be called "sports fan" history, where our team is always noble and valiant and their side commits only fouls and aggressions, where our motives are always benign and theirs are always malignant. The point is not that the other side did not commit the fouls but only that both sides commit fouls. *Our Oldest Enemy* rightly denounces Jacques Chirac for his links to Saddam Hussein, for example, but says nothing of Reagan's and Cheney's links to that very same dictator. (We knew that Saddam at one point had "weapons of mass destruction," after all, because we and the Europeans had sold them to him.) Deploying rhetorical sleight of hand, the book assures us that "a full accounting of Iraqi weapons became available only through American resolve and battlefield success," conveniently forgetting that the "full accounting," such as it was, was realized only through massive destruction and that it revealed not the presence but the absence of the promised weapons of mass destruction.

Written at a moment of administration optimism about Iraq, *Our Oldest Enemy* confidently proclaims that "Regime change in Iraq has made the world a decidedly safer place, though the French are loath to admit it." A few years later, majorities, even in the United States, think that the war, far from making the world safer, has made the world more dangerous by turning Iraq into a hornet's nest of terrorists and insurgents. The book ends with a loaded rhetorical question—"Will the French continue to follow a path of narrowly defined self-interest or will they aspire to a foreign policy based on the shared values of the West?" One would never guess from their phrasing that the "shared values" of most of the West, as expressed in the massive worldwide antiwar demonstrations of February 15, 2003, including in countries whose governments officially supported the war, entailed a virtually universal rejection of Bush's preventive war.

Our second example of highly selective denigration comes from a wide-ranging jeremiad against the United States by the Spanish writer Moncho Tamames. The title of his book—*La Cultura del Mal: Una Guia del Anti-Americanismo* (The Culture of Evil: A Guide to Anti-Americanism)—obviously plays on the phrase "axis of evil." After a few perfunctory nods to great American leaders—Abraham Lincoln, Woodrow Wilson, Franklin Delano Roosevelt, George Marshall, Martin Luther King, John F. Kennedy—the book offers more than three hundred pages of sheer denunciation of the United States, its foreign policy, its history, and its people. Illustrating our idea that the "pro" toward one country is intimately linked to the "anti" toward another country, Tamames describes anti-Americanism as the unifying force that gives Spaniards meaning:

> Anti-Americanism is the "pro" of our culture, the "pro" of our values, the "pro" of our economy, sovereignty, style of life and so forth. Anti-Americanism is a constructive, positive, healthy, cultivated and massive ideal, whose single goal is to say "let us live according to our own way of life and you go and do whatever you want." (p. 19)

Here Spain and the United States are constructed as opposites with absolutely nothing in common. Tamames writes that American history "is bathed in blood and corruption like no other, with constant elements of fundamentalism, genocide, political crimes, economic and military tyranny toward the rest of the planet." To which we can say only that, yes, these are important elements—although hardly the only elements— of American history. But unfortunately for Tamames's national vanity, the single finger that rightly points toward the United States also hides four other fingers that point back toward Spain, because his terms also provide an excellent description of aspects of Spain's own history: the violence of the eight-century-long reconquest of Spain from the Moors, the fundamentalism of the Inquisition, the genocide of the Indians of the Americas, the cruelty of transatlantic slavery, the plundering of the resources of various continents, the political crimes of various Spanish monarchs and dictators, and the economic and military tyranny over the Spanish colonies. The extremely important difference, of course, is that the United States is still invading and dominating other countries, while Spain has moved toward respect and collaboration. Indeed, the United States added the "insult" of American imperialism in Latin America to the "injury" of Spanish and Portuguese colonialism.[6]

The United States can be guilty of many of the crimes with which it is charged and at the same time function as a scapegoat for Europeans eager to forget Europe's own crimes. It is one thing for the actual victims of U.S. policy to charge the United States and quite another thing for those Europeans, many of whom were in historical terms fellow victimizers and colonialists, to charge the United States. Tamames, for example, paints a rosy picture of racial tolerance in Latin America and intolerance in North America, but what his denunciation hides, and here we see the narcissistic function of some bashing of the United States, is the Spanish role in the genocide of the indigenous people of the Americas. If Tamames were to count the native victims of the Spanish conquista the same way that he counts the native victims of the Anglo-American conquest, the Spanish figures would dwarf even the inflated figures that Tamames provides for the United States.

Already in Columbus's time, the Spanish priest Bartolome de las Casas—one of many courageous Spanish jurists and clerics critical of the conquest—witnessed and denounced the massacres of the Indians by the conquistadors and described them in 1520 in a book addressed to King Charles V titled *The Devastation of the Indies: A Brief Account*. De las Casas recounted a massive genocide that reduced the native population in the first thirty years after Cortez's landing from twenty-five million to six million souls. He estimated that in forty years, the "infernal actions of the Christians" had led to the unjust slaying of "more than twelve million men, women, and children."[7] De las Casas described Spaniards taking "infants from their mothers' breasts ... [snatching] them by the arms and [throwing] them into the rivers, roaring with laughter and saying as the babies fell into the water, 'boil there, you offspring of the devil!'"[8] Although Tamames describes Americans as grossly materialistic, what impressed the indigenous peoples back then was the irrational **Spanish** lust for gold, for which they were ready to kill en masse (and "after messe").

One wonders if Tamames has ever really studied the history of his own country or is just reciting the fables he learned in school. A Franco-era high school history book—*Historia del Imperio Espanol y de la Hispanidad* (Madrid, 1943)—taught Spanish history as a fable beginning in Eden and ending with the Generalissimo Franco: "The future of Spain united, after three centuries, to the destiny of the past! ... The ancient procession has not ceased. ... This is the grand task that God has saved for the Spain of today. ... An exceptional destiny. ... Through the Empire to God."[9] The job of critical intellectuals, one would think, is to question the conventional wisdom and to contest, to borrow a title from James Loewen, the "lies our teachers taught us."

Spain is now a quite progressive country in political terms, especially when compared with the United States, and the point of this catalog of horrors is not to ignore the myriad positive elements in Spanish history or culture—from Cervantes to Almadovar, from the first Golden Age to the latest film or novel—or to suggest that North American whites were not equally culpable of genocide, but only to point to the "bad faith" of Tamames in stressing only the crimes of the "Anglo-Saxons" while downplaying the crimes of his own ancestors. Various European powers oppressed the indigenous peoples of the Americas. The point to be made about the *leyenda negra* (the Spanish term designating the "black legend" promulgating English denunciations of Spanish atrocities) is not that it was untrue about the Spanish but rather that it was equally true of other Europeans. It was the Spanish and Portuguese who initiated not only transatlantic slavery but also the genocide and plunder of the native peoples—to the point that later colonizers such as the Dutch, French, and British envied their wealth and success and emulated their practices.

Tamames's attempt to describe British colonialism alone as violent and racist, in other words, is grotesque. All the European powers were oppressive to Native Americans and diasporic Africans. Indigenous activists in the Americas do not distinguish between the "good" colonizers in South America and the "bad" colonizers in North America; they denounce European conquest and domination in general, whether the product of the Spanish, Portuguese, Dutch, French, or British. In a speech, Evo Morales, the recently elected indigenous Bolivian president, denounced U.S. imperialism, but he also denounced five hundred years of indigenous oppression and the "culture of death represented by the West."[10] The responsibility of intellectuals is to denounce the massacres perpetrated by our own countries, along with the massacres perpetrated by others. Anything less is simply an exercise in diversion and self-flattery.

The same "you're worse than we are" selectivity applies when it comes to questions of race. Tamames paints the United States and other "Anglo-Saxon" countries as virtually the only racist countries in the world, while painting Europe and Latin American as friendly, mestizo places unblemished by racism. Because we have written on these issues elsewhere, we will not bother to refute such a superficial analysis here.[11] Suffice it to say that anti-indigenous racism is found throughout the "Red Atlantic," just as antiblack racism is found everywhere around what Robert Farris Thompson and Paul Gilroy have called the "Black Atlantic"; that is, everywhere in Europe and all the Americas. Police brutality against people of color can be found in the United States, Great Britain, Brazil, France, Spain, and many other countries. Tamames, apart from apparently not knowing his own country's history, reveals his profound ignorance of both Latin America and the United States. Almost no contemporary Brazilian scholars on race, for example, would defend the idea of Brazil as a "racial democracy."

British and American colonialism, Tamames claims, had the historical peculiarity of being "democratic." But here he creates a distinction without a difference. French, Dutch, and British colonialism also combined relative democracy at home with brutal domination in the colonies, a paradox summed up in oxymoronic phrases such as "Colonial Republic" and "imperial democracy." And here we see that ultimately Tamames is defending, even if only indirectly and implicitly, the Spanish colonization of the Americas by creating a supposed contrast with British colonization. Imperialists, including American imperialists, always see their own particular imperialism as having, as it were, a sweeter scent. (We, in contrast, would condemn them all as variant forms of domination, rather like diverse forms of garbage each with its own specific consistency and odor.)

While making minimal acknowledgment of Spanish crimes, Tamames implies that the supposedly happy state of intercultural relations in Latin America today redeems the violence of the past. As if to clinch his point, he writes, "Unlike the atrocities committed by the Spanish after their arrival in the Americas, nowadays we see in Mexico, Brazil, or Colombia, Indians and mestizos and whites and blacks. But has anyone ever seen an Indian in the streets of New York?" This assertion is almost comic in its self-confident ignorance. New York is by now a majority nonwhite city, composed of people from all over the world, including from Latin America and the Caribbean. The labor leader who paralyzed the city through a transit strike in December 2004, for example, was a Haitian American bearing the revolutionary name of Toussaint. As a result of this cosmopolitan mixture, one sees in the streets of New York more or less the same thing that one sees in the streets of Mexico, Brazil, or Colombia. First of all, one sees some of the hundreds of thousands of Mexicans, Brazilians, and Colombians who have immigrated to New York; that is, the same Indians, mestizos, and whites and blacks that one sees in Latin America. Indeed, virtually every Latin American country has a sister community in New York City. There are three million Spanish speakers in the larger New York metropolitan area. (One of them, a Cuban American, just became the senator from New Jersey.) Bolivian flute players grace the sidewalks as they do in many world metropolises, and some of the one hundred and fifty thousand Mexicans in New York are of indigenous origins, as is obvious from their physiognomies.

But one also sees *Indians*—the term itself derives from Columbus's mistaken impression of having traveled to Asia—in the form that Tamames means the term—that is, Native Americans, thousands of whom live in New York City. Some celebrate powwows at the tip of the island. Across the street from the New York University's Tisch School of the Arts, where we teach, is the American Indian Community House. Many Native Americans, moreover, have studied at NYU. Leota Lone Dog, a student in the American studies department, is writing her PhD thesis, titled "Native New Yorkers," on the subject of Indians in New York City. Chris Eyre, a graduate of our school, became the first Native American to direct a widely shown fiction feature film, *Smoke Signals*. In 2005 our colleague Faye Ginsberg curated a film series at the Museum of Modern Art titled "First Peoples, First Features," consisting of the first feature films by indigenous peoples: Native Americans, Inuit, Maori, Aborigines, and so forth. The Museum of the American Indian near Battery

Park has a running show on native artists in the city, including a film about Spiderwoman, an outrageously carnivalesque all-woman native group with Brooklyn roots and close links to the downtown avant-garde. In 1992 some four hundred Native American groups went to the United Nations to protest the quincentennial of Columbus's arrival, and Native Americans and their allies made antiquincentennial films with titles such as *Columbus on Trial* and *Columbus Didn't Discover Us*. Native American books sell by the hundreds of thousands. Native Americans were not exterminated in North America to any greater extent than they were in Latin America. So yes, one does indeed "see Indians in the streets of New York," although they are not wearing feathered head-dresses and therefore might be invisible to "Spanish eyes" that filter out anything that does not fit the preconceptions.

The word *Anglo-Saxon* appears on virtually every page of Tamames's text and thus calls for analysis. The word provides a key to a general slippage between legitimate political critique and illegitimate culturalist generalization. Despite the book's up-to-the-minute feel, Tamames and European writers like him are at the same time fighting very old battles that go back to interimperial rivalries in the Americas, including in what is now the United States. Spain had an enormous empire but lost it first to the British, then to the independence demands of their own Creole settlers, and finally to the United States, leaving only a few enclaves in Morocco and Equatorial Guinea abandoned by Franco. This shrinkage of the empire has been a source of lingering resentment in Spain.[12] It is no accident then that Tamames reserves his anti-imperialism for its British and American forms. Lurking in the background is European resentment over the Monroe Doctrine, which forbade European interventions in the Americas while facilitating U.S. domination, and over the Spanish-American War—when the United States ended Spanish imperialism but substituted its own.

Haunting European debates about the Americas is the vague (and perhaps even unconscious) idea that for many Spaniards, Florida, Texas, and California would have been better off staying Spanish, that for many French people, New Orleans would have been better off French, and so forth. On the U.S. side, the often unconscious converse assumption is that British colonization was better than Spanish, an assumption that undergirded the Monroe Doctrine and its Teddy Roosevelt corollary.

For our part, meanwhile, we would condemn all these colonialisms in exactly the same measure, while noting nuances in the precise forms of domination and while recognizing that it is American imperialism, especially, that dominates the contemporary epoch.

The fact that Tamames denounces the English alongside the Americans, and that he does so in cultural and political terms, suggests that he is replaying the old cultural quarrel between "les Latins" and "the Anglo-Saxons." This polarity was invented by the French during their nineteenth-century incursions into Mexico—Cinco de Mayo, after all, celebrates Mexican victories against the French—as part of an attempt to create a broad anti-U.S. alliance. But to our mind, both terms are misnomers: Latin America is not exclusively Latin, and North America is not only "Anglo-Saxon." (We will return to this point in another section.)

Tamames's book constitutes a decidedly mixed bag, mingling a legitimate critique of contemporary unilateralist U.S. foreign policy and of certain alienated aspects of the dominant forms of the American way of life—a critique we share—along with completely misfired cultural caricatures. Tamames conflates the American government with the American people: for him, both are paranoid, egocentric, childish, ignorant, irritable, greedy, and arrogant. Giving himself the right to generalize about the attitudes and state of happiness of some three hundred million people, Tamames offers the following gems of "scientific judgment": "friendship does not exist in a natural form in the United States" (p. 55); "A young Berliner, Milano, Lisboan, Sevillian, or resident of Marseille, can go out with four friends and have more fun than an American in his entire life" (p. 59); "Americans, and to a lesser degree the English, do not smile; they merely market themselves" (p. 54); and "White Americans have always lacked invention and creativity" (p. 159). Everything—priests molesting children, critical points made by Noam Chomsky, the behavior of drunken British hooligans in Spain—becomes grist for Tamames's mill.

The desire to stress only the negative things about Americans often leads Tamames into blatant contradiction. Thus to denounce the American system, Tamames argues that it is really a "dictatorship"; but to denounce the American people, he argues that the United States is not a dictatorship but a democracy, in which the people are responsible for the crimes of their leaders. He argues that Americans are never critical of their government, yet he relies largely on American critics for his evidence about American offenses. He derides the United States as puritanical but also denounces the American obsession with plastic surgery. The very same practices—Internet chat rooms, for example—are seen as reflecting negatively on Americans and positively on Europeans: a symptom of loneliness and alienation in the United States, they are a sign of openness to progress in Europe. For him and anti-Americans like him, Americans are simultaneously extremely stupid and yet diabolically clever, to the point that they have managed to dominate and seduce the world. What explains the contradictions is the desire to always speak ill, and to hell with the contradictions.

In Tamames's case, the national narcissism moves far beyond politics to include crude affirmations of a general cultural superiority. Just as Henry Higgins, in *My Fair Lady,* asked, "Why can't a woman be more like a man," and just as some provincial and arrogant Americans ask, "Why can't everyone be like us?" Tamames seems to wonder why America "can't be more like Spain." Tamames even makes the self-advertising boast that Latins are better lovers. (His picture is on the jacket, should anyone be interested.) Young Europeans, Tamames assures us, see the "Anglo-Saxons" as the worst seducers in the world, because "young Americans have trouble appreciating the beauty of young women" and both Brits and Americans pay no attention to the verbal side of seduction.

> We have all heard the jokes and anecdotes, especially about the English, who live more close to us. It is rare that a young Frenchman, Spaniard, or Italian would ever fear any Anglo-Saxon competitor for the affections of a young girl. The American would miss out through slobbering over the girl and lack of interest in verbal approaches, while the Englishman, after the woman has already escaped his grasp, would not realize that he should have told her something nice. (p. 42)

So in the end, the discussion comes down to this: the Spaniard thinks that the Iberian chorizo is more *saboroso* than the Anglo-Saxon wiener! But perhaps women and—to move beyond the pale of Tamames's apparent orientation, gay men—should have a say about these issues and also about whether they want to seduce or be seduced and whether they might be interested in conchitas and chorizos. And shouldn't what is essentially a political and ideological debate be pitched on a different and higher register than that of putative national personalities?[13]

Our evaluation of Tamames's book anticipates some of our points about certain forms of anti-American writing. First, anti-American writing is often primarily directed at the writer's national interlocutors or compatriots: Tamames, for example, is indirectly attacking the neoliberal Spanish right (and here we probably have more in common with him than with them). Second, some European anti-American writing mingles a politically left critique of American foreign policy and American-style capitalism with a culturally elitist and stereotypical view of Americans as vulgar, superficial, and materialistic. Third, some European anti-American writing is politically left in the sense of being anti-imperialist and anticapitalist yet politically conservative in its opposition to progressive movements such as feminism, multiculturalism, and gay liberation. Fourth, in methodological terms, such writing mingles the methods of materialist analysis of power arrangements with a static culturalist analysis of presumed "national personalities." Finally, such writing—and here Tamames is worse than most—crudely equates the U.S. government with the American people.

Our main point is to score the narcissism both of American superpatriots and of some of the anti-American writers. Indeed, we argue against pernicious forms of nationalist and ethnoessentialist modes of thinking in general. For us, nations are complex, conflictual, and multiple. Peoples everywhere have an obligation to participate in politics, but they also cannot be reduced to the horrific things that their governments do. Moreover, we all have a lot to learn by a parallax view, seeing ourselves through the eyes of others, both those within and those outside of our own countries. At this point in history, many Americans could learn a good deal from European and Latin American analyses of the "American way of life," which although prosperous and energetic also seems terribly unequal, stressful, militaristic, and ultimately cruel, including even, as Hurricane Katrina showed, for its own citizens. At the same time, French people could learn from Americans and Brazilians, together and separately. For our part, we discuss patriotism not simply in relation to one nation-state, or even as part of a bipolar comparison between two nation-states, but rather within a multilateral and polycentric perspective. What happens when we look at political systems and representation through discrepant histories of citizenship? What do we see that we might not have otherwise noticed?

But before we get to what our three nations have thought of each other, it is important to discuss what they have thought of themselves. It is to that question that we now turn.

U.S. Exceptionalism: The City on the Hill

We are in a unique position because of our unique assets, because of the character of our people, the strength of our ideals, the might of our military and the enormous economy that supports it.

—Vice President Dick Cheney

We are the indispensable nation. We stand tall. We see further into the future.

—Former Secretary of State Madeleine Albright

The United States has been the greatest force for good in history. [It] provides the single surviving model of human progress.

—President George W. Bush

Many reasons have been advanced to explain the American belief in the "exceptional" status of the United States: the country's privileged geographical position, its sense of providential destiny, its rejection of aristocracy, its status as a "nation of nations," and its distinctive political institutions. What has been called "American exceptionalism" promotes the idea of the United States as uniquely democratic and destined to exercise benevolent power in the world. The United States, in this vision, is the "city on the hill" or a "beacon to the world." One of the original disseminators of this idea was the French writer Alexis de Tocqueville, who in his *Democracy in America* (1830) gave a European imprimatur to a view of the United States as the premiere avatar of democracy. Ever since then, exceptionalists have argued that the American system is not only the best in the world but also exportable to the world at large. For Francis Fukuyama, at least in his "end of history" incarnation, history "ends" with American self-realization becoming the model for the entire world. Hidden within every non-American, within this perspective, is a potential American trying to emerge from the darkness into the light of American freedom and prosperity.

After its "city on the hill" beginnings, U.S. exceptionalism later mutated somewhat into a more materialist vision linked to the "American dream"; that is, the view of the United States as a model not only of democracy but also of upwardly mobile prosperity. "The house on the hill" became "the mansion on the hill." The United States, in this sense, was the "land of opportunity," where "success was available to the willing and able" and where "anyone could become president." A corollary leitmotif posited the United States as the "land of immigrants," the natural destination of the tired and oppressed "yearning to breathe free."

In the era of globalization, the exceptionalist idea mutates once again. Here the city on the hill becomes a set of economic policies—the idea that U.S.-style laissez-faire capitalism, expressed in the "Washington Consensus," with its faith in unregulated markets, reduced public spending, and International Monetary Fund tutelage, should be the model for the entire world. The fact that the model almost never worked, at least not for the countries of the "South," was not seen as a reason to reject it. But what all these variant versions of American exceptionalism share is the idea that the United States occupies a special position within human history, which derives from its having managed to escape the bitter class and religious conflicts and "entangling alliances" of Europe, on one hand, and the poverty and powerlessness of non-European countries on the other.

One of the clichés of anti-Americanism is the idea that the United States, and the Americas generally, are young and immature. But this idea of the United States as a "young country" is misleading. First, the United States has the oldest continuing constitutional democracy, so it is not young in political terms. Second, the United States is one of the oldest nation-states, predating even European countries such as Italy and Germany by about a century. Furthermore, all national identities are layered, with multiple temporalities and cultural strata. All the settler states of the Americas, in this sense, inherit the oldness not only of Europe (in the sense that they extend European modes) but also of Africa and indigenous America. In the United States, this multiple inheritance is reflected in place names such as Athens, Cairo, and Syracuse (drawn from the entire world), in architecture (e.g., the Greco-Roman style of monumental Washington), and in literary culture (the presence of Shakespeare in Melville's *Moby Dick*). More generally, the history of the Americas overall embeds the multiple and millennial histories of the indigenous peoples, of the countries of origin of enslaved Africans and indentured servants, and of the countries of origin of the conquistadores, *bandeirantes*, pioneers, and immigrants from all over the world.

And if Europe, by implication, is so "mature," one wonders how millennia of maturing could have led to some of the worst wars and holocausts of human history. Part of the shock of the Nazi onslaught for Europeans was that, for the first time since the eighteenth century, Europeans were doing to each other what they had habitually done to indigenous populations in Africa, Asia, and the Americas. As historian Tony Judt put it, "It was in the Second World War, then, that the full force of the modern European state was mobilized for the first time, for the primary purpose of conquering and exploiting other Europeans."[14] Francophone writer Aime Cesaire saw the Jewish Holocaust of the 1940s as a "crowning barbarism" that summed up the "daily barbarisms" of colonialism, tolerated and even applauded as long as they were applied only to non-European peoples.[15] Given the vast human costs of these practices, Europeans have reformed themselves and become relatively peaceful and democratic during the last half century or so, but let us hear no more talk about "maturity."

Within the American exceptionalist view, meanwhile, the United States accumulates a series of "firsts": it is the first "new nation," the first modern constitutional democracy, the first immigrant "nation of nations," and the only country based on opportunity for the individual. Its "manifest destiny," in the official view, was to conquer the land up to the Pacific and then to spread its power to the Caribbean,

Latin America, and the world. The idea is that the United States, blessed by providence with a unique purpose and fate, has avoided the petty foibles of others and thus somehow transcended history. The United States, from the Founding Fathers to George W. Bush, has displayed a specifically American form of "universalistic nationalism." America's cause, as Benjamin Franklin stated, "is the cause of all mankind." American internationalism, as conservative commentator Robert Kagan put it, is a by-product of the country's nationalism. In advancing its own interests, according to the dominant view, the United States advances the interests of humanity, whence the rather strange idea, on the part of some Americans, that the United States has the right to intervene anywhere in the world.

American exceptionalism refers to the complex of ideas that produces the United States as uniquely and providentially favored. English writer G.K. Chesterton wrote, "America is the only nation in the world that is founded on a creed ... [one] set forth with dogmatic and even theological lucidity in the Declaration of Independence."[16] Seymour Martin Lipset, one of the most widely read analysts of American exceptionalism, writing in the 1970s, listed five features of the American creed: (1) liberty, (2) egalitarianism, (3) individualism, (4) populism, and (5) laissez-faire. These features, for Lipset, emerge from a revolution and from the absence of feudal structures, monarchies, and aristocracies.

Lipset's taxonomy of features is quietly premised on a number of tacit norms and silent exclusions. Lipset assumes, first of all, that exceptionalism is universally shared by Americans. He assumes, in short, that there are no exceptions to exceptionalism. There is little room in his schema for the victims of American exceptionalism, whether at home and abroad, many of whom are understandably skeptical about exceptionalism. Did the Native Americans coming from communal cultures endorse individualism and laissez-faire in the same way white Euro-Americans did? And what is the relationship between the various terms in the taxonomy? Must liberty always be individualistic, or are there collective, communal, transindividual forms of freedom? How does laissez-faire rhyme with egalitarianism? Could egalitarianism possibly have meant the same thing for white slaveholders and for enslaved blacks? Do African Americans and European Americans respond in identical ways to patriotic holidays such as the Fourth of July? The former slave and intellectual Frederick Douglass famously answered in the negative. Did liberty mean the same thing for the frontiersman gaining land and the Native American losing it? Did American socialists and communists and anarchists in the 1930s endorse laissez-faire in the same way as procapitalist businessman? And did individualism mean the same thing for men as it did for women, when the latter for a long time were denied the vote and lacked personal liberties?

The myths that bind us are also often the myths that blind us. One danger in uncritical accounts of American exceptionalism such as Lipset's is that they encourage complacency. Myths of individual success and mobility, for example, lead us to glance over the fact that the United States is the most socially unequal of the first world industrialized nations, with 5 percent of the world's population but 25 percent of the world's prisoners, with more than 20 percent of its people living in poverty (compared to 7 percent in France), and with more than forty million of its people without health care (compared to virtually none in Canada). Contrary to right-wing myths, democracy and capitalism do not always work in tandem; they often work against each other. While democracy calls for equality, unregulated capitalism generates inequality. Capitalism can be **made** democratic in terms of distribution of wealth, as it has been in the Scandinavian countries, but it is not intrinsically so. (The German industrial capitalists who collaborated with Hitler had no problem with slave labor; after all, it held down costs.)

The American political system is dominated by corporate elites who laud individual effort and success even as they make the individual "success" of many others much less likely. It is difficult to reconcile Lipset's "egalitarianism" with increasing economic inequalities, where CEOs now often earn something like five hundred times what their own workers are earning. The issue of race, furthermore, runs through all these inequalities, because it is blacks and other "minorities" who are disproportionately incarcerated, impoverished, disenfranchised, and lacking in health care, and it is often they who are the workers (or the unemployed) rather than the CEOs. By calling laissez-faire capitalism an integral part of the American creed, furthermore, Lipset has subtly implied that socialism or even social welfarism within capitalism is "un-American," thus reinforcing the dominant ideology, failing to see the role of coercion from above in declaring more egalitarian social projects as "off-limits." In sum, Lipset's account of exceptionalism is itself exceptionalist. By idealizing American history, Lipset has not so much analyzed exceptionalism as provided an example of it.

From the beginning, the dominant political forces in the United States have carried out an exceptionalist ideology through expansionist policies that spread American power in ever-widening arcs of influence. This ideology was initially fueled by the conquest of the "frontier" (i.e., the appropriation of Native American lands). Historian Richard Drinnon traces the process by which white hostility toward "savages" has been recycled throughout American history. The process began with the "protovictims," the Pequots massacred in 1637, when the Puritans made some four hundred of them "as a fiery oven" in their village near the Mystic River and later finished off three hundred more in the mud of Fairfield Swamp, in an early example of the "righteous massacres" that have constituted one very violent strain within American history.[17] The aggressiveness subsequently expanded through Manifest Destiny and the "conquest of the west." At the same time that the United States was constructing a democratic system for whites, it was perpetuating slavery for blacks and dispossession for Native Americans. With the Monroe Doctrine, the U.S. power elite established Latin America as its sphere of influence, after which it was extended to the Philippines during the "imperialist binge" at the turn of the century, where many of the commanding generals had fought in the Plains and Apache wars.[18] Indeed, the model of frontier conquest in a way provided the dominant paradigm for the relations between the United States and much of the world. "The pigments of Indian-hating," writes Drinnon, "shaded off into coolie-hating, the Chinese Exclusion Act (1882) and the 'Yellow Peril' hysteria at the turn of the century."[19] At the same time, many of America's best writers—Mark Twain provides one example—denounced these injustices.

Another Asian war, the Vietnam War, also reverberated with echoes of the Indian wars. According to Frances Fitzgerald in *Fire in the Lake*, the American elite saw the war as the "painless conquest of an inferior race ... an achievement made in the name of humanity—the triumph of light over darkness, of good over evil, of civilization over brutish nature."[20] The very names of some of the military operations in Vietnam—Sam Houston, Hickory, and Daniel Boone—resonated with the memory, and the attitudes, of the American frontier history relayed in the Hollywood Western genre. For Lyndon Johnson, Vietnam recalled the Alamo. Even the "domino theory," according to Drinnon, "was an updated, internationalized version of the older fear of pan-Indian movements."[21] And during the first Persian Gulf War, General Schwarz-kopf compared Iraq to "Indian territory." The current "shock and awe" violence of the Bush administration has its historical roots in what historian Richard Slotkin calls the "regenerating violence" of conquest. And from a perspective opposite to Slotkin's, Robert Kaplan titled the first chapter of his recent ode (*Imperial Grunts*) to the romance of militaristic violence "Injun Country."

The U.S. claim to universality is rooted in the myth of "democracy in America," a myth formulated by de Tocqueville in the book of that title. Like France, the United States has sometimes deployed its claim of universality—the universal applicability of U.S.-style democracy and the "American way of life"—for imperial purposes. But while France spoke of its "civilizing mission"—whereby the colonized peoples were "lucky" to be granted the privileges of French civilization even as they lost their land and their rights—the United States spoke of "wars for democracy," which sometimes turned out to be wars on behalf of U.S. power. The quarrel in the United Nations over the Iraq War, in this sense, can be seen as a conflict between two imperialisms, one in ascension, and the other in decline, whence Donald Rumsfeld's cutting insult about France as "old Europe," even as he himself mimicked that continent's old imperialist ways.

The present-day neocons have refurbished the old idealistic language of Woodrow Wilson ("making the world safe for democracy"), but as with Wilson their idealistic language masks a clear will to power. The policy documents authored by the U.S. hawks in the Pentagon unabashedly declare an intention to dominate the world or at least to wage "preventive wars" aimed at foreclosing even the vaguest possibility of the rise to prominence of any rival powers. As neoconservatives Lawrence F. Kaplan and William Kristol put it, the foreign policy of the United States must be "unapologetic, idealistic, assertive, and well-funded. America must not only be the world's policeman or its sheriff, it must be its beacon and guide."[22] Such language always resonates with the idealistic nationalism of a certain part of the American public, but its results, as are obvious from the current mayhem in Iraq, are ambiguous in the extreme. Writer Robert Jay Lifton speaks of "superpower syndrome" to designate the feeling of omnipotence and false entitlement generated by being the dominant power. For George W. Bush, the United States represents the world's "single surviving model of human progress," an arrogant attitude that results in what some comedians have called "middle finger" diplomacy, mocked by the fake headlines of the satirical newspaper *The Onion:* "Bush asks UN Support for his I-Can-Do-Anything-I-Want-Policy" and "Bush Grants Self Permission to Grant More Power to Self." Or as fake reporter Ed Helms put it on the satirical news program the *Daily Show,* George W. Bush had the "balls" to appoint John Bolton, who despises the United Nations, to represent the United States at the United Nations. According to Helms, scientists claim that if George W. Bush's balls got any bigger, "they would be visible from outer space."

Religious historian Richard T. Hughes traces the origins of exceptionalism in the *Myths America Lives By.* While Lipset focuses on abstract Enlightenment ideals such as "equality," Hughes focuses on "myths," not in the pejorative sense of "lies" but rather in the sense of the stories that give us a sense of meaning and purpose.[23] A constellation of these myths, according to Hughes, shapes the collective sense of American belonging and destiny. The first myth is that of "the Chosen Nation," which can be traced all the way back to the Puritans but which gradually morphed from a communal bond of mutual support into a claim for an American redeeming role on the stage of world history. The second myth is that of "Nature's Nation," which emerged in the Revolutionary Era and conceived the institutions of the United States as being in accord with what the Enlightenment philosophers called "nature." This myth was used to justify both egalitarian and hierarchical institutions. The third myth is that of "the Christian Nation," which emerged with the religious resurgence called the "Second Great Awakening" and tried to impose a Christian stamp on the national adventure. The fourth myth is "the myth of the Millennial Nation," which evolved with American expansion and stressed the American vocation in ushering in a millennial age of freedom. (George W. Bush often speaks in the language of this myth, seeing "freedom as God's gift to the world.") The fifth myth, which emerged with the conquest of the west, is that of

Manifest Destiny, which Hughes sees as an outgrowth of the other four myths.

The majority of these myths, according to Hughes, hold potential both for good and for ill. The myth of the Chosen Nation reminds us of the "national covenant" binding Americans to God and to fellow citizens, but it also runs the risk of encouraging divinely sanctioned arrogance. All of the myths favor a concept that identified U.S. interests with those of the world at large. When they come to form part of patriotic discourse, Hughes points out, they entail an astonishing capacity to prettify the actual role of the United States in that world. Nurtured on these myths, many Americans assume that what our government does in the world is axiomatically good, and when it is not good, that badness is always a tragic exception, never the rule. While critical of all the myths, Hughes finds only one of them—the myth of innocence—utterly worthless, because it is grounded in self-delusion. Americans are asked to accept on faith that the hundreds of U.S. military interventions, from the Conquest of Mexico to the latest war in Iraq, have all been inspired by idealism. The contemporary mainstream American media, we would add, consistently frame the Iraq War as an "attempt to bring democracy to Iraq," eliding other, more material motives. The debates in the media tend to be more about technical and tactical questions—for example, are there enough troops?—than about the basic legitimacy of "preventive war," an idea clearly premised on American exceptionalism since it asserts a right that would not be accorded to any other state.

American exceptionalism and the myth of innocence, the idea of the "American Adam" wandering in a pristine paradise, we suggest, go hand in hand. Within a kind of fantasy of constantly renewed ethical virginity, the United States seems to be always in the process of "losing its innocence," whether with the Civil War, World War I, the assassination of John F. Kennedy, 9/11, or, most recently, the Abu Ghraib torture photos. But this "innocence" can thrive only in the magic kingdom of amnesia. Every lapse is portrayed as a momentary departure from a taken-for-granted benevolence. An integral part of the myth of innocence is its corollary—the myth of good intentions. Unlike other nations motivated by base and venal "interests," the United States has "ideals" and "values." Thus even the negative consequences of U.S. actions—for instance, the utter havoc in Iraq—is always seen a part of a well-intentioned effort. Thousands of deaths can be waved away with an "at least we meant well." The road to hell in Iraq was paved with what were purported to be good intentions.

For the George W. Bush administration, the torture in Iraq prisons or Guantanamo, even though traceable to the very top echelons of his government, does not reflect the "real" America, which for him always remains without blemish. Or as the mock reporter Rob Corddry put it on the *Daily Show*, "There's no question that what took place in that prison was horrible. But the Arab world has to realize that the U.S. shouldn't be judged on the actions of a ... well, we shouldn't be judged on actions. It's our principles that matter, our inspiring, abstract notions. Remember: just because torturing prisoners is something we did, doesn't mean that it's something we *would* do." Indeed, what Bush seems to be saying about torture is, "We do not torture, and further, it works!" Or, as summarized by another *Daily Show* report, "Everything we do is legal. Torture is not legal. Ergo (that's Latin for 'Bite Me') we do not torture."

But the problem goes far beyond Bush, and exceptionalism is not just a Republican or Democratic problem. Exceptionalist rhetoric forms part of the standard catchphrases of American politicians from both parties, who constantly embroider their speeches with ritual references to "this great land of ours," "the greatest nation in history," and the "greatest democracy on the face of the earth." Comic George Carlin jokes that the phrase "the most powerful nation on the face of the earth" is "usually thrown in just before we bomb a bunch of brown people."[24] The speakers at the 2004 Democratic Convention felt obliged to constantly reiterate the obvious: "We are here because we love America!" John Kerry, mimicking Republican machismo, tried to out-motorcycle, out-testosterone, and out-warrior-patriot George W. Bush, the man with the padded crotch proclaiming "Mission Accomplished!" But when the real thing imitates the fake, the real becomes fake as well. Surprising though it may seem to many Americans, political party rallies in other countries—with the exception of militarized regimes—do not necessarily feature such orgies of macho militarism. Nor do debates have to be shaped by false accusations of a lack of patriotism. Love of country should be assumed, as citizens simply make their political arguments, without the blackmail of Ann Coulter–style charges of treason for anyone who does not walk in lockstep with right-wing diktats. Any view of treason, such as hers, which would indict half of the country is, one would think, highly suspect. Does she really hope to put millions of Americans in prison, just so everyone understands that liberals can go to jail, too?

Some forms of American-style narcissism are submerged and might better be called ethnocentric solipsism rather than exceptionalism, in that they take the form not of explicit claims of superiority but rather of a lack of interest in other nations, even those in which the United States is intervening. And that problem cannot be blamed entirely on George W. Bush and the right wing. The U.S. educational system has become more and more U.S. centered, with less and less space for geography and world history. The U.S. media, meanwhile, have limited their foreign coverage to spectacular catastrophes or to direct challenges to what are presumed to be U.S. interests. In so doing, the media deprive American viewers not only of knowledge but also of self-knowledge based on comparative experience and relational perspective. Thus many Americans, who have never traveled or lived abroad and who therefore lack any concrete experience or knowledge of other social systems or cultures, who live in a society that denies them good schools, affordable health care, and transparent politics, naively believe that they are living in the best of all possible countries. And even more serious, those Americans who know almost nothing about the world find it quite normal for their country to dominate the very countries about which they know so little. It is this lethal combination of official arrogance and popular ignorance that has led many non-Americans to regard the United States, and by extension Americans, as so dangerous.

Dominated by corporate interests and preoccupied with ratings, the corporate media constantly flatter American narcissism and neglect the image in the mirror of the larger world.[25] As a result, it is within the United States that we find the greatest gap between self-image and reality. Although many Americans think of the United States as extremely generous with foreign aid, for example, in fact the United States, while the richest nation, is also the stingiest donor—transferring only 0.1% of its GNP (when the UN target figure is 0.7%)—even as it disproportionately drains the world's resources, for example, through the highest per capita use of oil. While most of the world sees the United

States as an imperialistic nation, most Americans do not. Already in 1927, renowned cultural commentator Walter Lippman wrote, "All of the world thinks of the United States as an empire, except the people of the United States."[26] And while the United States thinks of itself as promoting peace in the world, much of the world finds it bellicose. The ever-Orwellian "W" hailed Americans as "a peaceful people" even as he was rushing headlong toward a completely unnecessary war.

Thus an eveloping fog of self-infatuation blurs vision, standing in the way of seeing others with clarity and even of seeing our own problems and ourselves with lucidity. Delusion and narcissism go hand and hand, and self-aggrandizement is a sure sign of egomaniacal perception. And since neither the media nor the educational system foster knowledge of other countries and perspectives, this complacently self-congratulatory regard becomes a kind of discursive norm. And because neither the government nor the media explain what our government is really doing abroad and with what consequences, uninformed Americans are usually surprised by the angry "blowback" provoked by U.S. policies. The shock derives from the gap between the idealized self-perception and the unflattering reflection of oneself in the eyes of others.

American exceptionalist discourse is inherently paradoxical. While viewing the United States as positively exceptionalist, and thus different from the rest of the world, it also declares itself as a norm to be diffused and emulated; thus containing its very potential dissolution—from exception to norm. Lately the concept of exceptionalism has taken on a perverse new twist, the idea that the United States makes exceptions for itself when it comes to international law and human rights. Michael Hardt and Antonio Negri point out in their book *Multitude* that the term "U.S. exceptionalism" has two distinct and incompatible meanings. On the one hand, the United States claims to be the exception from the corruption and decadence and endless strife of Europe. In this sense, it sees itself as the beacon of republican virtue. On the other hand, American exceptionalism has now come to evoke the idea that the United States is "excepted" from international law. Thus the United States exempts itself from international agreements on the environment, human rights, and criminal courts, claiming that its military can ignore the rules to which others are subjected in terms of preemptive strikes, weapons control, illegal detention, and torture. But since the first meaning of exceptionalism—republican virtue—means nothing if it does not mean that "no one is above the law," then the second meaning, that is, that an imperial power is "above the law," stands in direct contradiction to the first.[27]

The United States incarnates a paradox concerning human rights. On one level, the United States, in the postwar period, set up an impressive international juridical apparatus meant to protect human rights and prevent the reemergence of totalitarian regimes. Yet the United States resists "complying with human rights standards at home or aligning its foreign policy with these standards abroad."[28] The United States was alone—except for Somalia—in refusing to sign the UN Convention on the Rights of the Child, presumably to protect its right to execute minors accused of capital crimes. Unlike 169 other countries, the United States refused to ratify the Convention on the Elimination of All Forms of Discrimination against Women, presumably to placate the Christian right, even though the United States often exploits the rhetoric of oppression of women in some parts of the Muslim world to justify its foreign policies. And in 2002 the United States tried to block a protocol strengthening the UN Covenant against Torture. Currently, the Bush administration, in the person of "Vice President of Torture" Dick Cheney, is pressuring Congress to make an exception for the CIA in its prohibition of "cruel, inhuman, and degrading punishment" of prisoners. While even the worst dictators hide the practice of torture, Cheney campaigns for it openly.

Italian political theorist Giorgio Agamben traces the lineage of the various "states of exception" and "emergency powers" and "full powers" that have been used historically to strengthen the state. The expression "full powers" refers to the expansion of the powers of the government and, in the U.S. case, the power of the presidency and the conferral on the executive of the power to bypass the legislature through unilateral decisions, which modify or abrogate the laws in force. This is exactly what happened, of course, when President George W. Bush decided to authorize the National Security Agency (NSA) to spy on American citizens without requesting a warrant. The administration has shown an eagerness not only to go to war but also to insist that Bush is a "wartime" president and "Commander in Chief" in a post-9/11 age and that therefore the old rules no longer apply. On November 13, 2000, the president issued a "military order" that authorized the "indefinite detention" and trial by "military commissions." The USA PATRIOT Act, meanwhile, had already authorized the attorney general to take into custody any alien suspected of activities endangering the "national security of the United States." What is disturbing about President Bush's order, Agamben points out, "is that it radically erases any legal status of the individual, thus producing a legally unnamable and unclassifiable being," within a legal situation comparable to that of "the Jews in the Nazi *Lager* [camps], who along with their citizenship, had lost every legal identity."[29] Although the media try to "normalize" what amounts to a serious constitutional crisis, its gravity keeps surfacing in various skirmishes between Congress and the administration, between the courts and the administration, between European authorities and the administration, and so forth. Although it would be hyperbolic to call the Bush–Cheney administration fascist, a clear authoritarian drift is perceptible in its pursuit of overweening power for the "unitary executive." The most unitary form of the executive, after all, is dictatorship.

On the international level, the United States in the postwar period has been both a major global enforcer of human rights and a major violator of those very same rights. For human rights theorist Michael Ignatieff, this kind of exceptionalism involves three separate elements: (1) the United States signs on to international human rights and humanitarian law conventions and treaties but then exempts itself from their provisions by explicit reservations, nonratification, or noncompliance; (2) the United States maintains double standards, judging itself and its friends by more permissive criteria than it does its enemies; and (3) the United States denies jurisdiction to human rights laws within its own domestic sphere. Exceptionalism, he argues, has become "exemptionalism."[30] The result is that the United States practices exactly the abuses that it denounces. It rightly criticizes others for abuses and then practices the same abuses in Guantánamo, Iraq, and Afghanistan. The United States rightly denounced the Soviet Empire for its gulag prisons yet now uses, even if not on the same scale, similar "black hole" prisons (reportedly in Poland and Romania). After supporting Saddam Hussein, it overthrew him, supposedly for torturing and gassing his people, yet the United States tortured Iraqis in Saddam's own prisons and has allegedly used chemical weapons (white phosphorous bombs) on Fallujah. And now even "our Iraqis" are complaining about the killing of civilians by American soldiers. And whereas the Sunnis, under Saddam, used to torture the Shia, now the Shia torture the Sunnis and vice versa. In June, 2006, Iraq suffered the slow-motion equivalent of 9/11—3,400 people dead. George W. Bush, who spoke from the rubble of Ground Zero, has reduced much of Iraq to rubble. "Stay the course" translates as "continue the bloodletting." Welcome to freedom—Bush-style.

The trajectory is thus from an early post–World War II period when the United States took a leading role in the drafting of the Universal Declaration of Human Rights, to a post-9/11 era when the Bush administration regards such rights as subversive. Geographer Neil Smith highlights the contradiction by suggesting that at this point President George W. Bush, at Guantánamo, has probably held more political prisoners in Cuba than Fidel Castro has.[31] And yet the administration seems surprised when it finds itself judged, for example, when other nations find the United States wanting in the area of human rights, whence administration outrage when Amnesty International accused it of creating a new "gulag" of extraterritorial and extralegal prisons. The Bush administration imagines that it need pay no price either domestically or internationally for establishing a whole extralegal system that institutes "military trials" for "enemy combatants"—a concept rejected even by many in the military and by the Supreme Court—and that practices extrajudicial "rendition" to countries that practice torture. It assumes that the rest of the world will not have the "bad taste" to point out the contradiction between claims of "spreading freedom" and these horrific practices. At this point, the same American government given to constantly lecturing the world on the beauty of its "values" is seen by that same world, ironically, as having no moral stature whatsoever. "The normative authority of the United States," as German philosopher Jürgen Habermas put it, "lies in ruins."[32] All of Ann Coulter's pseudo-patriotic rants cannot hide that crisis of legitimacy.

In economic terms, meanwhile, American exceptionalism means the attempted exportation of rampant deregulation and free market fundamentalism are the only viable options for the entire world, even when those policies are disastrous for "actually existing" human beings in countries such as Argentina and also, we would argue, for the citizens of the United States. The once wealthy nation of Argentina, after being praised as a model pupil following the rules of the Washington Consensus, turned into a kind of Enronlandia. The entire financial system collapsed, reducing the newly impoverished middle class to desperation, with some having to eat rats to survive. World economic management led by the Washington Consensus has fostered inequality both within and between countries. The conservative domestic program of what critics have called "private wealth and public squalor" has been transferred to the global domain.

In this sense, we must all "cry for Argentina." The American right wants to create a situation where the government has no obligation whatsoever for the welfare of citizens, "except for the ratcheting up of that military and police power that might be needed to quell social unrest."[33] In Argentina the financial elite preferred to crash the system rather than give up any of their power. And in the United States, as Social Security and pensions come under increasing attack, as corporations cook their books yet escape censure, we, like the Argentineans, cannot count on the banks, government, and corporations to help us out. And always that disquieting thought: what if all the military might and surveillance power in the hands of the government were turned directly on the American people? That, after all, is the ultimate logic of such concepts as the national security state and the "unitary executive."

Although the contemporary right defends both exceptionalism and globalization, there is a fundamental contradiction between the two phenomena. As Dutch social scientist Jan Pieterse puts it, "What does it mean when a country that by its own account is a historical exception sets rules for the world in general?"[34] Or to put it differently, how can a nation that regards itself as exceptional demand that others follow obediently in its tracks, if those tracks have already been defined as unique and exceptional? The corporate elite preaches universal "globalization" as a panacea, yet the asymmetrical power situation in the world, and the neocon wariness about any nation seeking even regional power, means that globalization tends to work only for the richest and most powerful countries. Despite George W. Bush's claims of the "American way of life" being the only "sustainable model" in the world, it is precisely the American way of life that is too expensive and wasteful to be a viable model for the world at large.

In fact events such as Hurricane Katrina demonstrate that the model is no longer viable even for the United States. If we can judge a society by how it treats the weak and the vulnerable, Katrina showed that our system and our corporate-adoring government have violated the basic social covenant of citizen protection. Few of the world's wealthy nations, furthermore, have themselves actually followed the formulas— that is, low tariffs, sell-off of public enterprises, and so forth—that the corporate globalizers recommend for poor nations. Washington itself, as the critics of neoliberalism point out, does not follow the Washington Consensus. The United States is caught up in a terrible contradiction; even as the elite "hawks" the American way of life, its policies make it impossible for most of the world to emulate that way of life. U.S.-led globalization theory of the 1990s, like the "economic takeoff" theory of the 1950s and 1960s, sees the Western nations, with the United States in the lead, as the pacesetters in a universally valid evolutionary process. But the expropriation of the labor and resources of the South, managed through "austerity policies" and the below-ground activities of "economic hit men," make it less and less likely that the poor nations could ever follow in the path of the prosperous Western nations. (We will return to the religious and class aspects of American exceptionalism in subsequent chapters.)

French Exceptionalism: Grandeur and *la Mission Civilisatrice*

France cannot be France without grandeur.

—from Charles de Gaulle's *Memoires de Guerre*

L'impossible n'est pas Français. (The word *impossible* is not French.)

—French saying

France, in some ways, represents the very paradigm of a grounded national identity rooted in a specific soil, expressed in a specific language, under the guidance of a powerful state. As one of the oldest nation-states in the world, France helped shape, realize, and formulate the idea of national sovereignty. Much of the theory of nation and nationalism has either been generated by French thinkers or concerned the French example. Like the United States, France, at least since 1789, has had a national creed. And like U.S. nationalism, French nationalism sees itself as universal. Janus-faced, French nationalism looks toward two distinct traditions: a rightist "blood and soil" nationalism and a more universalist idea of a global emancipatory mission for France. Like the United States, France sees itself as a model of liberty. In the words that are inscribed at the base of his statue on the Champs-Élysées, Charles de Gaulle spoke of the "immemorial covenant between the grandeur of France and the freedom of the world." Both French and American nationalism evoke this universal mission through metaphors of light. The United States sees itself as a beacon to the world. On the first anniversary of 9/11, George W. Bush mingled Enlightenment and biblical imagery: "The ideal of America is the hope of all mankind. That hope still lights the way. And the light shines in the darkness. And the darkness will not overcome it." France, meanwhile, speaks of itself as a beacon for humanity and lauds the *rayonnement* or "shining out" of its revolution and culture. The light metaphor, rooted in the already metaphorical idea of Enlightenment—*les lumières* in French—is a diffusionist one; the light spreads outward and brightens the world. The Great Seal of the United States, similarly, depicts a pyramid that the ancient Egyptians used as a metaphor for the tip of a beam of light. At the top of the pyramid is the all-seeing eye of the Egyptian sun god Horus, whose essence is light. The torch held by Lady Liberty, a French gift to the United States, similarly symbolizes this outward spreading of light.

French exceptionalism, like U.S. exceptionalism, stresses the political dimension of the national historical experience, here linked to the idea of the French Revolution as a model for the world. In this sense, France represents *liberté, egalité, fraternité,* not only for its own citizens but also for those who seek freedom in France as a *terre d'asile* (land of political asylum) and a *terre d'accueil* (refuge for the oppressed or impoverished). The American and French revolutions, as we shall see, were closely related through deep ideological and even personal links. Although many mistakenly think that the French Revolution preceded the American Revolution, an error perhaps rooted in the assumption that new ideas always originate in Europe, in fact the American Revolution preceded the French. Yet in the French view, the American Revolution was made possible by the French intellectual influence. In *The Old Regime and the French Revolution,* Alexis de Tocqueville argued that the American Revolution was the child, as it were, of French Enlightenment thought. (In our view, the Enlightenment was not exclusively French, or even exclusively European.) To the rest of Europe, the American Revolution seemed merely a novel and remarkable historical event, but for the French philosophers it was conclusive proof that they had been right all along. Indeed, the Americans, for de Tocqueville, "seemed only to be putting into practice ideas which had been sponsored by French writers, and to be making our dreams their realities."[35] This view expresses a kind of French intellectual paternity or ownership of the American Revolution, as if the Americans were merely giving birth to what had been a gleam in the eye of French philosophers.

Some of the tensions between France and the United States derive, then, from an intense duel over who represents the true universal and, relatedly, the true revolution. In a 1978 article titled "America and the French Intellectuals," French historian Pierre Nora wrote of a deep structural source for the "strange impermeability" between French and U.S. culture, one based on a struggle over the "idea of revolution itself." Which nation, and which political model, should be the universal model? (The answer "neither" is apparently not allowed within either French or Americanist national discourse.) French sociologist Pierre Bourdieu, in the same vein, speaks of United States–France relations as a case of confrontation between two "imperialisms of the universal."[36] The two countries struggle, in this sense, over who has the monopoly on the very concept of the universal.

The pretension to universality, in the case of France and the United States, forms a kind of "symbolic capital" (Pierre Bourdieu) that can be deployed in the service of two particular forms of imperialism: the harsh, militaristic American kind and the supposedly suave and cultivated (but historically also militaristic and often brutal) French kind. France claims universality based on its founding myth of the French Revolution as the model for any real revolution. The Marxist tradition of historiography, for Bourdieu, refurbished this myth by downgrading the American Revolution as less radical than the French Revolution and painting the Russian Revolution as the true heir of the French Revolution. (The conservative—or in French terms "liberal"—French historian Francois Furet called the discourse that links the French Revolution to the Russian Revolution "the Jacobino–Marxist vulgate.") The particularity of the French pretension to universality, for Bourdieu, is that it is both cultural and political; to be French is to feel oneself to have a right to "universalize" one's particular interest, this national interest that has as its particularity the trait of being universal.

Given this rivalry over ownership of the concept of "revolution," it is not surprising that familial metaphors lurk in the background of the France–United States relationship. Are the two revolutions siblings, as the metaphor of *républiques soeurs* (sister republics) suggests, or is it a relation between parent and child, mother and daughter, father and son? (The tropes of "mother" and "daughter" and "giving birth" are especially ironic because both revolutions barred women from full citizenship.) And who is the progenitor and who the offspring? Did the French Enlightenment give birth to the American Revolution, or did the American Revolution, as the first modern revolution, give birth to the French Revolution? Is America the legitimate heir of Europe or its bastard child? Or is it a Frankenstein monster, the creation that comes to haunt its creator? These questions reverberate even today as Europe oscillates between feeling itself to be the proud and then the disgusted forbearer of the United States, while the United States oscillates between being the rebellious and then the obedient child of Europe. The relationship, then, bears all the earmarks of the neuroses typical of dysfunctional kinship relations.

France too has its "myths that bind/blind." Historian Raoul Girardet, in his book *Mythes et Mythologies Politiques,* speaks of two "legendary narratives" in France: the myth of French unity and the myth of a golden age. The myth of unity papers over the endless conflicts typical of French history (and most national histories)—conflicts between religions (Catholic and Protestant), between aristocracy and commoners, between the secular and the religious, between the royalist and the revolutionary, between the native and the immigrant, between the right and the left, and so forth. Some analysts speak of the "bipolar" politics of France: "for and against the Monarchy, for and against the Revolution, for and against Robespierre, for and against the Constitutions of 1830 and 1848, for and against the Commune."[37]

The myth of a golden age, meanwhile, expresses nostalgia for a glorious past when all of Europe, and indeed much of the world, took its political, intellectual, and cultural cues from Paris. This kind of exceptionalism is often summed up in the word *grandeur*. Concretized in Parisian monuments, *grandeur* evokes power, prestige, eminence, lofty elevation, and an unabashed elitism. Within this discourse, past glories are invoked as inspiration for the present, as in Charles de Gaulle's "certain idea of a France" dedicated to an exalted and exceptional destiny. French grandeur is at once linguistic, cultural, social, and political. Linguistic grandeur evokes the idea of the French language as exceptionally rational—characterized by Cartesian "clear and distinct" ideas. Antoine Rivarol, in the symptomatically titled *Dictionary of the Universality of the French Language* wrote, in a kind of nationalistic tautology, "Everything universal is French, and everything French is universal." Just as France was the heir of the Roman Empire, so the French vernacular was the heir of the Latin language. The French language was seen as not only the royal language of aristocratic civility but also the crisply logical incarnation of Reason. France and its language, then, incarnate the rational quintessence of Europe. As President Georges Pompidou put it, rather wistfully, in the early 1970s, "Should French ever cease to be the primary working language of Europe, then Europe itself would never be fully Europe."[38] In 1995 President Jacques Chirac, after two decades of decline in the prestige of French, offered a new wrinkle in this discourse by defending French as the key to the defense of linguistic pluralism and cultural diversity in general. In proposing French as the vehicle for a broader linguistic resistance to English—why not Spanish, after all, or Wolof or Hindu?—Chirac was resurrecting the traditional claims for the French language as endowed with a special capacity to reflect ideas and feelings and to express a vision capable of inspiring universal solidarity and fraternity.

French grandeur has to do with achievements across a broad spectrum, which goes from high culture (achievements in painting, music, and literature) to the more quotidian culture of style and cuisine. Going back to the literary salons and courtly intercourse, elite France has been associated with elegant and witty conversation. Despite being only 1 percent of the world's population, France has given us brilliant intellectuals, extraordinary novelists, charismatic statesmen, audacious theater directors, and charming film stars. These cultural achievements have given France a vast influence completely disproportionate to French demographic reality.

In the past, French international "glories" were summed up in the phrase *la mission civilisatrice,* the idea that France was uniquely equipped to civilize the non-Western world. For centuries, French people were made to feel proud of their empire, a kind of prosthetic extension of Frenchness where freedom, culture, and assimilation were available to all. French imperialism, like most imperialisms, claimed that it was better than the others, less brutal, more civilized, less commercial, and more cultivated and thus entitled to speak on behalf of the world as a whole. Although France is currently critical of U.S. imperialism, France does not have clean hands when it comes to imperialism, neocolonialism, and exploitative forms of globalization.

Within Europe itself, France has historically practiced what Alain Duhamel calls a veritable "cult of sovereignty": "The venerability of the French nation-state, the first in Europe, Monarchical absolutism, Republican Jacobinism, and the authoritarian style of the Fifth Republic have maintained a religion of glorious independence, even if … it has become largely mythical. No matter: French people saw in this independence a source of pride and a guarantee of collective protection."[39] French exceptionalism in the aftermath of empire relays some earlier discourses of narcissism but also transmutes them into new, perhaps more modest, forms. If France no longer speaks for the universal, it does sometimes consider itself entitled to speak for Europe. This issue took on a new kind of geopolitical urgency during the disputes revolving around the Iraq War, where France was annoyed when some member states of "New Europe" refused to join the antiwar coalition and New Europe was annoyed at France for taking them for granted.

In terms of social policy, meanwhile, contemporary France represents a kind of "un-America." France prides itself on a humane social system, with guaranteed health care, unemployment insurance, paid vacations, and a short workweek. Many French people find the American system unfair, stressful, cruel, and punitive; they cannot imagine a government, especially in the richest country in the world, depriving its people of these basic social rights or understand the U.S. mania for massive incarceration as a social panacea. For the French, government is a way of solving people's problems—even if the solutions are not always equitably shared or efficiently executed—while right-wing Americans take exactly the opposite view: for them, the government, as Reagan put it, "is not the solution, it's the problem."

Yet the narcissistic process of selective memory operates in the French case, just as in the American case. Just as the exceptionalist view of the United States as a model of democracy and progress eliminates many "inconvenient" elements—genocide, the slave trade, xenophobia, violence, social exclusion, imperialism, and so forth—so the French exceptionalist view performs a tendentious "editing" of history. Like American exceptionalism, French exceptionalism masks and covers over all sorts of historical crises and injustices: an early history of religious persecution (against Jews and Protestants), the terror that ended the first phase of the French Revolution, the instability of French constitutions and political rule, the Napoleonic attempt to impose French-style revolution on Europe, the horror that was Vichy, and, most important, French colonial and imperial domination. Like the United States, France has been involved in Native American oppression, the transatlantic slave trade, and imperialism and neocolonialism. If the French are wise, T.D. Allman writes, "it is because their past foolishness has provided them with so many opportunities to learn."[40]

While France offers a much more solid welfare state to its citizens, it is easy to exaggerate the differences between the two systems. The French welfare state is also heavily bureaucratic and open to cronyism. The political system, meanwhile, is quite corrupt, although less dominated by corporate lobbies than the American system, and the educational system, while more standardized and equal than the American system, is still elitist and ethnocentric. There are subtle but unmistakable signs of discrimination in employment and housing based on race, religion, gender, and national origin. A solid one-fifth of French citizens support the racist right, and there is a pattern of prejudice against immigrants, especially against the children (and even the grandchildren) of Muslim, Arab, or African immigrants, leading to the violent rebellions of 2005. Even if these rebellions display nothing of the lethal magnitude of similar rebellions in the United States, where scores of people died, they still suggest that the French Republican model of "integration" is in deep crisis.

The 2006 protests over the New Employment Law, meanwhile, were revealing in a different sense. First, they showed the capacity of French civil society to mobilize millions of people and prevent an unpopular policy from being enacted. The American people, in contrast, have taken endless abuse from a right-wing administration that has constantly sided with the wealthy and with corporations. Second, the coverage of the protests in the United States manifests the right-wing pro-corporate slant of the dominant American media. The virtually universal line, from both conservatives and liberals, was that the protests were an irrational refusal of progress and reform, the self-defeating rejection of a measure designed to reduce unemployment by providing more flexibility for employers. Fine, but why did the media not also expose the other side of the question, that is, that the protestors were trying to preserve workers' rights that most Americans—except unionized workers—had already lost in corporate-dominated America; for example, the right not to be fired arbitrarily, the right not to have to juggle three or four jobs to survive, the right to pensions and health care, and so forth.

While U.S.-style arrogance, in Iraq, for example, takes political and economic form—"You Iraqis are incapable of governing yourselves so we will tell you how to do it"—French-style arrogance, especially in the wake of decolonization, often takes intellectual form—"You are incapable of thinking, so we will think for you"—resulting in what, to paraphrase French philosopher Michel Foucault, might be called the "indignity of thinking for others." Whatever their limitations, French cultural institutions have shown considerable openness to artists and artwork from other countries. On one level, this interest in the world is generous, productive, and cosmopolitan, but on another it sometimes takes the form not of listening to others but rather of telling others, often on the basis of minimal information, "who they are," a tendency that we will note in some of the French critiques of the United States.[41]

The 1989 bicentennial of the French Revolution brought all these trends to a grand and spectacular climax. The festivities began with a public reading of the "Declaration of the Rights of Man and of the Citizen" by French celebrities. The guests participated in the inauguration of three grandiose architectural projects—the Bastille Opera, the expanded Louvre, and the Arche de la Defense. In anthropologist David Beriss's analysis, the celebration symbolized both the foundation of the nation and the beginnings of modernity, the diffusionist spread of freedom and progress throughout the world: "In the parade's symbolism, France stood for the unity of the world brought together by the 'universal' values of the French revolution."[42]

At the same time, there are few parallels in the United States to the ways that the French government honors the cultural achievements of other nations. The 2005 "Year of Brazil in France" featured museum expositions, academic seminars, film festivals, book publications, and musical concerts. (France has come a long way since the racist "colonial expositions" and "human zoos" of centuries past.)[43] Whatever the exoticizing limits of the contemporary displays, they do still demonstrate an impressive openness toward other countries' artists and cultural achievements. In the 1980s François Mitterrand's culture minister Jack Lang gave expression to both tendencies—openness to others and praise of France—by encouraging collaboration with non-French artists and cultural industries while also stressing the cultural ambitions of France. In his 1984 "Projet Culturel Extérieur de la France," Lang described those ambitions as "probably unequalled in any country."

In the twenty-first century, French self-confidence is very much in crisis. In fact, French disillusionment with France is a "hardy perennial," expressed most recently in books with titles such as *La France qui Tombe* (Falling France), *Un Goût de Cendres* (A Taste of Ashes), and *Le Désarroi Français* (French Disarray). Alain Duhamel, in *Les Peurs Françaises* (French Fears), writes,

> France is full of self-doubt. She remembers what she was, she knows what she is no longer, but she doesn't know what she is becoming. She guards the memory of her past role, of her faded grandeur. She remembers having been the first power in Europe, having been the "oldest daughter" of the Roman Catholic Church, or having had the most renowned and powerful army of Europe. She remembers the pomp and circumstance and prestige of her kings, the colonial empire fashioned by her Republic, the influence of her language and culture, the astonishing spread of her political ideas. She has not forgotten that her revolution was

a universal thunderclap, that the imperial epic of Napoleon provoked admiration and disorder, fear and bitterness. She recalls
her status as a great power at the beginning of the 20th century.
She knows very well that she has made history, but she also real-
izes that she does so no longer.[44]

Writing from the neoliberal right, meanwhile, Guy Milliere denounces
what he sees as French ideological orthodoxy, composed of "a vague
mélange of soft socialism, insidious third-worldism and of old Pavlovian
reflexes drawn from Marxism–Leninism."[45] The French, he writes, "are
afraid: afraid of the future, afraid of war, afraid of the world." His wish
is that France, rather than taking the position of "an arrogant grand
Dame who has lost the means of her arrogance, rather look herself in
the face, and get rid of the myths ... which are asphyxiating her."[46] A
1999 poll had only 35 percent of French saying that they were proud of
their country. "The demise of [the] faith in the exceptional destiny of
the French nation," as one commentator put it, "eroded the belief in the
sovereign power of the nation state."[47]

With the partial erosion of the nation-state, national identity has
mutated into new forms. Some French have begun to consider transnational forms of identification, with the European Union for example, while at the same time defining France as a not-U.S. both in terms
of domestic options (the welfare state) and in terms of foreign policy
(preventive war). And at times, a refurbished republicanism situates
France as a kind of "third way" between European-style socialism and
U.S.-style market worship capitalism. As French politician Jean-Pierre
Chevenement put it in *Le Monde* (June 28, 1986),

> Between the market and socialism, there is place for something
> else: the Republic. Our task at the end of the twentieth century
> is not to invent socialism in the colors of liberalism. It is to revive
> the Republic, that French model of democracy ... France, in order
> to carry the message of democracy to the world, to give meaning
> to Europe ... has the need for the cohesion given by the belief in
> a project for its people.

But just as occurs with American patriotism and self-love, French patriotism waxes, and wanes, and shifts. It is not fixed or static; rather, it undergoes constant mutations. (We will return to the subject of French exceptionalism in the third chapter.)

Exceptionalism Light: God Is Brazilian

Brazilian exceptionalism is less universalist in its pretensions than that of either the United States or France. Since Brazil clearly exercises less economic, military, political, and cultural power in the world than France or the United States, Brazilians are less likely to indulge in megalomaniacal delusions of grandeur. Unlike France and the United States, Brazil has never been a major imperial power. And unlike the United States, Brazil has no bases spread around the world. In its present incarnation it invades no countries and envisions its role as that of a peacekeeper. At most, Brazil seeks a voice in world affairs commensurate to its significance as a power in the global South, a voice relayed in the form, for example, of a seat on the UN Security Council.

Brazilian nationalism also differs in its points of emphasis. While France and the United States highlight the originality and universality of their political models, Brazil did not invent a new political model and thus does not stress its political contribution. Brazil was first a colony then briefly an empire, and when it became a republic, roughly a century after the United States and France, it based its modern political system on antecedent French and U.S. models. Brazilian exceptionalism therefore stresses not sociopolitical accomplishments but rather, for example, God's gifts to the land itself. Only four countries in the world—the People's Republic of China, Russia, the United States, and Canada—are larger than Brazil. Indeed, the area of Europe would take up less than two-thirds of the area of Brazil, and many areas the size of France would fit into the Amazon region alone. But it is a question not merely of size but of quality. Brazil, especially in its romantic poetry and its nationalist discourse, is a paradisal garden where the air is sweeter, the bird songs are more melodious, and love is more ardent, in a land spared natural calamities such as earthquakes, tornadoes, and hurricanes and where, to quote Pero Vaz da Caminha's famous letter to the Portuguese monarch, "everything planted grows." Brazilian exceptionalism takes musical form in the lyrics of Jorge Ben's (aka Jorge BenJor) international hit song "Pais Tropical": "I live in a tropical country, blessed by God, and beautiful by nature."

Brazilians themselves are also quick to mock this Edenic view of Brazil, as in the following Brazilian joke, which asks, "What is the proof that Adam and Eve were Brazilians?" Adam and Eve were obviously Brazilian, the answer goes, because "they walked around without any clothes, had nothing but fruit to eat, and yet were convinced they were living in paradise." Of course, France and the United States are also proud of their variegated nature; France prides itself on the range of landscapes and climates within the Hexagon, and the U.S. anthem "America the Beautiful" speaks of "purple-mountained majesty" and "amber waves of grain." But French and American forms of national pride have never focused so disproportionately on facts of "nature"; they have always focused, from the very beginning, on social and political intellectual achievements, in short on facts of *culture,* a word that derives from the concept of cultivation; that is, the human transformation of nature. In U.S. "manifest destiny," the emphasis in the dominant ideology was placed on the transforming of the wilderness into a garden, whereas in the French *mission civilisatrice* the stress was on transforming "natural" colonized peoples into cultivated and assimilated French people *in potentia.* In Brazil, meanwhile, the emphasis is on the transformation of various elements—African, indigenous, European—into one national culture, the Brazilian.

Brazilian exceptionalism also features a distinct sense of temporality. More modest than French and American exceptionalism, it stresses not past accomplishments but rather future hopes: Brazil as the "country of the future." Like France and the United States, Brazil feels it is destined to play a leading role in the world—as evidenced in the current campaign to win a permanent seat on the UN Security Council—but that destiny is perpetually deferred, as in the oft-quoted and highly symptomatic joke "Brazil is the country of the future ... and always will be!" To put it rather schematically, official France is proud of its past and its present but worried about its future, whereas the official United States is proud of its past and present, and it plans to dominate the future in "a new American century," and Brazil tends to displace its faith onto an always receding future. Even the popular trope of Brazil as a "sleeping giant" presumes that a resource-rich and potentially powerful country will some day wake up and shake the world—but only in the future.

The implications of the sleeping giant metaphor—originally associated, ironically, with the United States—differs from those of the metaphor of "underdevelopment." While the development metaphor infantilized the Third World Brazilian toddler as "undeveloped," incapable of controlling his own body, the "dependency theory" of the 1960s and 1970s—in which Brazilian intellectuals such as Fernando Henrique Cardoso (later Brazil's president) played a key role—reversed that imagery. Now the image became one of foreign exploitation and vampirization—captured poetically by the Uruguayan writer Eduardo Galeano in his metaphor of the "open veins" of Latin America. In the new "dependency" and "world system discourse," Brazil's "backwardness" was blamed not on Brazilian immaturity but rather on the rapaciousness of the global North, seen as responsible for stunting Brazilian growth: "We are poor," in short, "because you are rich." Both Brazilian poverty and American wealth, in this view, were a product of the same dynamic of metropolitan enrichment and neocolonial impoverishment, a dynamic initiated by Portugal, then modified by British free-trade imperialism, and finally extended by American hegemony. At the same time, the dependency metaphor, by stressing Brazilian victimization rather than agency, continued the infantilizing trope even while trying to transcend it.

Nations tend to endow their histories with a sense of purposefulness or teleology, whether of unfolding and inevitable success (the United States) or at least of ongoing grandeur (France). In some cases nationalism cultivates a negative teleology of resistance to a perennial victimization (as in the case of Serbian and Israeli nationalism). In the French, Brazilian, and U.S. cases, these teleologies are subtly shaped by an underlying Christian and secularized Enlightenment heritage. Divine providence became secularized as "national destiny." Pero Vaz de Caminha, the sixteenth-century Portuguese scribe who accompanied Pedro Cabral, the Portuguese "discoverer" of Brazil, prefigured this providential idea when he suggested that God did not bring the Portuguese to Brazilian shores for no reason. The Southern Cross constellation, similarly, was seen as a sign posted by God in the heavens to point to the inevitable Christianization of the Southern Hemisphere.

In Brazil the ideas of natural wealth and providential destiny are strongly linked. Brazil is "the country of the future" precisely because of its God-given material riches. But the Brazilian version is less messianic than that conveyed by the religiously tinted discourse of the United States as the "city on the hill." In Brazil messianism was associated not with the top-down official view but rather with bottom-up millenarian peasant movements such as Canudos, the revolt at the turn of the century, registered in Euclides da Cunha's brilliant novel *Os Sertões* (Rebellion in the Backlands), a revolt brutally suppressed by the Brazilian army. The leader of that movement, Antonio Conselheiro, prophesied that the arid desert would become the teeming sea ("*O sertão vai virar mar*"); that is, that the poor would really inherit the earth. One detects millenarianism even in today's Latin American liberation theology, with its "preferential option for the poor" and its view that society's "first" shall surely be "last" and the "last" will be first. But millenarianism was never the official norm in Brazil.

A key element in the Brazilian positive self-image is the idea of Brazilians as peaceful and nonviolent people. The important grain of truth in this discourse derives from the fact that most of the political transitions within Brazilian history took place without major bloodshed. Thus there was no violent revolutionary War of Independence as in the United States—Brazilian independence in 1822 took place without bloodshed—and no revolution (or terror) as in France. Brazil achieved independence without bloodshed when the son of the Portuguese monarch decided to stay in Brazil rather than return to Portugal. Rather than the usual "liberty or death" proclamations typical of revolutions or republican independence movements, the Portuguese Brazilian leader simply said, "*Fico*" (I'm staying). Independence was decreed, in effect, by a Portuguese monarch. It is as if King George II had declared American independence in 1776. And Brazil had no civil war by which slavery was abolished, as in the United States. Even the coup d'état that overturned democratically elected João Goulart in 1964 succeeded without the firing of a shot. (Although the U.S. Navy was allegedly waiting offshore should force be required.)

In a broader perspective, this myth of nonviolence is linked to other Brazilian myths of "cordial" relations with the Indians, a relatively benign slavery, a generous abolition, a tolerant society, and so forth. In

Brazilian schools, pupils learn the significance of the colors and form of the Brazilian flag. The green rectangle symbolizes the riches of the jungles and forests; the yellow oval symbolizes Brazilian gold and mineral riches; the starred blue circle symbolizes Brazil's blue skies and the Southern Cross, suggesting divine blessing; and the white strip and the slogan "Order and Progress" ("*Ordem e Progresso*") suggests that Brazilians form an orderly and progressive people. Brazilian philosopher Marilena Chaui sums up the founding myths:

> We Brazilians form a new people, the result of mixture of courageous Indians, stoic black, and brave and sentimental Portuguese. Everyone knows that miscegenation gave birth to samba, which expressed Indian energy, African rhythms, and Portuguese melancholy. Who doesn't know that miscegenation produced our inimitable and easy corporeal style, the mark of our world soccer champions. And who doesn't know that as a mestizo people we shun all prejudices based on race, color, belief, and class? Who does not know that our history was written without the shedding of blood, with the exception of our martyr of Independence, Tiradentes, that the grandeur of our territory was due to the prowess of the brave bandeirantes, and of the noble moral character of the Pacifier Caxias, and the agile diplomacy of Rio Branco, and that forced by our enemies to make war, we have never been defeated militarily. We are not afraid of war, but we desire peace. In sum, we are a good, pacific, and orderly people.[48]

While there is a grain of truth in the discourse of a nonviolent and pacific Brazil, it is also partially a myth; Brazilian history has in fact often been horribly violent. Apart from the violence of Portuguese conquest against the native peoples and the violence of enslavement and the Middle Passage, one need think only of the military expeditions that crushed the maroon Republic of Palmares, of the *bandeirantes* who massacred Indians, of the military's crushing of Canudos, of the violence of the military dictatorship from 1964 to 1985, or of the present-day police and paramilitary violence against children and "marginals" and labor and environmental leaders. Death by firearms is much more prevalent than in the United States, and the Brazilian police kill a much higher proportion of people than do U.S. police.

Nonetheless, polls confirm the sense of Brazilian pride of which Chaui speaks. A 1995 Vox Populi poll showed that 60 percent of Brazilians were proud of their country and that only 4 percent were ashamed. Respondents listed the following as causes for pride (in decreasing proportions): the riches of Brazilian nature, the character of the people, sports, music, and carnival. Respondents described the Brazilian people as hardworking, combative, happy, helpful, and long-suffering. In a DataFolha poll in April 2003, similarly, 85 percent said they were proud to be Brazilian, 72 percent saw the country as exercising an important role on the world scene, and 61 percent thought Brazil was a good or excellent place to live.[49] Although Brazil has long been a magnet for immigrants from many parts of the world, in recent decades many Brazilians—a million and a half by some estimates—have emigrated to the United States, a phenomenon depicted in the telenovela *America*. But Brazilian emigration is compelled more by the stick of economic necessity and by widespread crime in Brazil than by the carrot of the "American way of life," the mainstream variants of which most Brazilians actually find less attractive than the homegrown model. And in 2006 Brazilian workers joined other "illegal immigrants" to protest the harsh immigration laws being proposed by the right.

One of the most famous literary avatars of Brazilian exceptionalism is the title character of Lima Barreto's novel *Policarpo Quaresma* (1911). Convinced that Brazil is destined to become the greatest country in the world, Policarpo proposes that Brazil adapt the Indian Tupi-Guarani tongue as its official language, since only Tupi-Guarani is adapted to the Brazilian brain and nature. (Tupi actually was the dominant language of Brazil, the *lingua geral*, up through the eighteenth century.) Within Policarpo's dreams of grandeur, Brazil is the world's "first country," whose people are "more courageous, more hospitable, more intelligent, and sweeter than all other peoples." Soon, Quaresma is convinced, "Brazil will become superior to England."

At the same time, the novel mocks its protagonist's claims, thus illustrating another side of the Brazilian national personality—its capacity for humorous self-demystification. Brazilian playwright Nelson Rodrigues has stressed this underside of Brazilian exceptionalism—the self-doubt that sees Brazil as exceptionally incompetent and even historically doomed. Rodrigues calls Brazilians "upside-down Narcissists," who spit on their own image. In much of the Brazilian literature of comparison with the United States, the orienting question—a rather humiliating one for Brazil—is what went wrong in the South that went right in the North? In everyday life in Brazil, the very word *Brazilian* is often used pejoratively, expressing, perhaps, not only a shrewd sense of self-abusing wit but also a neocolonized sense of inferiority. Every daily incident is read allegorically as typical of Brazilian incompetence or *ruindade* (badness). A late subway? "What do you expect—it's a Brazilian train!" Sometimes this negativity takes the form of a pervasive feeling that "things will never work out." The everyday phrase "*tudo bem*" (everything's fine) is often said with a resigned shrug and an ironic intonation. But this negative image, often linked historically to a Europhile prejudice regarding the black and Indian and mestizo character of Brazil, has usually been connected to Brazil's inferiority complex, first toward mother Europe and later toward Brazil's materially more successful cousin, the United States. In this sense, Brazil suffers less from exorbitant self-regard than from the opposite—an internalized sense of a lack of worth.

Unlike France and the United States, Brazil has generally not claimed to offer a universal political model. The election of Lula as president inspired hope in progressive circles around the world, but segments of the Brazilian left have begun to lose confidence in him after he became the darling of the International Monetary Fund and after his party became embroiled in political corruption scandals. But if Brazil does not usually propose itself as a political model for the world, some of its prestigious intellectuals, such as anthropologist Gilberto Freyre and novelist Jorge Amado, have proposed Brazil as a model for racial tolerance and a certain way of living together, one that is sociable, generous, and hopeful. What is almost universally acknowledged as a deep Brazilian hospitality to foreigners, for example, seems to have a double historical origin, one from the social "top" in the Arab-influenced patriarchal slave system described by Gilberto Freyre, the other from the bottom in the communal gregariousness of many of the indigenous and African source cultures of Brazil. Thus polls show that Brazilians are proud of their hospitality, their cordiality, their easygoing ways, and their gift for fluid, open communication. It is as if to the U.S. claim of being the "most powerful and prosperous country in the world," Brazilians answered with, "You Americans may be the most powerful, but nowadays nobody likes you, whereas we Brazilians are the most sympathetic and fun-loving, and everybody likes us." And then they add that devastating addendum (sometimes used by Rio de Janeiro residents to describe the residents of São Paulo), "You know how to work, but we know how to live." (Europeans, despite a different lifestyle, sometimes make the same claim.)

France, Brazil, and the United States all pride themselves on cultural achievements, but while French and U.S. narcissism focus on grandeur and political achievements as well as culture, Brazilian narcissism focuses on collective and popular culture. It focuses, for example, on the Brazilian capacity for clever improvisation, summed up in the word *jeitinho;* that is, a creative gift for surviving and even thriving in situations of poverty and disadvantage. Brazilian culture has often demonstrated an immensely creative capacity, doubtless the partial legacy of its subalternized populations, to improvise with scarce resources. We find this improvisational quality especially in the manifestations of Afro-Brazilian culture, where African Brazilians, working from a situation of material deprivation, have shown a capacity to turn everyday objects such as matchboxes into percussive instruments, to turn the throwaway parts of the pig into a delicious feijoada stew (the national dish, invented by Africans during slavery), or to turn even garbage into art. Brazilian intellectuals pride themselves in the country's "anthropophagic" ability to take the best of everything in the world and make it Brazilian. This kind of creativity has taken the artistic form of an endless series of innovative aesthetics, to which theoreticians have given many names: "anthropophagy," the "aesthetics of hunger," the "aesthetics of garbage," "Tropicalia," and "Dogma-Feijoada." Brazil also demonstrates an immense social and political creativity, which finds expression not only in what pop composer Caetano Veloso called the "most charming protest music in the world" but also in a rich repertoire of social movements—the landless movement (MST), favela community organizations, literacy programs, indigenous media, AIDS activism, human rights—many of which converged in the "World Social Forum" meetings held for several years in Porto Alegre.

Brazilian national pride was elaborated only slowly. It did not begin with a revolution or even with independence as in the United States, since, as was suggested earlier, there never really was a violent revolution or a full-fledged form of independence. Unlike France and the United States, Brazil was politically "exceptional" not in the sense of providing a possible model for revolutionary independence and constitutional democracy but rather in quite the opposite sense, of being the only monarchical "island" in a sea of republics in the Americas. But if political exceptionalism had this negative character, Brazilian writers were at the same time articulating a sense of cultural exceptionalism in the novels and poems of the nineteenth-century "Indianist" movement. This movement, in some ways parallel to its U.S. counterpart in the novels of James Fenimore Cooper and to its French counterpart in the work of Chateaubriand, fashioned stories in which native princesses such as Iracema, the heroine in the José de Alencar novel, wedded with Portuguese nobles such as Martim, giving birth to a symbolically aristocratic, but also mestizo, nation. These fictions stressed, if only indirectly, the pride of a nation built on the integration and synthesis of idealized whites and romanticized Indians.

Within romantic novels, the Indian was celebrated as a "brave warrior," as the naively good and deeply spiritual source and symbol of Brazil's nationhood. But the romantic exaltation of the Indian involved an element of bad faith toward both Indian and black and thus an element of white Brazilian narcissism. By celebrating the fusion of an idealized noble Indian with an equally idealized noble European, novels such as *Iracema* and *O Guarani* prettified the power relations inherent in white–Indian social and sexual relationships. The exaltation of the disappearing Indian was dedicated to the very group being subjected to a drawn-out process of cultural genocide. The Indians of Ceara celebrated in *Iracema* were virtually extinguished when Alencar published his novel. But although the actually existing Indian was destroyed, marginalized, or dissolved through miscegenation, the remote, literary Indian was idealized. Brazilian blacks, meanwhile, were seen at that time, by writers such as Alencar who were sometimes themselves slave owners, as purely a source of labor and an iconic reminder of the brutal heritage of slavery, hardly an image the elite wanted to project. To valorize blacks within a slaveholding society would necessarily be to cast whites as villains.

The ambiguous, so-called compliment toward the Indian thus became a means of avoiding the vexed question of slavery. The proud history of black rebellions, of Palmares and the *quilombos,* was ignored; the brave Indian, it was subtly insinuated, resisted slavery whereas the blacks did not. The romantics chose the safely distant and mythically connoted Indian over the more problematically present black.

The Indianist exceptionalism of the nineteenth century anticipated the patriotic exceptionalism of later epochs. In the President Vargas "New State" period in the 1930s, even the carnival pageant in Rio de Janeiro produced sambas that exalted Brazilian national heroes, in line with the nationalist contours of Vargas's New State ideology. It was in this period that Brazilian exceptionalism became informally fused with the claimed social achievement of "racial democracy." Brazil, it was thought, could be the model country showing the way toward racial harmony and understanding. Although the term *racial democracy* was first used in the 1930s, it was prefigured in those already-mentioned nineteenth-century Indianist novels, which figured Brazilian nationhood as a symbolic marriage of European and native. But this time the black Brazilian was included rather than ignored. Brazilian exceptionalist mythology developed what anthropologist Roberto da Matta calls the "fable of the three races"; that is, the view of Brazil as a happy amalgam of red Indian, black African, and white European. Intellectual historian Lúcia Lippi Oliveira puts it as follows: "If the United States is narrated as the result of the encounter of the European with the space of the frontier, realizing the designs of Providence, Brazil is recounted as the encounter of three races through miscegenation."[50]

In the 1930s Brazil had a quasi-fascist *integralista* movement that promoted a kind of right-wing *verde–amarelo* (green and yellow) patriotic euphoria. Three decades later the military dictatorship installed by the 1964 coup d'état also promoted a kind of patriotic euphoria. Slogans such as *"Brasil Grande"* (Great Brazil), *"Ninguem Segura este Pais"* (No one can hold this country back), and *"Brasil: Ame-o ou Deixe-o"* (Brazil: love it or leave it) proliferated. The media were censored, and even radio announcers during soccer matches would add, as part of the verbal stream of blow-by-blow soccer description, statements such as "Any well-intentioned people supports its government." A junior high school textbook for a required course (Morality and Civics) instituted by the military regime included the following passage:

> The very map of Brazil appears in the shape of a human heart. ... The heart palpitates with future greatness for a powerful Brazil, seeking courageous solutions, fiery and spiritual, a country that brings to a tired and aging world a new vision of strength. This is my country; I am proud to call myself Brazilian.

> The security of every Brazilian and the safety of every Brazilian institution is guarded by the nation's armed forces. There are two missions: defense against foreign aggression and vigilance against internal subversion. Brazilians do not seek territorial aggrandizement. Our people love peace. But the armed forces stand vigilant to repel any external threat. There stand other enemies within our midst: terrorists, subversives, and militants of communistic ideologies. The armed forces combat this menace, and remind us of our obligation for hierarchy and discipline.[51]

Such texts reflect the militarization of patriotism in the "national security state," a phenomenon not unknown, as we shall see, in the United States.

In the present period, presidents such as Fernando Henrique Cardoso and Lula refurbish the national ideals for popular consumption. The following is from Lula's inaugural address in January 2003:

> This is a nation that speaks the same language, that shares the same fundamental values, and that feels itself Brazilian. A nation where creolization and syncretism have been established and contributed to the world in an original way; where Jews and Arabs befriend each other fearlessly; where all migration is welcome, because we know that due to our capacity of assimilation and affection, each and every immigrant will become a Brazilian.[52]

In the same vein, the pop composer Gilberto Gil, in his inaugural discourse as the minister of culture, praised Brazilians as "a mestizo people which has created, over the centuries, an essentially syncretic culture, which is both diversified and plural ... and unified." Roberto da Matta points to the kernel of truth in the idea of Brazil as a model for gregarious and hopeful collectivity in a time of universal disenchantment:

> All this capacity of ours to synthesize, to connect and conciliate, to create realms and values related to joy, future, and hope; this capacity of ours to feel enchanted becomes something very positive, very important. Because this ability exists in a world which is more and more depleted of enchantment. We live in a world which keeps disappointing itself, instituting a boundless individualism which reduces collective values to mere appendages to individual happiness. ... Perhaps Brazilian society has a mission in encouraging this sense of possibility, which seems to be on a path of extinction in the western world.[53]

Like all national mythologies, the discourse of exceptional Brazilian tolerance contains an important grain of truth along with a dose of idealization. Marilena Chaui suggests the underside of the "enchanted" view of Brazil. The same Brazilian who can say in one context, "We are a people without prejudices and a nation born of racial mixture," Chaui points out, can say in another context, "Indians are ignorant, blacks are lazy, northeasterners are backward, the Portuguese are stupid, and women are naturally inferior."[54] Thus a country that has since its beginnings practiced what many Brazilians call "social apartheid" can cling to a positive and exportable image of fraternal unity.

All nations have their points of pride. Brazil prides itself on its polyphonic cultural diversity, on its great writers (from Machado de Assis and Mário de Andrade to Clarice Lispector and Guimarães Rosa), on its architects such as Oscar Niemeyer and Luiz Costa, on its musicians such as Villa-Lobos and Antonio Carlos Jobim, on its scintillating and infinitely variegated popular culture, and its caressing way of life. At the same time, Brazil has terrible social problems—grinding mass poverty, widespread corruption, omnipresent crime, police brutality, and all the other symptoms of what many Brazilians call an "undeclared civil war." Cristovam Buarque calls Brazil "a slave ship moving toward the future, with millions of the excluded poor in the hold, without food, education, health, on the one hand, and a corrupt elite on the other hand, with a high standard of living yet moving toward a disastrous future."[55]

Many Brazilians, meanwhile, speak of Brazil in the plural—*Brasis* (i.e., Brazils)—to evoke a sense of its marvelous multiplicity. The cliché phrase that calls Brazil "Belindia," (Belgium–India) that is, the combination of a prosperous Belgium-like south and an impoverished India-like northeast—a comparison that present-day India, now a geopolitical ally of Brazil, might find offensive—calls attention to this constitutive multiplicity of situations and ethnicities. It is this "many languagedness" that makes Brazil so well-equipped for comprehending both the global North and the global South.

In sum, the United States, France, and Brazil have all practiced and developed variations on the theme of national narcissism. Although all nations are narcissistic, they are narcissistic in their own way. To put it crudely: U.S. national narcissism is "armed and dangerous"; it is the narcissism of an overweening hyperpower; French narcissism, meanwhile, is that of a former imperial power, yet it is proud of its republic; and Brazilian national narcissism, finally, is that of a relatively disempowered, yet would-be power.

Having looked at how the three nations love—or sometimes hate—themselves, we will now look at the diverse ways that the Brazilians, the French, and some Americans have loved, not loved, or even hated the United States.

2. Variations on an Anti-American Theme

Sibling Rivalries: Anti-Americanism in France

Our introductory discussion of exceptionalism in the United States, France, and Brazil has prepared the way for a more direct discussion of anti-Americanism in traditionally allied countries of Europe and Latin America. We will not stress the repertoire of pro-American commonplaces praising the United States—the United States as a cosmopolitan "nation of nations," as a successful democratic experiment, or an economic powerhouse and the "land of opportunity"—since that is not our focus here. Despite the fact that the United States and France historically saw themselves as two "sister Republics," despite the fact that France served as midwife to the emerging U.S. nation-state during the American Revolution, despite the fact that the United States helped rescue France during two world wars, and despite the Marshall Plan, which catalyzed French recovery from the devastation of World War II, many commentators have suggested, and polls have confirmed, that France is one of the most anti-American of European countries. Indeed, *anti-Americanism* is the only instance in which the French language joins the prefix *anti* to the name of a country. There is no equivalent term such as *anti-Italianism* or even, despite a long and painful history of conflicts between France and Germany, *anti-Germanism*. For many French people, the United States calls to mind savage capitalism, phobic Puritanism, gross anti-intellectualism, and naked hyperimperialism. Furthermore, anti-Americanism has been a kind of lingua franca in France; it unites rich and poor, religious and secular, left and right. For the French left (and even for some on the extreme right), meanwhile, the United States is also seen as the puppeteer orchestrating global homogenization, an irresistible force that imposes the English language and Hollywood blockbusters on the world and shoves Big Macs down French throats, tempting them to forget the subtleties of French cuisine.

The tensions between France and the United States, as we briefly suggested earlier, are linked to the fact that both have always assumed a right to speak for universal values. But stressing only the contrasts between French and U.S. republicanism tempts us to ignore the clear commonalities, in both the positive sense and the negative sense. On the positive side, both are democratic republics (in principle if not in practice), shaped by revolution and featuring constitutional regimes. Both insist, at least rhetorically, on equality of rights, equality before the law, the separation of powers, and the separation of church and state. On the negative side, both have sometimes been undemocratic, and both have been involved in colonial conquest, slavery, and imperialism. Indeed, the two imperialisms have historically sometimes been allied (Vietnam) and sometimes been in conflict (Algeria). Often the countries were internally conflicted about the other country's policies. With the advent of the Haitian Revolution, for example, politicians such as Thomas Jefferson sided with the French slave owners in Haiti, while mavericks such as statesman Thomas Pickering sided with the Haitian rebels.

Hypocrisy and contradiction, on both sides, have been frequent hallmarks of Franco-American relations. With the Monroe Doctrine in 1823, designed to prevent European intrusions in the Americas, the United States resisted European imperialism while creating an imperialism of its own in Latin America. With the Spanish-American War, France denounced American imperialism, while carrying on its own imperialist policies elsewhere. Later, Franklin D. Roosevelt (FDR) made anticolonialist gestures—and furthered U.S. interests—by hastening the end of the European empires. Although FDR had expressed support for Vietnamese independence in 1945, the United States after that consistently supported the French in Indochina, up until the Dien Bien Phu defeat in 1954, at which point the United States took over from the French, culminating in the calamitous United States–Vietnam War that ended only in 1975. The recent quarrels in the Security Council over the Iraq War, in this sense, provided just one more twist in a long history of ambivalences and oscillations.

But as many commentators have pointed out, anti-Americanism in France long antedates the recent tensions over the Iraq War. The tradition of anti-Americanism began largely as an elitist and rightist penchant and only later morphed into an equal-opportunity phenomenon. Anti-Americanism in France goes all the way back to the naturalist movement, where certain late-eighteenth-century philosophers such as Buffon and Reynal, neither of whom actually visited the New World, denigrated the American continent. The naturalists offered so-called scientific proofs that everything in the Americas—the land, the flora and fauna, the indigenous people, and the Europeans—tended to degenerate. Within this pseudoscientific discourse, the Americas in general were metaphorically immature and underdeveloped—a place where human beings do not live but only "vegetate" and where "even the dogs do not bark." In the work of the French naturalist De Pauw, America is putrefaction, full of monstrous insects and lizards, not the Promised Land but the Egypt of the ten plagues. (De Pauw's work illustrates the point that anti-Americanism is often linked to an internal French agenda, in this case aimed at dissuading potential French settlers from going to the Americas.) Such dystopian discourses offered the shadowy phobic counterpart to the euphoric utopian discourses of other Europeans such as Thomas More who saw the Americas as the site of the fantastic: of Eldorado, the Fountain of Youth, the Golden Age, the Seven Cities of Cibola, and other phantasmagoria of the European imagination.

The prejudice against America, in the beginning, was strangely transracial and panhemispheric; it embraced both South America and North America and both Native American "Indian" and Creole white European, seen as two groups resembling each other in their common "savagery." It is somewhat surprising that this discourse also demonized Europeans themselves, at least those Europeans who had "gone native" in what was seen as a barbarous and alien land. The naturalist discourse exemplifies a penchant, on the part of some Europeans, to underestimate the talents and capacities of the New World and its inhabitants. Thomas Jefferson respectfully rebutted such prejudices—while introducing some of his own—in his *Notes on the State of Virginia*. And Benjamin Franklin, during his November 1776 visit to Paris, wittily upended some French prejudices. According to Jefferson's oft-retold account, Franklin, after citing French opinion about the necessarily smaller physical stature of American men, gathered around him an equal number of Americans and Frenchmen and had all the men stand up. A quick check revealed all the Americans to be taller than the tallest Frenchman. But Franklin was celebrated by the French, despite the rudeness of his refutation—or perhaps because of it; indeed, France declared three days of official mourning when Franklin died in 1790.

Perhaps the most exhaustive study of the history of anti-Americanism in France is Philippe Roger's *L'Ennemi Americain*.[1] Roger meticulously delineates the historical origins of each of the constitutive elements that came to form part of that larger discursive complex called "anti-Americanism." For Roger, anti-Americanism is a palimpsest of prejudices drawn from different periods but with each stratum leaving traces in later periods. In a contextualized form of discourse analysis, Roger traces the long-term roots of French anti-Americanism back not only to eighteenth-century "naturalist" discourses but also to the Civil War. During that conflict, France sympathized with the Confederacy, partly out of regrets over the loss of its own slave kingdom due to the Haitian Revolution but also out of hopes for a fracturing of the United States that would prevent it from becoming a rival superpower. The French naming of the war as a "war of secession" betrayed the unconfessable desires lurking just below the surface—that is, the hope for a long, bloody, unwinnable war that would weaken the United States.

A presumably republican France, then, which had abolished slavery, nevertheless sided with a slaveholding Confederacy. The French apologists for the South were embarrassed, of course, by the Confederacy's endorsement of the "peculiar institution" of slavery, but they papered over the contradiction by claiming that (1) the war was not really about slavery but about economics, that (2) slavery would inevitably end anyway, and that (3) the North also did not treat blacks well. But the guilty secret pleasure, the schadenfreude, derived from the prospect of the disintegration of the American republic. It was the disappointment after the victory of the Union forces that triggered what Roger calls the "crystallization" of French anti-Americanism. The very term *Yankee* was borrowed from the U.S. South, seen from a French perspective as an early victim of Northern "Yankee imperialism." Within an opportunistic discourse of solidarity, Southern whites stood alongside the Indians as exemplary victims of the rapacious Anglo-Saxon North.

Roger mocks the bad faith inherent in some of these expressions of solidarity:

> A new nation was thus born in the French mindset: the "other America," which would now be regularly summoned to testify in the permanent trial against America's crimes. During the first half of the 20th century, men indifferent to the fate of peoples colonized by European powers would become passionate about American Indians and treat the blacks with astonishing solicitude—at least the blacks in Alabama or Illinois (and not in Senegal or Cameroon).[2]

The so-called solidarity with Indians and blacks, furthermore, did not entail any real affection or respect—their unique status was as victims of the "Yankees." Moreover, the black and red objects of paternalistic sympathy were not granted any intellectual agency within this process. The French writers, like their white Euro-American counterparts, simply assumed the right to speak in their place. Ultimately the only good Indians for their French defenders were dead Indians, in whose favor French commentators could elegize the lost paradise of a French America and denounce the horrible genocide committed by the "Yankees."

The French pro-Confederacy discourse saw blacks as the victims of the destruction of the "Latin" patriarchal south. But this discourse did not entail any particular sympathy for the black victims of slavery. In an exterminationist age, some thought that blacks would inevitably go the way of the Indians and "disappear" (Roger, p. 115). Thus the French anti-Americans hated white America yet shared some of white America's prejudices. France, like many European nations, participated in the "disappearing" of the Native Americans, even while their romantic Indianist writers mourned that "vanished" world. In terms of postbellum Reconstruction, one of the most progressive periods in U.S. history, meanwhile, the French right followed the cues provided by white Southern racists; they denounced the "bad behavior" of blacks and the "victimization" of the white race. One French *ami des noirs* (friend of the blacks) described blacks as "cheats, liars and lazy, they are still more depraved. They are obsessed with the idea of the white women, and this obsession frequently leads them to the most craven of crimes."[3] Roger sums up the topoi of nineteenth-century French anti-Americanism as the denunciation of the genocidal fate reserved for non-Yankees, the exaltation of a miscegenated French past in the Americas, and the notion of the "Anglo-Saxon" race as the dominating element in the United States. In cultural terms, the topoi included laments over the widespread bad taste, excessive power of women, and general platitude of conversation. But Flaubert, we would add, just around the time of the Civil War, in his classic *Madame Bovary*, also denounced the "platitude of conversation" in France itself. Provincial boredom is not an American monopoly.

It is also worth noting, finally, that the French are one of the few national European groups that did not migrate en masse to the Americas. The absence of a shared demographic connection has certainly played a role in French attitudes, opening the way to projections and fantasies. A habitual attitude since the time of the American Revolution among the ruling classes and traditional intelligentsia, the "perennial targets for rancor," as cultural studies scholars Andrew Ross and Kristin Ross point out, included America's "moralistic work ethic, its appetites for novelty in commerce and its simplicity in taste and manners, its hectic pursuit of materialism, its enthusiasm for a demotic culture and its embrace, however ambiguous, of multiracialism."[4] Indeed, French commentators have often become somewhat disoriented by the cultural and racial heterogeneity of the United States, for them a kind of Tower of Babel resulting from the proliferation of peoples and colors who have had their rendezvous on American soil. Some French commentators, giving expression to ideological currents common to many "Black Atlantic" countries, found not only Brazil but also the United States too "mongrel" for their taste. Much as the racist Conte de Gobineau applied "degeneracy" theory to Brazil, Nouailles suggested in relation to the

United States that the "pure-bred Anglo-saxon blood, already crossed with Germanic and Irish blood, would be lost in this promiscuous mixture with inferior races."[5] Every new batch of American immigrants, Émile Boutmy noted, was "morally and intellectually inferior to the previous one."[6]

In the same period that some conservative Brazilian commentators projected the United States as monochromatically white, while seeing Brazil itself as dangerously mixed, some French commentators saw the United States, like the rest of the Americas, as frighteningly miscegenated. The French rightist Georges Duhamel, in *Scenes de la vie future* (Scenes of Future Life, 1930), saw the U.S. populace as a "mongrel race" of "confused, mixed people," a kind of "typhus" that might later contaminate a presumably homogeneous France. Among the symptoms, for Duhamel, were the jazz of "monochord niggers" and the "promiscuity" of all the races in the world. A completely contradictory account denigrated the United States as simultaneously a Yankee-dominated monolith and a messy cultural hodgepodge. An "antiracist racism" denounced the United States in a discourse that was itself racist. The arrival of new immigrants, it was vaguely hoped, would bring the blowing up of the melting pot. Although the French right did not approve of the "vulgar" and even "barbarous" immigrants themselves, in other words, it did approve of their historical function as the exterminating angels of a mongrel America.

The question of immigration in the United States intrigued the French partially because the same question ultimately concerned France as well; that is, how to assimilate "alien elements" into a nation-state presumed to be homogeneous. Often, the observations come with a strong odor of anti-Semitism, as in this text by the writer André Siegfried:

> Surely you can lay claim to some Israelite uncle from London or Frankfurt? He is sure to turn up again in New York. Or even better, can you not unearth some Alsatian Jew, a Kike from Breslau, a "youtre" from Lemberg or Salonica, or even—I do not exaggerate—some Hebrew from Asia with goat-like eyes and a prophet's beard.[7]

Siegfried goes on to describe New York as no longer a Western city:

> When the lower city swarms with somber-looking secretaries, with hooked noses, when the narrow streets of the lower East Side pour out the hurried crowds of swarthy Levantines and hairy Hebrews, the impression is oriental, and the fluidity of the currents of these never-ending crowds, evokes the human tides of Asiatic metropolises.[8]

Within this train of anti-Semitic and what might be called "Orientaphobic" thought, immigration was a lose–lose proposition in the eyes of the anti-Americans: if the United States incorporated the alien elements, it would lose its coherent national identity, yet if it failed to incorporate them, it would explode from the pressure of the "unassimilables." These overwrought reactions to American immigrant cosmopolitanism anticipate and shape, we argue, some later French reactions to "American multiculturalism," in that they constitute monocultural responses to polyethnic societies.

Anti-Americanism in France has always mingled contradictory rightist and leftist currents. For the left, the United States has been seen as too unequal, too consumerist, too undemocratic, and too racist, while for the right, the United States was too egalitarian, too democratic, too vulgar, and too racially mixed. What is interesting for our purposes is that the various levels of anti-American critique can be politically "out of synch," reflecting an ideological "uneven development"; that is, the criticism can be democratic and progressive on a political level yet elitist and conservative on a cultural level. Even today, a leftist-style denunciation of U.S. class society and imperialism can sometimes mingle with a rightist-style cultural elitism. Historian Tony Judt describes contemporary French anti-Americanism, for example, as an admixture of "conservative distaste (America is ugly, rootless, and crass); anti-Globalization rhetoric (America is polluting the world); and neo-Marxist reductionism (America is run by and for the oil companies)."[9]

Much of the anti-imperialist discourse in France goes back to the Spanish-American War. As a direct confrontation between the United States and a European power, that war catalyzed the reactive dream of a pan-European Union to counter the swelling strength of the American eagle. France felt caught in a pincer movement between the thriving Americans on one side and the burgeoning Germans on the other, two powerful nation-states deeply convinced of their providential mission. It is at this point that anti-Americanism became a real "passion" among the French, one that paid social-national benefits in terms of unifying an otherwise disunited nation. As occurred in relation to Native Americans and blacks, the real French sympathy in the Spanish-American War went not to the Cubans, as victims of "Yankee imperialism," but rather to the other European imperialists; that is, to the Spanish, a token of inter-European solidarity hardly surprising in the light of a shared European colonial project.

Yet on another level, the French critics of the war were prescient in sensing the slow, inexorable solidification of U.S. hegemony, proceeding from the conquest of the West and the Monroe Doctrine in 1823, to the Spanish-American War in 1898, and on to Wilson's role in World War I. Although recognizing that American imperialism was atypical in its reluctance to annex land or directly administer the territories it dominated, these critics discerned the dim outlines of what was to become a new mutated strain of imperialism, one less interested in territories than in bases, markets, and influence, one that named itself not as "imperialism" but rather as "making the world safe for free trade and democracy."

With the French Vichy regime during World War II, anti-Americanism took on recognizably anti-Semitic overtones, as the responsibility for war was attributed to "Jewish banks." Vichyiste books such as Henri-Robert Petit's *Rothschild. Roi d'Israel et les Américains* (Paris: Nouvelles Etudes Françaises, 1941) rewrote the entire history of the United States as a kind of Jewish conspiracy. "Uncle Sam," as historian David Strauss puts it, "had become Uncle Shylock." Both Jews and Yankees, it was said, "had speculation running in their veins."[10] The Vichyistes deplored the "Judaization" of the United States, denouncing jazz as a black–Jewish collaboration and portraying the "Yankees" with the hooked noses of anti-Jewish caricature. Thus French anti-Semites projected the image of Europe's internal "other"—the Jews—onto America's own internal others—blacks—and onto white America as itself "other" to Vichy France.

If World War I was a minor humiliation for the French, the outcome of World War II was much more traumatic. On one hand, the war triggered a kind of civil war between Vichy and the resistance. But on a global scale, France in a short time went from being a front-rank imperial nation to being a nation on the dole. Here a key element was the Marshall Plan for European Recovery. At a point when the United States accounted for half of the world's manufacturing capacity and most of its food surpluses, the Marshall Plan showed magnanimity in victory, as an attempt to restore Europe to power, with the result that Europe could be a bulwark against communism to the east but also allow newly prosperous Europeans to buy American consumer products.

Although in the United States the Marshall Plan was seen as the product of idealistic New Dealers, a generous way of saving Europe after the debacle, many French were convinced that the plan was merely a plot to enslave and dominate France. The purpose of George Soria's 1948 book *Will France Become an American Colony?* in this sense was to destroy the myth of American generosity. The Marshall Plan, Soria argued, brought U.S. gains in terms of political hegemony and new markets. The Blum-Byrnes accords of 1946, by not allowing France to protect its own industries through tariffs, provoked a loss of national sovereignty for France. Some went so far as to link the United States and Hitler, on the basis that German industry in the interwar period had thrived thanks to "Anglo-Saxon" capital. (In ethnoessentialist discourse, money, like blood, carries ethnicity.) Emmanuel Mounier, the founder of the journal *L'Esprit,* even accused the United States of wanting to create a new Vichy. The culpabilization of the United States went hand in hand with a deculpabilization of France itself for its collaboration with Nazi Germany.

Yet as historian Richard Pells points out, "some of these complaints were disingenuous," since "the governments of Western Europe were as keen as Washington to rebuild and modernize their economies."[11] Soon, rancor developed against the overly generous benefactors, resulting in what Roger calls a "double denegation": denial of intention—"the Americans didn't do it for us"—and denial of fact—"they didn't really help us, anyway." This resentment had a phantasmal aspect and transparently functioned to heal wounded national pride. But nowadays even critics of U.S. foreign policy regard the Marshall Plan, with all its shortcomings and self-interested motives, as also a farsighted act of political intelligence.

France's ambivalent relation to the United States changes with the geopolitical winds. When the United States becomes too powerful, according to Roger, France hates the United States; when it is weakened, as with 9/11, France rediscovers a latent sympathy. It has become a commonplace to say that France's attitude toward the United States exhibits the Monsieur Perrichon syndrome; that is, people prefer those they have saved to those who have saved them. Both French and American commentators have stressed the theme of the "burden of gratitude." Narcissism thus plays a role not only in the strident nationalism of the hyperpower but also in the strident anti-Americanism of the newly relativized European power. In the postwar period, anti-Americanism becomes a kind of specter conjured up to make France feel innocent and, above all, not indebted to the United States. (A defeated Germany, meanwhile, had to deal with different issues, namely its undeniable guilt for the Holocaust, and was perhaps therefore less sensitive about the burden of gratitude.) But in France, the denial of any debt toward the United States became, after 1945, an essential gesture of anti-Americanism: "At exactly the time when the Marshall Plan was assuring the material survival of France," as Roger puts it, "de Gaulle contributed to this denial of indebtedness by speaking of 'Paris, liberated by itself'" (Roger, p. 330). In other words, de Gaulle massaged the French national ego by cultivating an illusion of self-sufficiency; Paris did not need liberators. At the end of the war, most Frenchman, according to polls, credited the USSR as the country that had done the most to defeat the Germans. The point was certainly accurate in the sense that the Soviet Union withstood the Nazi attack and suffered many more casualties— some twenty million—than the Americans did. Yet stressing the debt to the Russians was also a way of canceling the other debt to the Americans. It is almost as if many French wished that France had won freedom on its own but alongside other Europeans, as a matter of national and European pride.

The American rescue of France in the liberation in 1945 constituted an ironic turnaround in terms of French imperial mythologies. Imperial France, like the neoimperial United States, had been inordinately fond of colonial rescue fantasies, whereby French colonists rescued colonized women from their own men, for example, or rescued colonized countries from their own presumed childlike incompetence. Such narratives were standard fare within the *mission civilisatrice*. Being rescued by a more powerful country like the United States, with its own "mission," in this sense, was a particularly hard pill for France to swallow. How could the European "parent" suffer the indignity of being rescued by its New World child? And to admit even a need for rescue was to gender oneself as female and thus undermine phallic notions of national virility.

What is especially interesting for our purposes, however, is the alacrity with which the French described American influence in Europe as a form of colonialism. Not only was American help not really help, but it was the opposite: it was colonization. The paradox of the immediate postwar period was that "the peoples of Europe—who were hard put to govern or even feed themselves—continued to rule much of the non-European world."[12] Thanks to a kind of ideological legerdemain, French intellectuals, citizens of what was then one of the leading imperial powers in Africa, Asia, and the Caribbean, used the highly symptomatic metaphor of "colonialism" to evoke French victimization by the United States, precisely in one of the places where the United States was not acting in a colonial manner. Here we encounter a recycled, latter-day version of the metaphorical use of "slavery," around the time of the French and American revolutions, to refer not to the literal bondage of blacks but rather to the metaphorical bondage of whites, a metaphor deployed, sometimes, even by those who themselves owned slaves.

Whereas the French anti-American discourse of the *entre-deux-guerres* (between the two wars) period favored metaphors of invasion and conquest, the postwar period favored tropes of colonization. Thus Jean-Jacques Servan-Schreiber's best-selling *Le Defi Américain* (1967) and Jacques Thibau's *La France Colonisée* (1980) both develop the metaphor of France as colonized by the United States. Although France had until recently been a colonizing power, its feeling of being colonized by the United States generated a kind of retroactive (and in some ways opportunistic) identificatory projection with the "real colonized" and the nonwhite world in general. While many courageous French intellectuals (Francis Jeanson, Jean-Paul Sartre, Henri Alleg) really did identify with the Third World, in other cases, this solidarity with the nonwhite world was tinged, we suggest, with more than a touch of bad faith (*mauvaise foi*). The metaphorical portrayal of the United States as colonialist toward France had the function of psychically erasing not only

French colonialism but also the beginnings of neocolonialism. France was artificially made the equal in victimization with Third World countries, some of which it had itself colonized and some of which it was in the process of neocolonizing in the post-Independence period. The shift had begun away from a narcissism of the civilizing imperial mission to a narcissism of resistance to imperialism on behalf of the Third World oppressed.

As part of the same "France colonized by the Americans" rhetoric, one anti-American writer, Roger Vailland, constructed an imaginary dialogue in which American GIs speak in racist ways about the French, in a manner clearly calculated to evoke French racist discourse toward Arabs: "These damned Frenchies are robbing us ... they're so filthy there isn't even a bath in most of their homes ... Frenchies will always be Frenchies. ... That's why we're turning into the dirty Arabs, the kikes, the Polacks of the Americans."[13] Ironically, Vailland's lament in 1955 about American colonization of the French coincided with the period of the "Battle of Algiers," when future right-wing leader (and presidential candidate) Jean-Marie Le Pen was literally torturing Algerians, and when French soldiers were performing murderous raids (*ratissages*) in the Algerian countryside. Vailland was writing roughly six years before the Paris police, on October 17, 1961, slaughtered hundreds of Algerians in the streets of Paris.[14] Against this historical backdrop, certain forms of anti-Americanism, not unlike certain forms of Francophobia in the United States, can be seen to have a self-exculpatory function. The hyperbolic assertion of the colonial-style victimization of France subliminally wipes clean bad memories of colonialism and Vichy. The contemporary period offers a similar sense of false victimization when some French writers posit France as the victim of globalization, alongside the countries of the global South, as if dominant France were not, economically speaking, an integral part of the global North, as the representatives of some of the nations of the South, such as Brazil, tirelessly remind their diplomatic interlocutors from the North.

In the same period, French anti-Americanism was also linked to the gradual decline of French cultural hegemony. Because French amour propre has always been tied to the French language, the inroads of English in France also triggered especially virulent reactions. Etiemble's *Parlez-Vous Franglais?*, for example, fused pop linguistics with national paranoia. In an anguished tone of masochistic humiliation, the book delineates in excruciating detail what Etiemble saw as the complete humiliation of France by the presence on its soil of the English language. The historical irony, of course, is that English, thanks to the eleventh-century Normandy conquest, had long been half French, at least in terms of vocabulary. For Etiemble, it was shocking to see France reduced to the rank of colonial Indochina or Algeria. "The Atlantic Pact colonizes us," he writes, "exactly at a moment when we ourselves are dealing with the vicissitudes of 'decolonization.'"[15] As Roger points out, Etiemble places the word *decolonization* in apologetic quotes, as if it were merely a myth, but not the word *colonization,* thus implying that the American colonization of France had more ontological substance than the merely putative French "colonization" of Algeria and Vietnam. The special sensitivity about linguistic intrusion, in this sense, betrays both pride in French as a prestigious language and a paranoia about its overshadowing by English, including in the former colonized world. The French language, which like the English language has served to spread European ideas and justify colonial rule, is now seen through a doubly defensive grid, as the language that should have been the first among equals and that has become subjugated to an upstart English.

L'Obsession: Anti-Americanism after 9/11

One symptom of anti-Americanism in France, historically, has been the occasional expressed desire for a kind of salutary, pedagogical disaster for the United States, one that would tame American arrogance and generate a complex and tragic sense of life. French rightist Georges Duhamel in the 1930s wished for America the kinds of "terrible adventures" that would "make it a great people."[16] Half a century later, this wish for a didactic cataclysm found expression in the immediate aftermath of 9/11. The French at first showed remarkable solidarity with the American people, summed up in the famous *Le Monde* headline: "Nous sommes tous les Américains" (We are all Americans). For some French people, the United States had finally joined the human race, as it were, by realizing it was not immune to attack on its own native soil. It had come to know through calamity what Europe had always known, that no country is so "exceptional" as to avoid the "blowbacks" of history.

But while *Le Monde* expressed solidarity, others were more ambivalent. The ever-ironic and always-apocalyptic postmodern French intellectual Jean Baudrillard spoke in the same journal of the "prodigious jubilation of seeing the world superpower destroyed." For Baudrillard, "all of us" were accomplices of the attack, exhilarated not so much because the victims were American but because at least someone had responded to the evils of U.S.-led globalization. The jubilation was not the terrorists' alone; "they" did it but "we" wanted it. Baudrillard's parenthetical aside that "of course none of this diminishes the suffering and the death of the victims"[17] seemed perfunctory in the extreme. But then the whole French desire for the collapse of New York's skyscrapers had been expressed long before by poet Louis Aragon in 1925: "May distant America collapse with its white buildings amid absurd prohibitions."[18] (The American Beat writers had also conjured up such possibilities.) Another current, expressed in Thierry Meyssain's best-selling book *L'Effroyable Imposture* (the Frightful Imposture), claimed that the entire event was staged by the Pentagon, as if it were unimaginable that Americans could ever really be victims.

French publishing history has for more than a century been rich in titles that attach the adjective *American* to ominous nouns such as *menace* and *peril—Le Péril Américain, Le Cancer Américain, L'abomination Américaine*—all part of a general French obsession with the United States. Thus the United States has played an extraordinary role in the French imaginary; it has become the repository, the site onto which the French have projected "their hopes as well as their fears concerning the future both of their own country and of the world."[19] Anti-Americanism in France, while originally a symptom of haughty aristocratic superiority, slowly became a manifestation of rampant insecurity, a fear less of America per se than for the future of France. In March 1964 the French weekly newsmagazine *L'Express* declared that communism was no longer a threat: "There is only one immediate danger for Europe, and that is the American civilization."[20] And these fears could be incarnated in the most diverse objects: a bottle of Coca-Cola, a refrigerator, a Big Mac, the Internet.

Franco-American tensions encode conflicting notions of temporality. On the one hand, a favored cliché about anti-Americanism in France is that the United States represents a possible French future—consisting of savage capitalism and carnivorous McDonaldization—about which France is highly ambivalent, to say the least. With regard to globalization, the dominant discourses in both countries see the other country as backward looking, but in diametrically opposed ways. American neoliberal Francophobes portray the French as "behind" and "clinging" to an "outmoded" welfare state. Many French critics, meanwhile, see the right-dominated United States as moving backward in social and economic terms, back toward the pre–New Deal 1920s in economics and to an obsolete nineteenth-century nationalism, which France once practiced and has now disowned, in foreign policy. In both cases, the relation is specular: France looks in the U.S. mirror and shrinks in horror.

Thus France has often projected the United States as the dystopian incarnation of its own nightmares about its own future. This obsession is, first of all, somewhat unique, at least in relation to Europe. No European country, not even the former colonizer Great Britain or defeated Germany, has been as obsessed with the United States as France. The obsession is also asymmetrical in its concerns and emphases. Most Americans, at least prior to the recent wave of right-wing France bashing, tended to have a fond (if archaically uninformed) image of France as the romantic land of the Eiffel Tower, the Champs-Élysées, berets, baguettes, champagne, *savoir-vivre*, and amour, an image filtered through various genres: musicals and romantic comedies depicting American artists in Parisian garrets and *Irma-la-Douce*–like prostitutes with hearts of gold; imperial epics depicting the French foreign legion in North Africa like *Beau Geste*; and literary adaptations of French classics such as *Madame Bovary* and *Liaisons Dangereuses*. Even today, this romanticism is echoed in films such as *Before Sunset* and TV series such as *Sex and the City*.

As in the case of Brazil, the asymmetries of economic power and mass-mediated cultural diffusion create a cognitive asymmetry, so that French people generally know much more about the United States than most Americans know about France, even if the French knowledge is sometimes schematic and based on clichés: Americans are childish, money loving, puritanical, have no culture or history, and so forth. But the French educational system does at least stress world history and geography, so that most French people tend to be aware of basic facts about the United States. One suspects that most French people could not only name the president of the United States but also name any number of major American political and cultural figures, while one doubts that most Americans would be able to do the same vis-à-vis France. But then that cognitive asymmetry is not unique to France–United States relations. Despite or perhaps because of American power in the world, the world knows more about the United States than the United States knows about the world, a fact that makes the disproportionate power of the United States in the world even more troubling.

Although the French obsession with the United States dates back, as we have seen, to the two nation-states' ambivalent sisterhood and rivalry in terms of contested concepts such as nation, democracy, modernity, and individualism, French attitudes are hardly uniform or consistent, and France has known waves of obsessive pro-Americanism and anti-Americanism. Even up to the present day, both Americanophile and Americanophobic books have become best-sellers in France. The lines between "pro" and "anti" Americans, however, are not always so evident. Writer and former revolutionary (and now public figure) Régis Debray, widely regarded as one of the anti-Americans, is also a very lucid critic of some strands of anti-Americanism in France. These strands, for Debray, express the wounded amour propre of French intellectuals who resent their loss of status in the face of an American popular culture that prefers blockbuster stars to maîtres à penser, and video games and the Internet to books. The progression from "graphosphere" to "videosphere," for Debray, necessarily relativizes French literary intellectuals.[21]

French anti-Americanism, in other words, is a function of the different status of intellectuals in the two countries. French intellectuals are astonished at the lack of influence of U.S. liberal-leftist intellectuals, when neocon and conservative think-tank intellectuals dominate the political media and the public sphere. Although influential within the academe, critical left American intellectuals exercise little influence on politics and enjoy little presence on the media. Instead, partisan hack commentators such as Ann Coulter and Tucker Carlson, who are not experts but play them on TV, are invited by the media to vent reactionary spleen on subjects—such as Islam and foreign policy—about which

they transparently know absolutely nothing. Celebrity, rather than
expertise, has became the major prerequisite for an invitation to participate in a political talk show. Knowledgeable intellectuals, or Middle
Eastern studies academic scholars, meanwhile, are largely banned from
the airwaves.

While many French criticisms of American policies or cultural trends
are on target, other criticisms are rooted in ignorance or prejudices or
a calculated amnesia about France's own past. Here one factor is what
might be called an imperial nostalgia, the ex-colonialist cuckold's feeling of jealousy concerning the imperial succession, whereby France,
once a leading imperial power on three continents, has been forced to
yield to the new American empire. This imperial "lap-dissolve" was
quite concrete in the case of Vietnam, where the United States took up
the counterinsurgency cause, unsuccessfully as it turned out, after the
French defeat at Dien Bien Phu. But this lap-dissolve is also general and
symbolic in the sense that U.S. geopolitical gains have coincided with
French losses in terms of political, economic, and cultural influence.
Some strands of French anti-Americanism are thus quixotic, reflecting
the resentment of a power that went from being a first-rank imperial
dynamo in 1918 to being a second-rank nation in the present. (Interestingly, the feeling seems less strong in England, perhaps because its conservative elites feel aligned with the American empire.) Like Cervantes's
hidalgo, some French intellectuals manifest a submerged nostalgia for
France's belle époque of imperial domination. No imperialism, after all,
likes the imperialism that takes its place.

Imaginary Tribes: The "Anglo-Saxons"

Nationalistic discourse, as we have seen, often promotes myths of
ethnic essence. The most violent example, of course, was Nazi Germany and its myth of racial purity. Jim Crow apartheid in the United
States, the American counterpart of Nazi race thinking, also constructed a myth of essential white purity. Brazil's myth, at least since
the nineteenth century, has favored a contrasting myth of a paradoxically "essential mixedness." Not all projections of national essences are
self-regarding, however. Nations can project myths of racial purity onto

other nations. It is especially through the comparative framework that assumptions about identity get articulated, whether in published essays or in everyday life. When a Brazilian tells an African American or a Latino that he or she "does not look American" or when an American (United Statesian) tells a blond Brazilian that he or she "doesn't look Brazilian," the remarks inadvertently betray axiomatic assumptions of national and ethnic purity: that Brazilians are always black or mestizo, and North Americans are necessarily white. (One blond Brazilian friend tells us that he always throws the question back onto the interlocutor: "What, in your mind, does a Brazilian look like?")

Some French commentators, in this same vein, project the United States as an essentially white country, an idea encapsulated in that much-abused phrase "Anglo-Saxon" to characterize Americans. The term is very versatile, since it can qualify a culture, theory, fashion, political system, or section in a bookstore. Often, it is deployed as a term of abuse. French politicians, for example, wield the term to condemn legislation they oppose. The term has a long history. Initially, it served to link three of France's traditional enemies: (1) Germany, the place of origin of the Saxons, who defeated Napoleon at Waterloo; (2) England, the land where the Saxons and the "Angles" joined forces; and (3) the United States, the leading power among the "Teutonic" triangle of nations. Another pertinent fact, perhaps, is that Charlemagne, a privileged forebear of the French, massacred the Saxons back in the eighth century. At the end of the nineteenth century, at the very heights of racialized thinking, conservative French thought generated a highly racialized portrait of the "Anglo-Saxon Yankee."[22]

In the nineteenth century, when the French empire extended even into Mexico, official French discourse posited an alliance between all the "Latin" countries—that is, France, Spain, Portugal, Italy, and all of "Latin America"—implicitly against the Anglo-Saxon countries. In our view, however, both of the terms—*Anglo-Saxon* and *Latin*—are misnomers, since so-called Latin America is not only Latin—it is also indigenous, African, Asian, and so forth—and the United States is not only "Anglo-Saxon." The view of the United States as essentially Anglo-Saxon flies in the face of historical fact, since the United States was already in colonial times Native American, African, Spanish, Jewish, Chinese, and pan-European. Ironically, the portrait of "an essentially Anglo-Saxon"

America, around the turn of the century, coincided with the waves of immigration that were further changing the face of an already mixed American nation. The idea that the United States was essentially and normatively Anglo-Saxon was the product of racist imperialists such as Josiah Strong, who stressed what they saw as the natural and inevitable destiny of the Anglo-Saxons—to rule over dark-skinned people. Anglo-Saxonism was the North American version of Hegel's valorization of the European "spirit," before the breath of which native peoples simply extinguished themselves. The term *Anglo-Saxon* was articulated from within by the dominant group as a way of affirming its identity, and it was articulated from without, by the French, as a way of asserting a rival, "Latin" identity. But what is striking is that the promoters of the Anglo-Saxon–Latin polarity do agree about one thing: to wit, that the United States **is** essentially Anglo-Saxon and that the French (and Latin Americans) **are** really Latin.

The "Anglo-Saxon" discourse also contradicted other anti-American stereotypes, because the French right had also expressed disgust at a "mongrel" race, composed of the "mud" of all nations. Thus the United States was seen simultaneously as an ethnic monolith and a hodgepodge. Within anti-Yankee discourse, everything—from the aggressive policies and character of Teddy Roosevelt to the predatory character of industrial monopolies—was explained in racially essentialist terms of "native dispositions" and "the fundamental tendencies of the Anglo-Saxon race." In a time of Darwinian beliefs in social evolution and stages and national types, a racialized portraiture, not unlike that developed in Europe's colonies, constructed a typical Yankee jaw, visible, anatomical evidence of the Yankee's devouring ambition. It is this period that the clichéd judgment emerges: "the United States is the only nation that has gone directly from savagery to barbarism without passing through civilization." Again, the caricatural Yankee had the unifying function of the scapegoat: "We are all from the same race," it suggests, "as long as we are not American."

The popular currency of the term *Anglo-Saxon* in the writings of authors from many countries, but especially from Europe and sometimes from Latin America, calls for interrogation and analysis. As a first step in clearing the air for dialogue and lucidity, we argue, analysts (of whatever nationality) should drop the term *Anglo-Saxon* altogether when speaking about the United States (or even about England). The term creates only confusion and comes overlaid with ancient European hostilities and interimperial rivalries. If *Anglo-Saxon* is meant to refer to a political model, these models cannot be reduced to ethnicities, and all societies are characterized by a struggle over many possible political models. The English language, moreover, is itself hybrid; indeed roughly half of its lexicon is derived from the Latin languages. If language and culture are coterminous and mutually constitutive, as the Sapir-Whorf hypothesis suggests, than Americans are already half French. Present-day English speakers, furthermore, would need special training to read an Anglo-Saxon text such as *Beowulf* or "The Seafarer," and ninth-century English speakers would be baffled by present-day English words such as *pundit* (from Hindi), *caucus* (from indigenous American Algonquin), and *kibitzer* (from Yiddish).

The term *Anglo-Saxon,* then, elides American society's complexity and heterogeneity. Just as we should not call the French the "Gauls," the Portuguese the "Lusitanians," the Italians the "Etruscans," or the Brazilians the "Tupinamba," we cannot characterize any present-day people as "Anglo-Saxons." Ironically, it was the French-born writer J. Hector St. John de Crevecoeur who, as early as 1782, pointed to the ethnic heterogeneity of the United States. Speaking only of the European groups, de Crevecoeur called the American a "new man" whose "strange mixture of blood" was to be found in no other country. (He was obviously unaware that similar discourses were being elaborated in other parts of the Americas.) In America, de Crevecoeur argued, "individuals of all nations are melted into a new race of men."[23] The current circulation of the term *Anglo-Saxon* also leads us to forget the revolutionary hostility toward Great Britain, seen as the main culprit in American oppression. Because of this hostility, the fledgling U.S. republic never considered making English the official language of the United States. The American revolutionary Thomas Paine even went so far as to disavow any filial relationship with England, suggesting that Europe as a whole, rather than England, was "America's motherland." In this sense, Paine was a transatlantic pan-European.

In their dismissals of "American multiculturalism," contemporary French theoreticians sometimes deride "Anglo-Saxon differentialism," that is, what they see as a tendency to emphasize racial and cultural differences. The expression "Anglo-Saxon multiculturalism" is oxymoronic in the sense that the multicultural movement emerged primarily from the Native American, black, Asian, and Latino minority communities, rather than from Euro-Americans. The term is even borderline discriminatory in that it renders invisible all intellectual or political agency on the part of non-Anglo "minorities" in the United States. Thus the term *Anglo-Saxon* as characterizing anything that emerges from the United States has the effect of "whitening," as it were, what multiculturalist activists and intellectuals have worked so hard to "color." When deployed to discredit multiculturalism, the term *Anglo-Saxon* ironically reveals the vital necessity of a multicultural analysis. The term *Anglo-Saxon* obscures the multiplicity of the U.S. cultural formation, the constitutive presence of indigenous, African, European, and Asian cultures, especially at a time when more and more American cities are nonwhite-majority cities. Census reports show that it is only a relatively small minority that claims England as a point of origin; for example, more Americans claim African than strictly English origin.

The term *Anglo-Saxon* even erases the "Frenchness" of the United States, for example, the Frenchness of certain regions and dialects within the United States (the Cajuns of Louisiana and the Canucks of New England, among whom French is reportedly making a comeback). It sets aside all the ways a French culture of cuisine, couture, and boutiques has already been absorbed into American culture. (Those french fries served at McDonald's are really just *pommes frites* after all.) The term *Anglo-Saxon* also obscures the philosophical Frenchness of the founding fathers, whose ideas were embodied in the Declaration of Independence and the Constitution. In 1792, in a more generous era, when France and the United States were regarded as *républiques soeurs*, the deputies in the French parliament approved a decree declaring all philosophers and freedom fighters (e.g., Thomas Paine and George Washington) to be honorary Frenchman. By emphasizing the Angloness of the United States, French commentators, including supposedly leftist French commentators, inadvertently align themselves with the cultural conservatives in the United States, who make the same claim. Both Samuel Huntington and Arthur Schlesinger, in their writings, stress the values of Anglo-Protestant America. American historians, in this sense, often overemphasize the English element in the formation of the United States.

The Dutch contribution, for example, has been neglected, partly because the official version of early American history was largely written by New England puritans, who were locked in combat with the Dutch during most of the seventeenth century.[24] In historical terms, the notion of "Anglo-Saxon" was never really appropriate. The cultural heterogeneity of American cities dates back to the very beginnings of the colonial enterprise. The Dutch outpost New Amsterdam (later New York) was already in the seventeenth century a Babel of peoples—Native Americans, Africans (slave and free), Norwegians, Germans, Italians, Jews, Walloons, Bohemians—and tongues. Indigenous and African languages, Dutch, Spanish, and Portuguese were all spoken in addition to English. "In its very seeding," as urban historian Russell Shorto puts it, "New York was a melting pot."[25] Nor was New York unique in this multicultural tendency. Los Angeles "began" as a Spanish pueblo with a mestizo majority.

The term *Anglo-Saxon* risks turning what should be a legitimate political argument against U.S. imperialism into an illegitimate ethnic slur. If the term *Anglo-Saxon* is meant to refer to the English language, then the term obscures the fact that many "Americans" of immigrant background speak other languages. The residents of a single New York City borough, Queens, for example, now speak 116 languages, and in many parts of the country, Spanish has become the de facto second language. A recent trend in American literary studies is to stress American literature written in languages other than English. The *Multilingual Anthology of American Literature,* edited by Marc Shell and Werner Sollors, features American literature in Italian, Arabic, Lenape, French, Spanish, German, Polish, Russian, Welsh, Yiddish, Swedish, Norwegian, Navajo, Hebrew, Danish, Chinese, Hungarian, and Greek. At the same time, unfortunately, the racist right, the present-day heirs of the Manifest Destiny Anglo-Saxonists, call for "English Only" and for a wall fence to keep out Mexicans. To which we say: "Mr. Bush: Tear Down that Wall!"

The term *Anglo-Saxon,* in sum, is Euro-diffusionist; it seems to imply that a tiny North European tribe managed to completely dominate an extremely heterogeneous spectrum of peoples and that all the non-Anglos together, over four centuries of history, did not in any way dislodge or inflect Anglo-domination or change the dominant group. That is why we propose that all writers—except scholars writing about ninth-century literary texts in the Anglo-Saxon language—abandon the term *Anglo-Saxon*.

Brazil and the Colossus to the North

How do relations between the United States and Brazil as postcolonial New World "cousins" differ from those of France and the United States as transatlantic siblings? As with the France–United States comparison, the Brazil–United States comparison encodes a definite, and in some ways inevitable, asymmetry, but it is not exactly the same asymmetry. While the United States has intervened directly and indirectly in Brazilian affairs and indirectly in French affairs, neither France nor Brazil has intervened in American affairs. If this book does not feature a section on French or U.S. "anti-Brazilianism," it is partly in function of these asymmetries, a function, that is, of (1) the relative lack of power of Brazil, which has never really threatened France or the United States, and (2) the general ignorance about Brazil in both France and the United States. For most Americans and French, Brazil is the land of carnival, soccer, samba, and bossa nova, as encapsulated in the French film *Black Orpheus*. More recently, Brazil has come to be seen as the land of urban crime and social violence, as portrayed in films such as *City of God*. For a politicized minority, Brazil is Lula and the progressive World Social Forum. While both Americans and French are not generally well informed about Brazil, educated Brazilians, at least, are more likely to be informed about both France and the United States.

Brazil was not always the "poor cousin" of the United States, however. Indeed, the story of an early Brazilian visitor to the United States gives a sense of the unstable nature of international relations and comparisons. Hipolito da Costa, one of the first Brazilians to officially visit the United States, was received in Washington by President John Adams on January 1, 1799. The Brazilian visitor was shocked by the rude poverty and shoddy clothing of the Americans. He wrote to his Brazilian friends that suicide was common and "there were many Indians married to whites and vice versa."[26] Ironically, the Brazilian was shocked, not by American wealth but rather by American misery and miscegenation, two traits usually associated with Brazil. Da Costa's shock reminds us that comparative national traits and positions are not fixed and eternal. In the beginning Brazil was the older and richer country, enjoying a vast mineral wealth lacking in the United States. The later colonizers, such as the British and the French, envied the vast wealth of the earlier colonizers, such as the Spanish and the Portuguese, and strove to emulate their feats.

Nor have diplomatic relations been static. Although the United States in the twentieth century tried to repress Latin American revolutions, the United States of Thomas Jefferson's time was more interested in promoting them, for reasons both of republican principle and of mercantilist hopes of breaking European monopolies on trade. Jose Joaquim de Maia (code name "Vendek"), one of the prime movers in the first anti-Portuguese plot (known as the "Inconfidencia" or "conspiracy" in Brazil, in 1788–89), communicated with Thomas Jefferson in 1786–87, first by a letter lauding "your glorious independence," then in person (in Nimes, France) requesting support for the revolt.

As colonial settler states, Brazil and the United States shared certain social contradictions. The U.S. example, as Thomas Skidmore points out, was highly relevant for Brazilians, since the American Founding Fathers seemed to find it possible to write the Declaration of Independence and to own slaves.[27] Some of the Founding Fathers even contemplated a kind of confederation cum military alliance that would unite all the Americas against European colonial encroachments. In 1817 Henry M. Brackenridge was one of the first writers to sense the need for a systematic comparison between Brazil and the United States. While recognizing that the comparison entailed comparing a "young giant" with a "mature dwarf" that had not even achieved independence, Brackenridge emphasized that it was necessary to see beyond present differences to envision what the two nations might become in the future:

The only empires that one can compare to Brazil, in terms of size, are those of China, Russia, and the United States, and even though Brazil is today the smallest in terms of population, the day will come when it will be the largest. ... Although it might seem premature at this time to compare Brazil and the United States, the moment will come when such a comparison will seem natural, even inevitable.[28]

Contrasting the anarchic disunity of the Spanish-speaking nations in Latin America to "the unified and indivisible" Brazilian nation, Brackenridge concludes, "Given the vast capacities and resources of Brazil, it is not to be a visionary to foresee that this [Brazilian] empire is destined to rival our own."[29] As Brackenridge foresaw, both Brazil and the United States consolidated their territories and grew from strength to strength over the course of the nineteenth century, even if Brazil never achieved the rough equality in power implied by Brackenridge's comparison. But Brazil did become known as the "Minotaur of South America" comparable to the "colossus of the north." A century after Brackenridge, Theodore Roosevelt compared the Brazilian *bandeirantes* who opened up the Amazon to the American pioneers who opened up the West.

But the relationship was always asymmetrical. Because the United States tended to pay attention only to those countries it perceived as powerful or threatening, unaggressive Brazil was simply lumped together with what historian Frank McCann calls "an undifferentiated mass called Latin America."[30] For the United States, Brazil was a taken-for-granted minor power—but one with enormous resources—that was expected to automatically endorse the axiomatically benevolent intentions of the United States. But for Brazil, the United States was a major trade partner and geopolitical interlocutor, regarded with respect mingled with fear, a partner in a pragmatic yet very unequal alliance. (France, meanwhile, was Brazil's major cultural interlocutor through the nineteenth century up on through the mid-twentieth century.) At bottom, however, there were solid reasons for a United States–Brazil alliance; as Thomas Skidmore points out, the United States was quickly becoming the major economic partner with Brazil. Second, both Brazil and the United States shared their status as non-Hispanic countries; Brazil needed an ally to counter this Spanish-speaking block. Third, Brazil sensed an affinity with the other continental-sized country, the other country blessed with vast empty spaces and vast resources.[31]

Even if political anti-Americanism in Brazil did occasionally slide into cultural anti-Americanism, most waves of anti-Americanism in Brazil, as we began to suggest earlier, were triggered not by neurotic envies and phobias but rather by specific U.S. policies. Although the Brazilian elite sometimes absorbed European snobbisms toward the United States, Brazil also had many very concrete motives for resentment. Although France sometimes felt itself to be metaphorically "colonized" by the United States, Brazil was literally subject to American neocolonial and imperial policies. As historian Frank McCann points out, tension and ambivalence have been constants in the United States–Brazil relationship. As the United States became more wealthy and expansionist and, under the aegis of the Monroe Doctrine, more interventionist, Brazil began to worry about its powerful northern neighbor, especially about its aggressive business representatives and their designs on Brazilian territory and resources. Some Americans from the South contemplated shipping the black American population to the Amazon, while others thought of annexing the Amazon as an extension of "manifest destiny" and "freedom of the seas." In 1826 the New York–based South American Steam Boat Association sent a steamship to the Amazon. And in 1849 some Brazilian leaders warned of a U.S. land grab similar to the one that had taken Texas from Mexico. In 1855 the United States, alleging a right to make free use of the Amazon, confronted Brazil with a kind of ultimatum. But even though the Amazon was almost as difficult to control from Rio as it was from New York, the Brazilian government did not give in.

Despite such tensions, Brazil under Pedro II maintained the appearance, during much of the nineteenth century, of a cordial alliance with the United States. Pedro II inaugurated the centenary exposition in Philadelphia alongside President Ulysses S. Grant. But with the abolition of slavery in the United States in 1863, the Brazilian slaveholding elite began to worry about the "danger" of an abolitionist movement in Brazil analogous to the one that ended slavery in the United States. Like official France, Brazil too sympathized with the Confederacy. It was this official Brazilian preference for slavery and for the Confederate South that inspired roughly three thousand Confederate American Southerners to move to Brazil between 1865 and 1868, founding the town of "Americana" as a refuge for the cultivation of cotton and the maintenance of slavery. Yet emancipation in the United States, ironically, had by that time indirectly made abolition in Brazil virtually inevitable.

The more important point, however, is that it is less phantasmatic projections than actual policies—to wit U.S. meddling in the Amazon—that provoked what Brazilian diplomatic historian Moniz Bandeira calls "the first anti-American movement in Brazil."[32] Other Brazilian critics amplified their critique from the sphere of foreign policy and business practices to apply generally to the dominant social system itself. General Abreu Lima attacked what he called "mad Yankee ambition." No one, he said, should have to put up with the "imperious brutality of the North Americans, their habitual crudeness, nor the country's savage independence, not its aristocratic liberty. There is not on the face of the earth a more selfish or exploitative people."[33]

The United States–Brazil alliance became less formal and more real with the advent of the Brazilian republic in 1889. The Brazilian republicans multiplied signals of their admiration for the United States, basing their constitution and federal system on the U.S. Constitution, and even adopted the name "United States of Brazil" as an explicit homage. As part of a tacit alliance, official Brazil sided with the United States in grand international disputes while hoping for U.S. support in terms of Latin American disputes. Not all of the resistance to this tacit alliance came from the left. As in France, late-nineteenth-century Brazilian anti-Americanism was often a product of the right. Eduardo Prado's *A Ilusão Americana* (The American Illusion; 1893) provides a fascinating example of this current. A monarchist from the elite, Prado was so rich and elegant that he was treated like a prince when he traveled in Europe, accompanied by his English valet de chambre. Revealingly, Prado saw himself as combating what he regarded as a generally pro-American attitude in Brazil. Citing the oft-expressed admiration of some Brazilian intellectuals for the American republican and federal model, Prado, from a decidedly aristocratic and antirepublican position, forcefully rejected that model. For Prado, the Brazilian republic was a poor copy of a too hastily adopted U.S. model. Prado's criticism of imperialism was erratic and inconsistent. On one hand, he excoriated the Monroe Doctrine and the "Americanization" of Brazil. Yet he was also pro-British, then the supreme imperial power. And Prado's critical discourse concerning U.S. economic policies also drew on the racialist and eugenic discourse of his time; thus he credits the United States for its "energetic races," but excoriates its form of government as "an abomination for all the Americas."[34]

This is not the place to sum up all the North American offenses against Brazil. They can be evoked in shorthand by phrases such as "the Monroe Doctrine," "dollar diplomacy," "the big stick," "authoritarian" versus "totalitarian" governments, "counterinsurgency," "the debt trap," "austerity measures," the "Washington Consensus," and "Operation Iraqi Freedom." After a long history of imperial interventions in Latin America, the United States under Roosevelt launched the "Good Neighbor policy," leading to the most serious rapprochement ever between the two countries. A geopolitically motivated attempt to ward off any temptation, on Brazil's part, to side with Germany and the Axis Powers, the Good Neighbor policy shipped a series of celebrities and artists to Brazil—Orson Welles, Douglas Fairbanks, John Ford, Walt Disney—and invited Brazilian artists to the United States, ranging from erudite composers such as Villa-Lobos to popular stars such as Carmen Miranda. In the end Brazil sided with the Allies and even participated in the war. During this period the Office of the Coordinator of Inter-American Affairs became what Antonio Pedro Tota calls a "factory for ideologies" linked to a "seductive" form of imperialism.[35] The relationship, once again, was asymmetrical. As Frank McCann puts it, "Hollywood offered a diluted and whitened version of Brazil to North Americans ... while a few American soldiers and sailors married Brazilians, exposing their families to Brazilian culture. And Brazilian studies began in American universities."[36]

Brazil's hopes for U.S. gratitude for its help in World War II were quickly dashed once the Axis threat had vanished, however, and in the postwar period the United States returned to imperial business as usual. President Eurico Dutra was the first Brazilian president (if one does not count Emperor Pedro II) to make an official visit to Washington during the Truman administration. Later, Eisenhower opposed the creation of a nationalized oil industry in Brazil (Petrobras), whose slogan was "the Oil is Ours." In this period, the United States tried to enlist Brazilian participation in the Cold War. The Alliance for Progress, under John F. Kennedy, funneled aid and investments into Brazil, so as to undermine the communist-supported social democratic left and strengthen right-wing politicians such as Carlos Lacerda. The attitude was always paternalistic and insensitive to the Brazilian desire to protect its own resources. (For Brazil, the memory of earlier U.S. ambitions in the Amazon played a strong role, even though the North Americans saw such fears as "irrational.")

The absolute nadir of United States–Brazil relations came with American support for the 1964 right-wing military coup d'état, which deposed the elected president João Goulart and installed a military junta in his place. (Lincoln Gordon, the American ambassador to Brazil, officially recognized the junta even before Goulart had left the country.) The coup followed in the wake of other U.S. coups against democratically elected governments (beginning with Arbenz in Guatemala in 1954), but it also served as a dry run for the U.S.-supported coup against Allende in Chile in 1973. Prior to the presidency of Jimmy Carter, all the American administrations supported the Brazilian dictatorship. In the Reagan era, the right-wing UN ambassador Jeanne Kirkpatrick made her notorious distinction between good "authoritarian" governments—that is, "our dictators" or "our sons of bitches," such as Augusto Pinochet in Chile—and bad "totalitarian" governments—that is, "their sons of bitches," elected social democratic or socialist leaders such as João Goulart and Salvador Allende, who in fact were authoritarian and totalitarian only in the ideologically warped minds of people such as Kirkpatrick.

Yet Americans were deeply divided about such policies. Two groups—the U.S. government, with its counterinsurgency priorities, and the counterculture and the academic left—were operating at cross-purposes. Many American scholars of Brazil, the so-called Brazilianists, became vocal opponents of the U.S. support for the dictatorship in Brazil. Indeed, historian James N. Green has scrupulously documented the activist work of U.S. scholars against the dictatorship. American Brazilianist Ralph della Cava and others denounced U.S. policy in various religious and progressive magazines such as *The Nation, The Progressive,* and *Christianity Today,* after which even mainstream newsweeklies such as *Time* and *Newsweek* began to report on Brazilian human rights abuses. (The left was rarely given any credit for pointing out such abuses, which were often officially recognized only decades later.)

By the early 1970s Brazil had become associated in the American press and in the public mind with torture and repression. Some progressive intellectuals founded "the American Committee for Information on Brazil," which compiled a dossier on "Terror in Brazil." (It is noteworthy that "terror," at that time, referred to that of the state and not individuals or groups.) Well-known scholars such as Richard Morse of Yale, Stanley Stein of Princeton, and Thomas Skidmore (then of the University of Wisconsin) signed a statement called "We Cannot Remain Silent." At the "Second National Conference" of LASA (Latin American Studies Association) in April 1970 in Washington, a unanimous resolution condemned the Brazilian regime's violations of academic rights and called for an investigation on the ground in Brazil. (As a result, Skidmore was denied a temporary visa to Brazil.) Meanwhile Brazilian left activists such as Marcos Arruda, Anivaldo Padilha, and Jean Marc Van der Weid, a former president of the National Union of Students, toured American universities, denouncing the dictatorship. Americans, for their part, formed organizations such as the Committee against Repression in Brazil (CARIB) and founded the "Brazilian Information Bulletin." When General Medici, the leader of the junta, appeared in the United States, he was met everywhere by protestors: at the White House, at the OAS (Organization of American States), at the Brazilian Embassy, and at his Blair House visiting residence. As James Greene points out, activism concerning dictatorship in Brazil was the harbinger of similar movements against dictatorships in Chile and Argentina.

With Brazil's redemocratization in the mid-1980s, U.S. hegemony became more economic in nature, largely exercised through U.S.-dominated financial institutions such as the International Monetary Fund (IMF) and the World Bank, leaving little room for maneuver for social democrats such as Fernando Henrique Cardoso or for working-class leftists such as Luiz Inácio Lula da Silva ("Lula") who hoped to make Brazil more socially egalitarian, politically democratic, and economically independent. Many Brazilians are deeply mindful that the IMF- and World Bank–style globalization, for many synonymous with "Americanization," has exacerbated inequities both within and between nations. In such a climate, neocolonial resentment, perhaps unfairly but also inevitably, comes to affect anything seen as American, including even its resistant cultures and oppositional projects, resulting in a missed opportunity for international collaboration on the left.

The View from the South

Brazil, from its southern "perch," as a country at once Southern and Northern, Western and Eastern, indigenous, African and European, is well positioned to cast an ironic look at geopolitical affairs and at the dominant powers. We see this ironic "look from below" in a hilarious Brazilian musical comedy (*chanchada*) by Carlos Manga, made at the height of the Cold War, called *O Homen do Sputnik* (Sputnik Man, 1959). In the film a Soviet satellite falls into the backyard of a Brazilian farmer who as a result becomes the object of the solicitations of three world powers—the Soviets, the Americans, and the French—all desperate to examine the satellite. The Soviets try to intimidate the farmer with (literal) saber rattling, the Americans try to win him over with money and chewing gum, and the French, *bien sur,* use the weapon of eroticism, in the shapely form of Brigitte Bardot. The Brazilian actress Norma Benguel, in an impeccable impersonation of the French star, invites the farmer to come *beber* (drink) with BeBe (BB). Brazilians, the film's satire suggests, can adopt an ironic perspective, equidistant from the megalomaniacal pretensions of all the great powers.

Although elite forms of Brazilian anti-Americanism occasionally coincide with French elite prejudices, it would be misleading to see them as two versions of the same phenomenon. If one sets aside the Europhile Brazilian critics of American "vulgarity," Brazilian anti-Americanism generally has a completely different history and expresses different tendencies. Most of the major sources of neurosis within Franco-American relations are absent in the case of Brazil. In metaphorical terms, there is no issue of paternity (since both the United States and Brazil were the political "children" of Europe), no sibling rivalry since Brazil and the United States did not have competing revolutions (since Brazil never really had a revolution), and no competing imperialisms (since Brazil, although once nominally a Portugal-centered empire, never became a major imperialist power). There was no dispute over who speaks for the universal, since Brazil, within the neocolonial division of intellectual labor, has never even been allowed to pretend to speak for the universal. In short, each of the countries has a different relation to established world power, and the neuroses that accompany that relation. To generalize somewhat crudely, the United States has the neuroses typical of those who exercise overweening power in the world, France has the neuroses typical of an extinguished imperial power, and Brazil has the neuroses of a disempowered would-be power.

Anti-Americanism in France, as we have seen, has often been linked to a backward-looking nostalgia for empire and a forward-looking panic about the future. Historically, it was originally more a product of the right than of the left. Although anti-Americanism derives from concrete issues such as neoliberal globalization and Pentagon militarism, some aspects of French resentment are also phantasmatic in nature, whence its peculiar pathos, its occasional undertones of hysteria. Brazilians, in contrast, have had concrete historical reasons for their anti-Americanism. Although the United States and Brazil began as allies and never went to war against one another—indeed they even fought together as allies during World War II—the geopolitical tensions generated by neo-imperial policies in Latin America have long undermined any deeply amicable relationship between the two countries.

Yet the tensions do not lead to neurotic projections to the same extent. For one thing, Brazilians are not cursed with the "debt of gratitude," since the United States has rarely done Brazil any real favors. Apart from vague hints at a possible revolutionary Brazilian–American alliance against Portugal in the eighteenth century, and despite the largely symbolic gestures of the Good Neighbor policy in the twentieth century, official U.S. policy never helped liberate Brazil from any menace. The U.S. government, in fact, abetted the oppressors of the Brazilian people by supporting the military junta during the 1964 coup. Unlike the case in Europe, the United States never offered Brazil a Marshall Plan to get it out of an economic crisis—the Alliance for Progress was much more invested in undermining the left and supporting U.S. multinational corporations—and, through unfair trade practices and IMF structural adjustment programs, the United States has often directly and indirectly contributed to poverty and inequality in Brazil. As a result, Brazilian resentment at the United States does not function as a way of scapegoating the United States for its own failures or as a means of exorcising any burden of gratitude. And unlike the once powerful France, only recently stripped of its imperial domains, Brazil has long had to live with its relative powerlessness in the world and therefore is less resentful than France. And yet recently, with its new alliances with such intermediate powers as India and South Africa, Brazil shows signs of becoming a more and more powerful representative of the global South.[37]

Brazil, as the self-designated "country of the future," is less likely to project the United States as a nightmarish version of its own future. Like the United States, Brazil is in a sense the historical product of the optimism typical of the spacious settler/immigrant nations of the Americas. Unlike the French, the Brazilians do not necessarily feel that their best times are behind them. Polls show that Brazilians are more proud to be Brazilian than French people are proud to be French. Although neocolonized, relatively powerless Brazil displays, ironically, a certain cultural self-confidence. Brazil seems more certain that it will always remain Brazilian in cultural terms, despite the country's "peripheralization" by those who wield economic and political power in the world. The very definition of Brazilian culture as syncretic, multiple, and "anthropophagic" means that new influences are perceived not as threats but as opportunities. The transparent anxieties of some French intellectuals, in contrast, seem to suggest that French culture is so fragile that it could easily be washed away by the tsunami of U.S.-led globalization or corroded from within by the immigrants who wash up on French shores. Since the idea of French culture, unlike Brazilian or American culture, has until recently been assumed to be more or less homogeneous, outside "foreign" influences are seen as more threatening.

For many French people, globalization looks like a bulldozer mushing Camembert into Velveeta cheese. But while many French felt extremely threatened by Euro Disney, McDonald's, and even the Internet, Brazilians see such processes as part of a much longer history, whereby Brazilian have managed to indigenize elements of other cultures, including popular American mass-mediated culture. Because absorption of the foreign is a Brazilian habit, American culture becomes just one more element to be absorbed and nationalized. Unlike the situation in France, where calls for boycotts of American products or institutions usually come **before** their arrival—and where the boycotts often give way to acquiescence—in Brazil the calls for boycotts come **after** the entry of the product, as a form of protest against specific U.S. policies.

While France sometimes seems increasingly to define itself as a "not U.S.," plus the welfare state, Brazil, despite certain neocolonized feelings of inferiority and despite frustrations about the corruption of the political system, still manifests a powerful sense of cultural self-confidence and is deeply fond of its own way of being. Even if Brazilians begin to eat McDonald's hamburgers, it is felt, all the cultural imponderables, such as the conviviality around the table, will still remain the same. It is as if there were always the knowledge that globalization, even as it worsens social inequities, will never destroy the music and carnival, the *jeitinho,* and the cordial way of life. Brazilian popular music has shown itself to be paradigmatic of this confidence by demonstrating a powerful capacity to indigenize and Brazilianize global currents such as jazz, soul, reggae, hip-hop, and countless other international trends, but always with a Brazilian bass note. And although on some level such confidence might serve as a psychic compensation or rationalization, or a nostalgic denial of historical change, on another level it points to the "periphery" daring to place itself at the "center" within the negotiation of production and consumption. Globalization, within this view, impacts the local, but the "locals" have a good deal of agency in shaping the contours of globalization.

And there is another factor, often unacknowledged, at play in the differing attitudes toward the United States. Although Brazil in many ways defines itself against the United States—seen as a distant, arrogant, hegemonic power with a very different and in some ways opposite culture—the two countries still share the commonality of belonging to the Americas. Both feature the presence of a deeply shared cultural substratum, far below conjunctional political oppositions. They display, that is to say, the shared traits of two continent-sized "New World" countries composed of indigenous peoples, imported Africans, and immigrant Europeans. Even for Americans who have very little information about Brazil, the country feels familiar in its spatial grandeur and ethnic multiplicity. It is not an accident that there is such a vast literature comparing the two countries. It is as if Brazilians project the United States as both the "other" and the "same."

In his memoir *Verdade Tropical* (Tropical Truth), pop star Caetano Veloso eloquently recognized these parallels:

Brazil is the other giant of the Americas, the other melting pot of races and cultures, the other paradise promised to European and Asian immigrants, the other. The double, the shadow, the negative of the great adventure of the New World. The epithet "sleeping giant," first applied to the U.S. by Admiral Yamamoto, would be taken by any Brazilian as a reference to Brazil.[38]

Caetano's own life and career illustrate the radical disjunction between culture and politics, in so far as the United States is concerned. As an adolescent and young man in the 1960s, Caetano hated the American political role in Brazil—specifically its neoimperialism and its support for dictatorship—yet loved Ray Charles and Nat King Cole.

Caetano also calls attention to another ambivalence within Brazilians, one involving the three countries under discussion here. He speaks of the psychic divide between what he himself calls a "Frenchified elitist education" and the daily experience of a popular culture, and especially musical popular culture, which intimately intermingled Brazilian and North American elements and synthesized samba and cool jazz, funk and maracatu, repente and rap. On the basis of these deep and often misrecognized commonalities, Caetano speaks of being surprised at his feeling of being "at home" on his first visit to New York in the 1980s:

> I felt surprisingly at ease, in a way that I never felt in England or even in continental Europe, including even Italy and Iberia. I instantly understood why: I was, as in Rio or São Paulo, in Salvador or Santo Amaro—in the Americas. It is complexly stimulating, for someone who knows himself to be, as an occidental, profoundly southern European and Catholic, to feel at ease in the Anglo-Saxon capital of the World empire. (p. 504)

Even though Caetano picks up again that old misnomer *Anglo-Saxon,* a term more in use in France than in Brazil, he does at least recognize that North America, and not only South America, is, as he puts it, "inevitably mestizo, inevitably engaged with … the non-whites decimated and enslaved by colonization" (p. 270).

Caetano thus rejects the myth of American whiteness. The "deep miscegenation" typical of the "Brazilian racial confusion," he writes, "also inevitably occurs among North Americans, despite the fact that they pretend … that it is not happening" (p. 505). Thus unlike some Brazilian critics of the United States, Caetano does not "otherize" or caricature the United States; he recognizes shared commonalities, including very negative commonalities such as genocide, slavery, and discrimination. In this sense, Caetano's perspective is close to that which animates this book. The point for us is not to deny the clear cultural and political differences separating the two largest nation-states of the Americas, nor is it our goal to propose a sentimental political alliance—some refurbished repackaging of the Good Neighbor paternalism of the 1930s and 1940s. Rather our goal is to point to a common struggle within all the Americas, not only against U.S. hegemony but also against internal racial and class stratification in all the countries. Our call is for us "United Statesians" to abandon unilateralist arrogance and cultural provincialism to "join the human race," as it were, or at least to see ourselves as part of all the Americas, to see a community of shared differences and challenges.

Recently, Caetano released his CD *Foreign Sound,* a collection of American standards (from George Gershwin to Bob Dylan and Kurt Cobain), consciously designed to combat the wave of anti-American sentiment in Brazil in the wake of the Iraq War. In interviews Caetano said repeatedly that while he was completely opposed to the war in Iraq, he did not approve of the recent wave of anti-Americanism. Caetano is thus less pro-American than "anti-anti-American." Perhaps having in mind the contribution of American popular music and the musical comedy to world culture, a Caetano song ("Os Americanos") credited American popular culture with providing a good deal of the *alegria* (happiness) available in the modern world, while also mocking certain rigidities in the middle-class American style of being. The U.S. government, however, was not so appreciative of Caetano's subtle distinctions. When Caetano applied for a visa for his 2004 concert tour promoting *Foreign Sound,* the immigration authorities allowed him only a ten-day visa rather than the usual multiple-entry artist's visa, even though Caetano owns an apartment in Manhattan and has a long history of performing in the United States. The charge against him was that in an interview, in which he had also condemned the 9/11 attacks, Caetano had committed the sin of calling bin Laden "handsome." (But then we should remember that the foreign policy establishment in the United States also used to see bin Laden as one of its "darlings.") In the interview Caetano noted that bin Laden physically resembled many members of his family and that when he (Caetano) visited Israel, where there are many Jews of Yemeni descent, people told him that he looked "Yemeni." But this purely aesthetic and cultural observation was too much for the immigration authorities (much as Bill Maher's denying that the 9/11 hijackers were "cowards" was too much for the ideological patrols of ABC). Thus does the U.S. government shoot itself in the foot, targeting even the cultural anti-anti-Americans with its ideological zeal.

The anti-Americanism, or better the anti-American policyism, of some Brazilian intellectuals does not prevent them from also having a nuanced and ironic attitude toward French cultural preferences. In an editorial column in the daily *Globo* (April 8, 2000), Brazilian writer Luis Fernando Verissimo showed a sensitivity to irony similar to Caetano's in his analysis of the paradoxes of French attitudes toward the United States in the wake of the war in Iraq:

> Today France, which did not support the invasion of Iraq, represents for everyone the preferred antithesis for the truculent Americans. France represents the Reason that resists the strident calls for war, the power that didn't lose its mind, and it is hoped that she will lead the civilized alternative to the bellicose world that the U.S. seems to want. Which is ironic, since the French always had a weakness for the American way of being and acting, a certain enchanted fascination with the barbarians. Ever since de Tocqueville returned to France to explain the Americans to the French, France has not known whether it should criticize or imitate the U.S., that strange land full of novelties which made the revolution before them.

Verissimo goes on to say that the French, in their mania for the new and for gadgets and in their search for rationalization,

> are more American than Cartesian. The culture of taming the forests that accompanied the growth of the U.S.—first of the savage frontier in conquering the continent, then of savage industrialization and new industrial arts which came with it, everything that was rough and vulgar in the American experience—both horrified and fascinated the French, but the fascination always won

out. The best jazz critics in Europe are French, the best authors of series noir, that other American art, are French, and despite the supposed resistance of French gastronomy to culinary barbarism, fast food reigns among the young. France invented the cinema and always had a strong film industry, but the heroes of the New Wave directors and critics were Samuel Fuller, Nicholas Ray and other savages. Nothing typifies the French attitude toward American culture better than the difficult romance between Simone de Beauvoir and writer Nelson Algren, a notorious drunk and poker player who was a kind of anti-Sartre, and who, they say, didn't even take the cigar out of his mouth when he kissed her.

It is perhaps inevitable, in this context, that Verissimo brings up the French cult of Jerry Lewis:

And then there's Jerry Lewis. The admiration of French critics for Jerry Lewis has by now become a joke. A theory about the larger meaning of his films, easily mocked but still intriguing, centered on the idea of the "destruction of the set." In his comedies, always more physical than verbal, Lewis always ended up destroying the set, the structures which represented the limits of invention and of art, and of social repression, or an entire society. Who knows if Bush is not the next Jerry Lewis of the ambiguous French fascination? In terms of destroying the set, he seems to be the artist of the moment.

Verissimo thus puts two world powers "on the couch," dissecting their obsessions and fascinations, analyzing the complex dynamics of the Franco-American relationship from the "peripheral" perspective of a cosmopolitan Brazilian.

Other Brazilian commentators, however, less indulgent than Verissimo toward Bush's "destruction of the set," denounced the United States in terms not so different from those of the French. One of the most popular writers in the world, Brazilian writer Paulo Coelho (*Folha de São Paulo*, March 8, 2003, p. A13), addressed the following series of ironic "thank-yous" to George W. Bush:

Thank you for revealing to the world the gigantesque abyss between the decisions of governments and the desires of their people. For making it clear that Jose Maria Aznar and Tony Blair do not give the slightest importance to the votes they received. Aznar is able to ignore the fact that 90% of Spaniards are against the war, and Blair ignores the largest public demonstration in thirty years. ... Thank you for managing to do what few have succeeded in doing in a century: uniting millions of people, all fighting for the same idea, although this idea happens to be exactly the opposite of yours.

Like some French intellectuals, some Brazilian journalists and intellectuals responded with glee to the 9/11 attacks on the World Trade Center. Many Brazilians saw the attack as a well-deserved rebuke to American arrogance, even if they did not endorse the exact form of the rebuke or its particular agent. Some very prestigious figures, such as economist Celso Furtado, defended the rather improbable hypothesis that the U.S. government itself was behind the attack, comparing it to the Nazi burning of the Reichstag in 1933.[39] Brazilian liberation theologian Leonardo Boff told *O Globo* that his only regret was that more planes had not crashed into the Pentagon. (He was presumably less enthusiastic about attacks on more clearly civilian targets such as the World Trade Center.)

Such responses raise questions about the pitfalls of certain forms of anti-American thinking. In the Boff case, one wonders how a Christian liberation theologian, himself a victim of the Vatican ayatollahs who forbade him to speak publicly on political issues, could applaud a fanatic Islamicist who, in the name of a twisted interpretation of the religion, want to eliminate infidels (i.e., Jews, and Christians such as Boff himself) and convert the entire world to Islam. Nor does one understand why leftist Brazilians would cheer a fundamentalist sect that, if it were to have its way in Brazil, would probably ban not only Judaism and Christianity but also Afro-Brazilian religions such as *candomble* and *umbanda* and prohibit the samba and substitute burkhas for the native Brazilian-style string bikinis (tangas) on the beaches of Ipanema. Around the time of the beginning of the Iraq War, Brazilian carnival filtered the bad news from New York and the Middle East through its comic-grotesque sensibility, mocking the antibody prohibitions typical of many of the world's religions. Within a mock-orientalist imaginary, the Rio carnival after 9/11 featured "bin Laden's Harem": Brazilian women lifting their burkhas to reveal the "dental-floss" bikinis underneath.

Just as the American right befriended Muslim fundamentalists because they were the enemy of right's enemy—secular nationalists, third worldists, and socialists—so Brazilian leftists sometimes applauded the terrorist enemies of the United States. Such are the aporias of the "enemy of my enemy is my friend" thinking. An upside-down version of Bush-style Manichaeism, this strand of thought risks transforming every enemy of the United States into a third world knight in shining armor. Saddam Hussein becomes a reincarnation of Ho Chi Minh, and bin Laden becomes a new Che Guevara. But being an enemy of the United States does not automatically make a leader a hero. Saddam Hussein was a bloody dictator, and bin Laden (and Zarqawi) are not secular revolutionaries like Che Guevara, who believed in popular liberation and socialism, but rather reactionary and murderous fundamentalists, ready to kill even those Muslims who do not share their exact version of Islam.[40]

Some Brazilian artist-intellectuals, aestheticizing human suffering, praised the 9/11 attacks as a beautiful "avant-garde work of art." Although few Brazilians went that far, most Brazilians did express hostility to U.S. foreign policy in both Afghanistan and Iraq. A few weeks after the attacks, a Datafola poll revealed that 79 percent of the Brazilian population were against any U.S. attack on the countries that harbored those responsible for the attack, with more educated people even more opposed than the less educated. The war against Iraq, similarly, generated overwhelming majorities against the war. Phrases such as "the U.S.A., most detested country in the world" became common in the press. In the Brazilian style, carnivalesque humor was also enlisted against U.S. foreign policy. Carnival floats in Rio read, "Bush, find an intern; make love not war" or, in a reference to Lula's missing finger (lost during a factory mishap), "Better a president without a finger than a president without a brain." A leitmotif in the press was that in just a few years, Bush destroyed the good reputation of the United States. The media were also full of indirect antiwar messages. A PT (Worker's Party) government public service announcement for Lula's "Zero

Hunger" campaign said, "This war, unlike others, is worth fighting," the "other wars" being a transparent allusion to the war against Iraq.

Most Brazilians saw the Iraq War not as a campaign for democracy but rather as a crude power play aimed at taking over Middle Eastern resources. In the background of Brazilian opposition to the war was the historical memory of U.S. attempts to appropriate Latin American resources. (Protest banners asked if the Amazon was next on Bush's list.) The antiwar feelings also spilled over into a general reluctance to collaborate with the United States. A poll in the daily *Jornal do Brasil* asked if there should be more cultural and educational collaboration between Brazil and the United States. Sixty-three percent said no. Since the United States (at least prior to Carter) had supported the Brazilian and other Latin American dictatorships, Brazilians were skeptical that the United States would really go to war for "democracy."

Although some Brazilians had warmed to Bill Clinton as the sunny advocate of globalization, the anti-American attitudes generated by the imperial bullying of the Bush administration inevitably spilled over and fed into hostility toward anything perceived as American. The attitude was "your arrogance has made us suspicious of anything that comes with the American label." But in clear contrast to some vindictive Americans who went out after 9/11 and beat up anyone of "Middle Eastern appearance" (a phrase that describes much of the world, including Sikhs, Indian Hindus, and even the Latin Americans misrecognized as Arabs or Muslims), Brazilians generally maintained their traditional hospitality toward foreigners, including toward the Americans in their midst, thousands of whom joined them in various forms of antiwar protest.[41] (After the London bombings, the London police killed a Brazilian living in England, presumably assuming that he fit the description of "a person of Middle Eastern appearance.")

When American intellectuals tried to contextualize the 9/11 attacks while denouncing them, they were denounced by the U.S. right as "blaming America first" and "siding with the terrorists." Needless to say, the right-wing charge was egregiously unfair to the international experts and Middle East scholars who were doing nothing more than providing historical background for horrible events. American commentators such as Chalmers Johnson had long been warning, even before 9/11, of domestic "blowback" for shortsighted foreign policies, should not be penalized for being right. And on one level the partisans of the "United States had it coming" perspective did make a number of thought-provoking points: the U.S. government had itself caused much death and suffering in the world (Hiroshima, Nagasaki, Vietnam, Chile, El Salvador, and so forth); many Americans had rarely showed sympathy for those non-Americans who died in U.S.-led wars, funded by their tax dollars; and Americans deserved no more sympathy than other victims. And in one way or another, the World Trade Center attack was partially "blowback" for U.S. military interventions in the greater Middle East.

On another level, however, while "blowback" explains the 9/11 crime, it doesn't make it less of a crime. For some less careful anti-American critics, who tended to see international politics as a kind of spectator sport, any blow to the opposing side was to be welcomed. But a new anti-American crime, involving the brazen murder of thousands of people, does not wipe out earlier crimes committed by Americans; it just adds another atrocity to the list. Although the official United States in the abstract might have "had it coming," it is a dangerous leap in logic to assume that those three thousand people in the World Trade Center also "had it coming." Conversely, it is just as illogical to think, as some American pseudopatriots do, that the thousands of innocent victims of American violence in Iraq also "had it coming," that all those deaths are in some way "payback" for 9/11. Such cynical forms of vindictive reasoning are equally and specularly repulsive, leading us only into an endless and potentially apocalyptic tit for tat.

In any case, it is bizarre that some progressives could applaud a terrorist act whose practical effect, quite apart from its intrinsic immorality, was to push everything to the extreme right. Many political analysts believe that the 9/11 attacks "saved" George W. Bush, who was then plummeting in the polls because of various Enron-style corporate corruption scandals, by allowing him to pose as the legitimate avenger of an "aggrieved superpower." Thanks to 9/11, an unpopular Bush was transformed into the man with the bullhorn at Ground Zero, the born-again savior of American honor and the defender of the national body. Thus bin Laden offered a gift to George W. Bush. The attacks provided the administration with an excuse to aggressively push all of its preexisting social, economic, and geopolitical agendas—the invasion of Iraq, increased military spending, heightened surveillance, tax breaks for the rich and corporations, the privatization of Social Security, and reduced social programs for the poor. Prior to 9/11, the antiglobalization movement had made impressive strides, but the attack put the antiglobalizers on the defensive, allowing the fundamentalist right to delegitimize domestic and antiglobal dissent as twin forms of treason and anti-Americanism. (Some Homeland Security funds were allegedly even used to repress antiglobalization demonstrators in Miami.) Thus those who applauded the 9/11 attacks have to acknowledge its negative consequences for civil liberties, for peace, and for progressives everywhere.

In Brazil, the emotions generated by 9/11 entered a preexisting field of national ambivalence about the United States. Historian Frank McCann has described Brazilian attitudes toward the United States as a "mixture of respect, repulsion, fascination, and fear."[42] Although there has occasionally been envy of the more "successful" cousin to the north, the resentment against the United States has not generally been imbued with neurotic investments, paranoias, or denegations. At the same time, these specifically political resentments sometimes do become overlaid with simplistic cultural oppositions—many of them half-truths—such as "Anglo-Saxon" United States versus "Latin" Brazil, Protestant United States versus Catholic Brazil, puritanical United States versus carnivalesque Brazil, racist United States versus tolerant Brazil, and so forth. These contrasts draw overly clear lines between the two countries; they forget that the United States is also (and increasingly) Catholic and that Brazil is also (and increasingly) Protestant, to the point that even small Brazilian towns have their evangelical churches. Indeed, the Protestant presence in Brazil goes all the way back to the French Huguenots in the sixteenth century. These contrasts no longer apply so neatly, especially now that there are more than forty million (predominantly Catholic) Latinos in the United States and that many cities have nonwhite majorities.[43] (We will return to the question of comparative religion in a later section.)

We do not want to portray Brazil as the only country in the world that is miraculously free of all taint of narcissism. There is one area, for example, where Brazilian anti-Americanism sometimes does become involved with neurosis and bad faith, and that is in the area of race. In a certain sense, the Brazilian white elite needs a negative image of American race relations for its own narcissistic purposes. Historically, the United States has always provided a negative foil to Brazil's self-image as a "racial paradise." In this sense, the United States is the antithetical site that is always already "more racist" than Brazil. (Apartheid South Africa sometimes served the same purpose for Americans and Brazilians.) This racially defined anti-Americanism offers the elite's exceptionalist vision of Brazil, sending a falsely reassuring message to both black and white Brazilians. For blacks it says, "You see, you are better off here in Brazil." And for whites it says, "You see, we are not racist like those terrible Americans!" And here we agree; white Brazilians, when they are racist, are not racist like white Americans. Rather, they are racist in their own special, cordial, paternalistic, Brazilian way.

The comparison with the United States, in Brazil, although not wrong in denouncing the terrible racism found in the United States, has often had a repressive function. Ever since abolition, whenever blacks began to mobilize against racism in Brazil, some white Brazilians have been eager to accuse their black fellow citizens of introducing an alien American problem into an always and forever "cordial" Brazil, eternal land of "racial democracy."[44] At the same time, antiracist activists might both reject a black–white dichotomy seen as more typical of the United States and reserve the right to selectively adopt specific ingredients of the African American model of militancy such as affirmative action, reparations for slavery, multicultural and Afrocentric curricula, and so forth. And despite some resistance, it is exactly this kind of discussion that we find in present-day Brazil, less because of the importation of North American projects than because the issues related to the long-term sequels of slavery are common to the two countries.

From Francophilia to Francophobia

Our discussion of the trilateral relationship between the United States, France, and Brazil cannot be reduced to a simple story of unilateral anti-Americanism. The relations between France and the United States, like the relations between Brazil and the United States, have often been profoundly contradictory on both sides. The United States has also had its admirers in both countries. In that sense, we have yet to explore certain aspects that complicate the picture of a unilateral French anti-Americanism. In this sense, we have to deal with American ambivalence and with two of its opposite extremes—Francophilia and Francophobia.

Simon Serfaty (whose Hebrew last name ironically means "French") emphasizes the fraught nature of Franco-American relations:

> The relation between the two countries is a mystery. They are so distant and yet so similar, constantly quarreling but also peerless allies. ... The two countries have always had a certain idea of themselves, but also of the other. But these ideas have recently created a vicious circle, nourished by a reciprocal suspicion without any easy cure.[45]

On a more colloquial, journalistic level, Dave Barry summarized the mutually hostile regard between the two countries:

> Yes, relations are at an all-time low. The French view us as a bunch of fat, simplistic, SUV-driving, gum-chewing, gun-shooting, mall-dwelling, John Wayne cowboys who put ketchup on everything we eat including breath mints.
>
> Whereas we view the French as a bunch of snotty, hygiene-impaired, pseudo-intellectual, snail-slurping weenies whose sole military accomplishment in the past 100 years was inventing the tasseled combat boot.[46]

Barry ends on an optimistic note, stressing, "The fact that we hate each other does not mean we can't be friends!"

Despite present-day backbiting, there is a long tradition of pro-French feeling in the United States, whether encapsulated in the memory of Lafayette and the two "sister republics" or in such maxims as "When Americans die they go to Paris." It was Benjamin Franklin who said, "Every man has two countries, his own and France." Thomas Jefferson, on his visit to Paris, praised the French people as benevolent, warm, devoted, and hospitable. John Quincy Adams wrote in 1778 of the "politeness, the elegance, the sweetness, and the délicatesse" of the French and of a country "whose riches, magnificence and splendor are beyond description" (in Serfaty, p. 19). And much later, the African

American French citizen Josephine Baker claimed "deux amours. Mon pays et Paris" (two loves: my country [the United States] and Paris).

A certain American love of France has often been reciprocated across the Atlantic. In France, Benjamin Franklin became a cultural hero, his likeness seen on etchings and handkerchiefs, medals and lockets. Furthermore, the revolutionaries from both countries read each other's work. Writers like Rousseau and Diderot were popular in America, while Franklin and Thomas Paine were popular in France. Many American leaders, such as Washington, Hamilton, Madison, and Paine, were proclaimed honorary French citizens.[47] Franklin was saluted in the National Assembly for his service to France. Jefferson was given the keys to the Bastille, which he sent back to Washington, where they remain at Mount Vernon. Within this veritable love fest, Jefferson was even invited to comment on drafts of the first French Constitution.

Although some Americans now complain about French "ingratitude" for the United States' having saved them in two world wars, the French remind Americans of the gratitude owed them for having saved the American Revolution. Without the help of France, many have argued, the United States would not even exist, because it was French support that prevented George Washington and his men from losing the War of Independence. It is as if France saved the United States when it was an infant, while the United States saved France when both nations were adults. Even prior to the French Revolution, the French monarchy favored the emergence of the American republic, not out of any shared republican idealism, obviously, but rather out of self-interest. After the British victory over the French in the Seven Years War (1756–63), which drove French power out of India and North America and strangled French trade in the Caribbean, the French ancien régime saw in American independence a chance to avenge itself against Britain. In 1778 Louis XVI went to war to protect the fledgling United States against the British.

France became the major ally of the United States as it was "birthing," generating comradely sentiments between the two nations, feelings that were only strengthened with the success of the French Revolution. The fact that the Franco-American amity "held" under both the monarchy and under the revolution, as well as through other governmental shifts, suggests that the bond goes deeper than politics and ideology.

At the same time, we must resist any temptation to romanticize this "sisterhood," since French support for the United States, both during the ancien régime and after the revolution, also clearly had to do with a French geopolitical strategy of undermining its enemy Great Britain, and at various points in history the United States and France almost came to blows.

Nevertheless, at this moment of alliance many Frenchmen went to America to take part in the battle for independence. After Benjamin Franklin's visit to France as ambassador, Louis XVI authorized the delivery of one million pounds worth of munitions to Washington's armies. Much of the gunpowder used in the Revolutionary War came from France. During the harsh winter of 1777, when the revolutionary forces were under siege in Morristown and weakened by desertions, Washington was saved by French aid. In 1778 France signed a treaty of commerce and friendship with the United States, thus guaranteeing its independence. (The signing had serious consequences, in that it triggered war between England and France.) Many high-ranking French military officers intervened to help Washington and the rebels. The first French fleet, commanded by Charles-Hector d'Estaing, was sent to block the English in New York harbor in 1778. In 1777 the Marquis de Lafayette became one of the commanders of the revolutionary forces. Starting in 1776 he had persuaded Louis XVI to send an expedition of six thousand soldiers to fight alongside Washington. In 1780 the French fleet commanded by Admiral de Grasse blocked the English army in Virginia. There, the Count of Rochambeau confronted the English general Cornwallis, who surrendered on October 1, 1780, with U.S. independence now guaranteed. For historian William Doyle the victory over the British at Yorktown in 1781 "was more French than American."[48] Needless to say, this history irritates contemporary American Francophobes, who dislike the idea of any American indebtedness to France. But then such denials form a normal part of the narcissistic process—on both the American and the French sides—since narcissists hate to admit that they need anyone, when in fact all people, and all nations, are constitutively in need of other nations and peoples.

The France–United States relationship began, then, as a kind of mutual love affair, at least between a certain strata in the two countries. The Founding Fathers, and especially Jefferson and Franklin, praised

France as the homeland of freedom, and French revolutionaries returned the compliment to the United States. The influences were reciprocal; French Enlightenment thinkers inspired the American revolutionaries, but the American Revolution also inspired French thinkers. The French declaration of the Rights of Man of August 1789 was partly inspired by Virginia's Bill of Rights. The love affair was "consummated," as it were, by the applause for the public embrace of Franklin and Voltaire in the Academy of Science in Paris. Some American political figures were penalized for this embrace of France. Jefferson's enemies, for example, accused him of being at heart a "Frenchman," foreshadowing similar attacks on John Kerry more than two centuries later.

The American cultural elite has often looked not only to England but also to France for ideas. Thomas Paine, Henry Wadsworth Longfellow, Ralph Waldo Emerson, Nathaniel Hawthorne, Frederick Douglass, Henry Adams, and Edith Wharton all visited France and wrote about it with affection. France formed an essential and particularly romantic part of the "grand tour," for the American elite, at first, and for the middle class later. For both the United States and Brazil, France provided an alternative European cultural model to the dominant colonizing powers (Great Britain in the U.S. case, and Portugal in the Brazilian case). As in Brazil, one finds in the United States as well homegrown versions of all the (partially) French literary movements such as romanticism, realism, naturalism, symbolism, and modernism. The Franco-American cultural dialogue was registered brilliantly in the novels of Henry James, where American democratic optimism and naïveté wrestled with French aristocratic cynicism. Nor was the influence exclusively literary. French socialist and utopian political movements had American imitators: the transcendentalists' Brook Farm near Boston and "La Reunion" in Texas were both French-style Fourierist communities.[49]

In the twentieth century, Francophilia was expressed both in American popular culture—for example, in the countless Hollywood films that made France the site of art, romance, and joie de vivre—and in erudite culture: the Francophilia of the American avant-garde. Many expatriate writers (Ernest Hemingway, Gertrude Stein, James Baldwin) and filmmakers (Joseph Losey, Orson Welles, Jules Dassin) found in France a haven from American chauvinism, racism, and McCarthyism. When American intellectuals became disillusioned with the United

States, France was the preferred destination for expatriation. Indeed, France has had a long history of welcoming American cultural and even political exiles, serving as a refuge not only for persecuted filmmakers such as Orson Welles but also for experimental or underfunded avant-garde artists such as Robert Wilson.

France has also played a special role in the life of African Americans. The first African Americans to arrive in Paris were probably Thomas Jefferson's slaves, one of whom, Sally Hemings, became the mother of at least one of his children. (Their story is told in the film *Jefferson in Paris*.) In the twentieth century, some one hundred and sixty thousand African Americans, beginning in 1917, served in France, and they received a warm welcome. As Tyler Stovall points out in his *Paris Noir: African Americans in the City of Light,* black American adoration of Paris was often a by-product of the sorry state of "race relations" in the United States: "African Americans shared the surprising realization that at least some whites could treat them with affection and respect, that a color blind society just might be possible after all."[50] Yet as occurred with black Americans in relation to that other presumed racial paradise—Brazil—blacks also discovered that the situation in France was in fact much more complicated than at first appeared. It is intriguing, in this sense, that a black intellectual such as Frantz Fanon could go from a French Overseas Department, Martinique, to the "mother country" France only to "discover" French racism, while black American intellectuals such as Richard Wright went from the United States to "discover" exactly the opposite.[51]

The role of Paris, as Tyler Stovall puts it,

> was both fascinating and deeply ironic. After all, the city was the seat of one of the world's great colonial empires, a place where anonymous French officials supervised the subjugation of millions of Black Africans ... [yet] more so than in the United States, even New York, African Americans found that in Paris the abstract ideal of worldwide black unity and culture became a tangible reality. ... French colonialism and primitivism thus paradoxically combined to foster a vision of pan-African unity.[52]

Harlem Black Renaissance writer Claude McKay actually took some of the black literati to task for praising France as the country of human rights—a useful stick to beat racist America with—to the point that they forgot the racist nature of French colonialism. The literati, McKay writes, is "well-informed about the barbarous acts of the Belgians in the Congo but it knows nothing at all about the barbarous acts of the French in Senegal, about the organized robbery of native workers, about the forced enlistment of recruits ... or about the total annihilation of tribes."[53]

In contemporary terms, neither France nor Brazil enjoys the same image of the "racial paradise" it once enjoyed among African Americans, a function of various factors such as (1) slightly improved conditions in the post-Civil-Rights United States, especially for the black middle class; (2) increased exchange and migration among the Afrodiasporas; and (3) greater awareness of racial hierarchies and discrimination in both France and Brazil. But even if African Americans are less enthusiastic about France than they once were, they are unlikely to become Francophobic. In sum, a certain affection for France, despite all these complications, still plays a significant role in African American culture and in American culture generally, despite and even sometimes because of the Francophobia of the right.

Anti-French Hysteria and the American Right

The current bitterness between France and the United States can be largely explained by long-term geopolitical tensions and by the hegemony of the right wing within the United States. Long after the amicable beginnings we described earlier, the relationship between the two countries worsened dramatically in the twentieth century, when the U.S. political, military, and corporate elite came to see France as a "shaky" ally. This anti-French tendency can be traced especially to the French defeat in May and June 1940, when the French armistice was considered a separate peace that obliged the United States to enter the war. The anti-French feeling was reinforced in the postwar period by what the American foreign policy establishment saw as the "intransigence" of de Gaulle, combined with the strong influence of the Communist Party in postwar France.

Other tensions revolved around U.S. ambivalence toward French colonialism. But then the United States, partly because of its own schizophrenic narrative of origins, has always been ambivalent about colonialism and imperialism. On the one hand, the United States came into existence thanks to an anticolonial revolution against Great Britain and is thus anticolonialist, but on the other hand, as a settler colony, the United States colonized and dispossessed indigenous people; imperialized Cuba, Puerto Rico, and the Philippines; neocolonized Latin America; and now tries to exercise empirelike hegemony in much of the world. Yet at certain points in its history—for example, with Woodrow Wilson's call for national autonomy for oppressed peoples and later during the long tenure of FDR—the United States did occasionally promote anticolonial policies, partly out of principle and partly for pragmatic reasons of opening up markets. For Americans, reared on the myth of anticolonial national revolution, direct rule over subject peoples has always been taboo. Yet the United States also exercises imperial domination, usually euphemized as freedom, democracy, and self-determination, simply granting itself the right to intervene anywhere in the world in the name of "preventive war."

Thus the United States constantly oscillates between the two poles of its historical formation as republic and empire, torn between the liberatory impulse of freedom against British colonialism and the opposite, colonial impulse of subjugating racialized minorities at home and imperialized subjects abroad. Bush administration rhetoric addresses only of one side of this history, however, seeing the occupation of Iraq, symptomatically, not as analogous to earlier colonial occupations like that of the British in Iraq or the French in Algeria, for example, but rather as the generous occupation of the magnanimous victor, like the U.S. postwar occupation of Germany and Japan. The neocons, especially, wed the rhetoric of republican freedom with the practice of empire.

Historically, the United States, as noted earlier, has been both critic and heir of French imperialism. It supported the French in Indochina, at least until the French defeat at Dien Bien Phu in 1954, but Eisenhower opposed the French (allied with the British and the Israelis) in Suez in 1956. At other times, the United States mimicked the mistaken imperial policies of the French, at times even on the very same terrain. In a kind of interimperial competition, the "best and the brightest" technocrat intellectuals of the John F. Kennedy administration were convinced that they could do a better job in Vietnam than the listless French. But like the French, the Americans left Vietnam with proverbial tail between proverbial legs. And most imperial powers made the same mistake of deploying armies against insurrections, which almost always becomes an exercise akin to killing mosquitoes with cluster bombs. The "collateral damage," meanwhile, is likely to turn the masses of people, even those who initially welcome the troops with flowers, against the occupier.

The United States opposed European imperialism for the same reasons that the British opposed slavery; that is, that it was no longer useful to them in furthering their own interests. The "anti-imperialist" United States of FDR, we cannot forget, was also well on its way to becoming a global quasi-imperial power. But while most of Europe accepted U.S. leadership in the postwar period, the French remained cool, even suspicious, developing an independent foreign policy that the official United States saw as aimed at developing a "third force" opposed to American power. On the other hand, this very resistance to American domination indirectly facilitated American aims by strengthening Western Europe vis-à-vis the Soviets, long a goal of postwar U.S. policy. And indeed, the United States recognized France as the unavoidable key player in developing European unity, since the two other great European powers were disqualified for the role—Germany by its Nazi past and Great Britain because of its "special relationship" with the United States.

In the Vichy period, anti-Americanism and pro-Europeanism had gone hand in hand. But the irony of history is that while French anti-Americans saw the construction of a new Europe as a defense against an expansionist America, it was the United States that served as midwife for the birth of the new Europe. In fact the United States favored European integration not only for real political reasons—with Europe as a counterweight to the Soviet Union—but also for ideological reasons. The new integrated Europe was seen as potentially an imitation of the U.S. federal system, a kind of "United States of Europe." When Reagan's strategy in the 1980s of outspending the Soviet Union in military terms to induce its collapse apparently "worked," the U.S. military and political elite thought it was time for France to simply acknowledge the overriding strategic wisdom of U.S. foreign policy and gracefully bow out of the geopolitical arena, abandoning the terrain to what by now was the world's only superpower or, in French parlance, "hyperpower."

In the George W. Bush administration's prosecution of a war and pursuit of procorporate policy, France has been a favored European enemy. If the Franco-American relationship began as a love affair, that love affair certainly "soured" later, to the point that Colin Powell compared the relationship to a couple undergoing two centuries of marriage counseling. The term *French anti-Americanism,* in this sense, distracts attention from the converse phenomenon—anti-French attitudes in the United States. While anti-U.S. attitudes in France are often shared by right and left alike, in the United States contemporary anti-French attitudes are almost exclusively the product of the extreme right, and especially of neocons such as George Will, Richard Perle, and Charles Krauthammer. Unfortunately, this politically-motivated animosity has spread far beyond the small circle that promoted them; they are now disseminated by talk shows and even sketch comedy shows like *Saturday Night Live.* As a result, millions of people with little knowledge or direct experience of France absorb the most absurd prejudices about the French. (A "Boondocks" cartoon has young Huey tell his grandfather about the "good news": African Americans are now only the third most hated group in the United States, "after the Muslims and the French.")

With the hawks of the Bush administration, Francophobia has reached monstrous proportions. Richard Perle, godfather of the neo-conservatives and one of the intellectual "authors" of the war in Iraq, suggested that NATO should add new members, and if that required any old members to be eliminated, he had, he said, in an obvious allusion to France, a candidate in mind. In this same vein, Mark Steyn, in *Jewish World Review* (May 1, 2002), wrote, punningly and venomously, that both the European Union and France's Fifth Republic were destined to "slip down the Eurinal" of history. Former secretary of defense Casper Weinberger in 2001 denounced a plot, presumably organized by France, aimed at dissolving the Anglo-American special relationship and undermining NATO.

In this same vein, the *toujours charmant* John Bolton, when he was at the State Department, warned the French not to be "envious and nostalgic" and to get in line behind American leadership. Amos Perlmutter wrote in the *Washington Times* (May 10, 2001) that the French were becoming the "only truly anti-American democracy." Repeatedly, the Bush government tried to humiliate France through acts of omission. When Cheney listed the allies in the antiterrorist struggle as consisting of Great Britain, Germany, Turkey, and Holland, he conspicuously failed to mention France. And a leitmotif in the Bush campaign against John Kerry was that he not only committed the cardinal sin of actually speaking French but also "looked French" (whatever that might mean). Such are the abysmal depths of stupidity to which know-nothing Francophobia can lead.

For the right wing, France constitutes an ideal enemy: in domestic terms it represents the hated welfare state—aka "big government"—and the resistance to neoliberalism, and in international terms it represents an independent foreign policy not servile to the United States. Often France has provided an ideal punching bag for right-wing ideologues, a way of shifting blame for mistaken American policies. When the United States failed to win Security Council support for the war in Iraq, and although the majority of the nations represented were opposed to the war, the Bush administration blamed it all on France, partially because it could build on preexisting stereotypes of the French as elitist, cowardly, and ineffectual. Scapegoating France drew attention away from other salient facts: that many Americans were also skeptical about the war, that Iraq's Middle Eastern neighbors opposed the war, that Saddam Hussein was sending signals that he was desperately hoping to avoid the war, and that the populations in many of the "allied" countries (e.g., Turkey) were massively hostile to the war. And now, while the administration, through its rose-colored glasses, sees "progress," most of the world sees present-day Iraq as synonymous with chaos and misery. If Iraq is the first positive "domino," auguring democratic change in the Middle East, one dreads the fate of the other dominos on the neocon hit list.

The scapegoating process usually entails the projection of one's own aggressions and the exorcising of one's own faults. An essay in the rightwing *Washington Times* provided a vivid example of this process when it claimed, "France has been sleeping with Saddam for decades," conveniently forgetting that Ronald Reagan, George Bush, Dick Cheney, and Donald Rumsfeld all also had been "in bed with Saddam" for decades as well. But what is most interesting for our comparative purposes is the clear parallel between the domestic and the international forms of right-wing populism, which simultaneously scapegoats "elitist" liberals at home and the "elitist" French abroad. The denigrating of France thus exists on a continuum with the denigration of U.S. liberals, as twin symptoms of right-wing (or one might say "white-wing") populism. The emphasis on elite, luxury items typifies, again, the strategies of right-wing populist discourse with its caricature of latte-drinking liberals and its ridiculous pretense of speaking up for ordinary people. In both cases, the right-wing economic elite deploys a bait-and-switch tactic, a transfer of hostility, under the guise of "antielitism." In domestic terms, the problems generated by the transfer of wealth from poor to rich are blamed on the "latte liberals." (The "elite" charge is linked, not surprisingly, to a European beverage.) In international terms, the worldwide condemnation of the war is blamed on the supposedly elitist French. And even then France was underappreciated; although France did not support the war in Iraq, it did collaborate with the United States in Afghanistan. And in still another sense, the Bush administration's broad-brush attack on "the French" seemed terribly ungrateful to the many pro-American French commentators and politicians in France.

The right's "Bill of Complaints" against France has not been limited to foreign policy. It also had to do with France's domestic choices. In the writing of George Gilder in *Forbes ASAP* magazine, any resistance to free market fundamentalism was labeled the "French disease." And here right-wing journalists performed the same up-is-down trick that they performed in relation to the United States. In a rather Orwellian turn, those who urged what would normally seem like egalitarian ideas like a more equitable distribution of wealth and the undermining of the real financial elite were portrayed as elitist. Roger Cohen, a European correspondent for the so-called liberal *New York Times*, consistently derided the French for "clinging" to their overly centralized welfare state, run by elitist technocrats. "France," Cohen suggested ominously, "has set itself up as perhaps the nearest thing the U.S. has to a serious ideological rival in the last decade of the 20th century."[54] Cohen portrayed the French as almost farcically irrational in their unwillingness to give up their inexpensive education, universal health care, short workweeks, long (paid) vacations, and guaranteed pensions. Why would any rational person, commentators such as Cohen insinuated, actually want the government to provide for people's needs, when "every man for himself" economics was working so well in America? The quiet implication was that "normal" people—that is, people like Americans—naturally prefer unaffordable health care, high-priced drugs, expensive education, long workweeks, short or no vacations, and vanishing Enron-style "now you see them now you don't" pensions. (Comic Wanda Sykes noted that it was much better to be mugged in the ghetto than to be mugged by Enron: "In the ghetto, they just take what you have on you; Enron mugs your whole future.")

In Cohen's wake, *New York Times* columnist Thomas Friedman, the euphoric apostle of globalization, contrasted the inexorable march of U.S.-led globalization with the small-minded obstructionism of the French. Friedman created a muddled contrast between the "conformism" of the French, clinging to their welfare state, and the daring of the neoliberal Americans. In his view, the French lacked the James Dean–like rebelliousness of the Americans, who are always ready to question conventional ways, since "the French system rewards people for their capacity to follow the path laid out to them."[55] Unfortunately for his argument, some of Friedman's articles were written around the time of a massive expression of French political rebelliousness—the 1995 street protests against the neoliberal measures being laid down by the French government—at a time when many Americans were passively swallowing whatever the corporate elite chose to inflict on them. Both Cohen and Friedman repeatedly fell back on the old stereotypes of the French as arrogant, snobbish, and grandiose. This convenient charge enabled the free market pseudopopulists to cast any resistance to globalization as "elitist," whence the appearances in TV commercials, in the 1990s, of caricatural representations of the closed-minded French, for example, in the commercials of American Express, foiled by forward-looking and open-minded Americans.

With the war in Iraq, know-nothing France bashing became a strategy for projecting the right's own vices onto others. In a classic case of guilty projection, Richard Perle—the advocate of preventive war against Iraq and a man repeatedly accused of profiteering from the war through his Trireme and Ahmed Chalabi connections—said in a *Guardian* interview (November 13, 2002) that it was not he who had "lost [his] moral compass" but Europe. An editorial in *Le Monde* (February 12, 2003) summed up well the American hostility toward France as seen from within France:

> We French are cowardly, Munich-style appeasers, singularly venal, rather anti-Semitic, and, it goes without saying, passionately anti-American. And let us not forget, we are also "old." That is how a certain American press sees us. One of the most prestigious columnists from the *Washington Post* writes that France has only cultivated one art since 1870, the art of flight and retreat. The *Wall Street Journal* publishes an article by Christopher Hitchens calling Chirac "a screaming rat" ready to transform France into "Saddam's whore." The most widespread assumption is that there can only be one explanation for the French position against the Gulf War—basely material interests, the whiff of gasoline—as if the official U.S. had no material interest in Iraq.

Seen in the speculum of United States–France "looking relations," Francophobia is here relativized from the perspective of its French "targets."

In the U.S. right-wing view, the ungrateful French constantly stab innocent Americans in the back, precisely those who saved France from its own murderous, suicidal, and anti-Semitic tendencies. At times, the right-wing hostility to the French becomes positively genocidal. In a new low even for the Francophobes, FOX anchor John Gibson regretted that the Olympic Committee had not chosen France for the Olympic Games: "The terrorists," he snickered, "would have blown up Paris, and who would have cared!" It is sad to think that even Hitler spared Paris from burning, but that FOX, in its Francophobic delirium, fantasizes about Paris in flames.

But there is one area where the U.S. right rarely criticizes the French—imperialism. It is highly symptomatic, in this sense, that the Pentagon screened the Italian Algerian film *The Battle of Algiers,* a classic denunciation of French colonialism in North Africa, as an object lesson for its bureaucrats in how to deal with an insurrection like the one U.S. forces are now facing in Iraq. Despite the proclaimed Francophobia of Donald Rumsfeld and despite the pretense of bringing not colonialism but only democracy to Iraq, when it comes to colonial wars the American military "naturally" sides with the French colonialists. A further irony is that historically the United States did not side with France in Algeria and that France was furious when the United States funneled arms to Tunisia, knowing full well that the weapons would end up in the hands of the insurgents in Algeria. Although the war in Iraq is called "Operation Iraqi Freedom," theoretically designed to "give Iraq back to the Iraqis" (or at least "our" Iraqis), when the Pentagon screens *The Battle of Algiers* it clearly identifies with the colonialist French paratrooper Mathieu and not with the revolutionary Algerian Ali-la-Pointe. Here we detect a tacit admission, if only by analogy, that what is now happening in Iraq, despite administration disavowals ("We are not an imperial power!") is not totally disconnected from France's colonial misadventure in Algeria fifty years earlier. Such are the unconfessable solidarities of rival imperial powers.

The United States has never really made up its mind about imperialism. Although the usual claim is that the United States is not imperialist ("We have no territorial ambitions" and "We covet not one square foot of foreign land"), some hawkish journalists and intellectuals have given the game away by calling explicitly for a kind of "stealth imperialism," all in the name of "freedom" of course. But here the United States is not different from earlier imperialists. Every European power claimed that its particular form of colonialism or imperialism was a benevolent enterprise bringing freedom and other benefits to subject populations. For Spain, colonialism was really about saving pagan souls; Portuguese colonialists bragged about their racial tolerance; British imperialism was only about trade and the "white man's burden"; French imperialism was part of the "civilizing mission"; and now American imperialism is about "spreading freedom." The Iraq War, in this sense, inevitably calls up memories of earlier imperial interventions, most notably the British intervention in Iraq in the 1920s. The Brits too bombed and invaded Iraq, they too had their colonial enclave, their "Green Zone." The revelations of torture at Abu Ghraib and Guantánamo, moreover, remind us of the clear links between other, earlier colonialisms and imperialisms and the current U.S. intervention. Some of the specific torture techniques—such as "water boarding" or forced near drowning—had scandalized the French press when they were used in French Algeria in the 1950s. The only novelty, perhaps, was the use of digital cameras to record some of the abuses, and perhaps the apparent lack of embarrassment on the part of U.S. officials such as Dick Cheney and Donald Rumsfeld.

The American form of imperial denial is to not see its own imperial self in the Magritte-like mirror of French imperial history. The United States looks at French history and says, "We are not imperialists like you." And indeed, United States imperialism is not exactly the same as earlier imperialism. Unlike former imperialisms, U.S. imperialism is an imperialism of bases, which usually begin as "temporary" yet somehow always seem to stay. The French form of imperial denial, meanwhile, is to say, "You Americans are imperialists," forgetting to add, "as we were in the past." What we find is an interimperial version of what Freud called the "narcissism of minor differences." Thus some of the tension between France and the United States bears on the usually undiscussed issue of denial and disavowal and the too-close-for-comfort repressed resemblances between two imperialisms.

Thus France looks in the U.S. mirror, especially at a time when the United States is behaving in an archly imperialist manner, and fails to see its own past self-haunting that mirror. In this case, the look at the reflection in the mirror provokes shame or at least disavowal. Dominant France looks at the United States and thinks, "We were civilized, cultivated imperialists, not barbarians like you; we did it better." Another broadly European form of denial is to see the United States as uniquely imperialist rather than as part of the broad and aggressive expansion, since 1492, of European power into the world, even though American power in some ways now goes against Europe itself. The official United States, meanwhile, looks at France and says, "We will be better, more efficient at domination." Thus much of the emotion generated by both right-wing Francophobia in the United States and anti-Americanism in France derives from an unstated intrawhite or intra-Western competition—our colonialism was more sophisticated than yours, our imperialism is more enlightened than yours, and so forth. The affinities are repressed on both sides, yet they return in their full paradox when Francophobic generals watch *The Battle of Algiers* and unabashedly identify with the French struggle against the insurgents.

Anti-Semitism, Misogyny, and the Neocons

The story of patriotism as love of country reminds us of the story of the stage gorilla in the film *Cabaret*—"if they could see her through my eyes, maybe they'd leave us alone." In the context of the film, the gorilla encodes a complex message of the "mixed mating" of ape and man, allegorizing the marriage of Jew and non-Jew in Nazi Germany:

When we're walking together,
They sneer if I'm holding her hand.
But if they could see her through my eyes,
Maybe they'd all understand.
(They waltz)
I understand your objection,
I grant you the problem's not small.
But if you could see her through my eyes,
She wouldn't look Jewish at all.

On a first level, the analogy to patriotism suggests the blindness of national narcissism: if other countries could see our country though our eyes, then maybe there would be no anti-Americanism or Francophobia, for example, for then everyone could see the irresistible appeal of each other's national ape.

But on another level, an interesting corollary of right-wing Francophobia has been the tendency to simplistically equate France with anti-Semitism but in a way that is almost allegorical rather than literal. Anti-Americanism has been conflated with anti-Semitism by analogy, as if the Americans had become the new targets of prejudice, in effect becoming the new Jews.[56] This tendency pervades right-wing commentary on France. "Even the phrase 'cheese-eating surrender monkeys,'" Jonah Goldberg wrote in the right-wing *National Review Online* (July 16, 2002), "is used [to describe the French] as often as the French say 'Screw the Jews.'" One has to "look to France," wrote neocon editorialist Charles Krauthammer in "Europe and Those People" in the *Washington Post* (April 26, 2002), to find "perennial anti-Semitism." Although France, like Europe generally, had indeed been the site of a long history of violent anti-Semitism, ranging from medieval pogroms and "blood libels" on through the Dreyfus case up to the Vichy government, which sent thousands of Jews to the death camps. On another level, the equation was also grossly unfair and historically imprecise. France was, after all, the first European country to offer emancipation to the Jews, and many French Jews reached high positions of literary prestige (Marcel Proust), political power (Leon Blum, Pierre Mendez-France, Simone Weil), and economic power (the Baron de Rothschild). Most of the American denunciations of French anti-Semitism centered on anti-Jewish attacks in France (some the product of classical right-wing anti-Semites and others perpetrated by Maghrebian youth scapegoating French Jews out of their own anger both about their own social situation and about political events in the Middle East). Violence against French Jews is usually followed by strong denunciation on the part of French government authorities and often by mass demonstrations of protest (as in the case of the torture and murder of Ilan Halimi, a French Jew of Maghrebian origin). The American denunciations also had do with the fact that France, like much of Europe, was very critical of the Israeli occupation of the West Bank and Gaza, an attitude taken as emblematic of anti-Semitism by elements of the U.S. right wing closely associated with the Israeli right. Here again France provided a convenient scapegoat, allowing the hawkish American right to blame France for the worldwide unpopularity of Israeli policies toward the Palestinians.[57]

Interestingly and symptomatically, the same neocons who portrayed France as a hotbed of anti-Semitism had no problem with the anti-Semitism of the American religious right and the "Christian Zionists." Nor did the neocons make the same accusation against other European countries that opposed the Iraq War. German opposition to the war never led to neocon denunciations of German anti-Semitism, despite the infinitely more "touchy" history of anti-Semitism in that country. As Nina Bernstein points out in an op-ed piece in the New York Times (September 28, 2003), Germany, unlike France, never became the target of rage for the right: "no one poured schnapps down the toilet, renamed sauerkraut or made prime-time jokes denigrating German manhood. Only France can evoke that kind of frat-boy frenzy." Could it be that this more indulgent attitude toward Germany, on the part of the neocons, partially derived from the fact that Germany, which has paid reparations to Israel, had generally been more pro-Israel in its foreign policy? Taking note of some very serious anti-Semitic incidents in France, the commentators sometimes failed to note the equally frequent anti-Muslim incidents or to note that the racist leader Jean-Marie Le Pen hated both Arabs and Jews with equally pathological fervor.

The past decades, then, have seen an extraordinary amount of transatlantic sniping. "The criss-crossing perceptions between France and the U.S.," as Denis Lacorne puts it,

> form part of a propaganda war in which each of the protagonists tries to improve its own image while lowering that of the transatlantic counterpart. "Atlantic Man" [sic] exists only in so far as he is torn between two worlds which observe each other, admire each other, critique each other, and sometimes roundly detest each other.[58]

More and more, one heard in the United States disparaging terms about Europeans such as "Eurotrash," the "Euroids," "the peens," and the "Euroweenies." On the American right, anti-Europeanism especially targets France, seen as the key rebel against U.S. hegemony and values, a kind of "bad influence" in the European neighborhood. For many in the United States, including liberals, the war in Bosnia reinforced the impression of European weakness and lack of moral fiber, because Europe was unable to prevent ethnic cleansing by Serbia, and France was subtly pro-Serbia. Europe in general, and France as its quintessence, were seen as weak, ineffectual, cowardly, and selfish, in contrast with an efficacious, brave, and generous United States, ready to assume its "responsibilities," saving Europe from itself.

But apart from concrete policy differences, a number of tropes and leitmotifs structure this Francophobic discourse. One is age. Europe is described as an "old people's home," "old Europe," or "museum." Another is appeasement. France is positioned as resembling Chamberlain (or Petain) in its response to terrorism, while the United States is cast as the virtuous anti-Nazi country characterized by intestinal fortitude, despite the Nazi sympathies of people like some right-wing Americans such as George W. Bush's grandfather Prescott Bush. Yet in fact France was quite effective in preventing terrorist plots and arresting terrorists—and this without launching into "we are at war" rhetoric, demagoguery, and politically opportune color-coded alerts. Bush, Cheney,

Rumsfeld, and Ashcroft, meanwhile, were "asleep at the switch," ignoring repeated warnings and CIA briefings concerning an imminent attack in the United States. In fact the administration did almost nothing against terrorism prior to 9/11 and, some argue, after 9/11 as well. (Although Stephen Colbert offered a tongue-in-cheek defense of the administration by pointing out that its distribution of security "pork" was a clever way of combating Muslims.)

The language of anti-French critique, in this sense, is deeply embedded in the masculinist imaginary. Commentators such as Frank Costigliola, Walter Russell Mead, Irwin M. Wall, and Charles Kupchan have all signaled the highly gendered and sexualized aspects of American Francophobia. While the French themselves had idealized France in the form of a woman, Marianne, who evolved from "young, active, sexually desirable single woman to the self-controlled, dignified matron of post-Commune France,"[59] the American right-wing portrayal of France mingled the traits of a venerable old lady, a wrinkled prostitute, and a flamboyant pansy. In contrast to a young, virile, and heterosexual United States, France was supposedly weak, frivolous, hypersensitive, and unrestrained; in short, France is characterized in terms stereotypically associated with the feminine and the queer. But this Francophobic gendering was hardly new. In the postwar period, a widespread sexist prejudice in American high schools saw French as an effete language meant for girls and German as a manly language made for boys. In August 1945 Brigadier General G. Bryan Conrad interpreted French anti-American resentment in terms of the neurasthenia and hypochondria of the grande malade, who was "flat on her back but hypersensitive to remedies suggested by U.S. doctors and unable, so far, to cure herself."[60] More than five decades later, the Wall Street Journal portrayed Chirac as a "transvestite" and a "pygmy Joan of Arc."[61] Francophobic discourse proliferates in such gratuitous disparagements of French masculinity. In an all too typical jibe, Dinesh D'Souza argued that Americans cannot take French criticism seriously "coming as it does from men who carry handbags."[62]

The "gendering" in fact goes even further back, to the common British foiling of the commonsensical, practical, and hardworking English with the flighty, sissified, and frivolous French. Superimposed on that contrast was a tacit religious contrast, which pitted a muscular, iconoclastic, and "rational" Protestantism against an effete, decadent, image-ridden, and sensuous Catholicism.[63] Within the international division of commerce, meanwhile, the French have long been linked to "superfluous" export products related to cosmetics and fashion (haute couture), associated in the imagination with frail and self-indulgent femininity. Properly "manly" countries, as it were, do not eat quiche or create perfume; they produce steel-made planes and automobiles, linked to phallic hardness, torque, thrust, and horsepower. (This discourse ignores the fact that France also exports cars and planes.) When Secretary of State Powell refers to America and France as being in marriage counseling for 225 years, we understand very well the gender of the two participants. For Frank Costigliola, meanwhile, the United States has long regarded the French as a "flighty, not-so-capable female; emotional, hypersensitive, frivolous, impractical, unrestrained, too concerned with food, drink, fashion, art and love," unlike the "rational, calm, pragmatic, and efficient" Americans.[64] During the Iraq War, the caricature took on homophobic overtones; one cartoon portrayed Chirac as a transvestite "bottom" caught in a "compromising position" with Saddam—or as Bush Pere pronounced the name "Sodom"—Hussein.

This mockery of French "girlie men" emerged from a highly hetero-masculinist U.S. right wing, a movement that is itself hostile to women and gays, and opposed to abortion, family planning, affirmative action, and equal rights. By linguistically coding the French as "womanish and thus requiring the ministrations of a healthy, implicitly masculine superpower," as Costigliola puts it, "Americans legitimated and reinforced the practice of belittling France and trivializing its perspective and concerns."[65] It is ironic, in this sense, that French writers have traditionally indulged in similar prejudices about American men, whom they portray as henpecked and overly "feminized" or queer. In The End of Empire, Emmanuel Todd repeatedly describes American society as gynocratic and American women as "castrating" and "domineering." Thus macho men on both sides of the Atlantic portray their opposite numbers as feminized. (We will return to Todd in a subsequent section.)

Neoconservative Robert Kagan of the Carnegie Endowment, in an article titled "Power and Weakness," argues that in an inversion of the old nostrum of the peaceful Americans and the endlessly warring Europeans, Americans are now from Mars and Europeans are from Venus.[66]

For Kagan, Europe, as a result of its own powerlessness, has moved into a Kantian world of "laws and rules and transnational negotiation and cooperation," while the United States still inhabits a Hobbesian world of the law of the strongest, where military power is seen as the key for achieving both liberal and illiberal goals. Each continent defines itself diacritically against the other, each regarding its own model as superior. Europe, as represented especially by France, defends peace, the welfare state, and negotiation of the Middle East crisis, whereas the United States practices militarism, the neoliberal shredding of the safety net, and blind support for Israeli policies. The result is what Charles A. Kupchan in *The End of the American Era* calls in Huntingtonian language a "clash of civilizations," not between the United States and the Muslim world but between Western Europe and the United States. Although the Cold War united Europe and the United States against the Soviets, the case of Israel and the Palestinians and the war in Iraq sets them on opposite sides in a cold peace.[67]

Equally interesting features of this Francophobic discourse were its omissions, its "structuring absences." The Bill of Complaints against France was terribly superficial; symptomatically, it never seemed to include more serious "lapses" such as French colonialism, imperialism, or slavery, whether because of ignorance or because right-wing Americans admired these so-called achievements. Or was it perhaps because such accusations might remind Americans of their own historical complicity with those evils? That Francophobes never brought up imperialism as a blot on French history, but only military weakness, implied that they did not see imperialism as a blot. The idea that cowardice prevented the French from joining the anti-Iraq coalition, moreover, was errant nonsense, since it would have required very little courage for France to join the most powerful army in the world against one of the weakest. It took a great deal of courage, in contrast, to resist the hectoring of the most powerful nation on earth.

American Francophobia reached its paroxysm with the France–United States tensions in the Security Council. Although virtually the entire world opposed the invasion of Iraq, France alone became the designated scapegoat for the bellicose right wing. At the same time, the hostility toward France also indirectly revealed the Bush administration's scorn for democratic public opinion. Bush presumed, revealingly, that the French government should simply ignore a public opinion over-whelmingly opposed to the war. And this from the same leader who told us to "trust the people, not the government."

Franco-American tensions have been fueled by preexisting prejudices rooted in a long tradition of cordial misunderstandings. France's opposition to the war unleashed the most xenophobic growls from within the belly of the right-wing beast. The French were seen as traitors for not blindly following the U.S. lead. American restaurateurs poured French wine into the gutter. The Congress Cafeteria renamed french fries "liberty fries." (Congressman Walter Jones, who proposed the renaming, has since repented and come to oppose the war.) The terms *french kiss, french toast,* and *french dressing* also seemed doomed to disappear. Bumper stickers read "Iraq first, then France." Florida Republican Representative Ginny Brown-Waite introduced a bill to bring the bodies of World War II soldiers who had been buried in France back to the United States, so that they would not be buried in a country that has "turned its back on us." In Las Vegas an armored vehicle symbolically crushed french bread, bottles of French wine, Perrier, a tourist guide-book to Paris, and xerox copies of the French flag. (And TV spectators all over the world thought, "Don't waste that wine. Send it to us!")

Talk shows also specialized in jokes at the expense of the French. Deploying a somewhat archaic musical stereotype in the age of French rap music, General Schwarzkopf compared "going to war without France" to "deer hunting without an accordion." Talk show host Jim Cates listed the following products that should be boycotted: Evian, Yoplait, the Club Med. American war veterans sent their medals back to France, and relatives tried to repatriate the mortal remains of American soldiers buried in France. After a minor diplomatic incident in the summer of 2000, Senator John McCain declared, "I hate the French." Charles Krauthammer proudly flaunted his Francophobia: "I thank God I was born American. And not French." *New York Times* columnist Thomas Friedman, another veteran France basher, suggested that the French should lose their seat in the Security Council. There was even talk of returning the Statue of Liberty, or at least expressions of regret that it had been a French gift. Some suggested that readers boycott everything French, "from their gooey cheeses to their overpriced wines."[68]

What is most striking in all this is the near-retarded level of the debate on the U.S. side. While most French anti-Americans at least offer a somewhat informed (even if at times misguided) analysis of American society, most American Francophobes seem not to know enough about France even to analyze it. Furthermore the denunciation is strangely and tellingly consumerist in its emphasis, that of people who are less likely to have read Flaubert or Jacques Derrida than to have tasted Camembert and imbibed Beaujolais. In a kind of reverse fetishization, the critics simply list France's various export products and then insult them, as if in effigy for the French government. The Francophobes show not the slightest familiarity with French history or with French debates. French history is for them nothing more than a trace-the-dots pattern of infamy. Often the phantom of French betrayal becomes a diversionary decoy. When FOX's Bill O'Reilly, in fall 2005, began to lose the debate with Jon Stewart on the *Daily Show*, O'Reilly started attacking "our enemies" the French (for which he was roundly booed). Francophobia has become an argument of last resort for desperate right-wingers on political talk shows.

Most of the Francophobic frenzy was orchestrated from the top, not only by the hysterical talk show hosts of the FOX News right but also by media magnates such as the Australian Rupert Murdoch. It was Murdoch's *New York Post* that spoke of the Franco–German alliance as the "Axis of Weasels." It was on Murdoch's FOX News channel that right-wing nudnik extraordinaire Bill O'Reilly said "good-bye to Roquefort dressing ... au revoir to Yves Saint Laurent. ... France has now hurt the U.S.A, and for many of us, payback time has arrived." Indeed, some suggest that Murdoch's motives for France bashing were not so lofty. The hostility to France on Murdock news outlets, as Clementine Wallace points out, was rooted in Murdoch's anger for not being allowed to extend his media empire into France. While Margaret Thatcher facilitated Murdoch's acquisition of the *Times* of London, and was consequently lionized in Murdoch papers, French politicians opposed a planned merger in 1999 between Murdoch and Canal Plus, Europe's leading pay TV broadcaster. While Thatcher helped Murdoch overthrow the press unions in Great Britain, the printers' unions in France helped prevent Murdoch from acquiring a significant press presence in France.[69] Hell hath no fury like a media magnate scorned.

Meanwhile the comedians have started to talk back. Stephen Colbert has clearly modeled his satirical persona on Bill O'Reilly, but this time one who loves all things French. The ads for the *Colbert Report*—pronounced with a silent *t* à la *Française*—remind viewers that the name *Colbert* is "French, bitch!" as if directly addressing Colbert's satiric prototype himself and reversing the gender and sexual dynamics by making O'Reilly the symbolic "bottom." And many Americans appreciated the French opposition to the war. They inundated French official organs with thank-yous for France's antiwar stance in the Security Council. Signs at antiwar demonstrations in the United States read "Thank You France" and "Chirac for President!" Some antiwar journalists such as Jonathan Schell implicitly contrasted the outspokenness of the French leadership with the passivity of wimpy Democrats. While politicians in the United States had given up their role as a "loyal opposition," he suggested, the French "have been better Americans than we have been." And in retrospect, it must be said that France, whatever its motives, has often been right in its critiques of U.S. imperial misadventures, even if not always from the noblest of motives but only because they had learned from past mistakes. And in retrospect, after the loss of fifty-five thousand American lives and millions of Vietnamese lives, who can say de Gaulle was wrong? In an open letter to George W. Bush, Michael Moore admonished Bush to stop blaming the French, reminding him that the French saved the American Revolution and had usually been a stalwart ally. Although some French people were terribly annoying, he wrote, in the end the French had "only done what good friends do—tell the truth."[70] And one of Bill Maher's "new rules" was: "No more bitching about the French" since they, unlike the Democrats, were at least standing up to Bush.

U.S. Francophobia, in sum, is the specular double of Americanophobia in France and displays all the same earmarks of ethnoessentialist thinking. Once again we find the same ignorance, the same rigged balance sheet, the same processes of scapegoating and projecting, and the same blindness to one's own faults. We have been trying to suggest that it is possible to go beyond such sterile exercises in the blame game. Having explored the contemporary manifestations of these tensions, we will now explore the ways that they are rooted in very old debates about revolution and citizenship.

3. Discrepant Histories of Citizenship

New Debates about Old Revolutions

Many of the tensions between France and the United States, as we have seen, are historically rooted in the claim of both countries to speak for universal values. At this point in history, U.S. politicians are more likely than the French to wrap themselves in the mantle of the universal. Thus George W. Bush speaks for the "civilized world," as if he were its divinely appointed spokesman, even when the vast majorities of peoples and governments in the world reject his actual policies. France, meanwhile, in the wake of the loss of its empire, has generally played a more modest role. While speaking intellectually for the universal, it nowadays tries to speak politically for Europe and sometimes for the global "South." The piqued reaction of "New Europe" to France's attempt to lead the opposition to the Iraq War revealed the limits of French influence even in Europe itself. Increasingly, "world public opinion," meanwhile, is also calling attention to the gap between Americans' own professed ideals and American behavior (e.g., torture; extralegal detentions in Afghanistan; Guantánamo, Cuba; Iraq; and now Eastern Europe).

Understanding contemporary attitudes requires a detour into a much longer history. The present-day geopolitical rivalry between the United States and France, for example, reconfigures the older rivalry over revolution. The American Revolution founded a republic and constitution that has lasted more than two centuries; the "young" country, paradoxically, has the "older" revolution. Yet the U.S. republic was haunted by slavery, which led to the bloody Civil War almost a century later. The French Revolution, meanwhile, overturned the ancien régime, but that overturning quickly gave way to a reign of terror. Since 1789 France has tried a wide array of political regimes, including republics, empires, constitutional monarchies, emergency committees, and dictatorships, along with hybrid forms like Vichy. Although the United States too has at various times been tempted by "national security state" thinking, the United States has never become completely repressive, although current trends—military trials, enemy combatants, secret prisons, stolen elections, spying by the National Security Agency (NSA), presidential "signing statements"—are worrying in the extreme.

One danger in drawing overly clear contrasts between the political histories of the two countries, however, is that the contrasts obscure much larger commonalities. Both republican France and the United States are quintessential products of an Enlightenment dominated by French figures such as Montesquieu, Rousseau, Voltaire, and Diderot. Both were founded on the notion of citizens' "rights": the Rights of Man and the Bill of Rights, a principle actually established by the U.S. government after the French, although the French project was modeled on an American state precedent (Virginia). Both insisted, in principle at least, on equality before the law, equality of rights, and equality of opportunity. Both societies were democratic in principle; both elected leaders legally obligated to conserve freedom for all citizens. Both spelled this principle out in written constitutions. Both separated citizenship from ethnicity and ancestry.

On the negative side, both France and the United States were simultaneously oppressive to some groups. The U.S. revolutionary government was oppressive in its relation to Native Americans, to enslaved Africans, and to women, all of whom were denied the vote, but it was relatively tolerant toward Jews. The French revolutionary government emancipated the Jews but was oppressive at home to those denied the vote and oppressive abroad toward the indigenous peoples of the Americas, enslaved Africans, and the colonized, generally. Despite their radical rhetoric, both revolutions were, initially at least, largely elite movements dominated by rich, propertied white men; even among "citizens," only a happy, wealthy few could be active, participatory citizens. Indeed, many historians have questioned just how revolutionary the two revolutions were; in both countries the revolutionaries at first sought compromise with established power, whether with the British king or with the ancien régime. While the American Revolution liquidated British colonial rule, the French Revolution tried to liquidate the vestiges of a monarchical system that had lasted for centuries. While the American Revolution overthrew one colonial power only to found another, the French Revolution was a social overturning of the ancien régime and the continuation of an empire.

Part of the "universality" shared by the United States and French democracies was the notion of human rights and *les droits de l'homme et du citoyen,* which was later extended by the United Nations as "The Declaration of the Universal Rights of Man." Yet there are important differences in the notions of rights. While U.S. official ideology stresses the individual, French official ideology stresses the citizen. The two terms are interesting in their different affect and emphasis: *citizen* implies a civically involved participant in a political community, while *individual* implies a striving, self-affirming monad pursuing personal goals. Although the word *citizen* also forms part of American political discourse, it is less popular than *individual.*[1]

Both the French and U.S. republics originated in violent revolutions, but neither the revolutions nor their consequences were identical. After a number of twists and turns, postrevolutionary France emerged with a social contract more heavily weighted toward equal distribution of wealth, so that a relative social equality was seen as being at the core of freedom. The U.S. Revolution was also antimonarchical, but it was more national-territorial than social. Although there were social tensions among the American revolutionaries concerning attitudes toward slavery, social inequality, and so forth, they were less preoccupied with equality than with freedom and property. When social welfare policies were later established in the United States, for example, by Roosevelt's New Deal, they could be portrayed by the right as the spawn of the special circumstances of the Great Depression rather than as emerging clearly and organically from the Constitution. (Roosevelt's "Second Bill of [social and economic] Rights," as we shall see in a later section, was an attempt to graft a more expansive and material view of rights onto the original Constitution.) Indeed, the American Revolution was ambivalent toward equality. While the Declaration of Independence spoke of equality, the Constitution emphasized property. And whereas on one hand the government supported slavery and class superiority, on the other hand the dominant mores, at least among whites, respected manual labor and favored a rough equality (at least among white people), something that had already impressed de Tocqueville.

A look at the parallel destinies of the two republics helps illuminate how we arrived at present-day ambivalences. The essentials of French republicanism have to do with the following ideas, many of which Americans too would support. First of all, the republic is a state of laws; that is, no one, even the most powerful politicians, is above the law. (As his policy regarding warrantless NSA spying attests, George W. Bush seems to doubt this basic principle.) While George W. Bush seeks the "unitary executive," French law is unitary in a different sense, in that it applies universally throughout France, from Alsace to Corsica, while in the United States only federal laws apply throughout the country. In the United States the states are even called "sovereign," even though they cannot declare war or sign treaties. The individual states control specific issues such as capital punishment, for example, which is legal in Texas but illegal in Wisconsin. In the French system, the national trumps the local, whereas the United States offers a complex, almost Byzantine system characterized by struggle between the claims of the municipal, the state, and the federal governments.

The unitary French republic entails one language, one penal code, and so forth; it rejects anything that might fragment the civic society. The differences between the two systems have to do with federalism à la the United States versus centralization à la France. Although the phrase "one nation, indivisible," occurs in the Pledge of Allegiance, it does not appear in the Constitution. In France, however, the term *indivisible* occurs in every French republican constitution. And the idea of indivisibility predates the republican era, since it goes back to royal absolutism. (The debates about centralism and federalism are taking place again in relation to the constitutions of both Iraq and the European Union, where both the French and the American systems have been points of reference.)

According to the French Constitution, sovereignty "belongs to the people, who exercise it through its representatives" and "no section of the people nor any individual can appropriate the exercise thereof," a clear claim that the central government is supreme over all other powers. The U.S. Constitution, in contrast, grants some powers to the federal government but delegates all remaining powers "to the states or to the people." In the United States the republic is indivisible only in the sense that states cannot secede from the Union—the point of dispute in the Civil War—but America is politically and administratively plural. The French system rejects federalism. The "departments" in France, including overseas departments such as Guadeloupe and Martinique, are not like the separate states in the United States; they are part of a unified national system. The departments do not form independent states, although the colonial departments overseas were characterized in the past by the "special laws" typical of racialized rule.

While federalism allows for flexibility, it also leads to endless battles over turf and rival jurisdictions. At times, it has led to conflicts—Civil War, the battle over segregation in the South—between states' rights and the federal government. The tensions also came up during the 2000 Gore–Bush election, as to whether the State of Florida or the Supreme Court had jurisdiction to decide on electoral procedures in Florida. The robed politicians of the Court opportunistically went against the usual stated states' rights principles of the majority of its members to provisionally support the pro-Bush antistates' rights position. The challenge for both the American and French revolutions was to forge unity within a diverse nation. In the United States federalism was a compromise, a way of having a fractured, minimalist unity rather than having no union at all. Race was at the heart of the issue and of the threat of disunion. In France the key issue was not race but rather region and politics; statist republicanism was seen as a bulwark against regional fracturing. Although the weakness in the U.S. Constitution has to do with a potential for various branches working at cross-purposes, the weakness in the French Constitution is exactly the opposite—hypercentralization and what might be called the "fetishization of the number one"; that is, the emphasis on unity at all costs.

Régis Debray's *La République expliquée a ma Fille* (The Republic Explained to My Daughter) offers a French perspective on the two political systems:

> We share a number of values with the U.S. It's the pioneer republic, older than our own, which served as an example for our own revolutionaries, and which offered us a strong helping hand on two historical occasions. But just as there were in an earlier period all kinds of monarchies—elective, hereditary, absolute, constitutional—now there are all kinds of republics—conservative, social, plebiscitary, and multicultural. The U.S. Republic is federal, like Germany, Brazil, and Mexico, while the French republic is unitary.[2]

In France a centralized state arbitrates private conflicts and ensures the cohesion of the country, developing a single educational model, a normative view of language (*l'Academie Française*), a single system of justice, and so forth. The common good overrides private interests, and the state is assumed to have a role in guaranteeing some fairness in the distribution of goods. In the area of culture, the French state assumes the responsibility for museums, theaters, and orchestras, while in the United States philanthropic foundations are expected to assume that responsibility. From a certain French point of view, the U.S. system seems dangerously individualist, market dominated, and even chaotic, while from a certain American point of view, the French system seems too paternalistic, statist, and elitist. (An ideal system, needless to say, would combine the advantages of the two systems, along with ideas borrowed from other systems.)

In the Name of God and the Republic

This constitutive centralism, we suggest, lies in the background of the general French hostility to multiculturalism, seen as going against the very grain of the founding principles of the French nation-state. For many French people, all specific ethnic or religious claims evoke a politically threatening aspiration to form a rival power to the authority of the state. It is perhaps for this reason that the French, projecting their own fears about national unity, have so often imagined an imminent disintegration of the American republic whenever it was challenged by secessionist or immigrationist movements, whether through what in France is symptomatically called the "war of secession" or through the influx of immigrants at the turn of the twentieth century. France's stress on unity, furthermore, sometimes feeds into some contemporary right-wing racist currents. Right-wing anti-immigrant Le Penism describes itself, after all, as a form of French republicanism: "La France aux Français."

France, Brazil, and the United States all perform variations on a theme of religious freedom. All practice the separation of church and state, although that separation is more and more under threat, in the era of "faith-based initiatives," within the United States.[3] Although the relation to the state differs, in all three countries the world's religions are practiced freely. The issue of Islam, obviously, is more central in France, with its high proportion of Muslims, than in the United States and Brazil. The official attitudes toward religion in the French and U.S. systems, meanwhile, are roughly comparable but also slightly different in drift. Both countries see religious freedom as the touchstone of republican values but with a slightly distinctive emphasis. To summarize crudely, the stress in the United States is on "freedom of religion" while in France it is "freedom from religion." Thus the French are shocked to see U.S. schoolchildren reciting an oath to the flag that includes the phrase "under God"—a phrase actually added only in the 1950s as part of the Cold War struggle against "atheistic" communism. Americans, meanwhile, are shocked to see the French government ban all ostensible signs of religious faith in schools.

For most Americans the head-scarf decree seems like a denial not only of religious freedom but also of individual choice. And since American federalism leaves educational policy up to the states and municipalities, the occasional local instances of such restrictions never become a national policy. As Blandine Chelini-Pont and Jeremy Gunn put it, the banning of the veil in French schools "as part of the structure of dogmatic French secularism whose historical ultra-modernity has by now become conservative."[4] If the United States faces the problem of the political manipulation of religiosity, France has the problem of a militant secularism, which at times becomes a "secular fundamentalism," an attitude of arrogant astonishment that anyone might ever willingly choose to be religious. Here we find a new, secular version of Montesquieu's mocking question: "Comment peut-on être religieux?" (How can one possibly be religious?)

Both the U.S. and French systems, in theory at least, protect religious practice from abuses by the state. The wariness toward established religion in both countries derives, indirectly at least, from a hostility to certain abuses by established religions. In the United States, the suspicion is rooted in the historical role of Anglicanism and Catholicism as state religions that oppressed some of the Protestant (and other) minorities, which fled to America for religious freedom. In France the suspicion is rooted in the Jacobin hostility to the church's links to the ancien régime. It is often said, correctly, that French people are less religious, overall, than Americans (and we add Brazilians), and that France is more consistent in its anticlericalism and in the separation of church and state. Unlike American presidents, French presidents do not place their hand on the Bible as they take the oath of office. In the French conception, religion is a matter of private faith, not of public engagement. The French republic is not clerical but secular, almost obsessively so.

Yet supposedly secular France also bears the traces of Christian religious hegemony. Christianity is inscribed on the national life in the form of holidays drawn from the Christian calendar. The French concept of *laïcité*, often translated as "secularism," furthermore, seems to suggest hostility to religion, yet the term itself, paradoxically, has a religious origin, since it refers to "lay people"; that is, baptized Catholics who were not members of the clergy. Thus the very term quietly encodes a Christianized set of values and distinctions.[5] France commemorates the deaths of presidents with religious masses in the Cathedral of Notre Dame. A Christian cultural substratum thus undergirds French life, even when strong majorities no longer attend church or Catholic Mass.

Religious double standards also pervade the discussion of secularity. The abstract "citizen" in France is treated very differently if he has a Muslim name, if she wears the *hijab*, and so forth. The wearing of crosses by high school students is not seen as a provocation, while the wearing of Muslim head scarves is seen as a threat to the secular principle. Even the 2004 law banning religious insignia in general was widely regarded as especially targeting Muslims rather than Christians and

Jews. Discrimination against Maghrebian immigrants and the reluctance of many French to welcome Turkey into the European Union surely also have something to do with a subtle pro-Christian and anti-Muslim bias. While some Europeans accuse Turkey of "human rights abuses" in Turkey as a reason for the exclusion of Turkey from the European Union—and such abuses certainly do exist—many suspect that the real reason has to do with Turkey's status as a Muslim-majority nation.

Anti-Semitism sometimes enters the picture. When a French politician, after a 1990s terrorist attack in Paris, said, "Some Jews were killed, but no Frenchmen were hurt," he was obviously imagining his French nation as essentially Christian. The anti-Semitic (but pro-Israel) Christian right in the United States, meanwhile, calls for an official labeling of the United States as a Christian nation, an offense to Jews, Muslims, agnostics, atheists, and the practitioners of all other religions such as Buddhism, Santeria, Vodun, and so forth. Thus, without falling into the neocon caricature of an essentially anti-Semitic France, we can note the quiet operations of an unspoken yet powerfully normative Christianity in both France and the United States.

But religion also asserts its presence in more subtle, almost subliminal, ways. Many national traditions accord to their country a special often religiously anointed place within world history. This quietly religious normativity applies to all of the countries in question here, whether in the U.S. form of "manifest destiny" and "Americans as chosen people," in the Brazilian form of a "nation blessed by God" and "God is Brazilian," or in the French form of being as endowed with a quasi-evangelical "mission"—the word choice is hardly accidental—to "civilize" the world. The Enlightenment was, after all, a secularization of Christian principles. "Providence," for example, became "progress."

The Christian right, meanwhile, has been trying to rewrite history to paint the United States as a Christian nation. Phrases such as "Nature's God," "Supreme Judge," and "Divine Providence" in the Declaration of Independence and the Constitution, for the religious right, show that the Founding Fathers saw the United States as a "Christian country at heart." In fact, however, the Founding Fathers were secular deists, for whom "God" was not the Christian or Jewish God but rather the rational clockmaker deity of the Enlightenment. Indeed, at the time of the American Revolution, many foreign commentators saw the United

States not as religious but as "godless." Under the Constitution, one critic complained, it is possible for "a papist, a Mohamatan, a deist, yea an atheist" to become president of the United States.[6] And roughly a century later, a Spanish newspaper *El Pensimiento Espanol* (in September 1862), described the United States as "founded on atheism." The text of the Treaty of Tripoli in 1796, signed by George Washington, pointed to a secular American republic (Article 11):

> As the government of the United States of America is not in any sense founded on the Christian Religion—as it has in itself no character of enmity against the laws, religion or tranquility of [Muslims] and as the said States never have entered into any war or act of hostility against any Mehomitan nation, it is declared by the parties that no pretext arising from religious opinions shall ever produce an interruption of the harmony existing between the two countries.[7]

The sentiments expressed here, confirmed again when Jefferson approved the treaty in 1806, are remarkable not only for their assertion of the nonreligious character of the United States but also for their lack of hostility to Islam and Muslims. The treaty was signed by John Adams and ratified, moreover, by two-thirds of the Senate.

Jefferson, ironically one of the political figures most admired by the right, was not a man of faith but rather a man of science and reason. Jefferson explicitly rejected the biblical God. He did not believe in divine revelation, the virgin birth, the Trinity, heaven and hell, or other basic tenets of Christianity. In a letter to his nephew Peter Carr, Jefferson advised him to "read the Bible but as you would read Livy or Tacitus."[8] Indeed, Jefferson's political rivals accused him of being a French infidel and atheist, citing his own words in his essay "Notes from Virginia" to the effect that "it does me no injury for my neighbor to say there are twenty gods, or no God." Jefferson was categorically opposed to public profession of religious beliefs by public figures or government officials. Jefferson also regarded himself as an Epicurean for whom the "pursuit of happiness" was consistent with an innate moral sense. Jefferson rarely attended church and associated what he called that "irritable tribe of priests" with despotism: "history furnishes no example of a priest-ridden people maintaining a free civil government."⁹ Rejecting the anti-Semitism of some of his compatriots, Jefferson was proud that the United States was the first country "to prove that religious freedom is most effectual and to restore to the Jews their social rights" (p. 60).

In his *Orient-Occident, La Fracture Imaginaire,* (Orient/Occident: The Imaginary Fracture) the Lebanese Christian writer Georges Corm finds substantial evidence of a deep Christian—and now Judeo-Christian—substratum even within secular European nations such as France. While modern European nations (including the United States) imagine themselves as having escaped the hold of religious irrationalism, what Corm calls "trompe-l'oeil secularism" hides the fact that traces of religious discourses, schemas, and modes of explanation subtly inform the general discourse. Current political discourse, for example, is saturated by religiously connoted terms such as *crusade, credo, axis of evil,* and so forth. The current hostility to Islam, for Corm, is founded on an artificial "us–them" division, which pits Jews and Christians on one hand against Muslims on the other. Muslims, the third "people of the book," have been ghettoized, as if they shared nothing with Christians and Jews. The ills of colonialism, for Corm, are ultimately rooted in a salvationist project: "It is the concept of Salvation that has nourished all the conflicts. It is this history of Salvation which is at the origin of colonialism. I have a history and you do not; therefore, I will introduce you into my history. Here is the theology of the history of Salvation. I possess the truth; you do not. You are in error; I will force you into the true path."¹⁰

Foundational Contradictions

In the United States, love for the Constitution, as the founding document of the country, is a taken-for-granted part of patriotism. But while the Constitution is regarded as a sacred text, surrounded by a mystical aura, the right and left disagree about what it portends for the present. A number of recent commentators, moreover, have questioned the premises undergirding this civic religion of the Constitution. The paradox for the left, at this point in history, is that it must simultaneously defend the Constitution, the Bill of Rights, and the separation of powers from political enemies and defend the separation of church and state from theocratically minded fanatics, yet at the same time it must probe the problems and limitations of that very same Constitution in terms of social and economic rights.

International constitutional debates are also haunted by the question of comparative national narcissism. This question is relevant to the discussion of both patriotism and to anti-Americanism, not only because constitutions have been favored objects of civic pride but also because many of the current strengths and weaknesses of the social systems can be traced to the strengths and weaknesses of their constitutions. A comparative study of the French and U.S. political systems, in this sense, reveals both common problems and distinct paths and solutions.

The United States, France, and Brazil, at this point in history, are all constitutional republics, but they arrived at that point via very different routes. The U.S. Constitution was written in 1787 and approved on March 4, 1789. Twenty-seven amendments were then added, including the Bill of Rights (1791), the Thirteenth Amendment, which abolished slavery (1865), the Fourteenth Amendment, which granted citizenship to former slaves (1868), and the Fifteenth Amendment, which granted former slaves the right to vote. The Sixteenth Amendment passed in 1913 allowed Congress to impose an income tax, the Seventeenth Amendment (1913) provided for the direct election of senators, and the Nineteenth Amendment (1920) provided for female suffrage.

Debates about constitutions in one country, furthermore, have historically had a way of becoming entangled with debates about constitutions in other countries. Many constitutions have been bricolage syntheses borrowed from previous constitutions. De Tocqueville, for example, proposed a brand of American democracy as an alternative to the then monarchical institutions of the French restoration. At the time of the French Revolution, French and American intellectuals corresponded about their respective constitutions. At various points, French intellectuals and politicians argued that France should adopt aspects of the American system. As far back as the 1780s, debates raged between the *Americainistes* and their rivals over whether France should adapt a bicameral legislature, the separation of powers, and checks and balances. The Americanophile Waddington called, in 1875, for a U.S.-style Senate. Others pointed to the American system's congenital defects, such as its "impotent" presidents, as a reason to reject the American political model. Here again individual nations are not separable; they exist in relation, even in a juridical sense.

Some of the American Founding Fathers, such as Alexander Hamilton, favored a system closely resembling the French model; that is, one featuring a fully sovereign central government whose rule would extend to the farthest reaches of the realm. The Federalist Hamilton would have liked to abolish the notions of states and states' rights in favor of relatively powerless French-style departments. That is why the name "The Federalists"—chosen by the right-wing group that tried to impeach Clinton—is a misnomer. The actual historical Federalists favored a strong central government, not a weak one that the present-day Federalists favor.

In Brazil the partisans of a republic were inspired by both the French and American revolutions, with some seeking to imitate the American way and others arguing for a parliamentary system. The vast power of the United States has occasionally placed it in a situation where it could impose, or at least strongly influence, the constitutions of other countries. This was clearly the case with Germany and Japan in the wake of their defeat during World War II, and it is currently the case with Iraq. The various European and the U.S. constitutions also form the backdrop for and concretely influence the discussion of a possible constitution for the European Union. In this sense one might speak of a "constitutional intertext" and of diverse forms of mimicry, emulation, and even plagiarism between constitutions.

The meaning and value of the Constitution have been contested throughout U.S. history. The abolitionist William Lloyd Garrison, at a New England antislavery meeting, burned a copy of the Constitution, calling it "a covenant with death and an agreement with hell."[11] All of American history can be seen as a struggle over the meaning of the Constitution, rooted in the tensions between the "all men are created equal" clause of the Declaration of Independence and the slaves as property clauses enshrined (albeit euphemistically) in the Constitution. It is as if the United States were haunted from the beginning by two competing political models, one democratic—as exemplified by the public commons and the town hall—and the other tyrannical—as epitomized by the slave plantation and the "big house." The fate of the country has ridden—and still rides—on which model will exercise the greatest influence.

To this day foundational contradictions haunt the uneasy wedding of revolutionary ideals and colonial reality. Since historically there was little open debate about the contradictions between republican constitutions and actual practices in Brazil, we might better speak of the larger issue of citizenship, both before and after the republic founded in 1889. How was citizenship seen in Brazil over the course of Brazilian history? Because there was no revolution in Brazil equivalent to the American or French revolutions, there was also no equivalent in Brazil to the debates about the contradictions between republican Enlightenment principles—"all men are created equal" and the "rights of man"—on one hand and colonialism and slavery on the other. At the time of Brazil's independence in 1822, for example, the issue of slavery was not debated as it was during both the French and American revolutions. Yet the questions were posed in other ways, not at the centers of government decision making but in concrete forms of symbolic (and real) performative actions by those oppressed by the regime in place. The various forms of indigenous (Indian) resistance to conquest, black resistance to enslavement in the form of the various *quilombos,* or free black rebel communities (the most famous being the seventeenth-century maroon Republic of Palmares, which resisted Portuguese and Dutch attack for almost a century) are all ways of taking a position on fundamental issues of justice, both in spoken (and sometimes written) words and through concrete actions.

Brazil and the Hazards of Citizenship

Like the United States and like the other "multination states" of the Americas, Brazil is a European settler colony. The rhetoric that classifies Brazil as "Third World" and part of the "South," while true on some levels, obscures important commonalities with other settler states in the Americas. The various independence movements in both North America and South America adopted an ambiguous stance on slavery, often ending up by supporting it out of respect for property and for slaves as property. The American- and French-inspired revolutionaries who led the abortive eighteenth-century revolt against Portuguese rule that took place in the inland state of Minas Gerais (the "Inconfidencia Mineira") contemplated abolishing slavery but ultimately chose to maintain their own white privileges. As occurred with the American Revolution, the goal of Brazilian revolutionaries was not to free slaves but only to liberate the white Creole ruling elite from economic servitude to European powers. The 1798 revolt in the northern state of Bahia, in contrast, involved lower-rank soldiers, artisans, and slaves, who wanted not only to get rid of Portuguese colonialism but also to eliminate slavery and white domination. But even after independence, Brazil suffered from the inertia of a colonial period characterized by the genocide of indigenous Brazilians and by slavery internally and by foreign domination externally.

Independence in Brazil was the result of a relatively pacific process when compared not only to the United States of North America but also to Spanish-speaking Latin America. Brazil claimed no great "liberator" figures or leaders of armies like the North American George Washington or the South American Simon Bolivar. Independence consisted of installing a member of the royal Portuguese family as emperor of a nominally independent Brazil. Independence came just a few decades after the Haitian Revolution, which frightened the plantation owners who dominated Brazilian politics. The 1824 constitution ignored slavery, as if it didn't exist, even though the slavery system pervaded the entire country. In 1827 England obliged Brazil to sign a treaty abolishing the slave trade, but the treaty was not respected, whence the popular expression concerning laws "made only for the English to see" (*para ingles ver*); that is, laws passed as a pure formality to please foreigners, with no real intention of carrying them out on the ground. (Interestingly, the French too sometimes pretended to respect laws against the slave trade, again literally "for the English to see," precisely since the British formed the vanguard of the movement to end the slave trade, much as they had been in the vanguard of the slave trade in an earlier period.)

The final abolition of slavery in Brazil took place at a time when many blacks were already free and when other slaves had already voted "with their feet" by fleeing from the plantations. As a result, there were very few remaining slaves—only 5 percent of the population—at the time of the "golden law" abolishing slavery in 1888. Yet in an earlier period, slavery had been even more widespread and entrenched in Brazil than in the United States, and even the *quilombos* or maroon rebel republics were obliged to come to terms with slave society. Slavery was so ingrained that when some slaves became free, they themselves acquired slaves.[12] (This also occurred occasionally in the United States.) The values of individual freedom as the basis of civil rights, so (often hypocritically) dear to European modernity, held little sway in Brazil. While in the United States abolitionism could base itself on the Declaration of Independence with its talk of "inalienable rights" and "all men are created equal," in Brazil abolitionists could make no such appeal. Rather, they appealed to more pragmatic arguments: that slavery was no longer viable, that it was an obstacle to progress, that it blocked the development of the labor market, that it was an embarrassment in front of enlightened Europe, and so forth.

That both Brazil and the United States, indeed the Americas as a whole, are more socially unequal than Western European social democracies has everything to do with the European legacies of conquest and slavery. While the United States is haunted by the big house and the slave quarters, Brazil is haunted by their Brazilian counterparts: the Casa Grande and the Senzala. Brazil remained a slaveholding society for almost four centuries, so that the power arrangements and discursive norms of slavery, as historian Angela de Castro Gomes puts it, "penetrated all the regions of the country and all the social strata from the richest to the poorest. ... Slavery became a terrible inheritance which doubtless marks even today the historical process of the construction of citizenship in Brazil."[13] At the time of independence, within a population of five million, eight hundred thousand were Indians and one million were slaves. A class of free people was interposed between the slave owners and the slaves, but the free blacks lacked all the necessary conditions to practice their freedom. The slave owners, meanwhile, were free but not really citizens, because they were the excessively entitled masters of the country, those who were "more equal" before the law. Justice and the legal system served not as guarantors of civil rights but simply as instruments for projecting personal power. The first constitution in 1824, meanwhile, recognized the civil rights of all "free men," including those "of color," who were granted equality before the law. Even if not really applied in practice, because it left a lot of people still enslaved, this law at least did provide the legal grounds, later, for dele-gitimizing enslavement or segregation based on color, much as the "all men are created equal" phrase from the Declaration of Independence helped discredit slavery in the United States.

Brazil followed the republican course relatively late, since Brazil was first a colony, then a monarchy and empire, and finally a republic, founded in 1889. The republic, a synthesis of the French and the U.S. political models, did not fundamentally alter the basic patterns of social and racial hierarchy in Brazil. Top-down abolition was made by and for the Brazilian white elite; it relieved whites not only of the embarrass-ment of slavery but also of the burden of responsibility for the physical well-being of the newly freed blacks. Nor did the republic attempt to aid slaves in the transition to freedom. The government opted to do almost nothing for blacks, choosing instead to have a European immigration "whiten" Brazil.

In the United States the Freedmen's Bureau at least attempted to edu-cate slaves after emancipation, even if the progressive period of Recon-struction ultimately gave way to the horrors of Jim Crow segregationist racism. By 1870 in the United States there were 4,325 schools for freed blacks, including one university—Howard. The liberal republican con-stitution of 1891 freed the state from providing primary education, which had been guaranteed to free men by the 1824 constitution, just as abolition freed white slaveholders from taking care of older slaves. In the United States blacks never got the promised "40 acres and a mule," but in Brazil such promises were never even made. Newly freed blacks were not provided with schools, land, or jobs. In many respects, then, the republic was a step backward for Brazilian blacks, much as the American republic had been a step backward for African Americans more than a century earlier.[14]

With the Brazilian republic, the U.S. model was adopted in the name—"the United States of Brazil"—and partly even in the flag, which at that time also consisted of stripes, but this time of green and yellow. The Brazilian Constitution copied the U.S. Constitution in its federal-ism, its presidentialism, its tripartite division of power, its bicameral legislature, and its separation of church and state. Yet in other ways the new constitution was a bricolage document combining elements of presidential, federal, democratic, and republican forms of government.

The revolution of 1930 installed a provisional government, which lasted from 1930 to 1934. The second republic lasted from 1934 to 1937, when it was interrupted by Vargas's populist/fascist Estado Novo, which ruled from 1937 to 1945. The third republic lasted from 1945 to 1964, when it was interrupted by the U.S.-supported coup d'état that overthrew the popularly elected João Goulart. After two decades of military dictatorship, the fourth republic was announced in 1985, with a new constitution in 1988.

The so-called Citizen Constitution in 1988 was remarkably progressive. Unlike previous constitutions, which were penned by a relatively small body of electors, the 1988 constitution was drafted by the entire Congress of 559 members, pressured by a wide spectrum of activist human rights organizations whose demands left a strong imprint.[15] The constitution provided for extensive protection of human, social, and economic rights, including rights to an education, social security, maternity leave, and so forth. The constitution also guaranteed the land rights of the indigenous peoples. The inertia of social injustice and unfair land distribution, unfortunately, partially overwhelmed the new constitution's good intentions. At the same time, it might be argued that the progressive ideas of the constitution unleashed many kinds of activism, such as the struggle for quotas for the poor and the black.

In Brazil laws and constitutions have historically had a different function than they have had in both the United States and France and therefore have a different meaning. In France and the United States, the law is the law; it applies universally and goes into effect immediately. (George W. Bush's "signing statements" challenge this tradition of respect for the legislature). Admittedly, both countries have had their share of political corruption, but in many cases the scandal is more in what is legal than what is illegal. In Brazil, in contrast, the law is more like an expression of pious wishes, hopes, and intentions, whence the famous saying in Brazil: "for my friends, everything; for my enemies, the Law." As this maxim implies, the law, which should be the universal guarantor of equality and a defense against arbitrary power, becomes in fact an instrument deployed by the ruling elite, which uses it to protect friends and punish enemies. As a result, the 1988 constitution, to all appearances a very progressive document, did not guarantee the actual enforcement of its many provisions.

The unequal application of the law in Brazil results in the problem of "impunity," whereby very powerful people escape from the consequences of their acts. As a result, many major crimes—such as the assassination of labor leaders or rural activists—go unpunished. There are even special prisons for people of higher status. As Brazilian legal scholar Roberto Kant de Lima puts it, "Different laws rule relationships among distinct layers of citizens, and they are not enforced between the distinct classes but only internally, among peers."[16] But all these contradictions are both social and racial, since the perpetrators who commit the crimes tend to be light skinned and at the top of the social and racial hierarchy, while the victims are darker and at the bottom. Nor does formal democracy necessarily guarantee progress in the social realm. As cultural critic George Yudice sums up the situation,

> There have been lawsuits to enforce laws against discrimination, but Brazilian society and culture have not undergone a civil rights revolution, nor does the judiciary operate to the benefit of most Brazilians, nor is there a welfare safety net that does justice to the concept, nor is consumption a viable medium for even rhetorical democratization. To this day, no one has been found guilty for the murders of street children, which number as high as nine hundred per year for São Paulo alone.[17]

Brazilian anthropologist Teresa Caldeira calls this situation one of "disjunctive democracy"; that is, a situation where formal democracy coexists with myriad social abuses: narcotraffic, police brutality, illiteracy, hunger, lynching, the massacre of children, and the class and ethnic cleansing of the cities.

But these situations are not unique to Brazil. In the period of neoliberal ascendancy, "disjunctive" or "oxymoronic" democracy is becoming a kind of norm in many countries. The combination of fortified rich enclaves and crushing poverty, as she points out, are as much a feature of Los Angeles and Paris as of São Paulo, even if there are many differences of degree and policy. Yet the Brazilian situation is in some respects worse. Comparing police violence in six regions in the Americas, among them Los Angeles, New York, Buenos Aires, and Mexico City, Chevigny (1995) found that São Paulo was worse even than apartheid South Africa. In 1992 São Paulo's police killed 8.5 times more than South Africa's apartheid regime did in its worst year.[18]

From the beginning, then, democracy has been compromised and endangered in all three countries. In the United States democracy was initially compromised by Native American genocide, by the enslavement of Africans, and by the political and economic marginalization of women. Later, democracy was threatened by right-wing political fanaticism, in moments of the "red purge" in the 1920s, of McCarthyism in the 1940s and 1950s, or of the repression of activists in the 1960s, on up through the post-9/11 outrages to the Constitution inherent in the misnamed PATRIOT Act, with its assault on civil liberties and free speech, and Admiral Poindexter's provisionally aborted "Total Information Awareness."[19] What used to be called "free speech" in the United States, moreover, has now become very "expensive speech," where corporate propaganda, regarded as the equivalent of personal expression, has more or less snuffed out public speech.

In France and Brazil democracy has also often been threatened. At diverse points, as we have already seen, French democracy has given way to monarchic restoration or to quasi-military regimes (e.g., Vichy, de Gaulle). Brazil, for its part, has often oscillated between authoritarian and democratic regimes, the most recent oscillation being between the democracy that held sway from 1945 to 1964, followed by the two decades of dictatorship inaugurated by the U.S.-supported coup d'état, which segued to the period of *abertura* (opening) and redemocratization in the 1970s and early 1980s, leading to the indirect election of Tancredo Neves in 1985 and the direct election of Fernando Collor in 1989 (subsequently impeached in 1992). This all culminated in an election in 2002 that was much more "clean" and much less corrupted by the power of corporate money than was the American election of 2000 and that was much more progressive in its results than the 2002 French election, where the racist Le Pen won second place in the first round and Chirac ultimately won the election.

Constitutions and Their Discontents

In both France and the United States, scholars are questioning certain founding myths of the nations, in ways clearly resonant in the present.

Scholars in France have debated the validity of the French Revolution. Undermining the classical view of historians such as Jules Michelet, some historians argue that the "terror," far from being an accident, was inherent in the revolution itself. As conservative historian Simon Schama puts it in *Citizens*, the terror was "merely 1789 with a higher body count."[20] Other historians argue that the French Revolution was not a real rupture, since political momentum had long been shifting under the ancien régime. Still others suggest that the French Enlightenment was very bourgeois, hardly revolutionary at all.

The bicentenary of the French Revolution triggered a massive outpouring of scholarship, some denouncing the revolution or even defending its enemies. Pierre Nora's monumental book *Lieux de Mémoires* (Places of Memory) was consciously presented as a kind of "funerary monument" for the universalist claims of the French Revolution. Meanwhile historian François Furet, one of the most influential figures, proclaimed that the French Revolution was "over." For Furet, the French Revolution was a liberal revolution, not a first step toward socialist revolution, as Marxists tended to claim. As Sunil Khilnani puts it, "1789 was identified as the origin and source of modern democratic culture, not a proleptic figure of the Russian revolution."[21]

In the United States, meanwhile, "critical law," "critical race," and feminist scholars have analyzed the class, gender, and racial biases in the American Constitution, showing the ways that the legal system is rigged against the poor and the black. The fields of critical law and especially critical race theory, as represented by scholars such as Derrick Bell, Patricia Williams, Richard Delgado, Regina Austin, Paulette Caldwell, Randall Kennedy, and Kimberly Crenshaw, among others, have unpacked these contradictions with passionate precision and literary power. Critical law shows that the system is arranged to favor the powerful and the propertied. Critical race theory, meanwhile, shows that racism in American law and society is not aberrant but rather normal and hegemonic. The movement explains how a white supremacist regime was created and maintained and how that regime affects the "rule of law" and "equal protection." For critical race theory, the law constructs race by reproducing the structures and practices of racial domination, often in disguised form by embedding the appropriation of Indian land and the appropriation of blacks as "property."

Despite the wave of bicentennial critiques—from very diverse points on the political spectrum—many French intellectuals still see the revolution as a source of inspiration for the present and as a viable alternative to the American Revolution. Alain Joxe, for example, in *L'Empire du Chaos* (The Empire of Chaos) denounces what he calls the "chaos" fostered by the American empire.²² A republic, for Joxe, cannot be an empire. Although republican democracy requires openness, accountability, and good governance, an empire requires secrecy, executive privilege, and the concentration of power. (The American conservative Pat Buchanan, ironically, made a similar argument in his book *A Republic, Not an Empire: Reclaiming America's Destiny*). The empire of chaos, for Joxe, derives from a "new morphology of power," where transnational corporations dominate the world "according to exclusively financial criteria and nation-states become the 'rational' agents of the destruction of their own economic and social sovereignty." The U.S. Federal Bank, General Agreement on Tariffs and Trade, the G-8, the International Monetary Fund (IMF), the World Bank, Davos, and the World Trade Organization, as global technical oligarchies, have effectively discredited the political realm. This situation threatens all the democracies that emerged from antimonarchical revolutions, including those of France and the United States, which aspired to national sovereignty and popular government. But for the new transnational globalizers, the sovereign people are little more than an annoying obstacle to their goals.

As an alternative to the empire of chaos, Joxe proposes the French "social republic," the roots of which go back to Article 21 of the "Rights of Man" in 1793: "Public welfare is a sacred duty. The society owes subsistence to its unfortunate citizens, whether by providing them with employment, or by ensuring the means of survival to those who are unable to work." The formulations of some revolutionaries were even more radical. For Robespierre, those who possess what is superfluous owe a debt to those who lack what is necessary. (We find here the class-conscious political translation, as it were, of Rousseau's more moralistic contrast of the overcivilized and decadent sophisticate and the indigenous "natural man.")

Joxe believes unabashedly in *l'exception française* (the French exception) defined by the deeply social character of the French Revolution, which makes it potentially more universal and progressive than that of the United States. While the United States deploys the universal as a means of domination, France proposes it, in Joxe's view, as helpful to all humanity, to which one is tempted to respond, "Sure, that's what they all say." When France exercised vast power in the world, it did not exercise that power any more benevolently than the United States does today. Both France and the United States were political oxymorons: colonial republics and imperial democracies. Joxe's well-meant idealizations do not really recognize France's historically exploitative role in the extra-European world, its role in globalization (e.g., the attempts by companies such as Vivendi to privatize water), or its protective tariffs for its farmers, policies that ultimately favor the North over the South. And official France, despite its occasional disagreements with the United States, often ends up collaborating, for example, in Afghanistan or in Haiti, with the same hyperpower denounced in its rhetoric, part of what might be called a good cop/bad cop schema.

For Joxe, French revolutionary thinkers were less invested, in all senses of that word, in the notion of property. Yet here too the picture is a bit more complicated. It is remarkable, for example, that the U.S. Declaration of Independence speaks not of the right of property but of the right to "life and liberty" and—on an astonishingly utopian note— "the pursuit of happiness." For Jefferson, *happiness* had a somewhat mathematical social meaning rather than a subjective one: the greatest good for the greatest number. But that interpretation does not exclude another possible interpretation, which detects a Native American resonance in the substitution of the term *happiness* for the Lockean *property*. Many eighteenth-century thinkers regarded the Native Americans as enjoying an egalitarian and gregarious kind of society that promoted the well-being and happiness of all its members. In the view of Thomas Paine, for example, the native peoples pursued happiness above all. In any case, that magical phrase "the pursuit of happiness" has served as a perennial cue for a peculiarly American form of socially minded utopianism, an alternative to a dreary pleasure-phobic Puritanism of New England pilgrims, in an earlier period, and to the anhedonia (the fear of having a good time) of the Christian right even today. (We will return to "the pursuit of happiness" at the end of our text.)[23]

At the same time, some U.S.-based scholars argue that the American Constitution and the American system are less hostile to social and economic guarantees than Joxe-style analysis suggests. Although it is true that the American Constitution does not create "social and economic rights" alongside political rights, that fact is much more ambiguous than first appears. Because ultimately the Constitution means what the Supreme Court says it means, as legal scholar Cass Sunstein points out, a modest change in the personnel of the Court could have resulted in social and economic rights, within an evolving concept of active and participatory democracy. Indeed, Sunstein challenges the sharp dichotomy between traditional constitutional rights and social and economic rights by showing that all rights depend on an active government and the expenditure of taxpayer funds. He also disputes the distinction between "negative" rights, that is, the various checks on government power, and "positive" rights or entitlements.[24]

Some of the framers, furthermore, were very much concerned about inequality of wealth. Jefferson sought to include protection against monopolies in the Bill of Rights, and late in life he warned against the usurpation of citizen power by "the aristocracy of our monied corporations."[25] Arguing that inequality brought "misery to the bulk of mankind," Jefferson in 1786 wrote, "Legislators cannot invent too many devices for subdividing property."[26] According to James Madison, the goal should be to "reduce extreme wealth to a state of mediocrity and raise extreme indigence toward a state of comfort."[27] (Conservative pundit Robert Novak would probably denounce Jefferson's words as suspiciously Marxist.) Jefferson, similarly, while acknowledging that an "equal division of property [was] impracticable," also worried about the "consequences of this enormous inequality producing so much misery to the bulk of mankind." A way of "lessening the inequality of property," he argued in an early version of a progressive tax code, would be to "exempt all from taxation below a certain point, and to tax the higher portions of property in geometric progression as they rise."[28] Madison denounced the "evil" of powerful corporations whose "growing wealth ... never fails to be a source of abuse."[29] During the early years of the republic, historian Eric Foner reminds us, the focus was not simply on "liberty" but on "equal liberty." Thomas Paine spoke of a "perfect equality" of rights. Noah Webster saw "a general and tolerably equal distribution of landed property [as] the whole basis of national freedom."[30] "Even a conservative like John Adams, who distrusted the era's democratic pretensions," Foner observes, believed that equal liberty required land ownership for every citizen.[31]

The U.S. form of government—republican, federalist, and presidential—has performed an almost incomprehensibly grand feat: it has provided a solid framework for democratic stability for more than two centuries. Yet some of its serious shortcomings became obvious at the time of the framing, and some of the Founding Fathers were not at all sure whether the experiment would survive. Other shortcomings became obvious only later, as it gradually became clear that the framers, as they themselves were aware, could not possibly foresee the subsequent course of history or its effects on the Constitution.

In his book *How Democratic is the American Constitution?* (Yale, 2002), Robert A. Dahl points to the remarkable strengths and the salient weaknesses of the Constitution. Although the framers' Constitution seems enlightened within the standards of eighteenth-century European authoritarianism, Dahl points out seven undemocratic features of the Constitution at the time of its first framing: (1) it did not forbid slavery and indirectly endorsed it through the "federal ratio" and the "Fugitive Slave Laws"; (2) it did not guarantee universal suffrage, leaving the matter of voting rights to the states; (3) it installed the undemocratic electoral college, leading to problems that would sprout much later, including in the 2000 Gore–Bush election; (4) it endorsed a system whereby senators were chosen not by the people but by state legislators; (5) it enacted the "Connecticut Compromise," giving each state equal representation in the Senate regardless of population, thus empowering certain "minorities" such as Southern slaveholders, who held a veto over any policy affecting slavery; (6) by failing to limit the power of the judiciary, it opened the way to the practice of judicial legislation—the courts indirectly creating law—as opposed to judicial review, that is, simply testing law against the Constitution; and (7) it limited the power of Congress to regulate or control the economy and thus promote the "common good."

Dahl also disputes the myth, fervently believed by many Americans, that the U.S. Constitution has been a widely adopted model for the world. In fact those countries where democratic traditions have lasted the longest have generally not adopted the American model. They have not adopted federalism, a strong bicameralism (the two legislative houses), unequal representation, a tolerance for financial manipulation of elections, or the U.S. way of electing presidents. And the Constitution did not prevent a fratricidal civil war or guarantee real equality for all its citizens. In terms of contemporary democracies, the United States ranks toward the bottom in a series of important issues, such as disparities of wealth, energy sufficiency, welfare safety net, electoral transparency, social expenditures, voter turnout, and foreign aid.

So Americans desirous of democratizing the United States are left in a quandary. On one hand, we have to protect the separation of church and state against the modern-day theocrats and cling to the rights guaranteed by the Constitution, rights increasingly under threat in the age of "faith-based initiatives," the "war against terrorism" and "national security." (The very phrase "national security," so popular with the Bush administration, has often been a virtual synonym for "dictatorship," for example, in Latin America in the 1970s.) The kinds of laws of exception, special powers, and military tribunals created by the administration have even more worrisome antecedents. On the other hand, we have to recognize the ways in which the Constitution actually impedes the democratization of the country.

The problems with the Constitution are very diverse in nature. Some derive from the Constitution's enshrining of property, from the anti-Democratic foundations of the Senate, from the favoring of the rural states, and so forth. Others derive from departures from the Constitution, for example, the gradual weakening of constitutional standards such as the right of Congress to declare war and the neglect of the requirement for congressional oversight of expenditures (ignored by a largely unaudited Pentagon and its congressional allies). Still other problems derive from developments not foreseen at the time of the framing, for example, the two-party system, the inordinate power of K Street corporate lobbyists, the power over the economy of a figure such as Alan Greenspan, and the power over the media of a figure such as Rupert Murdoch. It is hard to imagine that the framers could have imagined a situation, as occurred with Reagan in the 1980s and with George W. Bush now, where politicians use government to destroy government and where the government defunds its own agencies and hires cronies—as with the Federal Emergency Management Agency (FEMA), for example—precisely to sabotage their effectiveness.

Daniel Lazare's *The Frozen Republic: How the Constitution is Paralyzing Democracy* pinpoints some of the political problems generated by the Constitution, which for Lazare has led to the United States ending up with the worst form of politics in the advanced industrial world, the most inefficient government, the most self-serving politicians, the most punitive social policies, and the narrowest political debate. It is no accident, writes Lazare, that Americans have been "praising the Constitution and cursing the government" ever since George Washington took office. The problem with U.S. politics is not that "they are the flawed expression of a perfect [constitutional] plan, but that they are the all too faithful expression of a flawed Constitution."[32] The system is designed to protect property and prevent the country from becoming "too" democratic. A subtle yet powerful system of restraints makes it very difficult to alter the political structure in any fundamental way. Bottom-up popular movements for democratic change, in the end, tend to be co-opted, repressed, bought off, or dissipated by struggle fatigue.

Some French and Brazilian anti-Americans not only see the United States as an inherently reactionary power but also see Americans as inherently reactionary people. But if the Constitution is designed to thwart and contain popular power, as Lazare suggests, then there is a good probability that Americans are actually less conservative than the U.S. right (and some French and Brazilian anti-Americans) would have us believe. If someone like George W. Bush on one level expresses the American people, on another he oppresses them, in that his policies go against the interests and opinions of the vast majority of American people. According to recent polls, strong majorities think that George W. Bush does not share their priorities. The problem is that majority political views have trouble getting translated into effective power. The system seems rigged to favor the right, especially now that all countervailing powers such as unions and the opposition party have been so weakened. Yet the negative traits of American politics were not rooted, as some anti-Americans suggest, in some alleged defect, such as superficiality, conformism, naïveté, or lack of fairness, of the American people. Rather they are rooted in aspects of the system itself. Yet it must be acknowledged that systems also end up, by shaping the opinions and social stances of people, in a constant back-and-forth of social structure and individual agency.

While enjoying constitutional stability, then, Americans have also had to contend with endless fragmentation; vain disputation between municipal, state, and federal authorities; and powerful lobbying groups grappling over control of resources and power. The separation of powers, installed as a safeguard against despotism, has served an important function, but it has also facilitated a soft despotism of chaos and gridlock in a system where problems go unsolved yet where no one is blamed, as the buck is passed from agency to agency, from government branch to government branch, and so on. We find evidence of this trend in the buck passing concerning the malfeasance that allowed 9/11, in the faulty intelligence that led to the war in Iraq, in the blame-the-underling approach to the torture scandals, and most recently in the pass-the-buck game that ensued in the wake of Katrina. "When politicians complain about the blame-game," Jon Stewart quipped, "it's because ... they're to blame!"

Although many Americans are proud of the Bill of Rights and although many other Americans are uninformed about them, the fact is that the Bill of Rights has rarely been applied in the fullest sense. It has often been undercut by states' rights (sometimes in the defense of anti-black racism) and constantly been subverted by unfair social practices. Here again a comparative approach is revealing. Although the American people are presumably no more lawless than people in France, the United States incarcerates citizens at a rate six times that of France. "In no other economically advanced society," as Lazare puts it, again somewhat hyperbolically, "do the police go about with automatic weapons, bullet-proof vests, helicopters, and even armored vehicles. And in no other comparable society would officers successfully defend themselves against charges of police brutality on the grounds that official department policy required them to repeatedly club a speeder as he lay face down on the pavement, as four accused officers did in the Rodney King case."[33] Nor are these problems created only by the right wing or by Republicans; the triangulating Bill Clinton supported "ending welfare as we know it" and "three strikes and you're out."

As a result of all this, while "social Europe," Canada, Australia, and much of Asia have moved toward a social welfare state characterized by unemployment insurance, public pension laws, and universal health care, the United States seems stuck in a situation where many of the most basic features of the welfare state either have not been installed or are not even on the table for discussion. Among the industrialized nations, the United States was relatively late, having avoided such measures until Franklin D. Roosevelt and the Great Depression, and even then it adopted only a few basic features of the welfare state. In the postwar period, while Western Europe evolved toward a social welfare and social democratic model and peaceful relations with its neighbors, the United States has drifted toward social anomie, perpetual war making, and one constitutional crisis (not always recognized as such) after another—Watergate, the Iran-Contra affair, the voting irregularities in the 2000 and 2004 presidential elections, the war in Iraq, the PATRIOT Act, Guantánamo and enemy combatants, and NSA spying. The U.S. Congress, in this sense, has exercised one of the most invisible and unheralded powers—the power to do nothing within gridlock democracy.

Rather than move toward the protective social nets that have become the norm in most of the "advanced" countries, the American right wing has been trying to shred what remains of Social Security, while slowly disqualifying such programs as Medicare and Medicaid as unfair "entitlements" benefiting the lazy and the shiftless (aka minorities of color). The right, so enthusiastic about its own entitlement to tax cuts and advantages, prefers that the rest of Americans feel entitled to absolutely nothing. Even when their individual success depends on government contracts, rightists strike poses of rugged individualism, as when Dick Cheney, during the 2000 vice presidential debates, told Senator Joe Lieberman that his success as a businessman—almost entirely dependant on the contracts fostered by an incestuous relationship to the military–industrial–energy complex—"had nothing to do with the government." (Neocon "Democrat" Lieberman did not bother to contradict him.) The right-wing ideology places giant government-linked corporations in a win–win situation of happy codependency; if they succeed, they get tax breaks, and if they fail, they get government bailouts.

For the right, any help for less well-off people generates dependency, while any help for the rich and corporations creates prosperity. George Carlin has scored the contradictions of this ideology with his usual perspicacity. Have you ever noticed, he pointed out, that "conservatives say if you don't give the rich more money, they will lose their incentive to invest. As for the poor, they tell us they've lost all incentive because we've given them too much money." As Carlin's summary implies, this philosophy insults both the rich—seen as so greedy and lazy that they won't work without guaranteed profits—and the poor—seen as so lazy they will stop working the minute they get something for free. But that leads us to ask, if both rich and poor are lazy and corrupt, then why should we help only the rich? The right believes in the eureka bathtub principle: when fat cats bathe in champagne, we the servants get to lick the spillover on the bathroom floor. If we help the rich get even richer, then the wealth will "trickle down" to the rest of us. But as the homeless Robin Williams character in *Comic Relief* tells Whoopi Goldberg when she explains trickle-down economics to him: "I knew somebody up there was pissing on me!"

The right has successfully derailed all proposals for universal health care (or even insurance), despite attempts by Truman, Kennedy, and Clinton. While all the advanced industrial nations, not to mention some relatively poor Third World countries, have created some variant of a comprehensive and more-or-less free national health care system and even Tunisia, a poor North African country with few resources beyond phosphate, sardines, and tourism, offers its citizens free health care and education, the political representatives of the wealthiest nation on earth have forestalled equivalent benefits in the United States. The consequences have been terrible; according to Nicholas Kristoff, some eighteen thousand Americans die every year simply because they have no health insurance, and infant mortality for blacks is worse in the United States than it is in Sri Lanka.[34] Americans spend more on health care but get less in return. According to a 1999 study from the World Health Organization, France spends only 9.5 percent of its gross domestic product on health, compared to 13.5 percent spent by the United States, yet France was ranked first in the world for overall coverage, while the United States was rated a shameful thirty-seventh.[35] In France even foreigners who happen to be in France have the right to advanced, high-tech treatment, without being questioned about their insurance coverage.

While the right-dominated U.S. government spends billions of the national treasure on an effort to completely change another country's system by installing "democracy"—in their mind a pro-American regime, free markets, flat tax, and elections—we are told that our own government cannot respond to the basic needs of Americans at home. Expenditures of billions of dollars—for example, huge tax breaks to oil companies precisely when their profits are booming and Americans are suffering at the pump—are passed almost without debate. The huge deficit stretching far into the future makes it impossible to strengthen Social Security and Medicare commitments, even though they are paltry by European standards.

Given these problems, some American intellectuals have called for patriotic renovation of the principles of the Constitution. Lazare suggests that we appeal to one of the most progressive and founding sections of the Constitution: the Preamble. Since "we the people" are ultimately in control, since "we" ordained and established the Constitution and everything in it, we therefore have the right to change it in the name of justice, tranquility, welfare, and liberty. A vital next step, for Lazare, is to abolish the undemocratic Senate, where small rural states have the same representation as huge urban states, and turn the House, as the only truly democratic and representative institution, into a kind of parliament. That would end a situation where nine highly populated states, representing more than half of the U.S. population, account for less than 20 percent of the Senate vote and where senators from the smaller states, representing roughly one-fifth of the population, hold a majority, with the result that no law can be passed that is opposed by those senators. The right, in contrast, has called for amendments, for the first time in American history, that actually curtail rights, such as an amendment banning same-sex marriage.

Political discourse in the United States has always been ambivalent toward government. On the one hand it calls for government, in Lincoln's words, "of the people, by the people, and for the people," a formulation that implies that government per se can be a good thing. On the other hand, government is seen as a necessary evil, where the best government, as Thoreau put it, is "that which governs least." The more radical revolutionaries hesitated to create any central government and called for new rebellions—a kind of Trotskyist "permanent revolution" *avant la lettre*—

whenever the government no longer served the people. In this view government plants the seeds of its own destruction: it posits government as self-consuming artifact. In what is falsely presented as a zero-sum game, the government's loss is always seen as the individual's gain.

Although the United States has a strong tradition of antigovernment rhetoric—that is, rhetoric critical not of any specific government but rather of the very idea of government—French official discourse (even that of the Le Penist right) is statist in that it assumes that governments have affirmative duties to promote the general welfare. The disagreements are about what constitutes the general welfare. Unlike the United States, the argument in France (and Brazil) is rarely about whether government per se is good or bad or about "too much government" but about what the government can and should do for the people. The very framing of the debate as an issue of "too much government" is a framing victory for the far right, because in the neoliberal era every move against government is usually a move in favor of corporations, which rush to fill the vacuum left by government. The antigovernment rhetoric popular among American right-wing politicians would seem highly anomalous in Europe and Latin America, where the idea that the government should concretely help people seems like a no-brainer. In France and Brazil, for example, the critique—even on the right—is of government corruption or policy but not of government per se. The idea of a government shrinking from governing would see a giant abdication of responsibility.

Although clearly the most venerable of the three political systems, the U.S. constitutional system is not, in sum, without serious drawbacks. The weaknesses in the American Constitution, apart from its race, class, and gender exclusions, have to do with the potential for a kind of exacerbated individualism. In many areas the nation seems unable to muster the political will to solve what are manifestly serious, even lethal, national problems. Corporate lobbies corrupt Congress, with the result that consensus desires—universal health care, more equal education, environmental protections, progressive tax codes, a secure safety net—are not translated into public policy. A basic corruption has evolved over the centuries; what began as concessions to slaveholders and the slave states has now morphed into concessions to southern senators such as Tom DeLay and to corporations such as Enron and Halliburton.

We see some of the drawbacks of the American system in the area of elementary education. The fact that issues of education are reserved for the states results in an inchoate system where educational quality, largely based on property taxes, varies in function of the wealth not only of states but also even of individual neighborhoods. This system produces what educator Jonathon Kozol has long been calling "savage inequalities" and "the shame of the nation"; that is, enormous advantages for wealthy suburbanites but huge disadvantages for poor white or inner-city black children and thus for the nation as a whole, as human resources are squandered and dreams deferred.[36] (The same well-off people who throw lots of money to provide for their own children's education, Kozol points out, often object to "throwing money at problems" when it comes to the education of other peoples' children.)

The American political system, with all its advantages, seems to have difficulty in forging broad remedies for pervasive problems. Nor does the right wing see public education as something that deserves federal support. While education, including higher education, is quite inexpensive in France, Brazil, and many other countries, it is extremely expensive in the United States. American students go deep into debt to pay escalating tuition costs for an education they fail to recognize as a basic social right. Our American students are amazed when they meet Scandinavians who are actually paid to attend a university, on the assumption that an educated populace is a benefit to the entire country. The religious right, meanwhile, is dumbing down American education. The same Christian right that favors Social Darwinism and the "survival of the fittest" in social and economic policy refuses to teach the writings of Darwin himself. Meanwhile "creationism," or "intelligent design," is now being offered as an alternative consensus science about evolution, in the name of "diversity of opinion." The theocons, obsessed with the "survival of the fetus," care less about the fate of those "left behind." And the Christian right is more concerned with people going to hell than with the permanent hellish fires that might be caused by global warming here on earth. As a result of all these trends, the United States is becoming less attractive to international scientists and scholars, who are now turning more and more to Europe and Asia.

So while the French Constitution has the benefits and weaknesses of a kind of constitutional monologism, the U.S. Constitution has the strengths and weaknesses of exaggerated decentralization, resulting in a social system regulated less by democratic decision making than by corporate interests and elites. Democratic individualism as enshrined in the American Constitution has historically had trouble overcoming the vestiges of slavery and segregation in the past and lacks the political will to improve the educational and health systems in the present. If corporations and selfish near majorities see no immediate personal benefit in a given progressive policy change, they refuse to support it, even if that change would be of benefit to many individuals and to the country at large. (We will return to the question of individualism in chapter 6.)

Racism forms a key piece in the puzzle of the democratic paralysis and inequality. Forgetting that over the centuries most affirmative action measures—such as land grants—have benefited whites, the white middle class rejects affirmative action as unfair, thus preventing the nation as a whole from realizing the potential of all its citizens. If the white middle class somehow thinks it can get by on its individual resources, it sometimes resists supporting universal health care, even though health care is ultimately to the majority's own advantage. Who, apart from the superrich, would not prefer to be able to rely on guaranteed inexpensive medical care for all needs and emergencies? The moralistic individualism that sees individuals as exclusively responsible for their own well-being prevents progress in this area, as does the "self-made man" thinking that nourishes an illusion of self-sufficiency—"I did it my way!"—even as globalization makes such a route to success less and less probable. At the same time, such thinking projects blacks and other minorities as being needy and irresponsible and looking for a handout, as those who have not earned their way so as to "deserve" entitlements such as affordable health care. Racial narcissism, in other words, in the name of depriving racialized "others" of a fair slice of the pie, ends up penalizing whites themselves, especially poor whites, and preventing them from getting their own share of the pie. And on a more broad scale, the nation as a whole is penalized, as a vital part of its citizenry is left unattended in its needs and its vast creative potential is ignored and underutilized.

The crisis provoked by Hurricane Katrina brought all these issues to a boil, posing fundamental questions about our national priorities. Katrina not only ripped the roofs off Gulf Coast houses but also ripped the facade off the "national security state." The antigovernment rhetoric of the right, it turned out, has real-world effects. When you "drown government in the bathtub," to use conservative Grover Norquist's formula, real people drown. Katrina revealed with stunning clarity a federal, state, and municipal system unable to establish a clear chain of command or allocate resources to prevent a disaster. Our national security state left victims to agonize in hospitals or die on the street, even though the disaster had been gamed, predicted, and analyzed, as it were, to death and even though the administration knew early on the seriousness of the crisis. The incompetence of crony capitalism was revealed in all its horror. While thousands of desperate people screamed for help, "heck of a job" Michael Brown apparently worried more about fine dining and beautiful clothes than about the crisis in New Orleans. The catastrophically negligent response to Katrina, especially shocking in the richest nation on earth, exposed the limits of a faith-based and charity response to "natural" disasters, which outsourced relief to churches and Rotarians rather than to the government. If current trends continue, we will soon see a "presidential telethon" approach to disaster, where the government will simply lead the call for private contributions instead of using government resources to help the victims of natural disasters. Exxon and Mobil, gratified by all their tax cuts, will doubtless be as "helpful" as they always have been during disasters, while other energy corporations will perhaps provide a "thousand points of light."

The real problem is the government's failure to translate consensus desires into policy. Voters have little way of holding presidents or Congress responsible apart from elections, but the electoral debates tend to focus not on real economic issues but rather on trivial questions related to the personal qualities of performance, or Al Gore's earth tones or Kerry's patrician manner or Dick Cheney's mouthing of an obscenity. The deeper issues—corporate government and corruption, the manipulation of elections, the turn to "preventive war," the bloated Pentagon budget, unworkable "Star Wars" fantasies, and overstocked nuclear weapons—are barely discussed. Election debates hide rather than reveal the vital issues or the real intentions and policies of the candidates.

As the right was preparing to invade Iraq and rearrange the political map of the Middle East, the electoral debate revolved around Bush's call for "compassionate conservatism" and a "humble nation" uninterested in "nation building." And indeed that was one campaign promise that Bush kept. He did not engage in nation building; rather he engaged in nation destroying.

Despite being framed in misleading ways, the opinion polls provide a certain solace, in that they reveal the gap between the Beltway pundits and the majority of the American people. Poll after poll shows that Americans in general are more progressive than their representatives. Nine out of ten Americans, according to a 2002 Harris interactive poll, think corporations have too much influence on Washington politics.[37] According to a 2000 *Business Week* poll, 95 percent of Americans think corporations should "sacrifice some profit for the sake of making things better for their workers and communities," whereas 70 percent would prefer to buy from companies with good environmental practices.[38] The right wing can manipulate and game the system and brutally impose its policies, but it cannot make those policies truly popular. The right was hell-bent on creating a kind of national hysteria around Monica Lewinsky to impeach a popular president, yet polls consistently showed that most people were unswayed by it. The administration promoted a massive campaign to "reform" Social Security, yet the proposal became less popular the more people came to know about it, and it is now dead in the water. The political system and the media have veered dramatically to the right, but it is doubtful that the American people have moved right to the same extent. Polls consistently show majority support for a more progressive tax system, universal health care (or at least insurance), and so forth, yet the media rarely call attention to that fact, for they too are part of the problem.

The Crisis of American Freedom

The fortunes of American democracy have varied widely. On one hand we have constitutional democracy, and American mores, at least as far as white males were concerned, have generally been democratic and meritocratic. On the other hand democracy has always been compromised by racism and economic inequality. The old American promise that "any white person can grow up to become president" has had to be amended to "anyone with access to millions of dollars and approved by the corporate–military–mediatic establishment can be president." A truly "deep" democracy in the United States would have to have many levels. A first level would consist of formal, electoral democracy, a set of rules and procedures guaranteeing fair and representative elections on a one-person, one-vote basis. A second level would offer a truly participatory arrangement whereby the people can initiate popular policies from below rather than merely respond to what comes down from the heights of corporate or political America. A third level would offer social democracy in the form of popular entitlements involving health, education, retirement security, and so forth. A fourth level would promote economic equality, since economic equality and political equality go hand in hand.

At this point in history, democratic citizenship in the United States has been indirectly undermined by a number of factors: (1) the inadequacies of public education, which leave many citizens uninformed about basic social issues and thus incapable of informed participation; (2) the deeply corrupting power of corporate money in the "pay to play" system that has become known as the "best government money can buy," where money is the "mother's milk"—and the devil's poison—of politics; (3) the disproportionate power of the rural states, rooted in the constitutional definition of the Senate; (4) the assault on civil liberties in the name of "national security"; (5) the assault on freedom of the press and the right of journalists to keep secret the identity of "confidential sources"; (6) the obligatory two-party system and winner-take-all elections; (7) the transformation of serious news into infotainment, where a concern for ratings preempts any possibility of a critical discussion of issues and dumbs down the populace; (8) the shaping of an imperial presidency that presumes the right to detain citizens at will and without trial, completely outside of the American system of law and its traditional freedoms and "checks and balances"; (9) the passing of the (unpatriotic) PATRIOT Act, with its severe restrictions on free speech and assembly, rendering parts of the Bill of Rights a dead letter; and (10) widespread absenteeism at the polls, partially as a result of all the aforementioned factors.

But of all these factors, the most important is the role of the military–industrial complex in buying off politicians and enshrining preestablished funding priorities such as "defense." As Eisenhower warned a half century ago, the military–industrial–corporate (and we add "congressional" and "mediatic") complex now holds too much power in the country. In some cases corporations actually write the laws being passed by the legislature. Candidates from the two major parties have to make their peace with that complex before they can be considered "viable," whence the endless oscillation between populist rhetoric on the campaign trail and the endless returns to the corporate-dominated "responsible" center. Representative institutions, in short, have been short circuited and corrupted by institutionalized, and often even legalized, bribery.

In recent years the United States has seen a series of invisible and largely unacknowledged "soft" coups d'état that have severely threatened democracy: (1) the well-funded attempt (with the widespread complicity of the media) to entrap and impeach a popular, elected president (Bill Clinton) over a sexual peccadillo; (2) the exploitation of the proposition system in California to unseat an elected governor who had committed no crimes and misdemeanors and was guilty only of a budget deficit much less severe than that created by George W. Bush himself; and (3) and the mid-decade redistricting (gerrymandering) in states such as Texas, whereby politicians could choose their voters rather than vice versa to guarantee seats for Republicans and incumbents generally. As a result Republicans can win elections while receiving fewer votes. In the past three Senate elections, Democrats received 2.4 million more votes than Republicans, yet Republicans gained eleven more seats.[39] Another unfortunate trend is (4) the strengthening of executive power at the expense of the Congress, as reflected in Bush's warrantless spying on Americans and policy of "the unitary executive." Because of all these trends, the electoral system now resembles a casino rigged against its patrons, where evenly divided constituencies produce lopsided Republican victories. (Corruption, once a Democratic specialty, has now become a Republican specialty.)

All this came to a head in the 2000 and 2004 presidential elections. The 2000 election was deeply tainted by fraud—by the creation of a list of fake felons (largely black); by inadequate polling machines (whence the "hanging chads"); by thuggish Republican mobs chanting "stop the vote"; by the reliance on easily manipulable computerized voting machines, sold by corporations with links to the Republican Party, which leave no paper trail for recount; and by chicanery at the state (Katherine Harris and Jeb Bush) and federal levels (the role of a pro-Bush Supreme Court in stopping the votes from being counted and selecting rather than electing the president). All this indirectly rendered the 2004 election equally illegitimate, since it was premised on the unfair advantages of incumbency. That election too was corrupted by asymmetrical "spoilage" of votes so as to favor Republicans, by the rejection of Democratic provisional ballots, by uncounted absentee ballots, and by the suppression of the vote in black and Latino neighborhoods, and always to the benefit of Republicans. The right wing has created a situation where the left has to assume that millions of votes will be suppressed, "spoiled," or not counted due to partisan mischief, inconsistently enforced laws, computer vulnerability, local racisms, new versions of poll taxes (such as requiring photo ID or "proof of citizenship"), and other forms of disenfranchisement.

The overall process has been further corrupted by the commercially motivated nature of the dominant "infotainment" media, where celebrity scandals threaten at any time to preempt gory murders or serious political debates. Issues of individual morality preempt issues of systemic justice. The media generally treated the Democrats who protested the election results as "sore losers" or "crybabies" who should get over it, despite the clear evidence of fraud. Had such phenomena been registered in the Third World, Americans would have decried them as corrupt and typical of "banana republics." As a result of all these trends, a general sense of participatory citizenship has been eroded. Disempowered Americans have become mere spectators at the destruction derby called American politics.

At the same time, neoliberal discourse—that is, the view that favors laissez-faire free market capitalism, deregulation, and so forth—subtly undermines democracy. Although neoliberalism insists on the close links between capitalism and democracy, free markets and free elections, the relationship is actually much more fraught. When the ratio of average CEO compensation to workers' pay is more than five hundred to one—that is, thirty to fifty times what is the norm in Europe and

Japan—that disproportion clearly has political consequences in terms of who gets to influence politics. Capitalism can be forced to be democratic—as it has been in Scandinavia, for example—but it is not necessarily so. First of all, no capitalist society has ever proposed a plebiscite where people could truly decide if they wanted a capitalist system and, if so, what kind of capitalism they want. (The same is true of communist systems but not of social democratic systems where there is a spectrum of parties representing diverse views of capitalism and socialism, with negotiations about how wealth should be distributed.)

Second, capitalism can coexist with very diverse systems, from social democratic to fascist. The industrialists who collaborated with Hitler, for example, had no problem with slave labor; it was helpful to the bottom line. Jews and other slaves from the so-called inferior races were forced to work for the war machine. What has happened with contemporary American democratic capitalism is that most of the major economic choices have already been made for us by economic elites. Did we as a people ever have a vote about what would be done with the "peace dividend" that was supposed to come with the end of the Cold War and the disintegration of the Soviet Union? Were the American people ever really asked if they preferred to spend $300 billion—some claim a trillion—on a war of choice in the Middle East rather than spend it at home on education, infrastructure, health care, pensions, and deficit reduction?

The lack of democratic agency is reflected in the language of the dominant media. The media no longer speak of American citizens or even of the American people. Instead, old-fashioned *citizens* have slowly morphed first into *consumers* and then, at least on cable TV, into *investors* and *shareholders*. When a new domestic or international economic policy is announced, media journalists no longer ask about the reaction of average American working people. Rather they transfer political agency to that abstract (yet very real) entity called "the markets": they ask, "How will the markets react?" The markets have taken on the function of the oracles of ancient Greece.[40]

Despite the existence of various forms of corruption in both Brazil and France, the past Brazilian and French presidential elections were much more transparent and clean than the recent American elections. In the latest Brazilian election, computerized voting (with a paper trail) proceeded rapidly and without suspicions of fraud, and a wide variety of candidates were offered free and equal time on the media, an idea that has always been resisted in the United States, both by the media (which prefers to make money on political commercials) and by both major parties. (One can imagine the altered American political landscape if candidates from outside the two major parties—Ralph Nader, for example—had been offered free and equal time.) Although the French government has also known its share of corruption and although it too is currently pressured by neoliberal currents, globalization, and absenteeism at the polls, it is still slightly more socially minded, slightly more inclined to show concern for the "public good." The media in France, while partially privatized, still give slightly more voice to political debates about the electoral process—witness the lively 2005 debate about the EU constitution—than the right-wing dominated radio and cable media or the mainstream center-right network media in the United States.

The same is true in Great Britain. Unlike George W. Bush, Tony Blair had to actually debate his ideological opponents on Iraq. One of Jon Stewart's regular bits on the *Daily Show* has been to contrast the lively debates in the British media with the supine performance of American media journalists. After showing a British reporter frontally attacking Blair, Stewart asked, "Where can we get one of those guys?" After which he proposed a trade: "two Aaron Browns, one Brit Hume and one Van Sustern in exchange for one British journalist." On another occasion Stewart showed a clip of Soledad O'Brien asking a Pentagon official what was wrong with the United States' planting stories in the Iraqi press. Expressing astonishment, Stewart commented, "So a Pentagon public relations official has to explain the rationale for an honest press—to a journalist!" He was implying that it should be exactly the other way around. During the "cakewalk" and "slam dunk" phases of the preparations for war, when Americans were promised an easy, popular, and self-financing war, the media failed to note the direct contradiction between two basic arguments for the war: on one hand Iraq was immensely powerful, a threat to our very existence; on the other hand it was so weak that we could bomb it and impose a no-fly zone and an invasion would be a cakewalk. Nor did the media call Bush on the implications of his words or the contradictions between his various statements and positions. Bush promised during his 2000 campaign for the presidency to "trust the people, not the government," as if the people and the government necessarily existed in direct opposition. But in a democracy the government and the people are not supposed to be opposites; the former is supposed to represent the latter. It is possible, of course, that when right-wingers say "people" they really mean "corporations," which have the legal status of persons. At the same time, these "trusters of the people" have done everything they can to make democracy impracticable by undermining the political process through stolen elections, government secrecy, financial corruption, and the manipulation of the media through fake news and staged town hall meetings.

In keeping with his "don't trust the government" philosophy, Bush made the government really untrustworthy. By governing incompetently he demonstrated his own thesis that "government doesn't work." During the campaign Bush also argued that "government cannot plant hope in the hearts of the people," an idea that he amply "proved" while in office by crushing popular hopes. By empowering the NSA to spy on citizens and by unilaterally trying to redesign the geopolitical map, Bush ran roughshod over the much-vaunted people, including the Congress that supposedly represents it and that has had little say in the matter.

Right-wing antigovernment rhetoric is a charade. Ultimately the right cares more about power than about principles. To phrase it differently, the right's principles somehow always seem to reinforce its financial interests. The right is happy to amplify any form of government that it can dominate and exploit for its power. The important issue is not, as the right wing suggests, whether to favor big government or small government—indeed, government has never been bigger than under Bush, provoking concern even among some traditional conservatives. The real issue has to do with government for what purpose and for whose benefit. To stipulate the obvious, it is not "tax and spend" versus "no tax and no spend" but rather "tax whom and give tax breaks to whom and spend for whom and for what purpose?"

The contemporary right wing demonizes government in the abstract, while trying to take it over and expand it in the concrete. Orwellian to the core, the right uses antigovernment rhetoric to strengthen its control of government, while using it own power as a wrecking ball to destroy the kind of government it doesn't like. With Ronald Reagan, George H.W. Bush, and George W. Bush, the right has used the government to destroy government by weakening federal agencies by staffing them with corporate cronies who do not really believe in their stated missions. (The inept response of FEMA to Hurricane Katrina is only one of many such examples.) But whereas Thomas Jefferson's suspicion toward government was premised on humanity's "natural sociability," present-day conservative libertarian antigovernment rhetoric is premised on a kind of natural unsociability and dog-eat-dog viciousness that is somehow supposed to magically generate benefits for the larger society. The American dream of individualism here means that the poor and the indigent "must lack care or life support in the name of their own freedom."[41] We Americans, in this sense, are literally "freeing ourselves" to death.

Instead of the promised small government, the Bush–Cheney administration gave us big government, not for but rather **against** the people. It gave us big government for big war, big spying, big deficits, and big corruption. In all these senses, the administration really did "think big." The Bush–Cheney administration, and the right generally, eagerly carry out policies that polls tell us most people do not want (war, tax breaks for the rich) while stubbornly refusing to carry out policies most people want (health care, windfall profits tax, deficit reduction). We thus get all the disadvantages of big government—inefficiency, corruption, the suppression of rights—without the advantages—security, a safety net, protection from man-made and natural disasters. The right wing does favor big government, but only in terms of its repressive, punitive, militaristic, or procorporate functions, never in terms of its nurturing or life-sustaining functions. The Drug Benefit Bill was only an apparent exception to this rule. Ultimately a favor to pharmaceutical companies, the bill has resulted in a chaotic program that has left many impoverished people without their medicine.

It is a matter not of starving the beast but rather of feeding the beast only military food and offering the Pentagon a banquet, while starving the people of elementary benefits. The corporate right needs government to funnel public money into private hands. Stingy when it comes to disasters, stingy even in the much ballyhooed "war on terror," the right is infinitely "generous" when it comes to spending for war, partially because that spending is, ultimately, for the military and energy corporations with which the administration is embedded. Even in Iraq the U.S. military has been adept at destruction—in Fallujah, for example—and inept at reconstruction, even when American corporations are profiting from that reconstruction. The United States is swiftly acquiring the reputation of a country good at wrecking but bad at building, especially when it wrecks and builds in other countries. Despite all its "culture of life" rhetoric, the administration, like most of the administrations preceding it, sells arms and spreads violence around the world, and in this sense clearly demonstrates that it prefers death over life, destruction over construction, repression over freedom, and authoritarianism over democracy. Stephen Colbert implied as much in a witty question to Paul Krugman: "If Bush lied us into war, why can't he lie us out of war?" And the answer is that Bush lies only for war and not for peace because he does not want peace. Where would the joy be in calling himself a "peacetime president"?

Disjunctive Democracy

A comparative approach, we have been suggesting, helps illuminate questions of patriotism. What constitutes a patriotic response to glaring social problems? How do the problems and the responses differ from country to country, and how does this bear on both patriotism and anti-Americanism? In what way does national narcissism blinker the vision of those who criticize other nations' behavior but not their own? When do other nation-states become scapegoats, distracting attention from the nation's own crimes and social problems?

As "Black Atlantic" nation-states marked by the legacies of slavery and colonialism, Brazil, France, and the United States have all faced common problems having to do with discrimination and social exclusion. In the United States amateur video cameras repeatedly catch police brutalizing and even killing black people. In the Rodney King case, the acquittal of the policemen led to massive rioting in 1992. In France police hassle, racially profile, and humiliate the children of African and Arab immigrants, provoking the *banlieue* rebellions in November 2005. And in Brazil in 1997, amateur video cameras show the police systematically beating, robbing, and even killing favela residents in the neighborhoods Diadema (in São Paulo) and "City of God," the scene of the famous film of the same name.

A note of national narcissism often creeps into the media coverage of acts of rebellion and repression, thus the French media stress, with a certain schadenfreude, the racist dimension exposed by the American government's inadequate response to Hurricane Katrina. The American media, meanwhile, which rarely even report on events in France, relate with thinly veiled pleasure the tensions exposed by the rebellions in the *banlieue*. The same correspondents who show very little sympathy for black protests in the United States are strangely sympathetic to rioters in France. While in the United States, for example, during the large-scale and ultimately lethal Los Angeles rebellion of 1992, the American media criticize the rioters and highlight the danger to normal, upright, middle-class (white) citizens, when it comes to France they speak of discrimination, exclusion, and unemployment. This is what we mean when we refer to the nationalistic version of Freud's "narcissism of minor differences," where the conflicts in another country mask, allegorize, or displace the conflicts in one's own.

Our critique of the U.S. Constitution and political system, then, should clearly not be taken as letting countries such as Brazil or France off the hook. We do not mean to idealize any nation-state, especially not countries marked by colonialism and enslavement. In Brazil and France, as in the United States, the popular will is not always translated into governmental policy. The popular desire in Brazil to end hunger and lessen disparities of wealth is held back externally by financial institutions such as the IMF and internally by the inertia of the class structure. France, for its part, is not itself a colonial settler state, but it does share with the United States and Brazil its vestigial links to conquest, colonial settlements, and slavery. While France has a strong welfare state, with many guarantees for its citizens, it still remains a highly elitist country, dominated by well-schooled *enarchs* from prestigious schools and a country characterized by massive unemployment. France too has seen its share of scandals, whether in terms of financial corruption or of foreign adventures.

Some argue that French intellectuals scapegoat a vaguely defined "globalization" for problems that in fact resulted from French official pampering of a well-employed elite against millions of basically jobless people. Economist Timothy B. Smith, for example, argues that French public policy, "despite its rhetoric of solidarity, creates or aggravates as many inequalities as it corrects."[42] What is interesting about Smith's critique is that it does not come from the usual neoliberal position; he does not think France should move toward an Anglo-American-style social policy. Rather, he favors the redistributive Scandinavian-style approach, which spreads the wealth while also avoiding the widespread unemployment that plagues France and that helped fuel the *banlieue* rebellions. The rebellions suggest that the welfare state is not enough; citizens also need jobs, dignity, and space for cultural expression.

Although the French system has succeeded in securing the majority of the French population against the risks of capitalism run amok, it has not been as egalitarian or universal as it sometimes claims to be. French analysts, Smith claims, exaggerate the differences between the United States and France. In fact, the differences between France and Sweden are greater than those between France and the United States. The French, in other words, idealize their own system—and here again we see the symptoms of comparative self-praise—by contrasting it with a caricatured vision of the American system, defined only as the lack of a welfare state. The American right, meanwhile, idealizes the United States by contrasting it with a caricatured version of the French system, defined only by unemployment and bureaucracy. The dichotomy of neoliberal globalization versus welfare state egalitarianism is also simplistic. Some French are major participant "winners" from globalization. European transnational corporations now own Brooks Brothers, Random House, and the Los Angeles Dodgers. Denmark, Sweden, and the Netherlands are highly globalized in terms of trade and transnational corporations, yet they are internally egalitarian, with relatively little unemployment. Our story, ultimately, is not of "good" and "bad" nations but rather of differentiated commonalities across a spectrum of interactions. Any truly democratizing project requires lucidity about the advantages and disadvantages of different systems, without the blindness inherent in national narcissisms.

4. Political Sense, Cultural Nonsense

Exceptionalism Revisited: Socialism in America?

Many analyses of the United States, by both Americans and non-Americans, advance specific ideas about what are seen as essential traits of American culture in terms of religious and social attitudes. In this chapter we would like to unpack some of these views and explain how they are related at the same time to American narcissism—that is, how some Americans see their own nation—and to anti-Americanism—that is, how non-Americans look at the United States.

The notion of "American exceptionalism," for example, is sometimes deployed to explain the lack of socialism in the United States. The idea is that a series of factors—the enshrining of property values in the Constitution, the escape-valve function of allegedly unoccupied land being available on the "frontier," the role of antiblack racism in dividing the working class, and Horatio Alger–style myths of success—have served to weaken any popular, working-class movements in the United States. The two-party, winner-take-all political system, meanwhile, forced the "mainstreaming" of the two parties by marginalizing more radically egalitarian alternatives. As a result, some claim, the United States has no real class-based left that would be analogous to the Marxist left or even to social democracy movements in Europe and Latin America.

All of the factors cited do indeed play an extremely important role in American history, yet they do not exhaust the possibilities of analysis. Although class-based Marxist and socialist parties in the United States have never achieved the strength they achieved in Europe, American history has been marked by endless rebellions and resistance movements— from the Shays' Rebellion to the draft riots on to populism, the Black Panthers and the Rainbow Coalition—with clear class overtones. The premise of the Rainbow Coalition, for example, was to stress the "economic common ground" rather than the "racial battleground." One of the horrible specters for the elite, historically, has been the fear that the class victims of various colors might all get together to overthrow those at the top. When Irish indentured servants (i.e., virtual slaves) and black slaves escaped together from their masters, as sometimes occurred in the colonial period, their action symbolically prefigured a possible cross-class and cross-racial political movement. Indeed, a look at the history of New York City, and of many American cities, reveals that the dominant elite—going back to the panicked repression of the supposed 1741 conspiracy of blacks and radical whites and moving up through the fear of an alliance in 1968 between the white SDS (Students for a Democratic Society) radicals at Columbia University and the Black Panthers in Harlem—has often been frightened by the prospect of a black–white alliance.

The various populist movements in the United States, meanwhile, were often class based, although they were also often blind to race and sometimes even racist. The "anarcho-syndicalist" movements of the 1920s and the socialist and communist movements of the 1930s, similarly, were also based on a class analysis of the American social system. "May Day," after all, began as a tribute to the American working-class victims of police repression. In the 1960s the movement included the standard array of sectarian Marxist groups (Communist Party, Revolutionary Communist Party, Maoists, Trotskyites, and so forth), alongside race- and class-based groups such as the American Indian Movement, the Black Panthers, the Young Lords, the Brown Berets, the White Panthers, the Gray Panthers, and so forth.

Some critics point to the role of racism in dividing the working class as a cause for the weakness of socialism in the United States. The "whiteness" historians, for example, have shown how various immigrant groups, such as the Irish, Italians, and European Jews, were co-opted into the dominant group through the compensatory lure of "honorary white" status. The union movement was often divided along racial lines. This absorption into whiteness and division through race had the effect of cutting those "ethnic" groups off from blacks and cutting blacks off from their potential white allies. The idea of "no socialism in the United States," it must be said, is also partially a product of the dominant historiography, which naturalizes the soft hegemony of capitalism, forgetting the role of brute force and repression in putting down any and all radical challenges to the dominant system. As a result of a repression that was at once physical and ideological, socialist-style ideas in the United States have often been forced to take euphemistic form. Expressions such as "economic democracy" and "participatory democracy" point to a more economically equal society. Often vaguely socialist ideals are evoked not in explicitly political terms but rather in innocuous metaphors connoting social communality, such as "we're all in the same boat" or "it takes a village."

Political scientists and legal scholars distinguish between three kinds of rights: civil, political, and social (and now cultural), all of which take place within the frame of the nation-state, in the context of identification with a nation and loyalty to a state. First, civil rights bear on fundamental human rights to life, liberty, and property; to equality before the law; and to move, choose work, manifest one's thoughts, be religious (or not religious) in one's own way, organize, and benefit from fair and cost-free legal processes. The touchstone of civil rights is individual freedom in society. Second, political rights bear on citizen participation in government, whether through demonstrating, voting, or participating in elective office or other forms of representative government. Finally, social rights bear on participation in the collective wealth, whether in terms of education, work, a decent salary, health, or retirement, all of which require an efficient government apparatus. The French welfare state, the New Deal in the United States, and the Brazilian "New State" under Vargas were all very concerned with social rights. (In the case of Vargas, social rights came at the expense of political rights.) The basic principle was to use privately generated wealth to help needy people for the collective public benefit.

In this context the second-generation rights embodied in Franklin D. Roosevelt's New Deal betokens a more progressive side to American history. Roosevelt spoke of the "four freedoms": freedom of speech, freedom of worship, freedom from want, and freedom from fear. Roosevelt proposed the New Deal, as he explained, to prevent a revolution in the United States: "I decided half a loaf was better than none—a half loaf for me and a half loaf for you and no revolution."[1] In words that resonate even today, FDR saw excessive market freedoms as the root of the socioeconomic problems of the 1930s. Americans, he suggested in 1935, "must foreswear that conception of the acquisition of wealth which, through excessive profits, creates undue private power."[2] The duty of the state, not only during economic crisis but in general, was to use its powers and allocate the country's collective resources to eradicate poverty and hunger and to ensure safety and security of livelihood. Roosevelt thus moved from civil and political rights to social rights. He proposed the new rights without advancing a constitutional amendment, asking only that Congress explore the means of implementing an "economic bill of rights."

Roosevelt summarized these rights in his State of the Union Address of 1944:

> This Republic had its beginning, and grew to its present strength, under the protection of certain inalienable rights—among them the right of free speech, free press, free worship, trial by jury, freedom from unreasonable searches. They were our rights to life and liberty.

> As our economy has grown ... these political rights proved inadequate to assure us equality in the pursuit of happiness. ... We have accepted, so to speak, a second Bill of Rights under which a new basis of security and prosperity can be established for all—regardless of station, race, or creed.

> The right to a useful and remunerative job ...

The right to earn enough to provide adequate food and clothing and recreation ...

The right of every family to a decent home;

The right to adequate medical care and the opportunity to achieve and enjoy good health;

The right to adequate protection from the economic fears of old age, sickness, accident, and unemployment.

The right to a good education.

I ask Congress to explore the means for implementing this economic bill of rights—for it is definitely the responsibility of Congress to do so.

Although Roosevelt's New Deal was riddled with contradictions, especially in terms of the enormous concessions to white Southern racists, any serious look at this second bill of rights reveals how far the right wing, with the collusion of centrist Democrats, has taken us from our promise as a nation where all are created equal. While the United States, at least up until the 1960s and 1970s, was moving inexorably toward a more democratic and socially equal society, the movement since that time has been in precisely the opposite direction. FDR's economic bill of rights also reveals how social values now seen as typical expressions of European values narrowly missed becoming part of equally American values. The proposal for a second bill of social rights came, after all, not from an American "leftist" but from one of the most massively popular of all American presidents.

The goal of the far right, going back to the Republican Party platform in 1936, has been to dismantle all the "entitlements" that emerged directly or indirectly from the New Deal. But because these entitlements, for example, Social Security, have all become extremely popular ever since the people began to benefit from them, the right has to try to disguise their demolition job as "reform." Hurricane Katrina brought all these issues again to the fore, provoking calls for a "new New Deal." (The old New Deal, we recall, began with projects aimed at controlling floodwater.) But those who knew FDR know that George W. Bush is no FDR; rather, he is the antithesis, a man whose main goal is to do away with all the vestiges of the quasi welfare state set in place by the New Deal. The destruction and poverty left in the wake of Katrina are witness to what we have lost in the process.

Despite a history of political repression of the left in the United States—as exemplified in the antisocialist Palmer Raids in the 1920s, the anticommunist McCarthyism in the 1940s and 1950s, and the FBI campaigns against Martin Luther King, Malcolm X, the Black Panthers, and the American Indian Movement in the 1960s—certain aspects of American life are still deeply marked by a strong democratic ethos and feeling. That democratic and egalitarian sensibility is reflected in everyday mores, a feeling that everyone has a right to human dignity and a right to speak his or her mind, even if that right is more and more in danger in the post-9/11 era. American popular culture, from the Hollywood musical to Jerry Springer, is in the main hostile to patrician elites. Populist Hollywood musicals, for example, almost always side with the "low" culture of vaudeville or jazz against the "high" Europhile culture of opera and ballet. (French society, one might argue, is marked by a converse paradox, in that constant official homage to egalitarian principles of *liberté, égalité, fraternité* go hand in hand with an unabashedly elitist high culture.)

American mass-mediated culture is currently politically divided.[3] On one hand we find pockets of critical thought: Bill Moyers and *Frontline* and, on cable TV, critical and satirical shows such as Keith Olbermann's the *Countdown*, the *Daily Show*, the *Colbert Report*, and Bill Maher's *Real Time*, and on the radio, NPR and Air America. On the other hand we find the hate-spewing and administration-adoring FOX channel and social Darwinist reality shows, updated Robinson Crusoe stories where everyone wants to be "king of the island." Instead of FDR's "half a loaf," we get corporate trickle down, the contemporary version of "let them eat cake." The shark culture of devouring the weak becomes the ethos of the day.

The Protestant Ethic/Ethnic?

Many commentators have traced both positive and negative aspects of American society to a strong Protestant element within the dominant culture—which brings us back again to the issue of exceptionalism and what American and non-American analysts have done with this theme. In his classic work *The Protestant Ethic and the Spirit of Capitalism* (1920), sociologist Max Weber cited the writings of Benjamin Franklin as an example of the moralistic individualism typical of Protestant-style capitalism. The fact that most of the Protestant sects were congregational and egalitarian and not hierarchical, it was argued, fostered egalitarian, antielitist, individualistic, and populist values. The U.S. social formation favored voluntary associations rather than a national state religion. In a Weberian perspective, the Protestant emphasis on reading the Bible and on the "priesthood of every believer"—as opposed to a hierarchical state religion where truth is handed down a hierarchical ladder—also fostered attitudes very favorable to education. One of the results of these attitudes, to extrapolate from Weber, is a paradoxical nation, founded by intellectuals but often antiintellectual, and antielitist yet always passionately dedicated to education.

For Weber, the Protestant domination of the United States inspired values of honesty, hostility to corruption, and hard work. But if this account were partially accurate at some earlier point in history—itself a highly debatable point—the argument about "lack of corruption" certainly no longer applies. Although the United States is relatively free of the petty "palm-greasing" style of corruption common in Brazil, for example, it is now replete with corruption at the highest levels and on a very grand scale. Any serious look at the savings and loan scandals of the 1980s—in which George W. Bush's brother Neil played a key role—or at the Enron scandal, or the war profiteering by Halliburton, or at the K Street Project, or the careers of indictable politicians such as Tom DeLay or lobbyists such as Jack Abramoff casts doubt on any such narrative of financial and political innocence. The Bush administration, where virtually everything is based on cronyism and political favors and revolving-door links to military contracts, is a veritable cesspool of corruption, as is evidenced in the various waves of indictments and inquiries. Paul Wolfowitz, architect of the war in Iraq and head of the World Bank, is currently campaigning against corruption in the "developing world." Perhaps he should refocus his attention on the developed corruption scandals closer to home.

Speaking more generally, it is questionable if the "work ethic" now dominates American culture. Can such a complex and multiethnic society be reduced to a single ethic, not to mention a single "ethnic"? Although it is true that Americans are overworked, that probably has to do with the lack of a solid welfare system, which makes people work harder, not necessarily out of conviction but out of a kind of panicked fear of financial collapse. And these trends have more to do with neoliberalism and globalization and the insecurity they engender than with any ingrained cultural tendencies. More and more people are working more and more hours for less and less money. At the same time, hypercapitalist consumer societies such as the United States are inevitably ambivalent about the work ethic. First, the "get rich quick" ethos stresses easy wealth rather than work per se. Second, there is a tension between the "getting"—which involves work—and the "spending"—which involves pleasure.[4] While consumer societies stimulate the work ethic by increasing the desire to earn the money with which to buy consumer products, they also corrode that same work ethic with seductive commercials that stress leisure and consumption and the instant satisfactions available to the self-entertaining monad.[5]

Although the United States is religiously diverse, many commentators, whether pro-American or anti-American, still see the country as fundamentally Protestant, whether they see that trait as a blessing or as a curse. "Clash of civilizations" advocate Samuel Huntington, in his diatribe against Latinos and the Latinization of the United States—symptomatically titled *Who Are We?*—stresses the glories of "Anglo-Protestant" America.[6] Much as his earlier book *The Clash of Civilizations and the Remaking of World Order* was premised on irreconcilable differences between hermetically sealed off cultures internationally, so the later book is premised on the allegedly unbridgeable domestic gap between so-called normal Anglo-Americans and Latinos.[7] If the first book was partially set along an East–West axis, the later book is set along a North–South axis. At a 2004 conference at the Juan Carlos Center at New York University, in front of an audience largely composed of Latinos, Huntington defended his anti-Latino thesis. At one point Huntington suggested that the United States was "in danger" of becoming a bilingual country, prodding sarcastic audience applause, **not** for the wisdom of that idea but rather for what the audience saw as the positive prospect of a bilingual country.[8]

French and Brazilian commentators on the United States often assume a Protestant cultural dominance, an assumption that is partially valid but that also requires qualification. Although some Brazilian commentators, following Weber, see Protestantism and the work ethic as an overall positive, the key to U.S. "success" vis-à-vis Brazilian "failure," others see it as a negative source of puritanism, racism, and segregation. In fact both views have their grains of truth and of falsity. The point is that many comparative analyses flatten out the religious diversity that typifies all three countries. While the United States is usually seen as a Protestant country and France and Brazil are seen as Catholic countries, Protestantism forms a significant presence in both France and Brazil, and Catholicism is a significant presence in the United States. French Protestants, from the Huguenots to socialist president Lionel Jospin, have been extremely influential in French life. In Brazil, meanwhile, the Protestant presence goes back to eighteenth-century French Huguenots, and today evangelical Protestantism is spreading all around Brazil. The United States, meanwhile, becomes more and more Catholic because of immigration from Latin America, with "Latinos" now forming the nation's largest minority. Thus we see a pattern of religious convergence between the United States and Brazil. Overly schematic contrasts between the countries also elide the presence in all three countries of practitioners of religions other than the three "religions of the book" (Judaism, Christianity, Islam); that is, practitioners of Buddhism, Hinduism, Shintoism, Zoroastroism, Vodun, Candomblé, and so forth. (The 2004 ban in France on religious insignia, interestingly, totally bypassed the insignia of those other religions.)

If tensions in France revolve around the relation between Islam and the larger society, in Brazil some of the (minor) tensions revolve around the relation between Protestant evangelicals and Pentecostalists on one hand and the African-derived religions on the other, with the hostility largely coming from the Pentecostalist side. (The Catholic Church more or less gave up its struggle against African-derived religions in the 1960s.) African spirit religions, for their part, are not exclusivist and allow its adherents to simultaneously practice other religions. What is most striking in Brazil is the quotidian normality of the presence of African religions. References to Candomblé are common in everyday conversation, newsstands are full of magazines devoted to the *orixas* (saints), and millions of people practice the religions in every region of Brazil. Nor are such religions the exclusive province of the poor, the oppressed, and the "primitive"; in Brazil one easily encounters people who are simultaneously computer nerds and candomblé practitioners. It is misleading and simplistic, then, to call Brazil simply a "Catholic country," a point evidenced by Eduardo Coutinho's remarkable documentary *Santo Forte,* where virtually all the lower-class interviewees begin by declaring themselves Catholic but end up by revealing their deep immersion in Afro-Brazilian spiritist religions.

While African Americans largely adopted the formal robes of Christian religion—even if read in a critical, subversive manner and expressed in a transcoded African spiritualism—Afro-Brazilians managed to maintain clearly African and Africanized religions. Religious practice is also Africanized in the United States but in a different way. In isolated pockets going back to Spanish or Catholic colonization—New Orleans, South Carolina, the Gullah Islands—African roots were maintained. The black Protestant churches, meanwhile, favored the practice of a gospel trance called "getting the spirit" but without direct reference to the African *orixas.* While the dominant white mythology imagined the United States as a "New Israel" and Europe as Babylon, or the Egypt of the Pharaohs, African Americans saw the land of slavery in the Americas as biblical Babylon and the free territories to the north, or Africa, as the "promised land." Other black groups, such as the Black Muslims, meanwhile, rejected Christianity in favor of Islam, a phenomenon with few equivalents in Brazil, even though many of Brazil's enslaved (and the leaders of slave rebellions, such as those led by the Hausa) were Muslim.

The Biblical moralism bequeathed by the Puritans to some Americans has historically cut at least two ways, favoring self-righteousness and "God is on our side" wars on one hand and progressive reform and antiwar movements on the other. U.S. foreign policy, actually motivated by the realpolitik of economic interests, has often been wrapped in a Manichaean language of good and evil or in a missionary language of spreading the democratic gospel. Yet a concern with individual conscience and personal responsibility has also led to antiauthoritarianism and progressive civil disobedience, as Protestant activism "again and again spawned movements for social change and social reform."⁹ Every one of the innumerable American wars, usually couched by their advocates in an idealistic language, has generated powerful protest movements, equally couched in idealistic language. Religion in America is thus politically ambivalent. The right and the left, as occurs with all faiths, fight it out within the sphere of religion.

Recently a new mutant strain of fundamentalist pseudo-Christianity tries to persuade Americans—here we exaggerate but slightly—to hate rather than to love one's neighbor, to curse rather than to bless the peacemakers, to "sucker" rather than to succor the needy, to covet our neighbor's oil, and to "do others" before they even think of "doing" us. The Good Samaritan has been replaced by Scrooge. Their version of "Jesus Loves the Little Children" would not be "red and yellow, black and white," but "white and rich, and rich and white/They are precious in his sight." Thanks to this crypto-fascist strain, we now encounter an upside-down world where those who blather the most about Christianity are the least charitable, where those who prattle about "moral values" are the most immoral, where those who speak of "freedom" subvert civil liberties, where those who wax sanctimonious about "family values" actually undermine families, where those who denounce "moral relativism" engender fake news and disinformation, where those who preach "responsibility" to the poor refuse to take any responsibility for the consequences of their own actions, and where those who speak of the "culture of life" show depraved indifference to the human life of actually existing human beings, for example in Iraq. Right-wing pseudo-Christians now live in a world haunted by demons, where secular humanists are in league with latte liberals in league with Muslim terrorists in league with activist judges in league with tree-huggers and abortion-loving feminists in league with—you guessed it—the devil. "Christian Zionists," meanwhile, are engaged in a mutually exploitative *folie a deux* with the pro-Israeli right. Ready to fight to the last Jew, they see Israel as their proxy in the fight against the Muslim infidel. Gleeful spectators of the carnage in the Middle East, they read it as a sign that the rapture is near. They especially relish the prospect of the premiere of their long-awaited Biblical spectacular coming to a theatre near you—*Armageddon*!

One particularly noxious example of these tendencies is televangelist Pat Robertson, less a "man of God" than a man who thinks he's God or who at least thinks he has God's cellphone number. Confounding theology with meteorology, Robertson blasphemously claims the God-like power of steering hurricanes away from the faithful and suggests that America's high abortion rate might have provoked not only the 9/11 attacks but also Hurricane Katrina. More Zionist than Ariel Sharon, Robertson called Sharon's stroke a form of divine retribution for Sharon's "dividing God's land" and giving back Gaza to the Palestinians. (For some reason Robertson's God usually only punishes people; he rarely blesses or helps them.) Yet this greedy fanatic, who speaks of nuking the State Department, is treated by "The Situation Room" as a perfectly reasonable commentator on, for example, Israel–Lebanon relations. Bill O'Reilly, meanwhile, thunders on about the "war against Christmas," but if Jesus were to appear on *The Factor*—and we are admittedly being speculative here—O'Reilly would probably call him a traitor and kick him off the set. This new strain of Christianity accepts the almighty market as its personal savior. Rather than chase the money changers from the temple, the televangelists *are* the money changers in the temple: "just send those checks to …"

Misreading American Religion

The inordinate power of the religious right on the American political scene has led some commentators on the left to trace current U.S. imperial actions and regressive social policies to the country's puritanical origins. In a strange way their analysis coincides with that of the Christian right itself, although from an opposite political perspective, in that both the Christian right and such left critics see the United States as essentially Christian, and specifically Protestant and fundamentalist. The difference lies in the evaluation.

An essay published in the Egyptian paper *Al-Ahram Weekly* by Samir Amin, a political economist whose work we generally appreciate, exemplifies a religiously based misreading of U.S. history. Amin rightfully criticizes present-day U.S. foreign policy, but he goes on to suggest hardwired cultural reasons for the imperial turn. More specifically he blames U.S. neoimperialism on the country's origins in a particular form of Protestantism, tracing a direct line from the "New Israel" of the Puritans to the latest war in Iraq. On one level there is a grain of truth in this argument. This historical line does indeed exist, and it does indeed lead from the Salem witch trials to John Ashcroft and the PATRIOT Act. Indeed we ourselves trace a similar line in our book *Unthinking Eurocentrism*. Nor would we deny the religious and messianic character of George W. Bush's worldview or that a high proportion of Americans describe themselves as deeply religious. And we too are aware of the extremely dangerous alliance that currently links Bush, as a "born-again" president, to two retrograde political forces—the absolutely loony Christian far right and the anti-Palestinian pro-Israeli right; the axis, that is, of the "neocons" and the "theocons." While the neocons, such as David Frum and Richard Perle, call for military strikes to prevent a new holocaust, some of the theocons exult in the prospect of what is for them a devoutly desired Armageddon. This unholy alliance has penetrated the highest ranks of the government and wields a frighteningly powerful influence on foreign policy. Furthermore, a movement that David Neiwert calls "Christo-fascist" and that calls itself "Christian Reconstructionism" or "Dominion Theology" uses the Christian equivalent of madrassas to support a kind of neocrusade in favor of what can only be called a "theocratic" project.[10]

If that is true, then, what is our objection to what Amin is saying? The problem is that Amin ignores the extent to which the hyperreligiosity of Bush and company constitutes a break not only with the mainstream of American history but also with the mainstream of American religion. The lineage to which Amin points is only one line among many within the tangled and contradictory web that is U.S. religious culture. Already in the time of Puritan New England, some Protestants or agnostics argued against the Puritan position. In 1636 Thomas Morton, an anti-Puritan New Englander who collaborated and danced with the Indians, wrote the symptomatically titled *The New Canaan* (1636) precisely as an alternative to the idea of the New Israel. Nor can the origins of the country be traced exclusively to the Puritans; these "origins" are infinitely more complex than Amin—and the U.S. right—imagine them to be. Prior to the American Revolution, Puritan New England—which also happened to be one of the most progressive regions in its opposition to slavery—was not the only center of American culture. It had to compete with cosmopolitan, commercial, religiously tolerant New York, which began as a Dutch colony called New Amsterdam; with deistic, French-influenced Washington and Philadelphia; and with Catholic slaveholding states such as Virginia and South Carolina, states similar in culture to the French or Portuguese slaveholding territories or countries in the Americas, not to mention the not-yet-incorporated Latinized (Spanish and French) New Orleans and Louisiana.

The notion of a fundamentally Puritan America—which Amin takes as gospel—is partially the product of a dominant historiography written by New Englanders, whose take on history was strengthened by the North's victory in the Civil War. New Englanders exalted their own past and ignored all alternative narratives that might privilege other centers of influence, such as multicultural New Amsterdam or Africanized New Orleans. The early struggle, within the dominant group in the North at least, was between the Puritans on one hand and the secular Founding Fathers, deists such as Thomas Jefferson and Benjamin Franklin, on the other; that is, those politician intellectuals who were anticlerical and often antireligious very much in the manner of the French Enlightenment figures with whom they conversed and corresponded.

Amin's critique of a supposedly Protestant form of imperialism forgets that the first abolitionists were the Quakers, whose call for the abolition of slavery came during the American Revolution. It forgets that (presumably Protestant) nineteenth-century British abolitionists were far in advance of French abolitionists. Some Protestant churches, and especially black Protestant churches, moreover, have often played a very progressive role in U.S. history in opposing slavery and even imperialism. (George Washington Williams, a black minister, wrote the first full exposé of King Leopold's reign of colonial terror in the Belgian Congo.)

But the political history even of white Protestant fundamentalists is more complicated than might at first appear. Just a century ago, as historian Thomas Frank points out, the same evangelical Protestants who now form part of the religious right then formed part of the populist left. The populist William Jennings Bryan was a leftist socialist and a fundamentalist Christian, a combination quite improbable today.[11] And in the 1960s, university chaplains such as William Sloan Coffin were among the key organizers of antiwar protestors, often offering sanctuary to those fleeing the military draft, while the radical priests the Berrigan Brothers dramatized their opposition to the Vietnam War by spilling blood over Pentagon documents.

The current regressive policies of the United States are not an automatic result of some reactionary Protestant cultural "essence" of the United States. Rather they are the result of historical processes, of systemic defeats and political losses, where a resurgent and ruthless right wing has commandeered the American media (and Congress) and outmaneuvered a reactive left, in a situation where the United States exerts vast power in the world. The United States cannot be seen as having always been moving inexorably toward a predetermined religious goal. In fact, there have never been any national religious parties in the United States. The religious takeover by the religious right dates back not to 1776 but to the 1970s, at a point when the right was frightened by the spread in the media, the academe, and the country in general of what they saw as the "contagion" of leftism, antiauthoritarianism, antimilitarism, third worldism, and the countercultural anti-puritanism of sex, drugs, and rock and roll. The "culture wars" began as an attempt by the right to reverse those trends. The point is that although there are clearly discernable patterns within American history, the country cannot be reduced to one religion or tendency. American history is the product of various right and left turns, historical zigzags, and various steps forward and many steps backward.

The American Revolution, in this sense, already combined forward steps such as the Bill of Rights with backward steps such as the compromises over slavery. The Civil War constituted a forward step in preserving the Union, but it was followed by the backward step of Jim Crow segregation. In the 1960s the forward steps of the Great Society and the War on Poverty, which were clearly moving the United States toward a more solid welfare state and a more racially democratic nation, were undermined by the backward step into the morass of Vietnam. The present administration, and this is perhaps unprecedented, has brought us nothing but backward steps: war, polarization, deficits, inequality, and religious and racial bigotry.

That so many religious people in the United States now seem allied with the right, in this same sense, was not an inevitable working out of a predetermined telos but the product of shrewd and well-financed right-wing strategies worked out over decades. The power of the religious right really begins with the Moral Majority in the 1970s. Just a few years ago, as leftist writer Esther Kaplan points out, Paul Weyrich, one of the key figures in founding the Moral Majority, was despondent about the movement ever becoming truly popular. "I do not believe," he wrote in 1999, "that a majority of Americans actually shares our values."[12] While most white evangelical Christians favored the Iraq War, most Protestant denominations did not. Nor do most Protestant denominations favor neocon hyperimperialism. Bush's own denomination of the Methodist Church condemned his war in Iraq. U.S. religious figures, representing many different faiths, condemned the prisoner abuse at Abu Ghraib prison. In a thirty-second announcement broadcast on Arabic TV, networks Al Jazeera and Al Arabiya called the abuses "sinful and systematic" and expressed "solidarity with all those in Iraq and everywhere who demand justice and human dignity" (*New York Times,* June 11, 2004, A12). Progressive Protestant (and Jewish and Muslim) religious leaders have been frequent speakers at antiwar demonstrations, and Christian leaders published a full-page ad in the *New York Times,* directly addressed to George W. Bush, that read, "You say He changed your heart, now let Him change your mind [i.e., about attacking Iraq]." An ecumenical array of U.S. religious leaders condemned the torture and abuses in American-ruled Iraqi prisons. George W. Bush was met by protests at the religiously inclined Calvin College, where sarcastic protest signs read, "Who would Jesus bomb?" And in 2005 the National Council of Churches, representing some forty-five million mainline Protestants, launched "Faithful America," an attempt to engage progressive Christians, Jews, Muslims, and Hindus in e-mail activism for progressive causes.

Indeed the extremism of the Bible-thumping right has provoked a strong backlash even among some evangelicals. Jim Wallis, the leader of an evangelical group called Sojourners, argues, from within the evangelical camp, for an environment-friendly, antiwar, prounion, antiracist, anti-imperialist, antineoliberal, pro-human-rights version of Christianity. Wallis points out that the Bible mentions poverty thousands of time but mentions homosexuality only rarely. Like many religious people, Wallis scores Bush's inadequacies as a biblical exegete: "To continue to confuse the roles of God and the church with those of the American nation, as George W. Bush seems to do repeatedly, is a serious theological error that some might say borders on idolatry or blasphemy."[13] When politicians "play God" by trying to reshape the world in their own image, we add, what we get is a "god-awful" mess.

Both the neocons and the theocons are militaristic and antidemocratic, and their current alliance is extremely, even apocalyptically, threatening; it is a dagger aimed at the heart not only of American democracy but also of world peace. But that does not mean we should do "bad history." Amin's claim that American imperialism will be worse than the others has the corollary effect of rewriting European history as somehow innocent and nonimperialist. To our mind, the various imperialisms have family resemblances; the differences are of degree, not of kind. American imperialism, if it is more brutal—and that is a questionable point—is so only because it has more power available to exercise brutality. Anti-Americanism, Amin's essay shows, can lead even progressive thinkers on the "periphery," to use Amin's own term, into cleansing European history of its blemishes.

Praising the Catholic Church for its "universality," for example, Amin predicts that U.S. imperialism will "be even more brutal than its predecessors, most of whom never claimed to have been invested with a divine mission." Such a claim is astonishing in its historical blindness. Americans did not initiate the concept of a "divine mission." The religiously sanctioned genocide of native peoples in Spanish America, after all, was committed explicitly as part of a "divine mission." After all did Columbus rename the first Caribbean island he encountered "San Salvador" (Holy Savior) simply because he liked the sound of the words? Did Columbus not praise the Inquisition and present his voyages to Ferdinand and Isabella as an occasion to convert and enslave natives? Did not the *requiremento* that the Conquistadores read in Spanish to uncomprehending natives demand that they submit to Spanish rule, convert to Christianity, and give up their lands, and did it not stipulate that if they did not do so they would be destroyed and that all the destruction would be their own fault? (George W. Bush echoes this peremptory tone and language in his various ultimatums.) That was a "divine mission," with a (literal) vengeance, in comparison with which present-day U.S. interventions seem like marvels of secularism.

The concept of a "divine mission," in any case, goes even further back, to a period before Protestantism even existed. It was with the Crusades that Christendom defined the Muslim "infidel" as the universal enemy, as evil incarnate, the personification of the Antichrist. The popes called for their extermination, because killing infidels was not homicide but "malicide," a carrying out of God's will and a worthy homage to Christ's glory.[14]

Although we concur with Amin's general critique of the American social system and of foreign policy, and although we share Amin's fears about the religious right, we do not agree with the culturalist explanations of that policy or with his generalizations about the role of religion in the United States. The methodological problem begins with the title of his article—"The American Ideology"—where the "the" implies that there is only one American ideology, where the "American" implies that the ideology he describes is a universally shared national one, and where the "ideology," in the singular, implies that discourses can be univocal, monolithic, and all pervasive. Amin's binaristic method turns him into an upside-down version of what he opposes. Thus his discourse comes to mimic the Manichaeism of the same George W. Bush that Amin denounces as a contemporary Hitler. The paradox is that Amin, in his anti-Bush rhetoric, develops arguments that Bush and the religious right could also endorse—for example, that capitalism is the only legitimate American ideology and that the religious right represents the quintessence of America—even if he develops those arguments within an opposite intention.[15]

Methodologically the "American Ideology" essay slides between Marxist materialist and culturalist arguments; that is, between an analysis of material interests and an analysis of a supposed national core or American spirit. The essay presents one of those cases where we agree with the thrust of the critique made both of U.S. foreign policy and of the U.S. social and political system yet where we reject the uninformed historiography that marks the critique. Even if the United States is currently the worst behaved of the dominant nation-states, its bad behavior forms part of the five-hundred-year tradition of the bad behavior of European empires and colonial settler states in general. Even U.S. hyperimperialism must still be seen as part of a more general history of colonialism, slavery, and imperialism in which all of Europe took part. The white European and Euro-American powers—the Spanish, Portuguese, British, Dutch, French, Germans, Euro-Americans, and Euro-Brazilians—all behaved atrociously toward non-European peoples, often covering their atrocities with religious justifications. (Amin himself, ironically, is one of the thinkers who called attention to that general history.)

Even the present-day "well-behaved" social Europe of the postcolonialist era is still implicated in racism, neocolonialism, and top-down globalization. Just because Europe, shorn of its empires, is now comporting itself in a relatively civilized manner, one that the United States would do well to emulate, does not mean we should overlook the connections between the various forms of colonialism and slavery, between North American and European versions of the Enlightenment and the colonial project, or between a shared U.S. and European complicity in the global North's domination of the South. To make the United States bear the entire burden is an act of exorcism and historical amnesia.

Anglo-Saxons: The Sequel

As the foregoing discussion suggests, nation-states are usually "mixed bags," neither completely innocent nor completely guilty, although some, at specific points in history, might be guiltier than others. While we endorse certain critiques, such as Amin's, of U.S. foreign policy and the social and political system, and of neoliberalism and globalization, we reject the homogenizing drift of the argument. Here we will look at two other examples of this genre of writing, where utterly legitimate points about U.S. policy mingle with misfired generalities about American history and culture.

Our first example of this mélange of legitimate critique and aberrant nonsense comes from French writer Emmanuel Todd's *Après L'empire* (After Empire). Todd makes valid points about current American foreign policy, which he rightly sees as fomenting disorder and injustice throughout the world. "Everything occurs," Todd writes, "as if the U.S. were seeking, for obscure reasons, to maintain a certain level of international tension, a situation of limited but endemic war." But why would an educated and prosperous country, he asks, support perpetual war?

For Todd, the power elite in the United States is haunted by the prospect of its own irrelevance, and Bush's strident bullying actually betokens the end of the American empire and the end of American democracy: "At a time when the world discovers democracy and learns to get along without America, America itself begins to lose its democratic characteristics." The result is what Todd calls "theatrical militarism," designed not to solve problems but to keep them alive, as a demonstration of the need for the "indispensable power." The world's only superpower attacks a series of "micropowers" such as Iraq while developing a swollen military budget that makes it impossible for any country to challenge or even follow the self-appointed leader.

U.S. citizens, and the U.S. foreign policy establishment, have much to learn from French critics such as Todd. In an inversion of national stereotypes contrasting philosophically verbose French impracticality with American can-do pragmatism, in the case of the Iraq War it was the American neocons who indulged in high-flying fantasies of "cakewalk" triumphs and magical "domino" transformations of the political landscape of the Middle East. This cabal believed—or perhaps pretended to believe—in a fata morgana, a mirage. The same people who ridiculed Muslims for believing that suicide bombers would be greeted in paradise with sweets and virgins believed that their war would be greeted with pastries and flowers. The French, meanwhile, were more pragmatic, hardheaded, and prescient about the inevitable difficulties. Whatever their motives, the French did warn us against an unnecessary war, and all the neocon propaganda about the disloyal and cowardly French was in the end just so much hot air.

But French critics such as Todd also get it wrong. First, Todd seriously underestimates the dangers posed by the hawks. For him the United States is economically dependent on the rest of the world and is now simply managing its own declining relevance. But this might be whistling in the dark. While the United States is now undeniably in economic decline relative to other centers of economic power, the corporate–military elite might still try to dominate the world through exclusively military means, and the more delirious of the hawks, to wax speculative for a moment, might want to go out in a blaze of nuclear glory reminiscent of the violent "last stands" of the American western or of the missile-riding cowboy pilot in *Doctor Strangelove*.

But all that is in the realm of speculation. Todd goes more obviously wrong when he appeals to anthropology to explain American imperialism. Academically trained as an anthropological demographer, Todd speaks of an "initial anthropological code" that predetermines American politics. Sounding a bit like a nineteenth-century ethnologist dissecting a "primitive" tribe mired in archaic traditions, Todd writes,

> The Anglo-Saxon uncertainty about the status of the other is not a fact of modernity; it comes on the contrary probably from a certain anthropological primitiveness, from the appurtenance of the English to a historical-cultural stratum which was peripheral to the Old World, little or badly integrated into the successive empires of that world, and hardly mastering the principles of equality.

This account is disfigured by serious historical inaccuracies. England, with its Magna Carta and political philosophers, was often at the forefront of forging "the principles of equality," at least in terms of its own people. And Great Britain, moreover, was certainly an integral part of the "empire of the world." Todd's book is marred, furthermore, by a quasi-biological form of thinking. Calling attention to Todd's other books, historian Tony Judt points out in an essay that *After Empire* continues Todd's ongoing obsession with fertility, regime collapse, and genetic codes.[16] Telltale expressions—"cultural a priori," "familial structures," "the American mental system," and the "Anglo-Saxon mentality"—point to Todd's culturally essentializing schema.

As we suggested earlier, the United States cannot even be seen as fundamentally Anglo-Saxon. Even on a purely empirical demographic level, census reports show that English-descended Americans are a tiny minority of Americans. At this point there are more African-descended Americans than strictly English-descended Americans. In sum Todd sees international power struggles through the grid of ethnic typologies, a brand of thinking that constitutes a very retrograde form of stereotypical generalization. If it is the Anglo-Saxon mentality that explains the retrograde nature of the U.S. social system, Todd would also have to explain why even more thoroughly "Anglo" or Northern European or Euro-descended places such as Canada, Holland, Australia, New Zealand, and Scandinavia generally have not become so anti-statist and anti–welfare state as the Americans. (Even Great Britain and Germany—original home of the Saxons—have national health care.) How did they manage to transcend their hardwired genetic codes? In sum religious attitudes did not decree that the United States would have a weak welfare state. Thus Todd bumps up against the limits of ethnic, religious, and cultural explanations for social systems. Critics such as Todd assume that culture is permanent and fixed and determines sociopolitical structures. Without denying a cultural dimension within nationalism, we cannot ethicize and essentialize what are really, in the end, largely conjectural correlations shaped by historical struggles.

Alongside its valid insights Todd's book is marred by frequent lapses into cultural stereotypes. Todd repeatedly calls American women "castrating" and "menacing," as if he had personally researched the intimate lives and gender relations of all Americans. The charge clearly tells us more about Todd's anxieties than about a very diverse group of 150 million American women. Perhaps we should "reassure" Todd that the United States remains a sexist country, that millions of American women are still discriminated against, still underpaid, and still harassed and raped, including in elite military institutions; in short, that women are as disempowered in the United States as in much of the world. Lorena Bobbitt–style genital mutilation of men by women, he can be assured, remains a very rare occurrence. In sum Todd should not project his petty concerns about the fate of his own penis over a vast continent.

In a fascinating turn Todd scapegoats America for the phenomenon of scapegoating. He takes a broad human tendency—scapegoating—and restricts its reach to one nation—the United States. In a different, anthropological context, the French literary theorist Rene Girard takes the opposite approach in his work, seeing scapegoating and ritual sacrifice as cultural universals, characteristic of humanity as a whole. For Girard ritual sacrifice is at the very kernel of all religions—from Abraham and Isaac to Yoruba sacrifices, from Tupi cannibalism to the Christian Eucharist—and thus, indirectly, of all cultures. Yet Todd argues that the United States alone needs an "other" to scapegoat.

There is of course a grain of truth in the idea that scapegoating characterizes the dominant U.S. political system; indeed, we ourselves will elaborate on that point later. Yet cultures cannot be reduced to scapegoating, and scapegoating is in no way an American monopoly. To the extent that it exists, the United States simply "refined" the scapegoating that it inherited from Europe. Countless European analysts have signaled a historical tendency within Europe itself to scapegoat internal others (Jews, gypsies, heretics, and so on) and external others (the "infidel," Muslims, indigenous "savages"). In *La Peur en Occident* (Fear in the Occident), French historian Jean Delumeau speaks of Europe's obsessive fears concerning Jews, infidels, women, witches, cannibals, and so forth.[17] By suggesting that the United States is exceptional in its tendency to scapegoat, Todd forgets the European history of crusades against the infidels and the history of French anti-Semitism. Even today many on the French LePenist right (and sometimes the center left) scapegoat immigrants and minorities. In sum Todd himself has scapegoated the United States for a tendency shared by most cultures, including European cultures. The question, then, is not which nations scapegoat but rather how scapegoating functions within particular nation-states.

For critics such as Todd, "America" becomes a projective repository for everything Europe wants to forget about Europe's own history. Could it be that some European critiques constitute a displacement of what Europe has repressed—that is, its role in the colonial process? It is symptomatic that Todd appeals not to French imperial antecedents for American imperialism—that might have proved less flattering to national pride—but rather to classical Greek and Roman antecedents. Todd's method assumes a world where nations are static and homogeneous, unified entities dominated by a single "mental system." But in our view, nation-states and their peoples are not reducible to homoeostatic codes or systems; they are, rather, the site of endless contestation between rival forces and discourses. Culturalist analyses such as Todd's and Amin's, in their assumption of a single code or explanatory principle, miss the mutating complexities of social, cultural, and religious dynamics within and between cultures.

Les Mains Salles, or Dirty Hands

Everybody with half a brain knows about America's imperial interventions, except apparently quite a few Americans. In 1854 Henry J.

Raymond, founding editor of the *New York Times,* warned that "we are the most ambitious people the world has ever seen—and I greatly fear we shall sacrifice our liberties to our imperial dream."[18] As historian Thomas Bender points out in *A Nation among Nations,* Americans are often anxious to deny the relevance of empire to their history, usually relying on a largely imaginary contrast with Europe, yet the United States forms part of the larger history of white Western imperial domination of a richly "colored" planet. The turn-of-the-century "imperial binge" that took Cuba and the Philippines, in this sense, was not an exception to the rule of American history but a continuation of its Western expansion.[19] Already by the mid-nineteenth century, the United States had incorporated half of Mexico into its territory and "sent warships a staggering 5,980 times between 1869 and 1897 to protect American commercial interests and, increasingly, to flex its muscles in Europe."[20] And since that time, the direct or indirect interventions—unlinked to any officially declared war—only multiplied, encompassing countries such as Guatemala, Iran, Brazil, the Dominican Republic, Korea, Vietnam, Iraq, and so forth. For chauvinistic pseudo-experts like Ann Coulter, every last one of these interventions is axiomatically good, because the American nation-state, God-like, performed them, and they must therefore be found good.

Although France is currently critical of American imperialism, France does not have clean hands when it comes to imperialism, neocolonialism, and exploitative forms of globalization. In their demonization of the United States as the only imperialist nation, French critics such as Todd indirectly idealize their own country. And in denouncing U.S. capitalism alone, some critics forget that capitalism is the dominant system in the entire world. By nationalizing capitalism, by stigmatizing only its more aggressive U.S. forms, such critics let "normal" capitalism off the hook. Despite France's occasional pretense of speaking for the global South, for example, France's role is in many ways that of a subaltern neoimperialist, in that like the United States, France worsens conditions for the South by subsidizing its own farmers.[21] And France, like the United States, has worked hard to avoid being subjected to the judgments of an international criminal court.[22]

Many patriotic French citizens and intellectuals of all colors have explored these issues both in the past and in the present. Historians, for example, have dissected the contradictions inherent in a "republican empire." Scholars Nicolas Bancel, Pascal Blanchard, and Françoise Verges speak of an oxymoronic "colonial Republic":

> Republic. Colony. Can we even juxtapose those two terms? Can one speak of a Colonial Republic? ... A Republic is the place of expression of the sovereign people. It is inhabited by citizens. A colony is the place of expression of the arbitrary, of force. It is inhabited by subjected peoples.[23]

Yet French "republicans" often lauded embodied exactly this paradox, in that they praise a colonial empire where supposedly republican values would flourish. But these contradictions are not limited to the past. Thus many critics have addressed the neocolonial role of France in Africa as advanced by both the left and the right. François-Xavier Verschave, one of the most eloquent critics of French foreign policy, in his book *Françafrique: le plus long scandale de la République* (FrancAfrica: the Longest Scandal of the Republic), describes what some have called "FrancAfrique" as the dark underside of Franco-African relations. The exposed side is the "front" of *la Francophonie*, which invokes France as the "friend of Africa," the selfless promoters of "development, democracy, and independence." The hidden side, meanwhile, entails massacres, secret wars, electoral fraud, kleptocratic dictators, the debt trap, and the massive plunder of raw materials.

Verschave describes the close links between the French political elite and a long series of African dictators, who regularly call on France to intervene militarily to protect their interests. A whole racist and mercenary subculture becomes complicit with economic exploitation and torture. Yet despite the tensions between the Anglophones and the Francophones, a deep down alliance links the former colonizers and present-day imperializers, both members of what Verschave calls an international "mafiaAfrique." Verschave puns that "FrancAfrique" also means "France a Fric" (France of money).

Official France practices a cynical policy in Africa, which it would never have endorsed within Europe itself. The following are among the practices pointed out by Verschave: the use of laundered funds from Africa to finance major political parties; the corrupt role of the gas company ELF; the role of the French army in rescuing dictators; the French role in massacres in Cameroon; the presence of French mercenaries, linked to earlier wars in Indochina and Algeria, in the Katanga *gendarmerie;* and the massive French collaboration with apartheid South Africa. Both left and right have been implicated in these policies, carried out by the "leftist" François Mitterrand and his son Jean-Christophe, close to the Habyarimana family, and by the "rightist" Jacques Chirac, friend of General Denis Sassou-Nguesso, conqueror of the Congo and its resources. Both Mitterrand and Chirac befriended one of the greatest kleptocrats of all—Marshall Mobuto.[24] Hemmed in by globalization, Africans in the zone of French cooperation are mired in debt and ever more impoverished. Verschave cites a witty definition of development aid, one that applies equally to most of the South countries dominated by the global North: "Development aid consists in taking the money of the poor in the rich countries in order to give it to the rich of the poor countries." And Verschave adds his addendum, "because the rich of the poor countries give it back to the rich of the rich countries, who organize the whole operation."[25]

But what is especially interesting for us here is the interneoimperial rivalry between the French and the Americans (and their British allies), a rivalry that recapitulates early intercolonial and interimperial rivalries going back centuries. France supports Francophonic dictators and their massacres, in the name of defending French interests against the "Anglo-Saxons." Thus France favors certain dictators because they speak French, especially if their enemies speak English. A kind of "Fashoda Syndrome"—reminiscent of nineteenth-century Anglo-French rivalries—results in policies being decided not in the name of justice but rather in terms of always wanting the opposite of what the "Anglo-Saxons" want, whatever the negative consequences in other respects. "Horrible civil wars are triggered, exacerbated, or prolonged, only in order to expand the spaces of 'la Francophonie' to the detriment of the Anglo-Saxons" (p. 87 in Verschave).

Although many outside of France were aware of official French complicity in the Rwanda genocide, in France it has been covered over until recently. (Americans, similarly, are often the last to know about U.S. neoimperial crimes abroad.) Jean Carbonare, who tried in 1993 to warn the French government about the impending disaster in Rwanda, speaks of his shock at seeing "French military instructors at the military camp of Bigogwe ... hauling civilians away in trucks [who were subsequently] tortured and killed, then buried in a common grave."[26] Verschave highlights the narcissistic aspect of the French denial of complicity, rooted in the half-truth of France as "the homeland of the rights of man." The Rwanda genocide destroyed a mythic vision of French Africa. "Who among us, which ordinary citizens," Verschave asks, "tried to know what was happening over there [in Rwanda]? Who has raised their voice against the innumerable economic and political crimes inherent in Franco-African relations?"[27]

Like the United States, France is not an ideological monolith, and many courageous intellectuals such as Verschave have denounced these abuses and hypocrisies. Patrick de Saint-Exupéry, in his *L'inavouable: la France au Rwanda* (The Unconfessable: France in Rwanda), offers an eyewitness account of the Rwanda genocide.[28] The author uses the rhetorical/narrative device of addressing his account directly to "Monsieur le Ministre," Dominique de Villepin, then minister of foreign affairs and the current prime minister, denouncing him as personally implicated in the Rwanda affair: "[Because you went to Kigali in 1992] ... you therefore knew everything, Monsieur le Ministre. Since the beginning. This genocide, is also your story."[29] Saint-Exupéry explains how the French trained the Hutu army of assassins, including even the head of state. Paris ignored all warnings of an impending massacre, meanwhile, even as courageous functionaries such as Michel Cuignet were revealing the likelihood of such a massacre before the French Parliament. On December 6, 1990, the Rwandan newspaper *Kangura* published a racist anti-Tutsi document called the "10 Hutu Commandments." But despite these ominous signs, the French government increased its aid to Kigali, even though it was well-known that the "aid" would be used to construct an apparatus of extermination. Once the genocide began, the "socialist" François Mitterrand, in the summer of 1994, was quoted as uttering the following gem of master-race reasoning: "In those kinds of countries, a genocide is not a big deal." ("Dans ces pays-la; un génocide ce n'est pas grande chose.")[30]

Marie-Monique Robin, another courageous writer and filmmaker, in *Escadrons de la Mort, Ecole Francaise* (Death Squads, the French School)[31] has explored the role of the French secret services, at times in collaboration with the Americans, in exporting techniques of torture and assassination. From Indochina to Algeria and beyond, it was the French who developed the theories (and practices) of the doctrines of counterinsurgency against guerilla and revolutionary war, in a situation where the old battle-line tactics no longer worked. Then Lieutenant-Colonel Roger Trinquier published his book *La Guerre Moderne* (Modern War) in 1961, which later became the bible of all those specialists engaged in the struggle against Third World "subversives," from guerrillas in Vietnam to the IRA in Ireland to rebels in Argentina and Chile. Long before Donald Rumsfeld, these French theorists spoke of "new methods" and "exceptional laws" that would define the enemy so as to exist outside of the usual framework of national law; it is there we find the longtime origins of "enemy combatants."

Our point is not at all to "blame the French" for what the Americans did; indeed, the United States has committed all sorts of atrocities, or supported atrocities by others, during its interventions abroad, perhaps to an even greater extent than the French. In 1994 Joseph Kennedy said that the School of the Americas had trained more dictators than any other in the history of the world. But the United States, according to Robin, first became interested in the French theories of counterinsurgency earlier, during the Vietnam War, and invited Paul Aussaresses, the notorious special agent from the war in Algeria, to be an instructor at Fort Bragg. While official France was condemning the Latin American dictatorships and receiving their political exiles, some French special service agents were supporting those very same dictatorships, for example, in Argentina. The apparent rivalries and ideological differences between the French and the Americans are real, yet in terms of their secret services in certain periods of history, they have acted as colonizing brothers under the skin.

Submerged Narcissisms

We spoke in the opening chapter of "sports fan" histories, which demonize (or angelize) entire countries, citing the American example of *America's Oldest Enemy* and the Spanish example of *The Culture of Evil*. An essay by French writer Denis Duclos—"Délires Paranoïaques et

Culture de la Haine en Amérique" (Paranoid Delirium and the Culture of Hatred in America) published in *Le Monde Diplomatique* (August 2003)—provides a French example of the same tendency. Duclos makes a completely legitimate critique of social violence committed both within the United States and by the U.S. government in the world. But Duclos too makes the same culturalist mistake, tracing American violence to deeply ingrained cultural tendencies manifest since the very beginnings of American history. Throughout the essay the same telltale adjectives— "the intrinsic violence of the U.S.," "the essential violence which comes from the U.S."—become symptomatic of overly schematic thinking. For Duclos violence is inscribed on the very DNA of the American nation. But while true on one level, the same claim could be made about almost all nation-states and certainly about former imperial nation-states such as France.

Duclos reads history backward to find the *germ*—another symptomatically naturalizing, quasi-biologizing word—of later violence in Jefferson's words from the "Bill of Complaints" against Great Britain, for Duclos evidence of "paranoid delirium." Addressed to the British king, the Bill of Complaints was meant to justify the severance of the colonial bonds with England. While perhaps inconsistent or exaggerated, Jefferson's words are not paranoid. Duclos sees in Jefferson's passionate opposition to despotism only one element—an antisocial paranoia. One would never guess from Duclos's text that Jefferson's denunciations of despotism were themselves partially inspired by French Enlightenment thinkers, that Jefferson breathed the same intellectual atmosphere that created the French Revolution, or that Jefferson corresponded about such issues with Lafayette and other French leaders. Indeed Jefferson's enemies, as we have seen, called him a "Frenchman" and a "Jacobin." Nor does Duclos care to recall that it was the French Revolution, and not the American, that almost immediately lapsed into paranoia and tension. The selective analysis encodes, in sum, a surreptitious national narcissism that unlinks the interlinked histories of France and the United States.

The famous expressions associated with Jefferson—"All men are created equal" and "The right to life, liberty, and the pursuit of happiness"—suggest hardly paranoia but rather boundless optimism. Furthermore the founders did not see the alternative to despotism as a struggle of "each against each"; rather they saw society as the antidote to despotism. The republican society envisioned by Jefferson was to be held together by what the philosophes called "natural sociability"; that is, the "natural affection" between people. With both the French philosophes and the U.S. Founding Fathers, this view of natural sociability was partially inspired by the example of the Native American peoples, the Tupinamba in Brazil, and the Iroquois and the Huron in North America, paradigms of social equality and freedom not only for Montaigne and Rousseau but also for Jefferson and Payne. The Founding Fathers envisioned a New World free from the Old World's endless wars and paranoia. The problem with Jeffersonian discourse, then, was not its "paranoid delirium" but rather (1) the hypocrisy that led to the dispossession of native peoples and the enslavement of blacks, (2) a social-philosophical naïveté and optimism shared with many Enlightenment thinkers, and (3) a complicity with a racist element within Enlightenment thinking.

The operation, in Duclos's tirade, is one of tendentious selectivity and the overly clear drawing of lines. Duclos's "us versus them" logic obscures all commonalities, including even the "Frenchness" of the American Revolution. A series of examples—the massacres of the Indians, the enslavement of Africans, Jefferson's "paranoid" hostility to state despotism, the lack of a strong welfare state, the films *Bowling for Columbine* and *Gangs of New York,* and the indifference of U.S. troops as Iraqis looted Baghdad—are mobilized as examples to portray an essentially violent culture. "For three centuries," Duclos sums up, "within every communitarian formation in the U.S., the basic collective unit has been a group whose ferocious opposition to all enemies gives it the character of a band of vassals, led by a '*señor*,' riding toward glory and gathering booty and territories" (emphasis and translation ours). Duclos's choice of a Spanish word (*señor*) to sum up a supposedly American tendency inadvertently undermines his argument. Again, we are not denying the reality of the violence to which Duclos points, only to its exceptionalist positing as typically and uniquely American. Where Duclos sees only violence and vigilante mobs—certainly one element in American history—his compatriot de Tocqueville, like many commentators after him, discerned an American love of "associations," a prototype for what would later be called "civil society."

As critics of many aspects of the dominant American system, we of course recognize a partial truth in all these tendencies—indeed they have been the focus of much of our work—but we also recognize caricatures when we see them. Tendencies are not essences; tendencies are countered by other, even opposite, tendencies. The United States is at one and the same time the violent reality depicted in Michael Moore's *Bowling for Columbine* and the critical spirit that animates Moore's films, along with the enthusiasm of the hundreds of thousands of Americans who have made his books runaway best-sellers and his film *Fahrenheit 9/11* the most watched documentary ever made. During past years American best-seller lists have been crowded with left-wing books, including Moore's, that passionately denounce the domestic and foreign policies of the right. Jan Nederveen Pieterse, an equally harsh critic of American policy but one who writes without a culturalist animus, catches this sense of passionate debate, denouncing the anti-American caricatures that

> ignore the other America of the Civil Rights movement, "1969," social movements from the anti-Vietnam War to the battle of Seattle, and the polls that register majority positions on labor rights, women's rights, the environment, and other issues that are usually far more progressive than those held by media and political elites.[32]

What is missing in the essays by Amin, Todd, and Duclos, then, is a sense of conflict and struggle, the sense that all nations, the United States among them, form sites of perpetual conflict between progressive and regressive forces and modes.[33]

Within a rigged system, Duclos takes the best from one national tradition as evidence of inherently positive qualities and the worst from another as evidence of equally inherent negative defects. Duclos contrasts in a footnote Bush's warmongering with Brazilian president Lula's proposal for a "world campaign against hunger" as examples of two opposed "sensibilities." We certainly prefer Lula's politics to those of Bush, and we prefer a war on hunger to a war on people, and Duclos is right to point up the differences between the two leaders. In representative democracies it seem evident that presidents "represent" their nations. But on another level the comparison is misleading. Since Bush lost the popular vote to Gore by half a million votes (and to Gore and Ralph Nader combined by three and a half million votes) and since the 2000 election was stolen, would it not be possible to argue that Gore typifies the American nation more than Bush does? And just a decade earlier, Brazilians rejected Lula and chose Fernando Collor, a neoliberal who his ally George H.W. Bush called a Brazilian Indiana Jones. Does that mean that the corrupt, neoliberal Collor typified a right-wing and neoliberal Brazilian nation? In sum the comparison is rigged; every situation has to be assessed in terms of the larger trajectories and conjectural shifts of political struggle, not in terms of supposedly eternal characteristics.

Many critical essays about other nations, whether by Francophobic Americans addressing France or anti-American French writers addressing the United States, display a hidden, submerged, inferential provinciality and national narcissism. Thus U.S. journalists who ridicule the French welfare state implicitly idealize brutal dog-eat-dog American-style capitalism. Todd's tirades about "castrating American women," from the other side of the Atlantic, meanwhile, tacitly exalt what he sees as essentially "French" gender and sexual codes, where men are men, women are women, and *vive la différence*. (Todd also ignores the transatlantic intellectual dialogue between French and American feminists.) Duclos's denunciation of the paranoid antistatism of Jefferson "hides," as it were, a preference for the statism of the French Jacobin tradition. Duclos's essay, for example, reminds us of U.S. genocide and slavery. Yet Brazil and France were also implicated in native genocide and slavery. The French enslaved and killed Indians and enslaved Africans; they even did so in parts of North America (e.g., Louisiana) that now form part of the United States.[34]

Brazil, meanwhile, began slavery before the United States and ended it twenty-five years later than the United States. Present-day Brazil has close to the worst distribution of wealth in the entire world, exceeded only by countries such as Haiti and Zimbabwe, and Brazilian society has a much higher homicide rate than the United States. In May 2006 full-scale battles broke out between corrupt police and narcotraffickers in São Paulo, with hundreds of deaths on both sides. Yet for Duclos it is only in the United States that social violence and inequality indicate a basic tendency toward violence and injustice. For Duclos Brazil just "happens" to be violent—and besides it is a victim of U.S. imperialism—

while the United States is always, already, and intrinsically violent. If this is true, of course, U.S.-based progressives might as well commit suicide, since it is pointless to struggle against deeply ingrained tendencies; one cannot quarrel with one's genes. Or might we do better to look for a "genetically modified" form of politics?

Other French writers offer different, more nuanced analyses of U.S. politics and society. Tzvetan Todorov, a Franco-Bulgarian literary theorist and political and philosophical commentator, in his *Le Nouveau Désordre Mondial: Réflexions d'un Européen* (The New World Disorder: Reflections of a European) criticizes the American neofundamentalists who see the United States as an "elected" people blessed with the right to impose its notions of democracy on the world at large. Todorov, like Samir Amin, discerns a Protestant influence on contemporary America, but he does not make a reductive culturalist argument. In a twist on Max Weber, Todorov sees dominant ideology in the United States as a new, imperial version of the old "invisible hand" theory, whereby God guided wealth into the hands of the elect. For the Christian right, God now channels geopolitical power toward the hands of the United States. We add that in this case an old Calvinist tradition joins an upside-down version of left vanguardism—many of the neocons are former Trotkyists—to foment the idea of exporting revolution, in this case a capitalist revolution. Yet Todorov, more comparative and international in his approach, finds a French precedent for Bush-style unilateralism in the imperial vanguardism of Napoleon. The French emperor too, he points out, strove to impose the ideas of the French Revolution—liberty, equality, and fraternity—at the point of the bayonet. In an early version of the neocon "positive domino" theory, Napoleon too commanded "battalions of freedom" marching across Europe.

The Bush administration's goal of declaring war on political evil, for Todorov, is highly questionable because (1) it is unrealizable, (2) it would impose a situation of permanent war (thus reinforcing all the armies of the world), and (3) the resulting suffering is likely to outweigh the intended good results. (For our part, we are more skeptical about the idea that Bush and company really even want to spread democracy, given their dismantling of democracy at home and their inconsistent support for it abroad.) The American neoimperialists believe exactly what the right always accused the communists of believing—that the end justifies the means. Grand claims of installing "democracy" mask more crude national interests. If the United States is not strictly "imperialist," it is manifestly "imperial" in its planting of bases all over the world. But Todorov finds France somewhat hypocritical in its denunciations of the United States. Apart from having been an imperial power, France too has often ignored the will of the world as expressed in UN mandates. It did not ask for UN approval, for example, when it intervened militarily in the Ivory Coast. Todorov also reminds Europe of its dependency on U.S. nuclear protection for its own security; Europe, and especially France, protested American actions but rarely recognized its past dependence on the U.S. "nuclear umbrella."

Yet despite this more complex presentation, Todorov ends the book, unfortunately, with a tired recital of the wonders of what he calls "European values," a same-old same-old inventory of imagined intrinsic European virtues—rationality, justice, democracy, individual freedom, secularity, and tolerance—none of which are exclusively European and none of which really hold up to the light of historical critique. Although all of these traits have characterized a certain Europe at particular times, some can be found outside of Europe, and Europe itself has also displayed precisely the opposite tendencies: irrationality (witch trials, blood libels), injustice (of all possible kinds), tyranny (from autocratic monarchies to fascism and Nazism), slavery (practiced internally or abroad by most European powers), religious intolerance (anti-Semitism, the wars of religion), and racism against internal and external others, which Todorov has documented in *The Conquest of America*. Todorov's grid of qualities in this sense is selective; it narcissistically essentializes Europe as a positive force within world history.

Todorov roots some European values, moreover, in Christianity's supposed love of "individual liberty." But here we can lend an ear to Todorov's compatriot, the Lebanese-French writer Amin Maalouf. The following is Maalouf's more balanced assessment on the subject of comparative freedom within Islam and Christianity:

> Is Christianity essentially tolerant, respectful of liberty and inclined toward democracy? If you framed the question like that, the answer would have to be "no." One only has to look through a few history books to see that throughout the last 2000

years torture, persecution and murder have been carried out on a massive scale in the name of that religion, and that the highest ecclesiastical authorities, as well as the overwhelming majority of ordinary believers, accepted the slave trade, the subjection of women, the most heinous dictatorship and the Inquisition itself. Does that mean Christianity is essentially despotic, racist, reactionary, and intolerant? Not at all. You have only to look around you to see that it now lives comfortably with free speech, human rights and democracy.[35]

For Maalouf the historical paradox is that the Christian West, with its long tradition of intolerance for the "other," produced societies that ended up respecting freedom of expression and religion, whereas the Muslim world, which had long practiced tolerance and coexistence, has now at times become "a stronghold of fanaticism." The difference between the Maalouf approach and the Todorov approach is that Todorov's is static, positing an idealized and eternally freedom-loving Christian Europe, while Maalouf's is dynamic and conjunctural, taking history into account, without a priori idealizations. At the same time, Maalouf does project the current Islamic and Christian worlds as more homogeneous than they actually are. To complicate the analysis, we also have to add that Christian fundamentalism is also flourishing in the West (and is exported even to the Middle East through evangelical TV broadcasts) and is often uncomfortable with free speech and human rights. Grassroots struggles for democratization, meanwhile, also take place in the Muslim world.

Anti-Americanism: Dumb and Smart

Throughout this book we have tried to avoid both blind patriotism and blind anti-American critique. Blind patriotism proclaims "my country right or wrong," an idea as stupid as "my family right or wrong," or as English writer G.K. Chesterton put it, "my mother drunk or sober." Dysfunctional nations, like dysfunctional families, should not be defended at all costs, and, yes, a country should air its dirty laundry in public—that is what is meant by the term *democracy*—if only to get it cleaned. American superpatriots boast that they live "in the greatest country in the world," which Bill Maher compared to claiming that one's wife is "the greatest wife in the world." And for them that act of boasting equals love of country. But for us critique, one that is responsible, informed, and fair, a critique made not by perpetual malcontents or self-hating snobs but rather by those dedicated to a "more perfect union," is also a form of love.

An intelligent, political anti-Americanism need not slide, then, into an uninformed cultural anti-Americanism. While one can lament the spread of Big Macs and blockbusters, American culture(s) are not reducible to such phenomena. The United States forms a mélange of the world's cultures, a complex bouillabaisse, to borrow a French culinary metaphor, or a spicy gumbo, to borrow from New Orleans. People from all over the world feel connected to the United States, not only because of U.S.-spread consumerism but also because immigrants from every continent have made their home in the United States. In hating the United States in general at this point in history, moreover, one always partially hates oneself or at least one's relatives. Indeed Alexandre Adler, another Frenchman, makes a related point when he argues that "the hatred of America today can only be the most perverse form of self-hatred," because in attacking the "monstrosities" produced by American culture—obesity, hamburgers, the CIA—one is in fact "attacking occidental culture in general, of which the United States now forms the center."[36]

Adler's view, however, is both overly generous—because there are valid reasons for opposing American policy—and not generous enough, in that the United States cannot be seen as exclusively "occidental." The most intelligent critique of the United States, in our view, is a conjunctural, political critique that pinpoints specific administrations, policies, and elites, without making uninformed generalization about *les Americains* or *les Français*. Such a critique does not recycle cultural clichés and dialogues with those who are making similar critiques within the United States itself, precisely those who are accused by the right of being anti-American or of hating America. Those critical Americans deserve the solidarity not only of their compatriots but also of critics abroad, just as critics abroad deserve our solidarity.

Americans, as we have seen, can be called "anti-American" and even be anti-American. But it is important to distinguish between diverse types of American anti-Americanism. The first type is that of elitist Europhiles who have internalized the notion of American cultural inferiority and who are ashamed and embarrassed by the rowdy "vulgarity" of American popular culture. For this group, political critique is subordinated to a rejection of American "bad taste," as if the real issue were aesthetic rather than political. These critics echo perennial European stereotypes and encode a European sense of class superiority toward the lower-class people who chose to emigrate, along with a prejudice against Creole culture in the Americas. This kind of American anti-Americanism can be a form of self-loathing. Such American critics see America as *nouveau riche,* a put-down term that encodes an aristocratic scorn toward the "vulgar" and upwardly mobile.

The second type of American anti-American discourse is that of some ethnocentric leftists who mistakenly see the United States as the unique source of evil in the world. While the right-wing dominated United States is presently an extremely dangerous force in the world, to see it as the source of all evil seems to be not only excessively moralistic and ahistorical but also an inverted form of narcissism. It is right-wing Manichaeism turned on its head. An intelligent anti-Americanism, in contrast, assumes that no characteristic of U.S. policy is eternal or uncontested. It assumes that policies in the United States are set by powerful elites, even if the apparent "consent" of the people can be traduced after the fact.

A third type of American anti-American discourse is that of progressive leftists who have an emotional attachment to the place where they have grown up and live but who are revolted by systemic injustice and governmental corruption and neo-imperial policy, but who neither demonize the United States nor angelize Europe or the Third World. The real international coalition, for us, is that of people from all countries who combine a tough-love critique of their own countries with an openness to other countries and a readiness to engage other perspectives. While everyone (including Americans) has the right to be anti-American in any way he or she likes—such is the nature of free speech—the trick of the right wing has been to conflate progressive patriotism with the snobbism of the first position and the demonology of the second and to equate dissent with treason.

With a few exceptions, the right views itself as tolerant of dissent and free speech. Often when voices of dissent are heard publicly, the administration reassures the public that "We do not agree with them but they are entitled to their opinion" and "It's because the United States is a democracy that they can protest." But one wonders about these comparisons to nondemocratic states. The implication is that America essentially belongs to the right, which unilaterally "tolerates" the dissenting views. But no one is in a position to "own" a truly democratic system, and therefore no one should be in a position to "tolerate" dissent; conflicting views are simply part of a fair and equal public debate. Mark Twain addressed this atrophied view of dissent in a maxim that said that the three most precious things Americans possess are "freedom of speech, freedom of conscience, and the prudence never to practice either." Free speech is not a favor accorded by one group to another; it is enshrined in the Constitution as a universal right. When such comments are made by an extremely powerful administration, capable of spying even on domestic peace activists, *tolerance* begins to sound suspiciously like *intolerance*.

Although many Americans have been conditioned by a highly militarized system and a highly militarized media to accept war, they do not intrinsically love war. It has always required a huge propaganda effort to prod Americans into supporting war, and even then they ultimately become disenchanted, as is shown by the current majority opinion declaring the Iraq War a "mistake" and "not worth it." (The Korean and Vietnam wars also became extremely unpopular, and a number of U.S. presidents have won elections by promising, sometimes dishonestly, to end wars.) Today many young Americans are simply refusing to join the armed forces, and students are protesting military recruiting on campuses. Indeed the current recruitment crisis is so severe, the lack of enthusiasm so patent, that the military is resorting to lowering the requirements, bribing noncitizens with citizenship papers, and simply lying about the terms of enlistment (including, at times, not revealing that the "job" proffered is with the army). Those who "volunteer" for the military thus do so under a kind of duress, looking for a way to get what society has otherwise refused them—a good job, a good education, health care. And we taxpayers pay for the slick commercials that seduce our fellow citizens into risking their lives in an ill-advised war.

At the same time, the American military is resorting more and more to private contract labor—aka mercenaries of various nationalities—thus making a mockery of all the patriotic bombast about our boys fighting for their country in foreign strands.

The war in Iraq was only briefly, artificially, and precariously made "popular" through lies and manipulation. It was and is a war made by and for elites. Planned by a tiny cabal, the war was sold through sledge-hammer propaganda, mendacious advertising, and emotional blackmail. The lust for war did not bubble up from the grassroots streets of America; it "trickled" down from corporate and military boardrooms. In words that foreshadow the warmongering—it is hard to find any other word to describe the hawks' lust for war—Mark Twain observed the process by which initially reluctant masses of people are tricked into bellicose enthu-siasm for war. Writing at the height of another U.S. "imperial binge," Twain's account of militaristic demagoguery remains unsurpassed:

> The loud little handful will shout for war ... the great mass of the nation will rub its sleepy eyes, and will try to make out why there should be a war, and they will say earnestly and indignantly: "It is unjust and dishonorable and there is no need for war." Then the few will shout even louder ... before long you will see a curi-ous thing; anti-war speakers will be stoned from the platform, and free speech will be strangled by hordes of furious men who still agree with the speakers but dare not admit it. ... Next, the statesmen will invent cheap lies ... and each man will be glad of these lies [which] soothe his conscience; and thus he will bye and bye convince himself that the war is just and he will thank God for the better sleep he enjoys by his self-deceptions.[37]

The war in Iraq was a product, even in the commercial sense of that word, of a tiny band of "cheap liars" and "furious men," some with a direct financial interest in the war because of their links to energy cor-porations and military services. Many of the war's advocates had been trying to "sell" the war ever since the immediate aftermath of the first Gulf War. Can anyone imagine even for a second that Americans, with-out this mendacious marketing effort, would have spontaneously opted to risk so much life and treasure—treasure that might have funded jobs, education, mass transit, health care, pensions, and infrastructure repair—in such a costly fashion?

What makes U.S. power unique in the present day is the status of the United States as a "hyperpower" unchecked by any counterforce abroad and more or less unchecked by a strong domestic opposition party at home. But the United States did not invent imperialism. Rather it inherited and synthesized all the previous colonialisms and imperialisms. The network of U.S. bases, the areas of the world now subject to American military control or surveillance, are roughly congruent with the areas dominated by the colonial powers in the nineteenth century. When reactionary thinkers such as British historian Niall Ferguson argue that the United States should become frankly imperial, they do not say that the United States should become the first empire, only that it should imitate the last Great One—the British Empire. The United States has come to gather all the major "threads" of contemporary power—political, military, economic and financial, and informatic-cultural—that give it an unprecedented hegemony in the world. This conjunction of circumstances does indeed make the United States uniquely dangerous, and world opinion is not wrong in seeing a Pentagon-dominated United States as dangerous.

The hawks seem to want to place the world in a permanent state of emergency. Underneath the glove of "democracy" is the fist of military force, encapsulated in the old colonial nostrum "all they understand is force." Yet the right justifies this display of force by fantasizing, in a transparently self-exculpatory manner, a new "holocaust" supposedly threatening America. But the problem with overly concentrated American power is not that it is American, as Timothy Garton Ash suggests, but that it is power and that it is overly concentrated. No previous empire used its power exclusively for noble ends—the French and British certainly did not—and the same is true of the U.S. neoempire.

French writer and statesman André Malraux used to say that the United States was the only country that became imperialist without wanting to. However, with the neocons and theocons, that seems no longer to be the case: now sectors of the power elite, despite the rhetoric of "democracy," really want to be imperialist. Whereas *imperialism* used to be a negative accusation hurled by the left against the American foreign policy establishment, now many hawks openly proclaim imperialism as their ideal.[38] A *New York Times* headline (May 10, 2003) sums up the drift: "American Empire, Not 'If' but 'What Kind?'" Niall Ferguson, similarly, welcomes the new imperialism, seeing globalization, of which he approves, as simply a "fancy word for imperialism, imposing your values and institutions on others."[39] Donald Rumsfeld's office, according to a report by Dana Priest, "sponsored a private study of the great empires ... asking how they maintained their dominance?"[40]

Yet most Americans, including the soldiers who die or become sick because of Agent Orange (the Vietnam War) or depleted uranium (the two gulf wars) or even those who lose social benefits and health care partially because resources have been drained by the war, are also victims—even if rather uninformed and passive and in many ways guilty victims—of the imperial policies of the elite. Those policies do little for the masses of American people; they primarily help a well-heeled and well-connected minority. The Iraq War has been a disaster not only for all the Iraqis who have suffered but also for many Americans in terms of lost lives, maimed bodies, wasted resources, and lost liberties. This militaristic government does not even care about its soldiers; it gives them inadequate armor and cuts veterans' benefits, at the same time that it subjects soldiers to the ill-health effects of depleted uranium. George W. Bush does not attend the soldiers' funerals, since that would be "bad advertising." Rather than defend against a foreign enemy, as editorialist Lewis Lapham puts it, the establishment promotes "the protection of the American plutocracy from the American democracy."[41] It is almost as if Americans are ruled by an oligarchy—the people cartoonist Jules Feiffer used to refer to as "those same twelve guys"—that simply makes its plans without really consulting with the American people, which it sees only as a mass of gullible suckers to be spun like the buyers of useless consumer products.

Nor should it be assumed that Americans benefit evenly from globalization. Although the corporate elites of the world get rich through globalization, only a tiny minority of Americans benefits. During the Democratic debates for the 2004 presidential campaign, a number of candidates openly took their distance from globalization, with the most radical Democratic candidate Representative Dennis Kucinich even calling for the dismantling of the World Trade Organization. That the uneven benefits of globalization go disproportionately to management rather than labor forms the special theme of Michael Moore's books such as *Downsize This!* and his films such as *Roger and Me, The Big One,* and *Bowling for Columbine.* The benefits of globalization are disproportionately reaped; those who are "downsized" when a corporation moves to the Third World in search of cheap labor reap precious little from globalization, while workers in the Third World have low-paying jobs but few basic workers' rights.

Presumptively American multinational corporations and their CEOs have gotten vastly rich, while workers have gotten poorer and poorer. Indeed the American working class and middle class have been in economic decline since the 1970s, and the weakening of unions and the collapse of pensions can make things only worse. Tax breaks and off-shore shelters for corporations do not help ordinary Americans. In the reconstruction of Iraq, Halliburton, Dick Cheney's former firm, hired not U.S. citizens or even Iraqi citizens to do the building but rather cheap labor from Asia and Africa. (Yet if anyone should know how to rebuild Iraq it is the Iraqis themselves, who built it in the first place.) The Federal Emergency Management Agency followed the same modus operandi in Louisiana after Katrina, calling on cheap Mexican laborers rather than on local African Americans. Even the security of American ports was initially outsourced to a Dubai firm, leaving Bush caught on the horns of the contradictions of his own rhetoric and policy, which on one handed preached a clash-of-civilization anti-Islamic "crusade" against the Arabs/Muslims and which on the other hand practiced business-as-usual globalization and outsourcing.

The billions budgeted for the so-called Iraq reconstruction is money not spent on repairing levees or improving hospitals and schools in the United States. In fact as more and more funds get transferred to "security" in Iraq and as the funds for reconstruction run out or are swallowed up by corruption, the money is not even spent on hospitals and schools in Iraq. While Congress finances elections in Iraq, it cannot fix the broken electoral system or even the voting machines at home. The White House prods the media to show the "bright side" in Iraq, usually encapsulated in the cheery phrase "opening schools in Baghdad." But this notion of "opening schools" plays on naive assumptions both about American benevolence and about Iraqi backwardness. The media fail to remind us that Iraq did not need America to build schools; presanctions and prewar Iraq had functioning schools, national health care, and virtually universal literacy. While the media celebrates the sight of purple-fingered Iraqis voting, it is also clear that Iraq is currently going through a truly hellish situation. Whereas most Iraqis suffered under Saddam Hussein and the Baathists, many now live in terror of a whole range of catastrophes, in danger from ordinary criminals, terrorists, insurgents, American soldiers, militias, and contracted security guards (virtual mercenaries paid with our tax dollars).

Estimates of the human toll of the war as of September 2006 were 2,700 Americans dead and 43,000 to 112,000 Iraqi dead. That's an awful lot of deaths for a "culture of life" president. Our critique of U.S. foreign policy takes place within the general framework of our preference for smart rather than dumb anti-Americanism. The United States should not be made the unique scapegoat for all of the world's present-day evils. Ironically it is again the French intellectual Régis Debray, widely regarded as one of the "anti-Americans," who best articulates this point. Some strands of anti-Americanism in France, for Debray, constitute forms of magical thinking that heap on the United States all the evils of the world. This attitude is quixotic, the resentment of a power that went from being a first-rank imperial power to being a third-rank power. Like Cervantes's declining hidalgo in the throes of midlife crisis, France regrets its *belle époque* of imperial domination. No imperialism, after all, likes the imperialism that takes its place.[42]

Yet for Debray the phrase "French anti-Americanism" mistakenly implies that all of the French are anti-American and that French anti-Americanism is total and all embracing and goes "all the way down." This view obscures the ambivalence of French attitudes and the out-of-synch discontinuities between political and cultural attitudes. It was the politically anti-American Sartre, Debray points out, that made the French love jazz, Dos Passos, and New York City, while the politically "pro-American" Raymond Aron disdained American popular culture. Even as French leftists were denouncing American imperialism in the 1950s, French film critics were lauding American "maverick" directors such as Nicholas Ray and Samuel Fuller. Simone de Beauvoir and Jean-Paul Sartre, acerbic critics both of U.S. policy and of the American way of life, deeply loved American films and American music. (Think of the climactic ode to "Some of These Days" in Sartre's novel *Nausea*.)

Were he forced into exile, Debray adds, he would choose either Italy or the United States as his new homeland. In Africa he would be politically anti-French, given official France's alliances with neocolonial kleptocrats. An intelligent anti-Americanism, in sum, has to examine the hegemonic policies of the government rather than focus on a presumed national character.

Many would argue that insofar as the American people support the oppressive policies of the U.S. government, they too should be seen as responsible for those policies. And we cannot let the American people off the hook by placing the burden of responsibility only on the American government. We cannot be exceptionalist ourselves by opening up an "exception" for the American people. Americans should be judged on whether they resist or support oppressive policies. In fact all people around the world should be so judged. American citizens have the obligation to challenge the "preventive war" policies of the hawks. Nor are we positing a completely innocent American people, corrupted by the elite. Hegemonic elites always find accomplices. Any unfortunate hour spent with talk show hate radio in the United States reveals a significant number of good old-fashioned racists and sociopaths in America. But here one has to take into account the actual conditions of the possibility of resistance, since we "make history," as Marx famously said, but not "in conditions of our own making." We are not arguing that the United States is **better** than the critics say, only that it is infinitely more complex and variegated, characterized by many clashing perspectives.

Americans, in our view, are not inherently and eternally more reactionary that people elsewhere. Polls show that majorities of Americans share with Europeans a preference for the basic advantages of a welfare state. The polls reflect massive dissatisfaction with class inequality. Seven in ten, according to a 1998 poll, felt that "the rich just get richer while the poor get poorer," and 63 percent thought that "money and wealth in this country should be more evenly distributed."[43] The good news, then, is that egalitarian ideas are popular; the bad news is that there is little chance that these ideas will be translated into action, given the hammerlock of the right on public policy. Like a misaligned car that can only steer to the right, the system is rigged and needs an overhaul. The public and media debate in the United States is pitched far to the right not only in comparison with other nation-states in Europe and

Latin America but also in comparison to the past and in comparison to general American public opinion. The right-wing domination of the media debate, although the result of decades of well-financed efforts toward deregulation and corporate mergers, inevitably inflects the perceptions of masses of Americans.

As a result of the rightward shift in the dominant strata of the American body politic, the conservative French president Jacques Chirac, if one considers his policies on such issues as the death penalty, health care, and the war in Iraq, is now to the left of most American "liberal" politicians. Bill Clinton, painted by the right as a "sex, drugs, and rock and roll" radical, complained that his policies were so mainstream that they resembled those of an "Eisenhower Republican." Yet now, taken-for-granted entitlements—Social Security, unemployment insurance, Medicare, and Medicaid—are being put under suspicion by the right, portrayed as wasteful, even immoral. In retrospect even Republican president Richard Nixon, with his plans for a guaranteed annual income for all Americans, looks "liberal" compared to the present-day American right, at least in terms of welfare policy. In Europe, we remember, it was often conservatives who installed the basic mechanisms of the social welfare state, as a way of saving capitalism, just as the partisans of the New Deal saved the United States from the ravages of the Great Crash and the Depression. The current Bush program of "privatizing" Social Security, in its rush to take us back to the 1920s, forgets that Social Security was installed precisely because the markets and private investment were not working for most Americans.

An Arab American Dirge for 9/11

If the Frenchman Régis Debray represents intelligent critique from outside of the United States, the poetry of Suheir Hammad represents "intelligent critique" from within the United States. A Palestinian American who grew up in Brooklyn within a multicultural environment of blacks, Latinos, and East Europeans, Hammad's spoken readings are tinged with an African American accent, and one of her collections of poetry was titled *Born Palestinian, Born Black*. Hammad forms part of a burgeoning spoken-word movement among politically conscious young people of color as well as whites in the New York area. The multiracial coalition of poets generally combines percussive verbal-style, performative smarts and socially conscious lyrics. The movement gained media visibility through the cable TV program *Def Poetry Jam* and even briefly brought its poetry to Broadway.

In a poem titled "First Writing Since," written in response to the bombing of the World Trade Center, Hammad gives eloquent expression to the conflicting feelings of a Palestinian American New Yorker after the attacks. Hammad speaks first of her fear and shock and the lack of poetry "in the ashes south of Canal Street" and the lack of "prose in the refrigerated trucks driving debris and DNA." She speaks of the "sky where once was steel" and "smoke where once was flesh" and of her initial fears that the pilot might be Arab or Muslim, in short someone who "looks like her":

> First, please god, let it be a mistake, the pilot's
> heart failed, the plane's engine died.
> Then please god, let it be a nightmare, wake me now.
> Please god, after the second plane,
> please, don't let it be anyone
> who looks like my brothers.

The poet then tries to imagine what might have led such people to commit mass murder:

> I have never been so angry as to want
> to control a gun over a pen.
> Not really.
> Even as a woman, as a Palestinian,
> as a broken human being.
> Never this broken.

The poem scores the ignorance of those Americans who fear generic "orientals," who "do not know the difference / Between Indians, Afghanis, Syrians, Muslims, Sikhs, Hindus." But this scoring of ignorance does not preclude an affectionate homage to the multiethnic streets and people of New York, in this case the Koreans and their grocery stores:

> Thank you Korea for kimchi and bibim bob, and corn
> tea and the genteel smiles of the wait staff at wonjo
> the smiles never revealing the heat of the food or how
> tired they must be working long midtown shifts.

A verbal collage follows, based on words drawn from the shakily xeroxed printouts and photos of the disappeared of 9/11, whose names and physiognomies represent the most diverse gallery of ethnicities, posted by people looking desperately for their loved ones—"please help us find George, also known as Adel, his family is waiting for him with his favorite meal." The poet herself, meanwhile, is looking not for relatives but for peace and mercy and evidence of compassion. She thanks the white stranger who hugs her as she cries.

At the same time, Hammad is irritated by the e-mails from leftists and Arab nationalists who say, "Let's not forget U.S. transgressions." She feels resentful about such comments, because "I live here, these are my friends and fam, and it could have been me in those buildings, and we're not bad people, do not support America's bullying. Can I just have half a second to feel bad?" She also resents the Arab haters who ask if she knew the hijackers or those who say "they had it coming" but assume that "they" did not include the Arabs or Muslims or Mexicans who died in the World Trade Center. She denounces the media double standard where terror always wears a brown Arab face and white terrorists such as Tim McVeigh are forgotten. "When we talk about holy books and hooded men and death," she asks, "why do we never mention the KKK?"

And, then, in a sudden turn of association, Hammad makes what at first seems a surprising claim. No group of people, she writes, can better understand the grief of the victims in the terror attacks than the Palestinians: "if there are any people on earth who understand how New York is feeling right now, they are in the West Bank and the Gaza Strip." To those pro-Israelis who would say, "Now that you Americans have been the victim of suicide bombers, now perhaps you will understand us," Hammad answers, "No, it is Palestinians who understand this kind of victimization." At the same time, Hammad dissociates herself completely from bin Laden, whose "vision of the world does not include me or those I love." But she also knows who will end up paying in their blood for the attack: "in the world, it will be women, mostly colored and poor" and "in America, it will be those amongst us who refuse blanket attacks on the shivering. Those of us who work for social justice, in support of civil liberties, in opposition to hateful foreign policies."

The poet then expresses a kind of local, metropolitan patriotism— "I have never felt less American and more New Yorker." She worries about her Arab American brothers and sisters—"what will their lives be like now?"—realizing that "over there," that is, Palestine, is now "over here." She describes the aftermath of the attacks as life returns to a shaken kind of normality:

> All day, across the river, the smell
> of burning rubber and limbs
> floats through. The sirens have stopped
> now. The advertisers are
> back on the air. The rescue workers
> are traumatized. The skyline is
> brought back to human size. No longer
> taunting the gods with its
> height.
> ... I cried when I saw those buildings collapse on
> themselves like a broken heart. I have never
> owned pain that needs to spread like that.

Against those who might aestheticize violence, she writes, "there is no poetry in this" but only "cause and effects" and "symbols and ide-ologies," and there is life:

> There is life here. Anyone reading this
> is breathing, maybe hurting,
> but breathing for sure. And if there
> is any light to come, it will
> shine from those who look for
> peace and justice after the
> rubble and rhetoric are cleared
> and the phoenix has risen.

And refusing Bush's call to declare oneself to be with "us" or with the terrorists, the poet rewrites the choice as one not between "us" and "them" but between life and death:

Affirm life.
We've got to carry each other now.
You are either with life, or against it.
Affirm life.

"First Writing Since" gives an incandescent sense of what it is to live in the (multi)nation in the age of globalized error and globalized terror, of overlapping and conflicted loyalties to family and community on one hand and to nation-states on the other. But neither nation is unitary, and the "us" and the "them" are very much blurred. The Palestine that Hammad supports includes the fundamentalist fanatics that she abhors, and the United States, whose official policy she abhors, also includes peace-loving people such as herself. Such poetry exemplifies an intelligent critique of official actions, which scores the ugliness of terrorism, whether initiated by transnational cells or sponsored by states and whether done in the name of religion or in the name of "freedom." The poem sings the dappled, motley beauty of New York's (multi)culture. Its complex view exalts America's (endangered) civil liberties and revels in the polyglot dynamism of American cities while also being deeply critical of national chauvinism.

5. Contemporary Politics and the Crisis of Democracy

Pricks and Wimps

Having explored the complex and interwoven constitutional histories of the United States, France, and Brazil, along with their intricate emotional relationships as reflected in the various forms of mutual love, hatred, and ambivalence, we now return to the internal crisis that has shaped a sharply divided and in some ways disillusioned nation—the United States.

American history, like many national histories, has involved titanic battles between authoritarianism and democracy, racism and equality, injustice and justice. The rightward trend in the United States, we have been arguing, cannot be reduced to being the natural expression of some intrinsic right-wingedness inherent in American culture. Although the rightist trend obviously builds on certain abiding features of the body politic, it is also the product of a political crisis. The power of the far right is the concrete result of at least four decades of hard, well-funded, and often very dirty and manipulative work by right-wing ideologues, corporate executives, and lobby-friendly politicians. Our friends from abroad often ask, "How can Americans be so naive as to accept the right's lies?" There are a number of answers to that question. First, while millions of Americans do accept the lies, millions of other Americans do not. (The naïveté about "weapons of mass destruction" was partly a function of massive propaganda, collaborated in even by the *New York Times,* and of the lingering and disorienting trauma triggered by 9/11.)

But to the extent that Americans are in fact manipulated and confused, the explanations are multiple. Paraphrasing James Carville's famous election slogan ("It's the economy, stupid"), we offer the following answers: (1) "It's the media, stupid"; (2) "It's the educational system, stupid"; (3) "It's the political system, stupid"; (4) "It's the right's perverse brilliance, stupid"; and (5) and "It's the New Democrats' cowardice, stupid."

The media have tilted increasingly to the right, partly because its owners have links to the Republican Party, and even when they do not, tend to desire policies favored by the right, such as deregulation and corporate tax breaks. A political discussion dominated by what reformed right-winger David Brock calls the "Republican noise machine" deprives most Americans of the necessary perspective to make an informed judgment about imperial interventions presented as benevolent actions aimed at fostering democracy.[1] In such conditions the left fights an uphill battle against very powerful forces. The educational system, meanwhile, idealizes the American system as a transparent democracy and American foreign policy as benevolent and idealistic. By failing to educate Americans about world events or about other perspectives on those events and on America itself, it deprives Americans of the alternative knowledge base required to confront the big lies of the right.

Indeed one has to admire the right's ability to turn real historical lemons into propagandistic lemonade. Karl Rove, an ingenious alchemist, turned a habitual prevaricator—George W. Bush—into a straight shooter, a power monger into a compassionate Christian, an oedipal wrecker into a humanitarian, a draft dodger into a war hero (and the war hero, and antiwar hero, Kerry into a coward). Rove managed, at least for a while, to turn the dross of Bush's frazzled and sputtering mind into the gold of pseudostatesmanship, at least. The image makers even transformed 9/11, one of Bush's worst moments, into an apparent

Bush triumph. Over and over we see the same unequal Hannity-versus-Colmes duel between Republican audacity and Democratic timidity. Even as the White House was being buffeted by scandals of seismic magnitude—misleading Congress and the nation into war, profiteering from that war, approving torture, outing CIA agents—John Kerry was forced to prove that *he* could be trusted. What under Clinton would have been earthshaking scandals—for example, Bush's revealing his war plans to a Saudi prince before his own secretary of state—would last for a day and then just as quickly die, with the Democrats unwilling or unable to draw any advantage.

The centrist "New" Democrats, unfortunately, have internalized the "noise machine;" its theme songs constantly ring in their ears. The "duck and cover" Democrats, with a few exceptions, have become paralyzed by the fear of what the noise machine might say about them. Like schizophrenics who hear "voices," they cannot oppose any funds for war—excuse us, "defense"—because they hear the machine calling them "unpatriotic." They can't call for complete withdrawal from Iraq, because they imagine the accusations of "cut and run" and "abandoning the troops." They cannot redistribute wealth downward because that would be "class warfare." They can't oppose racism because the machine will call them "politically correct" or "reverse racist." They can't propose new government programs because that would be "big government" and "tax and spend." They cannot be economic populists because the right would call them "Marxists." They cannot speak of the administration's links to the oil and energy corporations, for that would be to indulge in "conspiracy theories." They can't oppose torture or "rendition," because that would be "coddling terrorists." They can't propose universal health care, because they will be called "socialist," or horror of horrors, "liberal," even though in most countries the word *liberal* means the opposite of *socialist*. Even though polled majorities support providing single-payer health care (65 percent), raising the minimum wage (85 percent), repealing tax cuts for the rich (60 percent), protecting the environment (87 percent), and ending the price gouging by big oil companies (87 percent), the New Democrats have trouble leading on any of these issues.[2] As a result of so many internalized taboos, the Democrats have triangulated themselves into irrelevance.

Frightened by the noise machine, the centrist Democrats have become their own worst enemy. While Democrats are haunted by their own internal Republican, the Republicans have no internal Democrat at all, resulting in what some have called "asymmetrical polarization." While the Republicans keep moving the goal post to the right, the centrist Democrats run sheepishly after it, but the Republicans denounce them as radical no matter what they do or say. The Democrats, with a few noble exceptions, have largely been pulled into the gravitational force field of the right. By moving not to the left but to the center, they have allowed the whole discourse to move rightward, leaving us without a serious, courageous, principled opposition party.[3] The political superego is pitched so far to the right of popular sentiment. As the right invents the conceptual grids—compassionate conservatism, small government—that justify the unjustifiable, the Democrats play defense. The right has captured all the key words: what *terror* is, what *democracy* is, what *strength* is, what *faith* is, what *patriotism* is, and so forth.

While the Republicans see politics as war, the Democrats see it as a graduate seminar. While the Republicans produce the Schwarzenegger-style blockbuster, the Democrats respond with their "balanced" PBS documentary—a style and genre that appeals to only a tiny segment of the population. Republicans fight to the death because they know billions of dollars are at stake for themselves and their corporate friends, while the Democrats hardly fight at all. A Mike Keefe cartoon (*New York Times,* December 25, 2005) dramatized the situation by showing a boxing match between a staggered Republican elephant, battered by Iraq, deficits, DeLay, and Katrina in one corner, confronted by a cautious donkey in the other, fearful of delivering the knockout punch. As his coach tells him to give the elephant his best shot, the donkey responds: "But what if I hurt my hand?"

Unlike Republicans, the upwardly mobile New Democrats are ashamed of their own base. While Republicans give ample red meat to their base, the Democrats restrict their base to a diet of bread and water.[4] While the Republicans display black people as props, the Democrats hide blacks in the name of a "middle class" coded as white, even though blacks are their most loyal constituency. In terms of labor unions, some Democrats feel they must show that they are not in the union "pocket." A half million people marching in New York City before the Republican Convention, in one of the biggest demonstrations in U.S. history, triggers only a noncommittal reaction among the New Democrats beyond "That has nothing to do with us, and please do not embarrass us by bad behavior." The unprecedented success of *Fahrenheit 9/11*, a film that reshaped the debates and probably added many votes to the Kerry column, elicited "We haven't seen it and don't plan to." The centrist Democrats are experts at dampening the enthusiasm of "vote and vomit" Democrats. They even think they can win elections by defining themselves against Michael Moore, even though he is probably much more popular than they are.

Time has shown, furthermore, that it was the left wing of the party that was ahead of the curve, since we now see that majority opinion has joined Michael Moore and the left against the war. Rather than cultivate the base, the New Democrat strategists—well-paid professional losers of elections—prefer to go for the undecideds, who appear (at least in their TV appearances) to be inarticulate and indecisive retards congenitally unable to make up their minds. Meanwhile the centrist Democrats apologize for their rhetoric—such as Senator Durbin's comparisons of Abu Ghraib to Nazi abuses—while the right refuses to apologize for the behavior that triggered the rhetoric in the first place. No weapons of mass destruction? "So what?" Thousands of innocent civilians killed? "Tough bananas! War is war!" Billions spent in a war that was supposed to pay for itself? "Big deal." Breaking the law by having the National Security Agency (NSA) spy on Americans? "I'd do it again." Being a Democrat, meanwhile, and we paraphrase the dialogue of the film *Love Story,* means "always having to say you're sorry."[5]

That is why Republicans draw blood when they say that the Democrats do not know what they stand for. Why didn't the Democrats lead the way in denouncing the PATRIOT Act, torture, and "preventive war"? Why was it Republicans like John Warner, Lindsey Graham, and John McCain who led the fight against "degrading, cruel, and inhumane punishment"? And if Democrats are not careful, the tiny moderate wing of the Republican Party may even claim the anticorruption and even the antiwar banners for coming elections.

The right is skilled in the theatrics of political combat. It shapes images and narratives proactively, narrating the stories that people want to hear and carefully tracing out the meaning to be drawn from the story. It knows that grids, prisms, and framing are more important than facts. The right connects with popular desire, framing the war first as a matter of basic self-defense and then as an idealistic matter of "spreading democracy." Democrats, in contrast, assume that events will reveal the meaning that the truth will simply emerge once the people see the negative consequences of the right's policies, at which point the people will see the light. But by then it is too late, because too many people have already been blinded by the propaganda barrage and will be reading even these negative consequences through the grids prepared by the right.

As a result of all these processes, the United States no longer has a functioning left opposition party. Instead of a left and a right, we have an extreme right and a right center. And given the winner-take-all two-party system, a minority can win elections by hook or by crook and then shove its programs down the national throat. A huge proportion of the electorate, which in a parliamentary system would have more voice, feels itself politically exiled. The situation recalls that which held during the Brazilian dictatorship, when the military junta banned all political parties except for two governmentally approved parties, promptly dubbed by critics the "Yes Party" and the "Yes, Sir! Party," which is more or less what we have too often had in the United States. But Brazilian politicians had the excuse of dictatorship; the New Democrats have no such excuse.

In politics as in philosophy, questions are more important than answers, and the Republicans have been aggressive at controlling the questions and defining the limits of debate. The war in Iraq? For the right, at least at the beginning, there was only one question: "Are we better off without Saddam Hussein?" Howard Dean was mauled for answering "not necessarily," but in the end he was right, but of course no one offered him an apology. But more important, there were many other questions the administration and the media could have asked: "Are the Iraqi people better off in the wake of the invasion?" Since the administration sells the invasion as being "for Iraqis," presumably Iraqis should have a say in answering the question. Few Americans know, for example, that hundreds of Iraqi educators had been assassinated, that many hundreds more have disappeared, and that some 84 percent of Iraqi institutions of higher education have already been burned, looted, or destroyed.[6] And are we Americans better off after such loss of American and Iraqi lives, with billions spent and a huge deficit and with the entire world resenting us because of our "preventive war" policies?

Subsequently, the Saddam question was replaced by other trick questions such as : "Will we be able to install democracy in Iraq?" This question is also misleading, beginning with the "we." A tiny cabal of neocons decided to create this war of choice, and yet now it is "we"—a highly fictive "we"—who are supposedly "in" Iraq. The question encodes the idea that "we" all support this effort and that the effort is aimed only at installing democracy, a formulation that assumes only benevolent intentions and obscures other questions such as the following: "What about the oil? Will the United States maintain permanent bases? And if so, can there ever be peace? And can democracy be installed by an occupation, which in most cases (with the exception of postwar Germany and Japan) is the opposite of democracy? And are 'wars of choice' ever justified?"

Unlike George W. Bush, who always ignores any question that annoys him or that he cannot answer and then reframes it to his liking, the Democrats too often fall into the trap of answering the question as posed rather than initiate their own questions. Right-wing questions are invariably the wrong questions, and the left needs to ignore them and pose its own questions instead. The talk show Democrats always seem to fall for right-wing debating tricks, which usually consist of a machine-gun series of lies followed by a wild accusation. Exaggerating only slightly, we say it goes a bit like this. The right-wing gasbag says, "The Democrats are socialists who want to fight terrorism with therapy. They want to wage class warfare and bring back the 1960s when everyone was burning books and flags and bras. They are not 'normal Americans' and, furthermore, they are all pedophiles." (Actually we made up only the last part.) Then the Democrat takes the bait by refuting the wild accusation—"No, only some of us are pedophiles, and you have your pedophiles too!"—leaving the original string of lies uncontested.

Ann Coulter, for her part, claims panoptical power to see into the hearts and minds of millions of liberals, leading to grand claims such as "Liberals want America to lose wars." She is like a debater who begins the discussion by accusing her interlocutor of incest and pedophilia, and then says, "Let's talk." What is particularly pernicious in her approach is that her accusations have nothing to do with what we on the left actually do or say but only with her mean-spirited speculations about what she imagines that we **want**. Thus those of us who did not want the United States to wage a preventive war, who did not want any Americans or Iraqis to die, are accused of "longing" for American troops to be shot at and humiliated. Thus, American soldiers are killed as a result of administration policy, but we are made responsible for their deaths, because Coulter has determined that that it was what we want. The left, meanwhile, usually focuses on what the right says and does: we do not say that the administration wanted black and poor people to die in New Orleans, only that such was the consequence of their neglect. We do not say that the administration wanted thousands of Americans and Iraqis to die in Iraq, only that that is the consequence of its actions. Thus, there is a terrible asymmetry in the rhetoric; we are supposedly responsible for what Coulter imagines that we "want," but the right is not responsible for what it actually does. Coulter denounces "godless liberals," but it is hardly clear what is "godly" about her. Could it be the lack of charity, the love of war, the scorn for the least among us? What is clear is that every news cycle dominated by debates about some outrageous Coulter assertion is a victory for Karl Rove. And the real question is not did she go too far, but rather, how in the world did such a malicious and partisan nonentity get on the air at all?

The Democrats' mistake in 2004 was to accept the right-wing framing of the issue of patriotism and then offer a servile mimicry of "us too" militarism. But the real point is to change the frame, even in terms of the sacred cow of "patriotism."

The contrast between the two parties was efficiently and wittily summed up in the following table from a Ward Sutton cartoon:[7]

Republicans	Democrats
Can take nothing and turn it into a Democrat scandal	Can take a Republican scandal and turn it into nothing
Go to great lengths to elevate their right-wing base	Go to great lengths to alienate their liberal base
Reduce complex issues to simplistic, dishonest mantras	Inflate simple issues into mushy, apologetic ramblings
Run on what they believe and win elections	Run on what they believe will win elections and lose

(continued)

Republicans	Democrats
When they're in the wrong they attack	When they're in the right they surrender
Promote their most outspoken and aggressive members	Sabotage their most outspoken and aggressive members
Adept at making their unpopular positions appear "mainstream"	Adept at making their popular positions appear "loony"
Define themselves by their own self-created myth of what they are	Allow themselves to be defined by the Republicans and then argue about it
Think standing for freedom means curtailing our freedoms	Think standing for freedom means never taking a stand
Prematurely sounding battle cries for next fall's election	Prematurely declaring victory in next fall's election
Have proven they are useless at protecting us from terrorists and hurricanes	Have proven they are useless at protecting us from Republicans

The Fine Art of Lying

As our first CEO president, George W. Bush not only has been a CEO and governed for the benefit of CEOs but has (along with Cheney) also resembled corporations in their infinite mendacity and soulless ambition. Bush and Cheney fit social critic Joel Bakan's definition of the corporation as "designed to be a psychopath: purely self-interested, incapable of concern for others, amoral, and without conscience."[8] They have turned the American polis into a company town. And when you have a government run by CEOs, you get government that works—but only for CEOs. And it is this CEO background that explains the brashness with which a CEO-dominated administration lies. It lies with the same bravado that cigarette manufacturers used when they said cigarettes did not cause cancer or that Union Carbide used when it denied responsibility for the disaster in Bhopal, India. Official mendacity is now modeled on corporate mendacity. When corporations are caught polluting, they do not acknowledge error and compensate the victims. Rather they go on the offensive, evading responsibility while blaming the victim. At the same time, they produce bucolic saturated-green commercials, underscored by New Age music and Andean flutes, about the corporation's sublime love of nature. Lately commercials have been using the music of the 1960s counterculture to give the impression that corporations are the new revolution: "You were a rebel then" (when you marched in the streets), "and you're still a rebel now" (when you buy the product we're selling).

Rather than lie, corporations simply mold impressions in a very misleading way. The administration's hostility to the "reality-based community" is rooted in the ethics of corporate public relations. The right, in this sense, has developed a propaganda industry, where the White House, as Frank Rich puts it, is the "NBC Universal or Time Warner of G.O.P. fictionalization, then the Miramax and Focus Features of the right are such nominally 'independent' satellites as Cybercast News, the Lincoln Group (which places fake news stories in Iraqi newspapers), the Rendon Group (which helped manufacture the heroic image of Ahmad Chalabi) and the now-dormant Talon News (the fake Republican-staffed news site whose fake White House correspondent, Jeff Gannon, was unmasked shortly thereafter)."[9]

The Bush administration has explored all the permutations of lying, using a very varied arsenal of techniques. The lies began with the 2000 campaign, a vast production designed to package the radical Bush as a "moderate" who would not disrupt the relative peace and prosperity of the Clinton years. One technique is the "flying in the face of the facts" blanket denial. As evidence mounts of torture by the U.S. soldiers, contractors, and CIA agents, the president responds simply, "We do not torture," while also implying "but it works." Another technique is simply changing the question. Accused of breaking the law by having the NSA spy on American citizens, George W. Bush simply asks himself a new question: "Will I defend the American people? Yes, I will." Asked by TV anchor Brian Williams if the reaction to Katrina would have been so ineffective had it affected a wealthy white suburb, Bush again changes the question: "Some people are saying that I'm a racist, but I'm not a racist." Donald Rumsfeld, for his part, asks himself his own rhetorical questions. Another technique is the bold, well-timed promise—"Bin Laden, Dead or Alive" or "We will rebuild New Orleans to be more glorious than ever"—followed by inaction, at best, and wrong action, at worst. Still another is the straw-man attack; for example "some say that we should give the terrorists everything they want ..." In fact, no one had made any such suggestion.

Another related technique involves the positing of false choices: for example, we either fight terrorism or retain our civil liberties, we either are prowar or are defeatist, and so forth. At times the administration lies through a kind of collage technique. It simply places two unrelated facts next to each other so as to imply a false causality. The administration used 9/11 as a pretext for doing whatever it wanted to do before 9/11. Just as TV commercials lie through suggestive juxtaposition—glamorous star plus hair product implies that the product endows the consumer with glamour—so the administration lied by constantly juxtaposing 9/11 with Saddam Hussein. The administration used 9/11 to explain away its failures or simply to distract attention. Catchphrases such as "the lessons of 9/11" and "we learned with 9/11" lead to arguments for the war in Iraq or justifications for bypassing the Constitution. The positively mythical idea that "everything changed on 9/11" was used to numb critical thought and justify right-wing economic policies—such as dismantling Social Security—that had absolutely nothing to do with 9/11.

Many of the right's lies are embedded—that is, the lie is not in what is explicitly said but in the assumption quietly embedded in the claim—thus allowing for "plausible deniability." When Rush Limbaugh says that Democrats are more afraid of Christians than of terrorists, we are meant to infer that Democrats cannot be Christian. The idea that Saddam would want to do something so suicidal as attack the most powerful country in the world, similarly, was patently absurd, yet that lie was the buried premise in all the warnings about what Saddam "could" do with a nuclear weapon or with just a tiny vial of anthrax. Like film director Alfred Hitchcock, the administration knows that the real terror is not in what we literally see—Hitchcock knew that placing a shot of a knife next to shots of a screaming victim is more effective than showing the actual stabbing—but in what we are induced to imagine on the soundstages of our mind. Calling Iraq "the central front in the war on terror," meanwhile, is less a lie than a self-fulfilling prophecy, because the war triggered extremist terrorism in a country where it had not existed before. (Although the Baathist regime terrorized its own citizens, the secular nationalist Saddam Hussein did at least hold Islamicist organizations at bay, which is why he was denounced by such groups as an infidel.) Gigantic fictions have been foisted on the American people, yet the perpetrators of the fiction have in no way been held responsible, even after the fictions have been unmasked.

While the Republicans have the "courage" to tell big lies, the New Democrats, again with a few brave exceptions, have too often lacked the courage even to tell the truth, for fear of the lies that might be told in response. When the majority, frightened by the propaganda about a "mushroom cloud," seemed to be for the war, the New Democrats were intimidated into supporting the war. But now that the majority is against the war, they still prefer to hear the voice of their internal Republican than follow public opinion against the war. And while the Democrats tell the truth shamefacedly, many Republicans lie routinely, with giddy abandon. Cheney even denies saying things that millions of people have seen him say on television. Such Republicans lie when they deny they're lying. And when others tell the truth, they accuse **them** of lying. They lie by commission and by omission, by implication and by association, reminding us of Mary McCarthy's devastating boutade about Lillian Hellman that "every word she writes is a lie, including 'and' and 'but.'" They lie out of habit, rather like the Brazilian character Macunaima, who says, "I didn't want to lie, but when I started speaking, I was already lying." It's not that the administration sometimes lies but rather, as Ronald Reagan's son Ron put it in an article in *Esquire*, that "they are a lie. They embody mendacity."

All that Republicans have going for them are a few basic ideas (dumb but clear, like no new taxes) along with fear, vote suppression, and lots of money to negatively define adversaries. That is why we have to cut through the completely irrational yet somehow persuasive trick arguments of the right. We need even to examine the role of proverbs and truisms in political debate. With regard to all U.S. wars, we always hear the same meaningless, yet somehow persuasive, clichés: we have to "finish the job," "better now than later," "better there than here," "better offense than defense," and so forth. But there is no point in finishing the job if the job was not worth undertaking in the first place. Offense is not better than defense if the offense is against the wrong target. It is not better to fight there than here if the fighting is making it worse both here and there.

Take what might called the "flypaper" argument; that is, the idea that our invasion of Iraq has attracted the terrorists who come to fight our soldiers and that it is therefore better to fight them there than to fight them here. Apart from the cynicism of using soldiers as bait—"Bring 'em on!"—and apart from the error of conflating the foreign terrorists (estimated to form only a miniscule part of the movement) with the Iraqi insurgents, the formulation forgets that the policy could mean that we end up fighting them both there and here, since Iraq has become a hands-on training ground for the terrorists who might still come here. (At this point even Brent Scowcroft, one of the architects of the first Gulf War, has said, "Iraq feeds terrorism.") But like any analogy, the meaning of the flypaper analogy can easily be reversed. Iraq is indeed flypaper, but the real flies are the American troops, who without the war would not have been available for killing by the terrorists and insurgents. Thus the reverse agreement would be that the Iraq War is allowing them to kill us over there, when they could not have killed us here. In fact most of the insurgents, as opposed to the terrorists, would have no reason to kill us here once we cease to occupy Iraq. And instead of the positive domino theory of democracy spreading outward from Iraq, now it is the negative domino of terrorism that is spreading from Iraq into neighboring countries.

"Patriots" usually fling the following gem of wisdom at antiwar demonstrators: "Our soldiers are fighting over there so you can be free to demonstrate over here!" Let us retire this piece of nonsense forever. Canadians, Swedes, Costa Ricans, and citizens of other free nations are free because they have collectively decided to be free and have installed the constitutional mechanisms to ensure freedom, not because their troops are fighting in some other part of the globe. While such a claim might have been true with respect to World War II, when the United States was massively attacked by totalitarian powers, it certainly did not apply with the Vietnam War, the Gulf War, or the Iraq War. Indeed many American wars made us less free, because war-making administrations lied to the people about the real causes of the war. The "Gulf of Tonkin" resolution passed by Congress to escalate the Vietnam War, for example, was subsequently revealed to have been a fabrication. Wars of choice, from Vietnam to Iraq, from Watergate to NSA-gate have often led to restricting the press, spying on citizens, and wilting civil liberties. More and more we came to resemble the enemy who "hates freedom."

Fear, Catharsis, and the *Daily Show*

As we suggested earlier, we do not believe that Americans as a people are intrinsically more paranoid or more inclined to scapegoat others than are the peoples of other nations. Indeed although some commentators (both within and outside of the United States) have spoken of a paranoid strain within American life, others have emphasized Americans' cheery optimism and our naive faith in humanity, our confident sense of ease and transparency in the world. To the extent that Americans have become paranoid, that is the product of a fear-mongering administration and media. A morbid panic about terror has been injected into the national bloodstream. Our point is not to deny the undeniable reality of terror, but only to point to the political uses to which it has been put. Indeed, two forms of scapegoating—one internal and the other external—have become an integral part of the American political system as it now functions. The internal form of scapegoating has do with a political situation where the right wing, whose "natural constituency" of the corporate rich is by definition miniscule and whose policies are profoundly unpopular once their consequences are understood, has to expand that constituency by scapegoating certain groups, thus persuading some people to vote against their own economic interests. Thomas Frank calls it a "French Revolution in reverse—one in which the sansculottes pour down the streets demanding more power for the aristocracy."[10] This upside-down revolution is led by the privileged and the enfranchised; instead of the *sans culotte* (the "pantsless" French poor) we now have the *sans pitié* (the pitiless).

To get the people to vote against themselves, the right emphasizes social wedge issues, which divide the electorate over hot-button passions about abortion, flag burning, affirmative action, or same-sex marriage. Sexual and racial minorities, needless to say, are especially useful in inflaming such passions. Hate radio is about raising the maximum rage to make listeners forget about raising the minimum wage. Just as the majority of Americans are losing out economically due to the administration's favor-the-rich policies, rightest hate radio begins to demonize Arabs, Latinos, blacks, and "illegal aliens." Through a massive confidence trick, right-wing populism channels hostility away from the people's real enemy—the corporate elite and the right—toward its real friends—the left. And up to a point the trick works, swelling the tiny natural constituency of the right with a boisterous coalition of the naive, the resentful, and the righteous.

On the home front, the right masterfully stimulates and exploits social resentment. It skillfully channels resentment over affirmative action, for example, by implying that undeserving blacks are taking away jobs that naturally "belong" to whites. Resentment is channeled downward, against those lower on the social ladder. Now it is time for the left to rechannel a much more legitimate resentment upward, against those who rip us off and dumb us down. It is the right, after all, that has benefited from its own form of affirmative action—not for blacks but for mediocre white people such as George W. Bush, whose legacy got him into Yale. Can we imagine a black, Latino, or Jewish presidential candidate running on Bush's mediocre record, after decades of being a drunk and a cocaine snorter? And what is crony capitalism if not affirmative action in reverse? Think of all those incompetents—the Tenets and the Rumsfelds and the Wolfowitzes—who "fail upward" into medals and promotions; that is, all the little "Brownies" that are (by definition) doing a "heck of a job." What is it about our system that makes it possible for ethically challenged people such as Dick Cheney to get to the top and crooks such as Jack Abramoff to get close to the top?

It is imperative that citizens tear the mask off the war-profiteering, budget-busting, women-hating, gay-bashing, immigrant-phobic, testosterone-crazed, death-loving, and antipatriotic maniacs who currently wield power over us. We have to show the frightened little boys behind the bullies. We have to learn how to generate legitimate emotion linked to old-fashioned values such as justice, equality, democracy, and peace, not to manipulate emotion but to recognize its legitimate place. Outrage at corporate tax evasion and price gouging. Outrage at the lies we are told. Outrage at the spoiled and sheltered such as Bush—Maureen Dowd's "man in a bubble"—who are somehow always entitled to have everything and yet do not want the rest of us to feel entitled to anything.

The external form of scapegoating, meanwhile, has to do with foreign policy, military budgets, and the manipulation of fear. After victory over real enemies (the Axis powers) in World War II, what Dwight Eisenhower called the "military–industrial complex" in the United States became more and more powerful and more and more in need of enemies as a justification for enormous expenditures. For almost half a century, the Cold War and the Soviet threat served this purpose. (Some conservative pundits such as George Will continued to warn that the "Russians were coming" even as the Soviet Union was on the verge of collapse.) The Cold War actually combined two wars: an early, largely legitimate one involving the containment of Soviet occupation and domination in Europe and later a much more problematic one involving proxy wars and low-intensity conflicts in the Third World, supposedly against the communist threat but really about control of resources and the warding off of nationalist, socialist, and social democratic governments (e.g., Arbenz in Guatemala in 1954, Mossadegh in Iran in 1955, Goulart in Brazil in 1954, and Allende in Chile in 1973). The point is not that enemies do not exist—and communist regimes were in fact totalitarian—only that the military–industrial system also generates a structural need for an enemy. As novelist Gore Vidal used to say during the cold war, "Whenever I hear someone say 'the Russians are coming!' I know that someone is about to pick my pocket."

With the demise of the Cold War and the military–political establishment's reluctance to pay the American people the much-promised "peace dividend," the search was on for new enemies, for "new axis of evil" that might justify expenditures exceeding those of any other nation and even combinations of nations. Bin Laden stepped into this vacuum. And although no one can doubt that bin Laden and bin Ladenism do represent very real threats, they are also exploited as a rationale for endless war and endless expense. The word *terror,* furthermore, is designed to trigger the private terrors of individuals, who project them onto the term. Some members of the military have pointed to the problems inherent in making the "war on terror" the linchpin of foreign policy. Retired general William E. Odom and Robert Dujarric point out that, first, terrorism is only a tactic, rather like arson or grenade throwing. Second, the United States itself has often used terrorism—Odom calls the United States "among the largest sponsors of terrorist operations since World War II." Third, terrorism is ultimately more of a "painful nuisance" than a major threat to U.S. hegemony. "To trumpet terrorism as a worldwide scourge," Odom writes, "is to confuse the public and misdirect diplomacy."[11] Since 9/11 many thousands of Americans have died—thirty-three times the number that died in the World Trade Center—not from terrorism but from the simple fact of not having health insurance. Yet we are told that we have to drop everything—civil liberties, national health care—in the name of "security."

The internal and external forms of scapegoating and fear mongering, furthermore, are intimately woven together. Media scholar Mark Crispin Miller notes a pattern of projected aggressions and preemptive strikes in both domestic and foreign policy. On the home front the right accuses the Democrats of planning to steal elections, and then it proceeds to steal elections.[12] On a foreign front the right, planning to attack Saddam Hussein, convinces itself (or pretends to convince itself) that Saddam himself is about to attack the United States. Second, the two forms of scapegoating are woven together by the "color line" (Du Bois). Both the internal scapegoat and the external enemy are as likely as not to be black or brown or of "Middle Eastern appearance." The shrinking of civil liberties in the post-9/11 period was first tried out on Americans with Muslim names or of Muslim religious background. Some of the reservists implicated in the abuse scandals in Iraq were assigned to Abu Ghraib because of their experience in American prisons. The face of the external enemy as well is likely to be brown or yellow, not only because of the bad colonial habit of racialization but also because "brown" countries—Grenada, Iraq, Afghanistan—are weak, attackable, or (in Cheney's word) "doable" countries, just as on a domestic level, blacks and browns, as we know from watching any *Cops* show, are abusable, while corrupt executives are not. (The premise of one of Michael Moore's satirical *TV Nation* vignettes was to show respectable three-piece-suited CEOs thrown down spread-eagle on the pavement, à la *Cops,* for crimes of corporate corruption.)

Fear has become the combustible without which the right cannot win elections or dominate the country. The right has injected morbidity into the body politic with the result that fear has become the default position of the most powerful nation on earth. James Madison, in a May 13, 1798, letter to Thomas Jefferson, in words that anticipate the recent attacks on our civil liberties, noted prophetically that it "is a universal truth that the loss of liberty at home is to be charged to provisions against danger, real or pretended, from abroad."[13] The word *terror,* furthermore, stigmatizes some forms of violence while exempting others. While the terrorism of a bin Laden is obviously horrendous and indefensible, we tend to forget that nation-state terrorism leaves innocent victims just as dead. Yet the former is seen as a manifestation of evil, while the other is seen as "spreading democracy," a distinction probably lost on grieving Iraqi families.

Domestically some of the ambiguities of the word *terror* were captured in a T-shirt picturing Native Americans armed with bows and arrows, with the caption "Fighting terror since 1492." For African Americans, meanwhile, the word *terror* evokes American forms of terror, such as Ku Klux Klan cross burnings and lynching, historically practiced against African Americans. The soldiers mindlessly grinning for the camera in the torture photos from Abu Ghraib, in this sense, were reminiscent of nothing so much as the giddy faces of the exuberant participants in the lynching of blacks in the American South. And in the United States and Iraq and Afghanistan, relatively disempowered poor white soldiers and "security guards" are granted power over black and brown bodies, available for scapegoating down the social ladder as emotional "compensation" for the guards' own oppression, all carrying out the implicit orders that come, both at home and from abroad, from the very top of the pyramid.

Fear and paranoia, it seems, often favor fascist and militaristic tendencies. The Nazi Hermann Göring said at the Nuremberg trials in 1946 that leaders who want to enhance their power, whether in a democracy or in a dictatorship, need tell people only "they are being attacked and denounce the pacifists for lack of patriotism, exposing the country to greater danger."[14] And while American right-wingers are not Nazis, they still do use fear as their basic political fuel. Fear was at the very heart of the right-wing message in 2004, conveyed not only by speeches but also by color-coded "terror alerts," which magically ceased once the election results were announced. The famous Franklin D. Roosevelt slogan in the wake of Pearl Harbor—"The only thing we have to fear is fear itself"—has been replaced, at least implicitly, by the new slogan "The only thing we have to fear is the end of fear itself." We are now offered the false choice of security or civil liberties, but as Benjamin Franklin said, "Those who would give up essential Liberty, to purchase a little temporary Safety, deserve neither Liberty nor Safety."

The Republicans have not only exploited fear mongering as part of their arsenal but also used ridicule, lampooning John Kerry, for example, as a windsurfer, a fairy, and a flip-flopper. But parody and ridicule can also be the privileged arm of the weak. Because parody appropriates a powerful discourse for its own purposes, it is well suited to the needs of the relatively powerless. It assumes the force of the dominant discourse, only to deploy that force, through a kind of jujitsu, against domination. Here the left could learn a lot from satirists such as Michael Moore and ironic parodists such as Bill Maher, Al Franken, and Jon Stewart. Stewart's *Daily Show,* for example, carries entertainment news to its logical conclusion by making the news truly hilarious. Yet it is paradoxical that this comic show serves up more of the truth than the conventional serious news. The program has been such a success that it has spawned spin-off shows and inflected other news shows and is by now regularly cited on "the real news." In fact surveys show that young Americans are more likely to get their news from Jon Stewart than from the "real" news.

As our pop culture deconstructionist, Stewart dismantles the contradictions of official discourse. Often Stewart uses the administration's own words and rhetoric against it. Bush, for example, rarely develops complex arguments; he speaks in a language of truisms and tautology: "I did it because it was the right thing for America." "If I have to defend America, I'll defend America every time." It is the kind of language that appeals to the obedient little fascist that dwells within all of us, exploiting our desire to accept on faith the words of the symbolic father of the country. Often Stewart simply interrupts Bush's more outrageous statements with a look of eye-rubbing amazement that says, "Did he actually say *that*? Did he actually argue *that*?" The *Daily Show* performers become satiric logicians who carry the logic of the administration's talking points to their absurd conclusions, as when Rob Corddry explained the logical illogic of the Iraq War, to the effect that "We invaded Iraq because we thought that they had a powerful army, but they didn't have a powerful army, so now we have to give them a powerful army, one which will be controlled by radical jihadists who will install Sharia law."

At other times Stewart acts out the meanness he senses behind the official mask of civility, exposing the nasty Id behind the self-righteous Superego by impersonating Cheney as growling maliciously or by making Bush grunt inarticulately, in the manner of Beavis and Butthead. At times Stewart exaggerates slightly by accusing Bush, Cheney, and Rumsfeld—and, in the spirit of fairness, this charge remains unproved—of strangling puppies, or by asking Washington insiders if Cheney is a "cannibal," or "if he drinks the blood of puppies." Stewart acts out the nasty thrust of their discourse and the spirit of the policies, the mean-mindedness usually hidden behind the shiny packaging of the rhetoric. Stewart's boomerang technique is especially appropriate to an administration that projects its own aggressions, often accusing others of planning to do exactly what it is already doing. Thus Bush accused Saddam of "defying the world" and "making a fool out of the United Nations," when that was exactly what he himself was doing. Stewart's boomerang technique sends back Bush's aggressions to Bush. One *Daily Show* episode showed Condoleezza Rice speaking of Saddam's regime as "obsessed with secrecy and ready to use force." Stewart simply repeated the words, making viewers hear them in a new way: "obsessed with secrecy and ready to use force ... hmm ... I won't even comment on the irony of those words." The clear implication was that the Bush administration too was equally "obsessed with secrecy and ready to use force." Another episode showed Bush describing Iraq as "a country under the control of one cruel man." Stewart's addendum, backgrounded by a photo of Rumsfeld and Cheney, was "And now it's under the control of two cruel men." (The insult also carried the implied charge that Bush was not really the president.)

Stewart also cuts through the mendacious idealizations so typical of Bush—"I am a patient man. ... We are a generous people"—by clarifying the incoherently narcissistic nature of the claims. At the same time, he exposes the euphemisms deployed to beautify what is cruel and ugly, as when he has Paul Wolfowitz call torture "freedom tickling." Indeed torture has been a recurrent motif on the *Daily Show*. One of the high-level memos authorizing the use of torture spoke of a "new paradigm" that might bypass the Geneva convention by authorizing certain forms of "pressure." Stewart commented, "What a relief! So it's not really torture; it's just a new paradigm. But you'll be better off if that new paradigm doesn't get attached to your balls!"

But the *Daily Show*'s commentary on torture became truly "torturous" around the time of the Abu Ghraib revelations. After describing what the photos revealed, Stewart said, "Surely it is time for the Defense

Department to speak out clearly and forcefully about these egregious instances of torture." The following clip showed Rumsfeld dodging the question by pointing out a legalistic nicety: "I'm not a lawyer, but my impression is that what has been charged so far is abuse, which is technically different from torture." Stewart's response was that he too was "not a lawyer" and that "in fact, he didn't know, technically, if [Rumsfeld] was ... human. But what we all saw, the photos and all that—that was fucking torture." Stewart prefaced a Bush apology to the Iraqis with a verbal echo of Bush's father: "George Bush wants Iraqis to know that we are kindler, gentler torturers." When Bush in his "apology" pointed out that one of the differences between democracy and dictatorship is that free countries confront abuses openly and directly, Stewart speculated that perhaps the Iraqis would prefer a system where there "wasn't any abuse at all ... a plutocracy perhaps." Correspondent Rob Corddry, meanwhile, explained that "the Iraqi people have to understand that the real America is compassionate, and that Bush has given them twenty-four hours to understand that, and if they did not understand that, he would bomb them and light up the place like a Christmas tree."

The satire continued with the *Daily Show*'s report on the hearings on Capitol Hill regarding Alberto Gonzales as attorney general. After a series of clips revealing Gonzales to be less than forthcoming during the hearings, Stewart stroked his chin maliciously, and in the manner of Hollywood gangsters or Nazis, hissed, "So ... he doesn't wanna talk, does he? Well, we know how to make him talk!" There followed a collage of the famous Abu Ghraib images, now superimposed on the face and body of Gonzales: Gonzales lurched at by attack dogs, Gonzales wired for electricity, Gonzales heaped onto a naked "guy pile." Through a simple mechanism of reversal, viewers were prodded to think about how Gonzales would react if **he** were left unprotected by the Geneva convention rules that he himself derided as "quaint." And in a later period, correspondent Stephen Colbert explained the apparent contradiction between Bush's claim that "We do not torture" and Cheney's effort to allow torture as follows: "Anything we do is legal. Torture is not legal. Ergo—that's Latin for 'Bite me'—we do not torture." Or as correspondent Ed Helms pointed out, "Sometimes to defend the Bill of Rights you have to create a Bill of Wrongs." And in his O'Reilly satirical persona, Colbert indirectly invoked medieval "trial by fire" as a model, asking a guest, "Why do we need the courts at all. Why don't we just torture people to see if they're guilty?"

Stewart often mocks the false pieties of the right. The day that Bush announced his "faith-based initiatives," the *Daily Show* had reporter Colbert praise an earlier very successful faith-based initiative in fifteenth-century Spain. Asked if he was talking about the Spanish Inquisition, Colbert mocked Stewart for "getting hung up on labels," when the important thing was that "they cleaned up Spain!" Often the *Daily Show* mocks the faulty logic of administration spokespersons who explain that "insurgent attacks are a sign of our success," for example. Ed Helms analyzed the rhetoric of President Bush's promises in the wake of Katrina, where Bush declared, "We're going to solve problems. We're problem solvers." Helms identified the structure as "We're going to AB because we're B-Aers. For example, 'We're going to eat zucchini because we're zucchini eaters.'"

George Bernard Shaw once defined Puritanism as "that terrible fear that someone, somewhere, is having a good time." Stand-up comics, for their part, have also mocked the puritanical phobias exploited by the right meant to create a pious climate more conducive to right-wing sermonizing. At the height of the hysteria about Clinton and Monica, part of a well-funded right-wing attempt to remove a democratically elected president, Jerry Seinfeld put the scandal in perspective. Clinton, he admitted, "lied about sex." But then he added, "Everybody lies about sex. In fact, without lies, there would be no sex!" And during the 2004 election, when the right was exploiting homophobia and the issue of same-sex marriage, Bill Maher declared himself baffled by the fuss, "since all marriages are same-sex marriages; you get married, and then you have the same sex, the same sex, the same. ..."

If Jon Stewart is pop culture's Derrida, Stephen Colbert is its Jonathan Swift. Who can forget Colbert's brilliant skewering of the president and the media at the White House roast? Mimicking the body language and the macho manner of right-wing pundit Bill O'Reilly, on the one hand, and the discursive tics and anti-intellectualism of George W. Bush on the other, Colbert ripped through the pretensions of both. As court jester, he spoke truth literally in the face of power, always in the guise of ironic praise. Stewart mocked the president for supposedly strong assertions of belief—a Karl Rove trick to make him look like a man of strength and conviction—by emptying the "credos" of all substance:

> I hold a simple set of beliefs that I live by. Number one, I believe in America. I believe it exists. My gut tells me that I live there. I feel that it extends from the Atlantic to the Pacific, and I strongly believe it has fifty states.

Since Rove constructs Bush as a man who takes strong stands, Colbert played with the word *stand:*

> I stand by this man. I stand by this man because he stands for things. Not only for things, he stands *on* things. Things like aircraft carriers and rubble and recently flooded city squares. And that sends a strong message: that no matter what happens to America, she will always rebound—with the most powerfully staged photo ops in the world.

Colbert also mocked Bush's rock-hard refusal to change with changing circumstances: "The greatest thing about this man is he's steady. You know where he stands. He believes the same thing Wednesday that he believed on Monday, no matter what happened Tuesday." But Colbert reserved his most cutting barbs for the spineless media reduced to, with a few notable exceptions, disseminating White House spin:

> Let's review the rules. Here's how it works. The president makes the decisions. He's the decider. The press secretary announces those decisions, and you people of the press type those decisions down. Make, announce, type. Just put 'em through a spell check and go home. Get to know your family again. Make love to your wife. Write that novel you got kicking around in your head. You know, the one about the intrepid Washington reporter with the courage to stand up to the administration. You know—fiction!

Through humor, then, these patriotic clowns have probed the most serious issues—mendacity at the top, the false rationale for the Iraq War, the hypocritical pieties of the Christian right—in a mode appealing to young people shaped by a media-saturated era. Bill Maher, to take another example, has effectively skewered the president in amusing ways on his *Real Time with Bill Maher* show. The following is his sum-up of the Bush presidency as of September 16, 2005:

> Mr. President, this job can't be fun for you any more. There's no more money to spend—you used up all of that. You can't start another war because you used up the army. And now, darn the luck, the rest of your term has become the Bush family nightmare: helping poor people. Listen to your Mom. The cupboards bare, the credit card's maxed out. No one's speaking to you. Mission accomplished.

> Now it's time to do what you've always done best: lose interest and walk away. Like you did with your military service and the oil company and the baseball team. It's time. Time to move on and try the next fantasy job. How about cowboy or space man? Now I know what you're saying; there's so many other things that you as president could involve yourself in. Please don't. I know, I know. There's a lot left to do. There's a war with Venezuela. Eliminating the sales tax on yachts. Turning the space program over to the Church. And Social Security to Fannie Mae. Giving embryos the vote.

> But sir, none of that is going to happen now. ... You've performed so poorly I'm surprised that you haven't given yourself a medal. ... On your watch, we've lost almost all of our allies, the surplus, four airliners, two trade centers, a piece of the Pentagon, and the city of New Orleans. Maybe you're just not lucky. I'm not saying you don't love this country. I'm just wondering how much worse it could be if you were on the other side.

The scandal, of course, is that the most trenchant critiques of the political system come not from the "serious" media commentators—although here Bill Moyers and Keith Olbermann, not to mention Amy Goodman, Laura Flanders and Rachel Maddow, constitute admirable exceptions—but rather from comics. While the mainstream journalists have been "spun" until they're dizzy, the clowns get it straight. Given the complicity of the media in administration mendacity, such comic shows serve, in lieu of an honest and critical media, as our balm and our stimulant; they tell us that the right's lies are laughable, that our leaders are crazy and dangerous, and that the emperor is naked! And the laughter from the audience tells us that we are not alone.

Sodomy, Sadism, and the Christian Right

Although it is obvious why the Christian right sees itself as being on the right, it is less obvious why it thinks of itself as "Christian." Perhaps the right is Christian in the same sense that the Crusades, the Spanish Inquisition, and the Salem witch trials were Christian. But the right is clearly not Christian in the sense of "love thy neighbor." For the right the word *neighbor* refers only to rich people living in one's gated community. Were Jesus Christ to become a political candidate, one suspects, the right would "Swift Boat" him in a second, debunking his claims about walking on water and denouncing his "wacky ideas" about poverty. They would deride Jesus' "give all you have to the poor" as Marxist class warfare. Televangelist Pat Robertson, as a very rich money changer in the electronic temple, might call for Christ's assassination for saying "it is harder for a rich man"—that means you, Robertson—"to enter the kingdom of heaven than for a camel to pass through the eye of a needle." Quite apart from Jesus' Jewishness, his ambiguous birth from a poor virgin, and his enigmatic sexuality, the Christian right—and here we speculate—would probably lock Jesus up on the basis of "three strikes you're out," with the first strike being his bleeding-heart love of the poor, the second strike being his "politically correct" tolerance—"judge not, that ye be not judged," "let he who is perfect cast the first stone," and so forth—and the third strike being his excessive love of peace ("Blessed be the Peacekeepers") and insufficient love of war—as encapsulated in the traitorous idea (borrowed from the Jewish Bible) that "Thou shalt not kill," a concept that for the right applies only to fetuses, leading to the following dilemma: when an American soldier kills a pregnant Iraqi, has that soldier performed an abortion?

A paradoxical feature of right-wing outrage, to wax more serious for a moment, is that it is directed more at images than at actions, more at symbols than at practices. It is more obsessed with insubstantial violations having to do with harmless images—Janet Jackson's breast, naked statues in the Justice Department, Internet porn—than with actual deeds that actually hurt real people. Right-wing fury is strangely iconoclastic, more desirous of keeping up appearances than of preventing certain kinds of brutal behavior. Thus the right is terribly unforgiving of the imagistic offenses of Hollywood films (even Clint Eastwood films) and yet so infinitely forgiving of very real abuses in Guantánamo, Iraq, and Afghanistan. Indeed the eighteen hundred images from Abu Ghraib, most of which Americans have not seen, revealed a startling feature. What was striking was the highly sexualized nature of the abuse, reflected in photo-op "guy piles," giddy female soldiers pointing to detainees' penises, rape, and forced fellatio.[15] All this alongside reports from elsewhere of women interrogators splatting (or pretending to splat) religious detainees with taboo menstrual blood or fondling their breasts to provoke the prisoners, demanding that the men masturbate, and so forth. Why exactly is it that the right gets so exercised (and possibly eroticized) about Janet Jackson's breasts, which never harmed anyone and which have presumably provided comfort to some, yet is so indifferent toward these other more violently sexualized and hurtful offenses? A suddenly sexually tolerant Rush Limbaugh, for example, dismissed the explicit images of the military police as "standard good old American pornography."

Yet perhaps one can explain what at first glance seems like this odd double standard that denounces Janet Jackson's harmless "wardrobe malfunction" and yet is so permissive toward these other, infinitely more violent transactions. First, the denunciation of Hollywood immorality forms part of the domestic "culture wars," where excoriating the "Hollywood elite" and black stars serves to divert attention away from the upward redistribution of wealth provoked by its economic policies. Second, for right-wingers the abuse of dark-skinned people in the Third World is not particularly shocking. If we are torturing them, they must be terrorists: why else would they be in our custody? It all depends on who is committing the abuse. Whatever abuses "we" commit—even to the point of detainees dying in military custody in what

Amnesty International called a new American "gulag"—are a priori justified, since they are committed against an indistinct and dehumanized "them" (foreigners, terrorists, dark people). It goes without saying that if "they" were to commit exactly the same abuses against "us," it would be read as a token of their barbarity. It is ultimately a question of framing and hierarchies of values. Patriotism is redefined as the right to commit unethical acts toward enemies: sadism in the service of a noble cause.

Nothing sends the religious right into ecstatic orgies of moral rectitude like the prospect of sodomy—that awesome encounter of a penis and an anus.[16] For the right the very idea of that encounter is so powerful that they try to mobilize it to win elections. (And didn't George H.W. Bush pronounce the word *Saddam* to sound like *sodom*?) There is of course some hypocrisy in this aversion to sodomy, since the White House had no problem employing James Guckert (aka Jeff Gannon), as a fake newsman-prop for its press conferences, a man who turned out to be working as a $200 per hour gay escort, who advertised himself as a muscular, masculine, and military "top" on the Hotmilitarystud.com Web site.[17] And there is one form of sodomy the right wing seems not to mind at all; that is, the sodomy involved when the penis belongs to an American soldier and the anus belongs to an Iraqi or Afghan detainee. U.S. military and Red Cross reports, the reports of former interrogators such as SPC Tony Lagouranis, and the photos from Abu Ghraib all offer ample evidence as to the practice.[18] Man loving man? That stinks to God's nostrils! But one of our soldiers sodomizing an Iraqi detainee? Our boys are doing a fine job!

What, then, explains the lack of right-wing outrage at this kind of sodomy? We think the discrepancy has to do with the fact that the sexualized torture of dark-skinned people, for the right, is seen not as a form of sexual abuse but rather as a part of what they see as a more lofty, almost religious goal—"disciplining" and "punishing." Thus what would normally seem worse—sodomy as an act not of love but of naked aggression—for them is actually better, because the torturer is administering, as it were, God's will toward the detainees, who deserve whatever they get. What they are approving is not the sex but the violence. And doesn't the right always prefer violence to sex? When the right complains about sex and violence on television, we all know that it's the sex they're really after and not the violence of, say, a Schwarzenegger blockbuster.[19] Nor is it the violence of sexual harassment that disturbs them but rather sexual pleasure itself (and especially that of women). For the right enormously violent crimes such as lying the country into war pale in malignity next to real crimes such as extramarital fellatio. (An Internet joke pointed to these skewed priorities: "Will someone please give Bush a blow job so we can impeach him!")

At times one is shocked by the sheer sadism and violence of some on the right. First, the obscenity of rushing to war, where any chance of peace through UN inspections or Iraqi concessions, was regarded by the administration as "bad news" that might slow the march to war. Or the very idea of a vice president lobbying for the right to torture. Or those Enron types recorded making fun of the elderly women who would suffer from their stage-managed blackouts in California. Or Republican lobbyist Jack Abramoff making fun of the "morons" from the Indian tribes that he was cheating. The right-wing imagination seems peculiarly violent: Bush talking about "smoking them out" and "bring 'em on," William Bennett speculating about "aborting all the black babies," Ralph Reed speaking of "spilling the blood" of Democrats, Bill O'Reilly fantasizing that al Qaeda might destroy San Francisco, John Gibson licking his chops over the imagined destruction of Paris, Rush Limbaugh suggesting that "it's not healthy to go without a war," Pat Robertson wishing death for foreign heads of state and destruction on those towns that fail to vote his way on "intelligent design," and Ann Coulter pouring poison into the public ether, with her endless fantasies of violence against "liberals," Muslims, and 9/11 widows.

Some critics have noted a sadistic bent within George W. Bush. Mark Crispin Miller has noted that the usually inarticulate Bush has no trouble with language when he is talking about violence or revenge. Psychiatrist Justin Frank, in his book *Bush on the Couch: Inside the Mind of the President,* describes a "lifelong streak of sadism" in Bush's life and career, going from inserting firecrackers into the bodies of frogs, to using a branding iron to maim young pledges in his fraternity at Yale, to smirking over the executions of death-row inmates, and on to the sadistic spree called the Bush presidency. Frank sees sadism even in the lack of a plan for postwar Iraq—the war itself was the point:

Like the explosives Bush unleashed in Iraq, the time bombs he
has planted in our future were inspired by the perverse combination of destructiveness and denial, righteousness and reckless-
ness, that marks the sadist mind-set.[20]

Our nation, Frank concludes, will be dealing with the legacy of this
sadism for years to come.

But then why are we surprised? The right's domestic and international policies are a form of sadism. Cutting taxes for the rich while
gutting social programs is a form of sadism. Allowing more than forty
million citizens to live without health care and thus putting them in
danger of death is a form of social sadism. Preaching chastity to Africans as a solution to the AIDS crisis is a form of sadism. Depriving those
devastated by medical emergencies a chance to use bankruptcy protection is a form of sadism. Favoring a punitive system that sends more
black men to jail than to college is a form of sadism. Sending young
people off to die without adequate armor in a misbegotten war is a form
of sadism. Profit-driven health care is a form of sadism. Offering a pre-
scription-drug benefit to seniors, which is ultimately a gift to the drug
companies, is a form of sadism. Spending billions for war and nothing
for peace is a form of sadism.[21] Devastating the infrastructure of other
countries is a form of sadism.

The militaristic patriotism of the right virtually requires enemies, an
"us" and a "them." The exaltation of the self runs tandem with the denigration of the internal and external enemy. In the United States the tradition of what Michael Rogin called "political demonology" specializes
in the creation of monsters through the "inflation, stigmatization, and
dehumanization of political foes."[22] What is especially striking about
some of America's enemies in recent decades—Manuel Noriega, Saddam Hussein, the *mujhadin* in Afghanistan (including bin Laden)—is
that all are former allies and partial creations of the United States. The
enemies were figures previously adopted by the United States, thus giving the hostility a strange, almost incestuous quality. The same Hussein
praised as "moderate" and "pragmatic" by earlier administrations; ally
of American policy and the darling of American, British, and German
corporations; the man whose hand was shaken so warmly by Donald
Rumsfeld in 1983 was transformed during the first Gulf War into a

reincarnation of Hitler, with the rapidity with which enemies for "Hate Week" were fabricated in Orwell's *1984*. A 1994 Senate investigation found that between1986 and 1990 the United States licensed companies to export $600 million worth of advanced technology and materials used by Iraq to make mustard gas, VX nerve agent, anthrax, and other biological and chemical weapons and that shipments continued after Hussein used chemical weapons to wipe out Halabja in 1988.[23] The same Dick Cheney who later vilified Hussein did business with him up through the 1990s. After the 1992 election, Halliburton rebuilt Hussein's war-damaged oil fields for some $23.8 million, even though Cheney, as secretary of defense during the first Gulf War, had been part of the military campaign that destroyed those very same fields. In fact columnist Nicholas Kristof of the *New York Times* wrote that Cheney-led Halliburton had "sold more equipment to Iraq than any other company."[24] Indeed Halliburton's profits have come in large part from rebuilding, at taxpayers' expense, what the U.S. military had destroyed.[25]

Scapegoats are hated for their presumed evil attributes but loved for their socially unifying function. Thus both Bush administrations whipped up hatred against Saddam Hussein, partially as a distraction from political problems at home. But one has to watch out for what one demonizes. There is always the possibility that the demon might turn out to be not "them" but "us." Thus George W. Bush, the sovereign above the law, performs a macabre dance with the terrorists, deemed below the law. Bush's righteous pronouncements about Saddamite evil ended up boomeranging against Bush himself when it was revealed that U.S. soldiers and contract interrogators had also tortured and killed, at times in the very same Abu Ghraib buildings used by the Saddam regime. Ronald Reagan denounced the Soviet Union, but just a few decades later Americans were reportedly using torture in "black sites" in the same East European countries where torture had been used earlier by the "Evil Empire." It now seems clear that the environment that made torture possible came from the very top of the administration, in legal memos giving advice as to how to get around the "quaint" Geneva conventions—a manifestation of the "We have met the enemy, and he is us" syndrome. Rhetorical vilifications have a way of yielding "strange fruit."

And what are we to make of a military mind-set that studies a culture—in this case Arab and Muslim culture—only to humiliate that culture? Relying on such Orientalist favorites as Raphael Patai's *The Arab Mind,* the administration decided that the U.S. military could use the supposed sexual disorders of Arab/Muslims to control them. Here we find the complete inversion of the civilized–barbarian trope. The CIA manual "KUBARK Counterintelligence Interrogation," produced in 1963, inventoried a number of "scientific" and "touch-free" techniques that could be used to elicit information. The chapter "The Coercive Counterintelligence Interrogation of Resistant Sources" includes the following observation:

> All coercive techniques are designed to induce regression. The result of external pressures of sufficient intensity is the loss of those defenses most recently acquired by civilized man ... relatively small degrees of homeostatic derangement, fatigue, pain, sleep, loss or anxiety may impair these functions.[26]

So there we have it: the goal of the highly civilized, technologically superior CIA is to induce a regression, on the part of detainees, from civilized norms, thus presumably proving that the detainees had always been subcivilized anyway and were simply reverting to type. The document, just one more monument, as German Jewish intellectual Walter Benjamin famously put it, to both civilization and barbarism, suggests that the job of the interrogator is to literally manufacture barbarian regression. Here we find proof of the interdependence of civilization and barbarism; the civilized master, imbued with feelings of superiority, produces the barbarian while in the process producing his own barbarity as well.

Patriotic Blackmail

Despite the United States' apparently impregnable geographical position between two oceans, despite our peaceful relations with Mexico and Canada, despite our overwhelming economic and military power, we Americans seem more and more on the defensive. Our country has become a national *in*security state. The United States is clearly a much more militarized country than most countries in the world. Our entertainment is more violent, our people are more armed, and our might is more awesome. We outspend all other countries on what used to be called *war*, which is now called *defense*. Over past centuries our country has been involved in endless wars and military interventions in Asia, Africa, South America, and Europe. Although it used to be said that the "business of America is business," it seems that now more and more the business of America is war, even as war itself is becoming more and more a business. "When war becomes profitable," as Chalmers Johnson puts it in the film *Why We Fight*, "we can expect more of it." And like other businesses the war business is carried more and more by the "outsourced" labor of a shadow army of thousands of people who in an earlier period would have been called "mercenaries." Even politics has been militarized in the permanent warrior state, to the point that the U.S. political system basically blocks anyone who is unfriendly to the military–industrial–corporate power structure from even coming close to the portals of power.

Patriotism, then, has become collateral damage in our government's wars of choice. Rightist politicians bully us into war and then eagerly proclaim "we are at war" as an excuse to ignore domestic priorities, bypass the Constitution, and strengthen the executive branch. Patriotism has been redefined as knee-jerk support for all wars, no matter how ill advised or counterproductive. Most of the recent U.S. wars, as Carl Boggs points out, "represent a flagrant violation of regional treaties and laws, not to mention the UN Charter itself, which explicitly prohibits military attacks against sovereign nations."[27] At this point patriotic jive has become the last refuge of scoundrel politicians, especially those with declining poll numbers. It is about time we Americans ask ourselves why our powerful nation seems to always be at war. The ritualistic repetition of the slogan "Global War on Terror," a war that risks morphing into World War III, is no longer sufficient.

We must, unfortunately, shed ourselves of this sham, militaristic patriotism, before we can even begin to speak of real patriotism. It is interesting in this context that the patriotic charge—"You have to support the troops in the name of patriotism," "You can't side with the enemy"—works only in relation to wars and foreign policy. The right cannot use patriotism to support its domestic policies—for example, "You must support offshore tax havens for corporations in the name of patriotism," "You must not have universal health care in the name of patriotism," or "You must resist campaign finance reform in the name of patriotism"—because in those cases patriotic logic might just lead in precisely the opposite direction.

The link between pseudopatriotism and militarism is a relatively recent development. Although U.S. history, like many nation-state histories, has often been violent, U.S. society and politics have only recently become militaristic. Militarism was not inscribed from the beginning on the hard drive of American history. In his Farewell Address (September 17, 1796) George Washington warned against "overgrown military establishments which under any form of government [were] ... inauspicious to liberty, and which are to be regarded as particularly hostile to republican liberty."[28] James Madison, the primary author of the Constitution, wrote,

> Of all enemies to public liberty, war is, perhaps, the most to be dreaded, because it comprises and develops the germ of every other. War is the parent of armies; from these proceed debts and taxes; and armies, and debt, and taxes, are the known instruments for bringing the many under the domination of the few.[29]

Nothing in the Constitution "commits or even encourages the United States to employ military power to save the rest of humankind or remake the world in its own image."[30] Militarism per se goes against the expressed wishes of the founders; it was not originally part of the national DNA. Before both world wars, the U.S. army was miniscule, and the American populace was generally reluctant to participate in foreign wars. Even after World War II Americans were eager to demobilize the army and return to domestic concerns, while the Pentagon wanted to get its troops out of Europe. When wars drag on, Americans tend to tire of them: the Korean and Vietnam wars, for example, ended with support levels of around 30 percent.[31] At this point, polls show that not only American citizens but even a majority of the soldiers in Iraq think we should leave. Yet the war goes on, as if its vast unpopularity were irrelevant to the decision makers, reminding us once again that democracy is a precious, but also precarious, thing.

The dominant media rarely give a sense of how strange, unusual, and recent the current militarization is. Many Americans seem unaware that not all nations define patriotism as an attitude favoring war and the military. Many countries have seen periods of military fervor, but they were usually linked to authoritarian episodes in the nation's history. France has known periods of militarism, but they were associated with France's colonial and imperial conquests. Brazil has also known such periods, but they were associated with (U.S.-supported) right-wing dictatorships such as the one that overthrew João Goulart in 1964.

In the United States militaristic patriotism has produced a vicious cycle. The military–corporate–governmental complex, or some faction within it or politicians linked to it, begins ill-advised wars—usually really about control of the world's resources but "covered" with fantastic warnings about imaginary dangers and ennobled by lofty slogans about freedom that hide the actual motivations. Once the war is started, the usual blackmail begins: "We must support our troops," "Leaving would be a victory for the enemy." After unleashing what even military officials call the "Pandora's box" of ethnic strife in Iraq, the politicians use the chaos as an argument for not leaving. Just when our international credit is depleted because of the Iraq War, we are told that we must continue the war because "our credit is at stake" and "we have to keep our word" and "backing down would send the wrong message." (And they say that only Asians are concerned with saving face!) And then the cruelest of all non sequiturs: "We cannot leave, because then our soldiers would have died in vain." In other words an even larger pile of corpses is required to prove that those who already died "will not have died in vain." "Camp Casey" and Cindy Sheehan and the "Gold Star Families against the War" have offered eloquent refutation of this argument.

As part of the usual marketing operations, most recent U.S. wars—no matter how misguided—have been packaged as replays of the one "good" war—World War II, where the United States defeated Nazism and installed the mechanism of a more peaceful and prosperous world order. The World War II analogy serves multiple purposes. First, it implies that all U.S. interventions are motivated, like World War II, by foreign attack. Second, it implies that the enemy is as evil as Hitler or Hirohito or Mussolini. Third, it implies that any postwar "occupation" will be benevolent and effective like those of Germany and Japan. The phrase "Islamic Fascism" serves the same function. Apart from attaching the name of a religion to a political ideology—rather like saying "Christian Nazism"—the phrase flatters the hawks by implying that a "war of choice" was not an exercise in imperialism but part of a noble fight against fascism. The phrase "Islamic fascism" also distracts attention away from the administration's own authoritarian policies (preventive war, manipulation of the media, extra-legal detention, torture, and overweening executive power). It is one more attempt to pin a label on a pseudocoherent enemy. Just as during the Cold War when all commies were deemed the same—despite massive disagreement between the USSR and China or between China and Vietnam—so now all terrorists are the same. It is as if the debates over recent American wars inevitably invoke two opposite historical paradigms. Those in favor of the wars see them—or at least pretend to see them—as replays of World War II, while their opponents see them as "tragic farce" replays of Vietnam. When the enthusiasm for the war flags, our leaders resurrect the tired old "Munich" charge, referring to Great Britain's falsely reassuring "peace in our time" agreement with Hitler, a form of rhetoric becoming less and less effective as the memory of Munich fades. Thus voices against the Iraq War have been repeatedly caricatured as Chamberlain-like partisans of appeasement, neatly forgetting the long U.S. official "appeasement" and even support of Saddam Hussein. The real image of appeasement is the 1983 photo of Rumsfeld shaking hands with Saddam. And now it is the United States that is threatening faraway nations. *Blitzkrieg* in German translates as "shock and awe" in English. And as the demonstrator's placards put it, "We're shocked, and it's awful!"

The official goal of the U.S. government, as outlined by the hawks in various policy documents, is global domination through absolute military superiority. That goal frightened the world when it was expressed by the Nazis, and it frightens now, even though Bush is not Hitler, even though the discourse is not fascist and racist but democratic, and even though Americans are not, by any stretch of the imagination, Nazis. (It is interesting that populist senator Huey Long predicted in the 1930s that America would have fascism but that "we will call it democracy.")[32] What we do have, if not fascism, is democratic rhetoric being used as a mask for highly authoritarian and undemocratic ends. Paul Wolfowitz proposed in 1992 that the objective of U.S. foreign policy should be to prevent "any hostile power from dominating a region whose resources would, under consolidated control, be sufficient to generate global power."[33] The Wolfowitz formula recalls that of Stanley Kubrik's satirical General Jack Ripper from *Doctor Strangelove:* "Trust no one!"

Within this Ripperesque logic, any nation aspiring even only to regional influence risks attack, because that nation's resources "might" conceivably, at some later time, generate an alternative center of power. Needless to say the right's equation of U.S. national interest with the universal interest has been met with skepticism and even anger outside of the United States and sometimes inside the United States as well. Why should a country representing only 5 percent of the world's population wield power over the other 95 percent? The dominant U.S. media normalize this state of privilege and entitlement, making it seem part of the natural order, euphemized as our "world responsibility." Naturalizing the U.S. global military presence, the media rarely explain precisely what our militaries are actually doing and why they are doing it, whence the protest T-shirt asking, "It's 10 p.m.; Do you know what your marines are doing?"

Columnist Charles Krauthammer of the *Washington Post,* meanwhile, calls for vivid demonstrations of American might: "America is no mere international citizen. It is the dominant power in the world, more dominant than any since Rome." Calling for a "triumph of the will" reminiscent of fascist discourses of the 1930s, Krauthammer goes on: "America is in a position to reshape norms, alter expectations and create new realities. How? By unapologetic and implacable demonstrations of will."[34] The problem with "implacable demonstrations of will," of course, is that they provoke other, equally "implacable demonstrations of will," taking us back to "might makes right." And in the case of the Iraq War, implacable demonstrations of will translated the wishes not of the American nation as a whole but only of a tiny elite, since the populace was persuaded to go to war only by misinformation and the strategic conjuring up of "mushroom clouds."

The Pentagonization of Patriotism

Thanks to the complicit media, few Americans are aware of the American military world abroad, a world dotted by hundreds of U.S. military facilities, often surrounded by a tax-financed subculture of golf courses and Learjets, with virtually no civilian oversight.[35] The same politicians who deplore "throwing money at problems" when it is a question of poor people at home delight in throwing money at the military both at home and abroad. Although many Americans actively, or more often passively, accept the outsized military budget, most would probably be shocked at the degree to which that budget penetrates all of our social and political institutions, at the social sacrifices made in its name, or at the degree of corruption it entails.

Contrary to the American Constitution, which stipulates a "regular Statement and Account of the Receipts and Expenditures of all Public Money," there is now little effective oversight or auditing of the Pentagon. In May 2001 the deputy inspector general at the Pentagon admitted that "$1.1 trillion ... was simply gone and no one can be sure of when, where, or to whom the money went."[36] Furthermore there is an inverse proportion between the seriousness of such crimes and the degree of the punishment. The theft of a wallet lands you in jail, but the theft of billions in defense contracts gets you some good land and a pleasant retirement. And the whole system is linked to the "crony capitalism" of an interlocked network of right-wing ideologues, retired military men, corporate executives, and congressmen and senators. And while during the Cold War this network merely influenced the government, with this administration, where key figures are linked to corporations involved with energy or the military, where the president is a former oilman, and where the vice president himself is a former military contractor, this network is now the government.

While lauding "markets" in principle, the corporate–military–political complex has constructed a perfectly well-oiled system based on automatic cost growth and pork distribution. A virtually unaudited Pentagon—despite constitutional requirements of oversight and accountability—dominates the country and enriches those at the top of the corporate–military ladder. It is rumored that Eisenhower, in his Farewell Address, thought of warning the nation against the military–industrial–congressional complex but dropped the word *congressional*.

Military spending is now woven into the very fabric of the U.S. government, as well as into the whoop and warf of the economy and the culture. Militarized video games, Hollywood blockbusters, military recruiters in schools, and Air Force flights over sports events all exalt the military and a military approach to problems. The profits from the system largely go to corporate–military kingpins like Bechtel, Halliburton, and the Carlyle Group, but they are also doled out to the states for electoral purposes. Thus relatively safe red states such as Wyoming or Montana get proportionately more "antiterrorist" funds than the truly vulnerable blue states such as New York and California.

Pseudopatriotic militarism sometimes takes very vicious forms. On June 23, 2005, Disney/ABC radio personality Paul Harvey, one of the most widely listened-to commentators in the United States, lamented the decline in warrior virility and called, at least by implication, for the use of nuclear weapons in Afghanistan and Iraq: "We sent men with rifles into Afghanistan and Iraq," he complained, "and kept our best weapons in their silos." Rather than being ashamed of the genocide and slavery of the Native Americans, Harvey saw them as proud moments in American history:

> We didn't come this far because we're made of sugar candy. Once upon a time, we elbowed our way onto and across this continent by giving smallpox-infected blankets to Native Americans. That was biological warfare. And we used every other weapon we could get our hands on to grab this land from whomever. And we grew prosperous. And yes, we greased the skids with the sweat of slaves.

The so-called family-friendly Disney corporation, the same corporation that found Michael Moore's *Fahrenheit 9/11* "too controversial" (but not the anti-Clinton television special "The Path to 9/11") and that markets superficially pro–Native American cartoon epics such as *Pocahontas,* apparently saw no problem with allowing eighteen million listeners hear a white-supremacist rant that literally echoes some of the precepts of *Mein Kampf.* Hitler, after all, cited the genocide of the Native Americans, alongside that of the Armenians and Tasmanians, as a model for the extermination of the Jews that he was planning.

The right likes to frame the questions in terms of "How much government?" and "The government against the people." In Brazil and France the debate is almost never pitched in such a manipulative way. The real question is "Government for whom?" And "What can governments offer their people?" And "What do we get in return for our tax dollars?" While other advanced governments offer their peoples health care, free education, and affordable housing, our government basically offers us endless wars, all "sold" as part of campaigns against a shape-shifting gallery of enemies: the Evil Empire or rogue nations and now axis of evils and a vaguely defined terrorism. Some enemies, such as Saddam Hussein, have been dictatorial thugs, but the actual designated enemies can be very diverse in terms of the social–political arrangements they represent. And even Saddam Hussein was regarded as an enemy not simply because he was a dictator but also because he ran a statist regime where oil was nationalized.

The concern with democracy has been highly selective. The administration had no problem with kidnapping and removing a democratically elected president—Jean-Bertrand Aristide—from office in Haiti. And the lack of democracy in friendly oil states such as Saudi Arabia or Kuwait has never been a problem. Recent U.S. interventions, as left commentator Michael Parenti points out, have targeted a wide variety of forms of government: (1) a populist military government (Noriega in Panama), (2) a Christian socialist government (the Sandinistas in Nicaragua), (3) a social democracy (Allende in Chile), (4) an anticolonialist radical reform government (Lumumba in the Congo), (5) an Islamic revolutionary government (Libya under Qaddafi), (6) a conservative but statist military regime (Saddam Hussein in Iraq), and (7) a Marxist–Leninist government (Castro in Cuba).[37]

The administration and the media offer a highly idealized and abstract picture of the U.S. war in Iraq. It is a matter not of never reporting bad news—how could the media not report suicide bombings, improvised explosive devices, and American casualties?—but rather of ignoring key issues. For example, one word rarely heard in Bush's speeches about the war or in the media is *oil*. And indeed if it was not at all about oil, why did Halliburton prepare a five-hundred-page document concerning what to do with Iraq's oil industry, several months before the invasion of Iraq?[38] The war is also about controlling the country that has the oil and thus wielding a powerful economic weapon against Europe and Asia, especially China. But even though many American presidents had spoken of U.S. strategic interest in oil, the media, following administration cues, have avoided the word. Since the war had been sold as a matter of removing a villain about to attack us, the O word cannot be used. The war is also about transforming Iraq, as a centrally planned economy, into a neoliberal market economy. As much a "business opportunity" as an ideological crusade, the Iraq War provoked a feeding frenzy for energy, industrial, communications, security, and prison corporations, all with their "contractors," a term that Neil Smith calls "a legal nicety for mercenaries."[39]

Despite administration coyness about the O word, some U.S. policy makers in the past were more frank about American interests. A long line of U.S. officials (including presidents) has acknowledged both privately and publicly that the United States needs oil and will use military force to secure it. During the Cold War George F. Kennan, the architect of the anticommunist "containment" policy, spoke candidly of the "necessary lies" that would ensure the consent of the American population and the world:

> We have about 50% of the world's wealth, but only 6.3% of its population ... our real task in the coming period is to devise a pattern of relationships which will permit us to maintain this position of disparity ... to do so, we will have to dispense with all sentimentality and daydreaming.[40]

In a similarly frank document, decades later, former army intelligence officer Ralph Peters spoke of a "new American century" in which

> we will become still wealthier, culturally more lethal, and increasingly powerful. We will excite hatreds without precedent ... the de facto role of the U.S. armed forces will be to keep the world safe for our economy and open to our cultural assault. To these ends, we will do a fair amount of killing.[41]

This astonishingly straightforward statement attaches words such as *lethal* and *assault* to the word *culture* and demonstrates the monumental chutzpah of giving a national name—*American*—to a century, as if a hundred years of complexly lived experiential time, shared by billions of human beings spread across various continents, could ever actually "belong" only to a single nation-state, as if all the "others" were living in the mistaken time of someone else's periodization. It is this kind of megalomania that has been served up, falsely, as "patriotism."

Democratic presidential candidate Dennis Kucinich compared the nostrums of the military–corporate elite to Marie-Antoinette's recommendation to the French common people on the eve of the French Revolution. The French aristocrats' "Let them eat cake," he suggested, has become the administration's "Let them eat war!" A country that represents a small percentage of the world's population accounts for half of the world's military expenditures and a high percentage of the world's arms exports. (Other countries such as France and Brazil are also involved in arms sales, although to a lesser extent.) The massive military expenditures, never really voted on democratically, simply cannot be reconciled with the government's fundamental responsibilities in the traditional areas of education, income security, health care, housing, and environmental protection, not to mention protection from disasters such as hurricanes, avian flu, and biological terrorism. We pay billions for defense and yet could not defend ourselves from 9/11. All those trillions in expenditures did not guarantee that the Pentagon, NORAD (North American Aerospace Defense Command), and the FAA (Federal Aviation Administration) could communicate and collaborate to respond to an actual attack. In asymmetrical warfare the attack depends not on missiles but on determination and box cutters or on local insurgents who infiltrate American mess halls in Iraq. Hugely expensive Star Wars–style defense systems now being proposed are clearly more or less irrelevant to the fight against these kinds of terrorism, which suggests that the huge increases in the Pentagon budget are more about profits than about terrorism.

The Katrina disaster, meanwhile, revealed that we are not prepared even for nonterrorist-related disasters, including "natural" ones such as hurricanes that had been predicted years in advance. And it is paradoxical that although U.S. military spending outstrips that of the rest of the world, all these expenditures do not generate a feeling of security in the American people. The result of the administration's militaristic bullying, ironically, is to have created an impression of the United States as a declining power. The more Bush struts and bullies, the more other leaders defy him and the more leaders in Europe and Latin America simply act and collaborate without him.

The more Bush beats up the world, the more he grinds his own hands into pulp. Unilateralism and militarism have accelerated the decline of U.S. power. The Bush administration fails to realize that not creating enemies around the world is part of national security. It is strange that the most powerful country is also a very insecure country, a place where the people feel "endangered." People in France and Brazil certainly feel some insecurity, especially about crime, yet they worry less, paradoxically, about being attacked, even though they spend infinitely less on defense. Is there a connection, one wonders, between our profligate military spending on "defense," and our "defensiveness" and between our hyperpower and our hyperinsecurity?

Trickle-down militarism helps not the American people but only the corporate–military elite. Chuck Spinney, a program analyst for the Pentagon, describes the system as a "self-licking ice cream cone," based on automatic cost increases. The military budget becomes what William D. Hartung calls a "giant cash machine" to reward friends and punish enemies.[42] All the rest of us get in return is the "outsourcing" of democracy and the privatization of war, as the United States becomes a "national security state" characterized by perpetual war and a frayed and fragile democratic process. Perhaps that is why the war's promoters seem so unperturbed by the chaos in Iraq. The chaos works for them by generating profits and (desired) deficits and maintaining a military presence in the region, one of the main goals of the mission. Yet on another level the relentless prowar propaganda staged by the administration and by sectors of the media constitutes a backhanded complement to the American people. Literary critic Edward Said often said that if Americans really knew what their government was doing, they would rise up in revolt. Indeed the concept of fair-mindedness is highly cherished by the people of the United States, which is perhaps why the government so often has to lie to them. That the administration has to disguise the destruction of Social Security as "saving Social Security" is similarly a backhanded complement to the popular intelligence, since it assumes that Americans do not want Social Security destroyed. Only the most massive forms of government and media brainwashing, by the same token, could win "consent" for a war in Iraq that many Americans accepted only reluctantly. The war became palatable to the majority only when it was framed first as a fight for "survival" and then as a fight for "democracy."

Indeed one can only be impressed by the massive effort required to persuade Americans to not want what they would ordinarily want—such as health care, mass transit, and inexpensive education—and to want what they would ordinarily not want. On one hand the system tries to convince us that we want war and its attendant horrors: death, killing, maiming, trauma, stress-related disorders, and so forth. On the other hand it tries to convince us that we do not want the social benefits offered by other industrialized democracies. They try to convince us that nothing could be worse than walking into a medical office and not having to fill out insurance forms, nothing worse than having guaranteed health care as part of a national health care system. Those poor Brits, they have to accept house visits from doctors—imagine doctors in your own home; what a terrible loss of privacy! We prefer being humiliated and ignored in the impersonal corridors of America's profit-oriented hospitals.

Right-wing hype tries to convince us Americans that we love going broke paying medical bills, that we adore being bankrupted by our parents' or grandparents' medical emergencies, and that we simply relish using the emergency room as our doctor of last resort. Above all we venerate those insurance companies—their TV commercials tell us how good-hearted they are—whose primary bottom-line goal is to not help us at all or, failing that, to help us as little as possible. And we absolutely love the power of the medical and pharmaceutical industries, which sometimes prefer not to actually cure diseases because, as comic Chris Rock reminds us, "the money is in the medicine!" By the same token, the right tries to convince us that we absolutely relish going into debt to pay for our education or our children's education. In the 1950s they tried to convince us that nothing could be worse than the European-style welfare state. The Swedes, we were told, were committing suicide en masse because their welfare system was taking care of them—horror of horrors!—"from the cradle to grave." According to right-wing nostrums, people who are taken care of from cradle to grave lose all initiative and even a desire to live. The ideal, apparently, is to be abused and neglected from cradle to grave.

The Demise of Reciprocity: A Fable from Megastan

One sometimes wonders if we Americans have been so spoiled by our overweening power that we have lost any sense of reciprocity and of the general human condition. As a matter of habit, we find normal and acceptable practices by ourselves that would provoke outrage were they practiced by any other country. Have we forgotten that ours is the only country that has ever actually used nuclear weapons? Even now our government flirts with the possibility of "mini-nukes," yet we wax self-righteous when other countries even contemplate developing nuclear energy programs. As Jon Stewart puts it, "Who do they think they are—us?" We find it normal to have American bases all around the world, yet we would be rightly outraged if Chinese, Russian, or French soldiers were stationed on American soil. We find it normal for the United States to rearrange the economic system of Iraq, but we would presumably not find it normal for any other power to impose an economic system on us. U.S.-based transnational corporations take over key industries in countries such as Argentina, but we are scandalized when China tries to buy a U.S. oil company such as Unicol. The right wing calls for closing our borders but at the same time expects all other countries to open their borders for U.S. businesses or the military. While we can literally invade other countries' militaries, we cannot tolerate what is, in the end, a merely metaphorical "invasion." The rule seems to be "Never let others do to us what we have done to them."

Let us explore this question through an analogy. Let us posit an imaginary country, located on the other side of the globe, called "Megastan." That country is roughly ten times as powerful as the United States. Megastan's military spending outstrips that of the United States and Europe combined. It has hundreds of military bases around the world, including in countries close to the United States. Megastan has an economic and political system that it believes is superior to that of others—let's call it the "Megastani Way of Life." The Megastanis know very little about the United States or about American history. Very few of them speak English.

Let us imagine, then, that a small group of neo-Megastanis, under the pretext that George W. Bush had stolen the 2000 election and become a dictator, decides to install a pro-Megastani government and Megastani-style economic system in the United States. These Megastanis claim that the United States is developing powerful weapons that threaten Megastan, even though Megastan is infinitely more powerful than the United States. For years Megastan has been bombing us, and two-thirds of the United States forms a no-fly zone. After economic sanctions that kill—here we extrapolate proportionally—five million Americans, Megastan invades the United States, killing another million. The Megastani army seizes the gold at Fort Knox and the oil deposits in Texas but stands by as rioters loot the Smithsonian, the Library of Congress, the Museum of Natural History, the Metropolitan Museum, and the Museum of Modern Art. (The Megastani secretary of defense dismisses concerns about the looting, insisting that it is a sign that freedom is taking hold.)

The Megastanis then install an interim government led by a Megastani proconsul who does not speak English but who exercises the real power in the country. They disband the army, the government, and the Democratic and Republican parties. Meanwhile the occupying government orders Megastani soldiers to seek out Republican "dead-enders." They destroy much of the infrastructure of the United States and then refuse to hire Americans to do the reconstruction, since Guatemalan contract laborers are cheaper. They break into our homes in the dark of night to arrest anyone found with suspicious Republican literature. Young Megastani soldiers in their early twenties now wield life and death power over our parents, brothers and sisters, and children. Meanwhile Megastani soldiers perform bizarre sexual tortures on arrested Americans, forcing Christians to urinate on their Bibles and mount each other like dogs, apparently with approval from the highest levels of the Megastani government. (Their secret agents have discovered that our culture makes us particularly susceptible to religious and sexual humiliation.) In response the American insurgents, including a few Ku Klux Klan–style and militia terrorists along with citizens of all political, religious, and ethnic persuasions outraged by the Megastani occupation, pick up arms.

The Megastanis respond by massive bombing that kills and displaces huge numbers of American civilians. In the case of Philadelphia, they virtually raze the entire city, kill thousands with phosphorous bombs, and oblige almost the entire population to find shelter in neighboring cities until the city has been declared terrorist free. Asked for statistics concerning American civilian casualties, the Megastani spokespersons declare that they do not do body counts. They say such numbers are of no interest to them, since it was all part of a liberation aimed at getting rid of Republicans and terrorists. Megastan installs a kind of government, but it is unable to control the violence in American streets. As the United States descends into full-scale war between various ethnic and political factions—to the point of the slaughter of more than a thousand Americans per day—Megastan officials are reluctant to call the situation one of "civil war." Some Megastani policymakers, meanwhile, envision dividing the United States into three autonomous, ethnically defined nations: Anglostan, Latinostan, and Negrostan. And even though polls conducted by Megastani pollsters themselves show that strong majorities of Americans want the Megastanis out, the Megastanis' refuse to leave, under the pretext that they have to help the American government "stand up," after which the Megastani army can "stand down."

One can easily imagine the howls of execration at such a comparison: There is no Megastan or even any country like it! Saddam really was a dictator! Bush is not! You can't talk about hypothetical situations! The United States really is in Iraq to promote democracy—just look at the elections! And so forth. And indeed our comparison is a bit of a stretch. Our point is a didactic one. Our aim is to prod prowar Americans into imagining, even if only for a moment, how it feels to live in an occupied nation. (Among contemporary Americans only Native Americans, African Americans, Mexican Americans, Native Hawaiians, and Puerto Ricans, and in a very different way, white Southerners, perhaps have a historical inkling of that feeling.)

How would we feel if non-English speaking foreign "experts," in league with an army occupying our country, were cooly pontificating whether we would be better off as one or three countries? In general, thankfully, most Americans have never seen foreign tanks rumbling through U.S. streets or foreign helicopters hovering over U.S. homes. We have never had foreigners barking orders at us in an alien tongue or shooting us by mistake at roadblocks on American streets. Citizens of a superpower lose the very capacity to imagine being in a less powerful position, yet such is the ordinary feeling of most people in the world. We have been top dog for so long that we forget how little dogs view the world. We see the war in terms of how it is going for us. The deaths of Iraqis are downplayed in relation to American deaths, even though the war was supposedly conducted for Iraq. The city of Fallujah was destroyed and its residents forced to flee, yet some Americans, as Naomi Klein points out, were more disturbed by a photo of a soldier smoking—a bad example for children!—than by images of soldiers killing.[43] We are told that all the bombing strikes are surgical and precise, yet how can we know without knowing the exact number of casualties?

This failure of the imagination reached a sick climax with the dismissals, by the right, of the importance of the revelations of torture in Guantánamo, Afghanistan, and Iraq. Such abuses have been a standard feature of counterinsurgency wars, whether in Vietnam, Algeria, or Iraq. Yet for radio talk show host Rush Limbaugh, the torture was the equivalent of a "fraternity prank," even though some detainees died from such "pranks." One can imagine Limbaugh's reaction had the positions been reversed, if Iraqi "insurgents" had been torturing GIs and forcing them to live in a puddle of their own urine and excrement. But that would have been torture of us, by the "barbarians." For that matter how would Limbaugh react if **he** were forced to strip naked in front of his enemies, if **he** were forced to masturbate or mimic homosexual behavior or to desecrate the cross or the Bible, or if aggressive dogs had been unleashed against **his** naked body? Would he dismiss that as a mere prank? Of course not, because then "real people"—that is, well-upholstered, drug-addicted, white Americans like himself—would have been on the receiving end. It was even a matter of indifference to Limbaugh that most of the victims were neither terrorists nor insurgents. (Some military intelligence officers told the International Committee of the Red Cross that in their estimate "between 70% and 90% of the persons deprived of their liberty in Iraq had been arrested by mistake.")[44]

It is all reminiscent of Huck Finn's answer to the question whether anyone was hurt in a steamboat accident: "No Ma'am, killed a nigger."

In other words no "real" people were hurt. Those who say torture is "no big deal" are the same kind of people who say "relax and enjoy it" about rape; they are people without a clue about the horrible physical abuse and soul-destroying violation involved. (As the example of the Senator John McCain case shows, there seems to be an inverse proportion between knowledge and experience of torture and enthusiasm for it.) Right-wing blowhards are not generally known as tolerant people, but in one area they have infinite tolerance—for other peoples' pain. One wonders if the right-wing Christians who were so moved by the torture of Jesus in Mel Gibson's film *The Passion of the Christ* would also be moved by the torture of Iraqis, not the Son of God admittedly, but still human beings made in the image of God. Joe Scarborough of MSNBC revealed his cluelessness on Bill Maher's HBO *Real Time* show by virtually defending "water boarding," the torture technique used by the French during the Algerian war, which consists of induced near suffocation and near drowning. The fact that the revelation of such practices caused a huge scandal in France in the 1950s and 1960s and yet are now seen as "debatable" in the United States certainly tells a melancholy tale about our much-vaunted "values." Other right-wingers see torture through the grid of macho bravado, comparing it to the ordeals of military boot camp, conveniently forgetting that in this case the abuse is administered by people who hate you and might kill you, in a situation where you have no idea if you will live or die.

The fact that the Pentagon itself has acknowledged that many people have died while being "interrogated," furthermore, completely undercuts the argument that torture is all about "information." Torture is sometimes about information, but in situations where a culture of torture develops it is almost always about power, humiliation, and sexual sadism. Furthermore, torture is the only issue that is always discussed in relation to a one-in-a-million possibility—the "ticking-bomb" scenario. No other issue is discussed in such terms. The people who are so flippant about torture have obviously never been tortured or known people who have been tortured. They seem to think torture is merely a passing bad moment, not a horrific degradation that results in lasting trauma for victims and even for their families. Many of those who seek political asylum in the United States—one hundred thousand of whom live in the New York area—are the maimed survivors of torture in their home countries.⁴⁵ And it is paradoxical that the administration still relies on accounts of torture as part of its arsenal of denunciation of others—how many times have we heard "Saddam tortured and gassed his own people"?—while asking for an exemption for its own torture.

The right is always denouncing the left for its "moral relativism" and its "postmodern" abandonment of truth, yet in the end it is the right that practices completely opportunistic and relativistic notions of truth and morality. When President Clinton lied about sex to a grand jury, the Republicans told us that it was the end of civilization as we know it—what would we tell the children? Yet when vice presidential Chief of Staff Scooter Libby lied to the grand jury, Republicans told us it was a "technicality" with "no underlying crime." With the right's defense of torture we find relativism, "with a vengeance." But for some right-wingers, the thought of American soldiers (of whatever color) tormenting brown bodies is part of the natural order of things, a reassuring return to law and order. Thus it makes perfect sense that former Senate Majority Leader Trent Lott, the same senator who had eulogized the segregationist Senator Strom Thurmond, would also defend the torture at Abu Ghraib. "Interrogation," Lott said flippantly, "is not a Sunday-school class. You don't get information that will save American lives by withholding pancakes."⁴⁶ The comparison of torture, which degrades both torturer and victim and which has lifelong traumatic consequences for its victims, to "withholding pancakes" is beyond obscene, especially when one remembers that most of the detainees at Abu Ghraib were innocent people caught up in an indiscriminate and vindictive dragnet. Torture, which used to be something that psychopathic Nazis did in Hollywood war movies, has now become, for the right and even for some "liberals," a legitimate part of the repertoire of violence, as long as it is not performed on "real people." To their eternal credit, many in the military and courageous senators have argued for a clear no-torture policy. Ignoring the Geneva Convention, they argue, undermines the prestige of the United States and endangers American troops. But why should it take courage to denounce an abomination like torture?

The U.S. power elite constantly packages its often aggressive policies in terms of lofty ideals such as patriotism, democracy, freedom, and sometimes women's rights, concepts to which most Americans vibrate. But idealistic language of this kind has often been an old colonial ruse.

In the admittedly very different context of Belgian colonialism in the Congo, King Leopold of Belgium presented forced labor and genocide to European audiences as forms of "philanthropy." Novelist Joseph Conrad in *Heart of Darkness* spoke of the lofty "redeeming ideas" that covered over the most brutal policies. Unilateral military interventions in the name of U.S. interests, in this sense, are often verbally redeemed by such grand ideas as democracy, keeping the peace, restoring law and order, or freedom on the march. The propaganda works, to some extent, because Americans really do believe in these ideas and are moved by them, even if their leaders do not.

It is interesting, in this sense, to contrast the lofty rhetoric of the speeches of American presidents engaged in war with some of their more informal exchanges with their intimates and advisors. Here we have President Nixon, press secretary Ron Ziegler, and presidential advisor Henry Kissinger in a dialogue recorded by the White House taping system on April 25, 1972, at the height of the Vietnam War:

President: How many did we kill in Laos?

Ziegler: Maybe ten thousand—fifteen?

President: See, the attack in the North that we have in mind ... power plants, whatever's left—POL [petroleum], the docks. ... And I still think we ought to take the dikes out now. Will that drown people?

Kissinger: About two hundred thousand people.

President: No, no, no. ... I'd rather use the nuclear bomb. Have you got that, Henry?

Kissinger: That, I think, would just be too much.

President: The nuclear bomb, does that bother you? ... I just want you to think big, Henry, for Christsakes.[47]

If this conversation had not been recorded, one would surely assume that it was dialogue drawn from a leftist satire, an invention of America haters, yet it is quite real. In another conversation Nixon said that he wanted to "cream" North Vietnam—a country that never attacked the United States—using maximum U.S. power against "this shit-ass little country." Thus our leaders talk to each other in the tone and manner of mafiosos but preach to us in the manner of pastors addressing a congregation or parents admonishing a five-year-old: "There's a bad man who eats children like you at the other end of the world, and Daddy has to stop him from eating them anymore." We can imagine what would have happened if Bush and Rumsfeld had tried to sell the Iraq War in this frank language of killing rather than in the language of overwhelming threat ("weapons of mass destruction") and radiant promise ("spreading democracy").

Yet some uninformed Americans take at face value the cynical war marketeering of politicians. In 1983, in a move that recalled the plot of the film *The Mouse That Roared*, Ronald Reagan managed to convince many Americans that the tiny Caribbean island of Grenada, whose major product was nutmeg, constituted a major strategic threat to the United States merely because the Cubans had helped Grenada build a badly needed airport. The invasion of Grenada took place shortly after an attack on marine barracks in Lebanon, in which more than two hundred marines were killed, and gave every appearance of a theatrical show diverting attention from the disaster in the Middle East. During the buildup to the Iraq War, George W. Bush and company similarly persuaded many Americans to believe that the militarily bludgeoned and sanctions-destroyed Iraq was on the verge of launching a nuclear attack on the United States. (Few in the media asked the obvious questions: exactly which planes would escape the no-fly zones to deliver the weapons, and how could a country that was so weak that it could not defend its own air space manage to attack the most powerful nation on earth?) The inflation of the threat served to unify the country around a policy that most Americans would have rejected had it been presented honestly and that they have in fact rejected once the dishonesty came to light.

Militaristic exceptionalism leads to endless theatrical interventions against small, relatively defenseless states, falsely packaged as major-league threats (Grenada, Panama, Iraq). The wars are buttressed ideologically by ever-shifting opportunistic ideological rationalizations—the war on communism, the war on drugs, the Evil Empire, the war on terror, the struggle for democracy—the only constant being the creation of pretexts for ever-increasing military spending. What go unsaid are the financial advantages for the politicians and corporate figures supporting the wars. Many of those who speak up in the media for military expenditures or wars personally benefit from those policies.

One would love to see a moving scroll of on-screen subtitles detailing the financial involvements of the war's advocates every time they appear on TV talk shows. Yet it is more or less taboo in the media—itself a corporate-dominated space—to acknowledge any link whatsoever between Bush's energy policies and his status as an oil executive or of Cheney's links to Halliburton and the defense contracting. That would be in bad taste. Although John Kerry spoke of "Benedict Arnold" corporations, he did not signal the direct financial interest of Bush, Cheney, Rumsfeld, and others in the economics of war. And when presidential candidate John Edwards brought up such issues, the media more or less belittled the charges or accused him of touting "conspiracy theories."

The Illiberal Media

At this point scores if not hundreds of brilliant analyses of the American media have been published, and there is no point in rehearsing their arguments again. Suffice it to say that despite the conservative tilt of the U.S. media, the right promotes the fantasy of the "liberal media," even though the right now directly or indirectly controls the debates about most issues resulting in what has come to be called the "illiberal media." The fact that it was Judy Miller, a reporter for the *New York Times*, who served as a legitimizing conduit for White House propaganda about weapons of mass destruction and the fact that the same *New York Times*, the "paper of record," held back a story about NSA spying on American citizens for a year because of White House pressure—a story that might have changed the results of the 2004 election—should help bury forever the myth of that paper's liberal standing. The very persistence of the myth of the liberal media, as many critics have pointed out, is a symptom of the right's overwhelming dominance. One Google search for mentions of "liberal bias" yielded 47,000 hits compared to 710 hits for "conservative media bias."⁴⁸ Yet in the two weeks before bombs fell in Iraq in 2003, only 3 out of the 393 on-air pundits interviewed on PBS's so-called liberal *NewsHour with Jim Lehrer* were antiwar, even though 34 percent of Americans at that time opposed the war.⁴⁹ Moreover there is no left-wing media empire equivalent to the *Washington Times*, the *New York Post*, and FOX, just as there are no left-wing foundations aimed at taking power, nothing comparable to Olin, Heritage, Cato, American Enterprise, and so forth.

Here again a comparative perspective is essential. The right-wing slant becomes obvious when one looks at the U.S. media in triply comparative terms: (1) in relation to the various media, (2) in relation to the past, and (3) in relation to other countries. In terms of comparative media, one is struck by the contrast between the publishing industry, which has generated hundreds of very smart political books (many best-sellers) critical of the right, on one hand and the major network media, where such criticisms are rarely given a serious hearing, on the other.

In terms of comparative time frames, the Republicans, and the media linked to them, are now far to the right of the Republican leadership of a generation ago. The Republican president Eisenhower regarded the kind of Republicans now in power as a tiny, crazy minority. The present-day right wing's attempt to liquidate the legacy of the New Deal would have been unthinkable for Eisenhower. In a letter to his brother, he wrote,

> It is quite clear that the Federal government cannot avoid or escape responsibilities which the mass of the people firmly believe should be undertaken by it. ... Should any political party attempt to abolish social security, unemployment insurance, and eliminate labor laws and farm programs, you would not hear of that party again in our political history. There is a tiny splinter group, of course, that believes you can do these things. Among them are H.L. Hunt (you possibly know his background), a few other Texas oil millionaires, and an occasional politician or businessman from other areas. Their number is negligible and they are stupid.[50]

Even in the 1970s it was Republicans who were pushing for environmental regulations, higher Social Security benefits, and increases in social spending for the poor. A liberal (but not left) consensus reigned up until the 1960s, in reaction to which the far right made immense (and largely successful) efforts to take over the media. The right managed to do so through Reagan-led "deregulation," through the 1984 law eliminating the requirement that cable operators provide local programming, through the ending of the "Fairness Doctrine" in 1987, and through the 1996 Telecommunications Act, which opened the door to greater concentration of ownership. The result of all these developments was the rightward slant we see now. In this sense the media have accompanied the move to the right not so much of the American people—James Stimson argues that Americans grew more liberal in the two decades after Reagan—but rather of the American political system.[51]

At this point in history, the media debate usually pits representatives of the far right against representatives of the timid center, aggressive right-wing barkers such as Sean Hannity against bland centrist wimps such as Alan Colmes. In comparison with the media in other liberal democracies, U.S. media politics are skewed far to the right. European and Latin American media rarely feature any commentators in the vein of the splenetic, perpetually outraged spokespersons of the American right wing. One rarely encounters the counterparts of Ann Coulter, Bill O'Reilly, and Sean Hannity—and we are not even speaking of right-wing hate radio—in social democratic countries. Although France has its fascist and racist Jean-Marie Le Pen, le Penistes do not dominate TV or radio, and the media, when it interrogates right-wingers, tend to be skeptical. Brazilian television features sensationalist crime shows, which tend to indirectly favor more repressive policies, but there are no equivalents to Coulter and O'Reilly.[52] Despite its oppressive social structures, Brazil has no Ku Klux Klan, no right-wing hate radio, no xenophobic minutemen patrolling its borders. Although it has millions of poor and black people, what it does not have is rabid talk-show hosts belittling and demeaning poor people, cruelly rubbing salt into the wounds of their oppression.

It often seems that the media are far to the right of the American people. (Programs such as Amy Goodman's *Democracy Now!* or Bill Moyers's *NOW* or radio's *Air America* obviously constitute exceptions to this rule.) When watching the 2004 presidential primaries on C-SPAN, we were struck by the gap between the smart, informed, and substantive questions asked of the candidates by ordinary American people and the dumb, superficial, "horse-race" questions asked by media correspondents. And that is one of the few areas where we agree with the right—the American media are indeed elitist—although not in the sense meant by the faux-populist right. The media seem deeply invested in making the American people look dumber than they are. They rarely show articulate everyday Americans; rather they usually exhibit stuttering, inane, confused Americans, perhaps so that they, the newscasters, can look by contrast like the "experts" that they like to think they are. But apart from the personal narcissism of journalists, this strategy serves the agenda of the right. The implicit contrast favored by the right is between the good-hearted but inarticulate people and the elitist liberals who supposedly oppress them. Articulate jobless people, activists, and union spokespersons, needless to say, do not fit into that picture.

Too often, moreover, the discussion revolves around the red herring of "bias," when the real questions have to do with power, policy, and framing. That some journalists vote Democratic is irrelevant; what matters is how the owners vote. Most of what we see, hear, and read is controlled by some ten corporations: AOL–Time Warner, Disney, General Electric, News Corporation, Viacom, Vivendi, Sony, Bertelsmann, AT&T, and Liberty Media.[53] Therefore the important question is not that of bias but rather what the grids, prisms, and filters are through which events are told and seen. What are the important issues that are **not** discussed? How are the media linked to the centers of political or corporate power? Who owns the media and sets down their basic orientation? How are they linked, for that matter, to war industries and the military–industrial establishment? (The case of General Electric is revealing in this regard.) Are the media public service or profit oriented? Who decided that the public airwaves should be used exclusively for private profit? What has been the impact of infotainment on American democracy? What did we not learn about the world or about our own country while the media were obsessing over O.J. Simpson, Kobe Bryant, Michael Jackson, and Scott Peterson? And did we learn anything of value from those scandals?

The biggest lies purveyed by the media are lies of omission. One key realm of omission has to do with economics. Unlike the media in most liberal democracies, the U.S. media rarely address economic policy or the implications of policy debates, to wit, basic issues of who benefits and who loses from any economic measure or policy. Economics is seen as a technical matter that is better left to businessmen and economists, not something that everyone is capable of speaking about, something that structures everyday existence by enabling or constraining the choices that make up our lives. The absolutely consistent procorporate bias of the Bush administration is hidden in the media by (1) never being explained and (2) by being rendered not in systematic but only in personal terms ("Coming up—those new tax provisions: why you might be paying less in taxes when April 15 comes around"). The class implications of corporation-friendly laws such as the recent bankruptcy bill, a favorite of the credit card industry, which made it harder for citizens pressed by medical crises or by natural disasters to declare bankruptcy, are barely debated in the media. Latin American and Middle Eastern media, however progovernment they might sometimes be, do at least constantly address complex economic issues such as monetary policy, devaluation, the International Monetary Fund (IMF), the national debt, and so forth, supposedly "dry" issues that the U.S. media avoids like the plague but that are infinitely more consequential for people's lives than celebrity trials and scandals. Economic issues in the U.S. media get shunted off to "business news," where the dominant point of view is that of big investors.

Indeed one could fill a book with crucial issues never debated in the U.S. media. Was there ever a real debate about military spending? About what to do with the "peace dividend" that was supposed to come with the end of the Cold War? Was there ever a sustained debate about the wisdom or morality of "preventive war"? About Star Wars? About the PATRIOT Act? Whereas France, and Europe generally, held a lively discussion about the economic implications of the new European Union Constitution, in the United States economics is not seen as part of a national debate. And this elision of economics serves the right-wing strategy of using moral- and cultural-wedge issues to divert attention from the consequences of their trickle-up economic policies.

Since the right always accuses us of complaining without making positive suggestions, here is our proposal for an ideal TV news program, whether local or national. It would be neither governmental—since that leads to the abuse of political power—nor corporate—since that leads to the abuse of economic power—but it would be public, in the sense of being publicly funded, rather like an interstate highway but this time dedicated to the "interstate commerce" of ideas. The program would be fascinating and entertaining because the discussion would be lively and it would deal with compelling issues, but it would not be infotainment, since it would not be concerned with ratings. It would not be a business, since, as Karl Marx famously said, "The first freedom of the press consists in its not being a business." The set of anchors would "look like America" not only in terms of race, class, and gender but also in terms of physical appearance: blow-dried glamour would not be a requirement.

Each newscast would have a full-spectrum news team with six or seven commentators, chosen more or less in proportion to the spectrum of political opinion in the community in question. But the show itself would not be partisan or feature only the two major parties. Rather, it would feature a broader spread in terms of far right, right, center right, center left, left, and far left, as determined not by party affiliation but by views on a whole series of issues such as health care, campaign finance, the death penalty, tax policy, and so forth. The show would not have sensational crime reports but have only a brief charting of statistical trends. Partisan gasbags armed with "talking points" would be refused entrance. The correspondents and anchors would begin by presenting the basic facts—for example, that a labor union began a strike against such and such corporation—after which the different newscasters would debate the meaning of those facts. The leftist would support the strike, the rightist would oppose it, the centrist would try to play both sides, and so forth, and the show could end with call-ins to amplify the debate. Discussion about events abroad would involve experts from the countries in question expressing diverse points of view. This way the news would be seen as something to be debated in democratic fashion; the elusive "objectivity" would consist not in dueling sound bites but rather in a polyphonic voicing of very diverse opinions.

The "illiberality" of the media becomes clear in the way world events are covered. The U.S. media foster narcissism by filtering world events through exclusively American preoccupations and interests. The result is a kind of cognitive asymmetry. Europeans, Latin Americans, and Middle Easterners usually know much more about the United States than Americans (except for specialists) know about those areas of the world. To which the American exceptionalist replies, "But, of course, we're America!" To paraphrase comedian Chevy Chase, "We're the United States, and you're not." American media correspondents in Iraq, to give another example of ethnocentrism, speak of "foreign fighters" to refer to *jihadists* from Jordan or Syria; the tacit implication is that

U.S. soldiers are **not** foreign, even though they, unlike the Syrians and Jordanians, are usually not Muslim, not from the region, and not fluent in Arabic. While the word *terrorist* is certainly appropriate to Zarqawi and his minions, it is less appropriate to those who oppose an occupation. The use of the word *insurgent,* meanwhile, is somewhat anomalous since it was the Americans who were trying to force regime change, shouldn't they be called the insurgents?

Even as the American media become ever more global in their technical reach and influence, they become ever more parochial in their perspective. People who know little about the world dominate the coverage of that world. On cable talk shows, political hacks with no knowledge of Arabic and no expertise in Iraqi history pose as "experts" on Iraq. Talk-show hosts who have probably never met an actual Arab/Muslim blithely claim that "the Arabs have always hated us." (Yet the hundreds of thousands of Americans who have lived in Arab/Muslim countries can testify to the hospitality with which Americans have usually been treated.) Rarely do we see Iraqi intellectuals or experts speaking about the situation in their own country. Suicide-bomb attacks on innocent civilians in London are rightly treated as major disasters worthy of comment by political leaders and as human interest stories about those who lost loved ones. Yet the similar attacks almost daily on innocent civilians in Iraq do not merit similar treatment. There are few follow-up stories about the impact on Iraqi lives, and there is no coverage of funerals or mourning of loved ones, little to convey the human cost. The inference is inescapable: Iraqi lives, for the dominant media, simply have less value than American or European lives, even though it is our government that put this series of events in motion.

By now conducting wars in almost total ignorance of the countries being invaded seems to have become a bad U.S. government habit. It is almost as if our Rumsfelds and Cheneys decide to invade countries just to learn about them. Rather than "travel broadens the mind" it's now "invasion and occupation broaden the mind." As correspondent Rob Corddry of the *Daily Show* put it in the wake of the torture scandals, "So apparently the road to Iraqi hearts and minds does not pass through their electrified genitals. So now we know! Lesson learned!" U.S. wars go on for decades without Americans learning anything of substance about the nations with which they are at war. The Vietnam War went on for decades, but the only Vietnamese word Americans learned was *Viet Cong,* the pejorative name for the National Liberation Front. The United States is deeply embroiled in Iraq today, but what Arabic words have Americans learned besides *jihad*? And just as American soldiers in Vietnam dehumanized the Vietnamese by calling them "gooks" and "slants," now soldiers reportedly call Iraqis "hajjis" and "towel heads."

While the U.S. media usually cover violent actions and the superficial aspects of Green Zone political developments in Iraq, they almost never explain the economics of the war, either in terms of the economic system being installed in Iraq or in terms of benefits and losses for Americans. How were the billions budgeted for the Iraq War actually spent? Whatever happened to the $9 billion that was "missing in action"? Why does the media never mention Cheney's personal connection to the war machine as a stakeholder in Halliburton and Lockheed? How might those funds have been spent at home? Who profited from that spending? Under Paul Bremer, the United States, with virtually no participation by the Iraqi people, changed all the Iraqi laws governing banking, investment, copyrights, business ownership, and taxes—all of which gives the lie, again, to the claims of advancing "democracy." One Bremer order privatized 192 government-owned industries. Iraqi reconstruction, meanwhile, has been firmly under the control of U.S. firms such as Halliburton, yet the United States has been unable to provide water, sanitation, and electricity at Saddam-era levels. The media generally avoid such issues, preferring to talk about the role of Islam, autonomy for the Kurds, women's rights, and so forth, all important issues but hardly the only ones.

Although the major TV networks make a good share of their profits from political advertising, during the 2004 election they lacked even the civic decency to use the public airwaves to cover the two party conventions. And while the far right is constantly represented on the political talk shows, one almost never sees their left equivalents. The left is vaporized, either absent or melting into the liberal—that is, centrist—category. With the Katrina disaster, however, the media suddenly seemed to find their voice. The gap between the realities the journalists were living and showing on the ground and the Pollyanna-like declarations of the authorities was too great, and the protective levees of spin constructed by Karl Rove were "overtopped" by a category-five scandal. Even mainstream media figures such as CNN anchor Anderson Cooper and NBC anchor Brian Williams showed anger at the mendacious incompetence of government at all levels. MSNBC anchor Keith Olbermann, in a rare editorial, lambasted the administration that had pressured the media to report good news from Iraq, that had won an election by implying that the other party would place us all in danger, and yet that was clearly unable to protect us. Had the coverage of the Iraq War been as honest and vivid as the coverage of Katrina, many mused, Americans would have howled for an exit from Iraq long ago.

The Wages of Exceptionalism

Our tale of the crises of narcissism and patriotism has revealed a partly phantasmatic encounter between various nationalisms, narcissisms, and exceptionalisms, each projecting its heroes and villains. Vainglorious debates about "my country is better than yours" and "my country right or wrong," we have tried to suggest, are a dead end.

European critiques of U.S. imperialism, in this sense, should be seen within the *longue durée* of five hundred years of colonialism and imperialism. Those Europeans who excoriate the United States as if it were the only racist and imperialist nation are in some ways sanitizing their own nation's past and present history. Europeans often write about the problems in the Americas as if their own past actions had nothing to do with those problems, when it was Europeans who laid down the basic structures of stratifications in those countries, even if Europe practices rough welfare-state egalitarianism at home. Even an imperial power such as the United States can become a scapegoat for "retired" or "emeritus" imperial powers. To say the obvious, we note that the United States, despite its oppressive present-day role, did not invent colonialism, capitalism, slavery, imperialism, or globalization; it only refined and updated what it inherited from Europe. Indeed there is hardly any current-day "American" evil that does not find a European precedent. The current situation, which places the U.S. corporate–military–political elite as judge, jury, and policeman of global offenses, is not new. Americans in Iraq? The British preceded them by many decades. Winston Churchill literally "gassed the Kurds" in the 1920s, long before Saddam Hussein did.

We have been especially critical of U.S. exceptionalism not because it is unique—all nations have their exceptionalisms, and all exceptionalisms are unique—but only because the United States at this moment in history is the most empowered nation-state, the one capable of doing the most damage, and if it chose to do so, the most good. Our "preventive war" government has quite literally become dangerous to the health of the world, to its inhabitants, and to American citizens, which is not to say that the United States is the only dangerous power or that it is only and always dangerous. The combination of an arrogant and fundamentalist president, warmongering neocon advisors, a passive electorate, and a supine media has been a formula for catastrophe.

American exceptionalism, we have suggested, hurts Americans themselves. On the domestic front the prideful idea that the United States has nothing to learn from other countries, as columnist Paul Krugman of the *New York Times* points out, prevents Americans from solving the health crisis, as the Hippocratic oath's "Do No Harm" runs up against the insurance companies' "Pay No Patient," which means, in reality, harm to the patient.[54] And on the foreign policy front, imperial nations die when they overreach. The cost of pursuing supremacy through militarism has financially (and morally) devastated the country. Dutch social scientist Jan Nederveen Pieterse, one of the most lucid critics of U.S. policy, puts it as follows:

> [America is now] undereducated, culturally backward and inward-looking, economically on its knees and dependent on foreign borrowing. ... With reliance on the military–industrial complex comes an authoritarian culture of threat inflation, and the stereotyping of the "rest" of the world. The price of primacy is ... the disempowerment of Americans.[55]

Although the war in Iraq has perhaps "worked out" in terms of unprofessed goals—dominating Iraq, installing bases, making money for corporations—it has certainly not worked out in terms of its professed goals. The Iraq War did not bring the promised cheap oil, democracy, enthusiasm for war, peace in the Middle East, or improved relations between Israel and the Palestinians. It overthrew the head of one of the "axis of evil"—Iraq—but it strengthened another—Iran. The Iraq War did not bury the "Vietnam syndrome"; rather it revived it. For every advantage gained through the administration's bullying approach, just as much, if not more, has been lost, *even in terms of its own stated goals*. Every provocative action triggers a reaction, and in response to U.S. hectoring, the nations of the global South are bonding together. Politicians all over the world know they can win elections by being more anti-American than their opponents. While the United States obsessed over the Middle East, all of Latin America moved massively left, creating new alliances unwilling to collaborate in U.S. designs. Argentina is getting loans from Venezuela instead of from the IMF. Bolivia is nationalizing its natural resources. Perhaps "preventive war" is not all it was cracked up to be.

While we have critiqued American narcissism, we have also pointed to the national narcissism at the root of some international critiques of the United States. Anti-Americanism sometimes serves to distract attention from the fact that other countries share many of our problems. U.S. society is deeply marked and structurally deformed by racism and the legacy of slavery, but these evils also mark most of the countries around the "Black Atlantic," including many in Europe and the Americas. U.S., Brazilian, and French societies all bear the traces of various forms of classist educational systems and inferentially racist cultural institutions, just as they all feature forces actively engaged in challenging those systems and institutions. Virtually all European countries, like the United States, have their racist and anti-Semitic movements (skinheads in Germany, Jean-Marie Le Pen in France). The French papers, including *Le Monde,* are full of news items about discrimination in France based on appearance, name, and national origin. Polls, meanwhile, show that a fairly high proportion of French citizens think there are too many immigrants or too many Arabs in France. And just as Katrina unmasked the poverty and racism buried beneath happy talk news and the American "opportunity" model, so the 2005 rebellions in the impoverished French *banlieue* (suburbs) and the 2006 mass protests against the New Employment Law reveal that the French republican model is also in deep crisis.

At this time all the global patriots need to go beyond provincial national vanities to collaborate with one another. The massive worldwide protests against the Iraq War; the dynamic anti–World Trade Organization demonstrations; the immense success of the "social forums" held in Porto Alegre, Mumbai, and Caracas, along with the many satellite forums elsewhere, including in the United States; and the proliferating forms of human rights advocacy point to the fact that millions of people believe that an alternative to unilateral militarism is possible. It is a question not only of where we are from but also of where we want to go. Transnational collaboration "from below" is now a matter of global survival.

6. None Dare Call It Patriotism

The Contradictions of the Right

Before we get to our final proposals about patriotism, it is important to point to some of the contradictions within the right's view of the subject. Here we can mention just a few of the myriad tensions within right-wing thinking. First, there is the tension between patriotism as love of country on one hand and the right-wing hatred of half of the people of the very same country supposedly being loved on the other hand. In fact for the right, patriotism is not a unifying idea at all. Patriotism for right-wing politicians is a "wedge issue," a weapon for exclusion meant to turn neighbor against neighbor, one-half of the country against the other half, all calculated as a way to win elections. It is not patriotism *for* but patriotism *against*.

Second, there is the tension between the right's antigovernment rhetoric—"Government is not the solution, it's the problem"—and the administration's demand for blind loyalty to a specific government—their own. The right is antigovernment when it's out of power—hence the attempts to impeach and humiliate a popular president like Clinton—but is progovernment once in power, at which point it demands total "trust us" loyalty while declaring all dissent irresponsible, shameful, and even traitorous.

Third, there is the tension between the right's antigovernment rhetoric on a domestic level—where "the government can't solve problems"—and the progovernment rhetoric in foreign policy—where the government can supposedly achieve monumental feats: overthrow dictators, plant democracy, transform economies, restructure whole regions, and so forth. Incapacitated in domestic issues, the government is all-powerful abroad; it is paralyzed nationally but megalomaniacal internationally. The right offers us big government for war and small government for our everyday needs. We can afford nothing at home— "There's no money!"—yet afford everything abroad—"Money is no object!" A clue to what's behind all these paradoxes can be found in a Balzac aphorism—"Money is the answer to every riddle"—or, to put it in our native idiom, "Follow the money." And in this case, the money is going to the pockets of well-connected corporations linked to a militaristic foreign policy.

Fourth, there is the tension within right-wing ideology between patriotism as a necessarily unselfish and collective idea—that is, the binding thread of "horizontal solidarity" that ties citizens to compatriots whom they do not personally know—and the right's valorization of possessive individualism, precisely that force that undermines horizontal solidarities such as patriotism. Is an individualist patriotism even possible, when patriotism is by definition transindividual? Patriotism ideally turns us into friends and allies, while possessive individualism turns us into competitors and rivals.

Fifth, there is the tension between the administration's "small government" and "trust the people" philosophy on one hand and its strengthening of the executive on the other. The right asks government to leave businesses alone and unregulated yet intervenes in our lives by trying to ban abortion, censor the media, and snoop voyeuristically into our lives (at the head of the spying is Dick Cheney, the man Maureen Dowd calls the "Grim Peeper"). On a financial level right-wing rhetoric speaks of trusting we the people with our own money but then proceeds to waste billions—if not trillions—of our dollars on a war that the American people never really chose in any legitimate sense.

Sixth, there is the tension between political nationalism and economic transnationalism. The administration touts "America first," yet the oil-rich Saudi Arabian monarchy or corporations from Dubai might weigh more in the balance of internal political power than the aggregate of oilless American citizens. A procorporate government, in this sense, can be only intermittently patriotic, since corporations respond to major stockholders, not to any particular government or people. Although companies such as Halliburton suck at the public teat for private gain, their own ultimate loyalties seem to be less to national communities than to the bottom line and to the profit margin, to the grand fatherland of corporate wealth. The provincial, nationalist discourse of political speeches hides the cosmopolitanism of the corporate interests.

Seventh, there is the tension within one of the major electoral blocks on the right, that is the tension between the Christian right's love of unbridled free markets and laissez-faire capitalism on one hand and its hatred for the mass-mediated culture (code words *Hollywood* and *pornography*) generated by that very same capitalism, which seeks profit wherever it finds it.

Eighth, there is the tension between the myth of rugged meritocratic individualism on one hand and the reality of mediocrity, nepotism, and crony capitalism on the other. While one can admire the struggles of individuals who succeed despite obstacles, one suspects that if one scratches some of the most vociferous "rugged individualists" of the right, one might just find a trust-fund baby, or the son of a president.

Ninth, there is the tension, already explored in detail in this text, between the rhetoric of "spreading democracy" abroad and the reality of subverting and shrinking democracy at home.

Tenth, there is the tension between democracy and theocracy, between the constitutional ideal of separation of church and state, and the eroding of that separation through "faith-based initiatives."

Eleventh, there is the tension between the "conservative" label and the administration's absolute radical contempt for traditional democratic governance, bipartisanship, and the separation of powers.

Twelfth, there is the tension between the right's moralistic "good and evil" discourse on one hand and its often completely cynical and amoral practices on the other. What exactly was the connection between Ralph Reed's Christian morality and his links to casinos and Jack Abramoff?

For the right, to put it rightly, might makes right, but its self- righteousness does not put it on the right side of history.

Finally, there is a fundamental contradiction between democracy and empire, a contradiction pointed out even by conservatives such as Pat Buchanan. An editorial in the procapitalist *Economist* magazine, appealing to the memory of the American Revolution, argued a similar position:

> Imperialism and democracy are at odds with each other. The one implies hierarchy and subordination, the other equality and freedom of choice. People nowadays are not willing to bow down before an emperor, even a benevolent one, in order to be democratized. They will protest, and the ensuing pain will be felt by the imperial power as well as by its subjects.
>
> For Americans the pain will not be just a matter of budget deficits and body bags; it will also be a blow to the very heart of what makes them American—their constitutional belief in freedom. Freedom is in their blood; it is integral to their sense of themselves. It binds them together as nothing else does, neither ethnicity, nor religion, nor language. And it is rooted in hostility to imperialism—the imperial rule of George III. Americans know that empires lack democratic legitimacy. Indeed, they once had a tea party to prove it.[1]

At this historical moment, true patriotism has become a subversive idea, as subversive as the idea of overthrowing British colonial rule.

Wrestling with Patriotism

Throughout this book we have wrestled with the issue of patriotism. We use the word *wrestle* advisedly to suggest that patriotism is never easy, simple, or unambivalent. Al Franken physically mimed this ambivalence on the audiovisual logo of his Sundance TV show by interacting awkwardly with various symbols of Americanism—an apple pie, a baseball bat, the flag. The audiovisual logo of the *Colbert Report,* meanwhile, mocks superpatriotism with its soaring, diving American eagles. Rather than sitting on their usual perch watching over the nation, these soaring eagles, rather like those in Hitchcock's *The Birds,* fly threateningly toward the camera, their claws aimed at the spectators and their beaks open as if ready to devour the audience. If Bill O'Reilly were a bird, he would be that kind of eagle. These eagles symbolize not the nation's quiet pride but rather the superpatriot's aggression against the people. We the viewers have become the eagle's prey.

When we question the right-wing view of patriotism, we are not speaking about the sincere, relatively powerless Americans who show the stars and stripes or display yellow ribbons to express solidarity with the victims of 9/11 or to show concern for the lives of soldiers. We have in mind the powerful corporate-friendly politicians who use patriotic bombast as a scam to justify war, suppress dissent, and transfer public money into private hands. All the American flags in the world decorating the stage behind right-wing politicians cannot obscure the cynicism of their policies.

Up to this point we have tried to clear away misleading notions of patriotism, but we have not really addressed our key term. Patriotism—we actually prefer the dictionary definition of "love of country"—is assumed to take certain forms. It is usually seen as taking the form of pride in national achievements, be they scientific, cultural, or social. It is also assumed as taking the form of pride in military victories or rooting for the national team in the Olympics or the World Cup. Patriotism can take the form of a comfortable feeling of belongingness when one participates in democratic rituals such as voting. But patriotism cannot be just a narcissistic "we are the champions" jingoism, a facile celebration of "us" as the best, a wallowing in a positive self-regard that refuses to imagine how we are seen through the eyes of others. Patriotism, we argue, is not looking at one's country and, God-like, finding it "good" or "the best" but looking at one's country and trying to make it better. Exactly what that "good" or "better" would be is the crux of the debate.

In times of crisis, in particular, patriotism can also take the form of anger and disgust, that ache in the pit of the stomach over crimes committed in our name. It is a sign of our love for a person, after all, that we can be hurt by that person. The same country with which we are intimate is the one that can hurt us the most. That is the country to whose fate we cannot be indifferent, the one that prods us into participation and hurts us into activism and protest. The opposite of patriotism is not anger or dissent but cynical indifference or opportunistic greed.

Patriotism can be summed up in a few words and principles: the love of one's country and compatriots, a hope for and activism on behalf of their collective well-being, and in the U.S. case loyalty to basic principles such as the Bill of Rights; the equality of all people; one person one vote; freedom of speech; separation of church and state; checks and balances; life, liberty, and the pursuit of happiness; and government of, for, and by the people. Patriotism means participating in the national conversation, not opting out or trying to close it down.

Patriotism is always conflicted, however, and especially so in the colonial settler states of the Americas, all of which—from the extreme north to the extreme south—were founded on the dispossession of the native peoples. Even the idea of the United States as a nation-state, and the Constitution, generate conflictual emotions for some Americans. Key words in U.S. history and civic discourse resonate differently for different groups, beginning with the word *land*. For many Native Americans the first object of loyalty has traditionally been land and community. According to native scholars such as Vine Deloria Jr., native patriotism means loyalty to a social system that preceded even the foundation of the U.S. government: "Tribal rights of self-government predate the Constitution and derive not from the American people or the Constitution but from the inherent sovereignty of a given tribe."[2] While this idea seems somewhat subversive of the nation-state, it is important to remember that the American Constitution recognized this separate tribal status in Section 8, paragraph 3, giving Congress the right to "regulate commerce" with "Indian tribes."

Throughout the history of United States-indigenous diplomacy, many native groups have generously allowed Euro-Americans to share the "basic rights that Indian and settler share as members of humankind."[3] The result is a different appreciation of the land. While Europeans claimed, "This land is mine," the Native Americans said, "This land is us." Whereas Europeans said, "This land belongs to us," many Native Americans said, "We belong to this land."

Or think of the distinct resonances of the word *free* for different people. Cultural critic Matthew Arnold said, "Freedom is a very good horse to ride, but to ride somewhere."[4] While the right wing lauds *free* enterprise, African American singer Nina Simone sings, "I wish I could know what it means to be *free*." Needless to say, the meaning of *free* is not the same in the two instances. Democracy is the debate about what *freedom* means, as seen from the varied perspectives of the American people. Since the African American past in the United States has been so bitter, black patriotism can hardly be a simple unreflecting love of country. American history, for African Americans, has been a long story of abuse, beginning with slavery, through segregation and lynching and the thousands of "sundown towns"—where blacks were not supposed to be seen after sunset—on up to the neglect and prejudice reflected even in the reaction to Katrina, where a country that could mobilize helicopters to save soldiers in Iraq could not mobilize to save citizens in New Orleans. Although there have always been decent white people in America, they have rarely been influential enough to make the system decent to African Americans.[5]

Despite all the abuse, African Americans are those who not only have fought in all the nation's wars but also have fought the hardest for freedom, not just for themselves but for everyone. All Americans owe African Americans a debt of gratitude for injecting meaning and substance into the abstract phrases of the Declaration of Independence. Although often denied education and even literacy, blacks have never stopped demanding full equality. As W.E.B. Du Bois wrote in the founding manifesto of the Niagara movement, "We claim for ourselves every single right that belongs to a freeborn American—political, civil and social; and until we get these rights we will never cease to protest and assail the ears of the America."[6] And as we witnessed in a particularly painful and illuminating sequence in *Fahrenheit 9/11*, black congressional representatives defended Al Gore and the integrity of the electoral process, even when Gore did not defend himself or the process.

What, then, does patriotism mean in the "multination" states of the Americas? Although these states have often used the native Indian as a figure or symbol of the new nation, they have all dispossessed the actual, living native peoples. Here Native Americans can be only ambivalent, to say the least, about the meaning of the founding of the country. In 1854 a Mohican Native American named John Quinny spoke of his ambivalence about patriotic celebrations in the United States: "It may appear ... a singular taste for me, an Indian, to take an interest in the triumphal days of a people who occupy, by conquest or have usurped, the possessions of my fathers and have laid and carefully preserved a train of terrible miseries to end when my race has ceased to exist. ... For myself and for my tribe I ask for justice—I believe it will sooner or later occur, and may the Great Spirit enable me to die in hope."[7]

Frederick Douglass similarly spoke of the conflicted feelings of a slave on the Fourth of July:

> [The fourth of July is] a day that reveals to him, more than all other days in the year, the gross injustice and cruelty to which he is the constant victim. To him, your celebration is a sham, your boasted liberty and unruly license; your national greatness swelling vanity; your sounds of rejoicing are empty and heartless; your denunciation of tyrants brass-fronted impudence; your shouts of liberty and equality hollow mockery ... [all] a thin veil to cover up crimes which would disgrace a nation of savages. ...
>
> This holiday is yours, not mine. You may rejoice. I must mourn. To drag a man in fetters into the grand illuminated temple of liberty, and call upon him to join in joyous anthems, were inhuman mockery and sacrilegious irony. I have no patriotism. I have no country. What country have I? The institutions of this country do not know me, do not recognize me as a man. I have not—I cannot have—any love for this country, as such, or for its constitution.[8]

Even today there is a huge gap between white and black understandings not only of history but also of perceptions of justice and opportunity in the United States, a gap shaped by the dramatically different realities lived by the two groups. Those who deny that gap have simply not looked very deeply at the matter. For some Americans, then, patriotism cannot be dedicated in any simple way to the nation-state as such; it can be dedicated only to the country's potential, part of a future-oriented patriotism aimed at reshaping the country into a more lovable form.

Echoing Walt Whitman's poem "Leaves of Grass," African American poet Langston Hughes gave eloquent expression to this future-oriented patriotism:

I am the poor white, fooled and pushed apart,
 I am the Negro bearing slavery's scars
 I am the red man driven from the land.
I am the immigrant clutching the hope I seek—
 And finding only the same stupid plan
 Of dog eat dog, of mighty crush the weak.

 O, let America be America again—
 The land that never has been yet
And yet must be—the land where everyone is free.
 The land that's mine—the poor man's,
 Indians, Negro's, ME—

It is up to Hughes's "red man driven from the land" to say what free-dom and a native patriotism might mean in terms of native land rights, cultural respect, and so forth.

For many African Americans to even begin to feel something like the same unalloyed enthusiasm for the larger country would require the empowered white majority in the United States (and in other "Black Atlantic" countries) to express, and more important to perform and act on, at least three key performative statements or commitments: (1) "We're sorry"—for the pain caused, for the kidnapping, for the middle passage, for slavery, for segregation, for police brutality, for utterly dis-proportionate incarceration, and for the political and economic injus-tices and inequalities that persist to this day. (2) "Thank you" for your work in literally building this country, for shedding your blood in its wars, for demanding democratic rights, and for creating the art that has inspired many throughout the entire world. We recognize the benefits and advantages that have accrued to white America thanks to black labor, intelligence, and creativity. (3) "Let's make it right." Let's go beyond apologies and thank-yous to create, by "any means necessary," real equality, justice, and democracy. Only then perhaps can the Fourth of July begin to mean the same thing for white Americans and for black Americans. It is not a question of a curdled and resentful white "guilt" but rather one of responsibility—because all this would not be a "favor" to black people but be a favor to the nation as a whole, a reconciling of white people with their better angels.

A love of country requires going beyond racial narcissism. An inclu-sive, lucid, and multivoiced patriotism means acknowledging these discrepant histories and their consequences in the present. If the past of the national "family" has been in some ways abusive and dysfunctional, any recovery requires facing up to those repressed memories, going beyond denial, and taking responsibility. Only then can a patriotic "sobering up" take place.

It is our belief that national narcissism, or in this case the uncritical love not of one's country but rather of specific administrations and groups and their policies, is a disservice to the country. When every legitimate criticism of policy is answered with shrill accusations of treason, then the country will remain stagnant; indeed it can become only more unfair, more unequal, more paranoid, and more imperialistic. Patriotism has been wrongly defined as loyalty to government policy rather than as loyalty to what one sees as the deeper interests of the nation. A critical patriotism, a "tough-love" patriotism, excludes blind, generic, quasi-fascistic endorsements of any and all governmental policies. Callers to radio talk shows often express an unalloyed blank-check faith in government. Thus one often hears such statements as, "I believe Bush [or Bill Clinton or any president] is our president and we should support him," "The government wouldn't put people in jail if they didn't do anything wrong," and "No law-abiding citizen has to worry about the PATRIOT Act; it's meant only for terrorists." Such citizens fail to recognize that many people are indeed wrongly jailed, that punitive measures are sometimes aimed at critics of the government or of corporations rather than at terrorists, and that if any one citizen can be declared an "enemy combatant" at a president's whim, then ultimately all of us can, and we no longer live in a free country. Such blanket-approval declarations carry ominous undertones of fascist authoritarianism; they are the antithesis of love of country. Blind faith in presidents who rewrite the rules as part of their commander-in-chief function, destroying the old checks and balances, bodes very ill for the future of democracy.

Those of us who criticize certain policies of the U.S. government are constantly berated for our supposed lack of patriotism. We are called "America haters" or the "Blame America First" crowd. We are portrayed as, in Newt Gingrich's words, "the enemies of normal Americans." Yet we are among those who actually care enough to be informed and participate and protest, to take seriously our civic duty to examine national debates. In our view the superpatriots are fake patriots and our superpatriot president has been guilty of "high crimes and mis-demeanors." The right constantly asserts that we "hate America," but we do not hate America. We hate only what right-wingers are doing to our democracy. We do not really even hate Bush and Cheney, only their abuse of the law and their illegitimate power over the rest of us.

The day after a huge antiwar demonstration in Washington, in the period leading up to the war, CNN news anchor Carol Lin reached a new low in pseudopatriotic demagoguery. She asked the following electronic poll question: "Do you think antiwar demonstrators should be regarded as traitors?" The very question was obscene, even, we say, unpatriotic, because it implied that a prohibition on dissent, the very kernel of a free society, was conceivable and perhaps desirable. Because treason is normally punished by death, it was as if CNN was asking the prowar faction of its audience to decide if another faction of its audience—those who were antiwar—deserved death. And yet with the passage of time, the supposedly "treasonous" antiwar position has become the majority commonsense position. Any definition of treason that turns a majority of Americans into traitors is, one thinks, rather problematic.

But in our view dissent is absolutely essential to patriotism. It is a question not of a paternalistic tolerance of dissent—an "allowing" of dissent that always carries a veiled threat that what has been allowed can just as easily be disallowed—but rather of democracy **defined as dissent**. The right's "hating America" charge is merely a crude attempt to censor opinion, since many critiques of policy are made in the name of love of country, and nothing is more patriotic than dissent. The right rarely debates the left on the facts; rather it just tells us we shouldn't say what we say, even if what we are saying is true. For us it is a matter not of making a place for dissent, as if it were an add-on, but rather of seeing dissent as at the very kernel of democracy, the very thing without which democracy becomes a hollow shell, whence the protest chant of antiwar demonstrators: "This is what democracy looks like!" What Democracy decidedly does **not** look like is fake town hall meetings, fake reporters at White House press conferences, photo ops, staged "chats" with soldiers in Iraq, and fake news reports planted in Iraqi newspapers. Democracy is not the taking of a prescribed position but rather the active participation in the debate; indeed it is the debate itself. Those who try to shut down debate, who tell us that "we have to watch what we say," in this sense, are clearly unpatriotic.

All this impugning of patriotism is just a (not very polite) way of saying "shut up!" Patriotism as wielded by the right has a repressive function; it is meant not to inspire us to sacrifice but rather to mute debate. We are no longer in the realm of "what you can do for your country" but rather in the realm of "what your government can do to you." Unable to deal with its critics on the level of argument, the right deals with them on the level of spying, slurs, and labels. Mark Crispin Miller puts it very well:

> Today in the United States, the highest crimes are somewhat less offensive than it is to talk about them publicly. A president "elected" by judicial fiat; "preemptive war" put over by official lies; tax dollars to fund religious groups that proselytize; "free speech" confined to "First Amendment Zones"; vital covert operations blown deliberately to punish disagreement with the White House; foreign nationals arrested without charges and indefinitely jailed; untold thousands tortured by U.S. troops and contractors, or sent to other nations to be tortured; Americans searched and arrested, conversations bugged and transactions monitored without a warrant; seemingly independent journalists paid surreptitiously to spout the party line. ... All such doings are profoundly un-American.[9]

The right for Miller has been intent on "cancellation of the Bill of Rights, radical abridgement of the Constitution, and a betrayal of the Revolution that was waged so that we might be free to rule ourselves, to hear the truth, to speak our minds, and to seek our happiness."[10]

The lack-of-patriotism charge, in sum, is a trick; the accusation implies that the accuser is the model of patriotism and devotion to country while the object of the accusation is painted as a public enemy, obliged to prove "innocence." It is much worse than the prosecutor asking the defendant, "Have you stopped beating your wife?"; it is a case of the actual wife beater asking the nonbeating spouse if he has stopped beating his wife. The accusation replaces the real issues—the wisdom of a policy or the justification and costs of war—with the irrelevant, manipulative, and distracting question of patriotism. Accusations of treason poison the air and preempt legitimate debates about policy; critics are implied to be guilty until proved innocent.

Personally we would rather have everyone's patriotism simply assumed, without patriotism even being part of the discussion. But since the right constantly denounces the liberal left as unpatriotic, here we will meet the charge head on, not by protesting our own patriotism but by analyzing what patriotism is and testing the superpatriots against our definition. It is not just that we do feel we must speak out of love for the country but also that we think the right has a warped, upside-down view of patriotism.

The right wing, to paraphrase an anti-Kerry Republican attack ad, has some "wacky ideas" about patriotism. The admittedly partisan James Carville has shown how the Bush administration has ignored the goals inventoried in the Preamble to the Constitution. While reluctantly acknowledging that the administration has "provided for the common defense"—but only if "invading countries for no reason" is seen as defense—Carville argues that the administration has not "promoted the general welfare" (but only that of the well-off), has not "secured the blessings of liberty for ourselves and our posterity" (since it has left posterity with a mountainous debt), has not "established justice" (given its disrespect for the Constitution), and has not "ensured domestic tranquility" (since it divides the country) or "formed a more perfect union" (since gaps in income have increased astronomically).

Who are these patriots who subvert the Constitution? How could patriots spend millions of taxpayers' dollars to entrap, impeach, and paralyze a popular elected president, against the clear wishes of most of the electorate? How could "patriots" try to destroy Social Security, the most popular and successful government program ever invented? How could patriots lie to Congress and spy on the American people? Why would patriots try to suppress the vote and cheat citizens out of political representation? Why would patriots shroud the people's business in secrecy?

Why the Superpatriots Are Not Patriots: A Test

By our definition the right wing flunks the patriotic test. But let us measure the right-wing superpatriots with more precision in terms of any reasonable definition of patriotism. What are the criteria for patriotism, and how does the right measure up? In commonsense terms one would think that any serious definition of patriotism or love of country would include, first of all, *loving the land;* that is, the contours and resources, the air and the water of the country. The word *land* means both "earth" and "country," and the two are deeply linked. Our national anthem speaks of "purple mountains' majesty" and "fruited plains." But "this land is my land" kind of love should also embrace the peoples who loved the land before "Americans" did; that is, the Native Americans. Indeed the very word *American* initially meant "Native American," so perhaps we all should become true Americans by adopting Native American attitudes toward the land, adopting native knowledge about how to really love, nourish, and protect the common land. While the colonists saw the land as "virgin territory" to be deflowered, fecundated, and owned, for the natives it was a "mother," the source of sustenance, "widowed" by European conquest. But Americans in general have learned a good deal from Native Americans. As Native American writer Vine Deloria Jr., tongue planted firmly in check, expresses it, "We have brought white Americans a long way in 500 years, from a childish search for mythical cities of gold and fountains of youth to the simple recognition that lands are essential to human existence."[11]

Ecologically minded critic Joel Kovel proposes a more open stance toward nature whereby human beings help "catalyze nature's abundance" rather than destroy nature in the name of profit.[12] Yet far from loving the land, the "patriotic" right wing, and the corporations that support it and that it supports, violates the land, strips it and sells it to the highest bidder, and pollutes the atmosphere with arsenic, polychlorinated biphenyls, and carbon monoxide. The right contaminates the soil and fouls the waters of America the beautiful and contemplates the use of so-called small nuclear weapons that would not only spread radioactivity on those targeted but also fall back on all of us. Its *Sound of Music* goal is to "Strip every mountain / Poison every stream / Pollute every rainbow / till [it finds its] dream."[13] The right prefers lordly dominion over the land to a loving collaboration with it. As "superpatriot" Ann Coulter put it with her usual thuggish brutality on the *Hannity & Colmes* show (June 20, 2001): "God gave us the earth. We have dominion over the plants, the animals, the trees. God said, 'Earth is yours. Take it. Rape it! It's yours.'" As a result of such attitudes and policies, we are on the verge of exceeding "the buffering capacity of nature with respect to human production, thereby setting into motion an unpredictable yet interacting and expanding set of ecosystemic breakdowns."[14]

Second, one would think that any definition of patriotism or love of country would include the idea of *loving the people of the country,* caring for their bodies and their welfare and having their best interests in mind in terms of their physical, medical, emotional, moral, economic, and social well-being. It is important to distinguish, in this sense, between "liking" and "loving." Patriots do not have to like all the people in the country of their birth or adoption; that is implausible, even absurd. In fact what Benedict Anderson calls the "horizontal camaraderie" of national belonging is premised on not knowing—much less liking—the vast majority of one's compatriots.[15] The Ann Coulterish right wing, which claims to be so patriotic, seems to hate at least half of the country, which it dismisses as traitors. It even hates politically incorrect widows of 9/11 and mothers who lost children in Iraq. Frankly we don't personally like effete snobs, racist rednecks, airhead newscasters, blustery talk show hosts, or lying politicians, but as citizens in a democracy we recognize their right to their obnoxious views. The patriot loves the people in the aggregate, in the sense of promoting their collective welfare. The current superpatriots clearly fail this patriotic test. If they really cared about the well-being of all the citizens, they would be fighting not only for security from terrorists but also for universal health care, workplace safety, affordable or free education, a progressive tax code, well-paying jobs, solid retirement programs, uncorrupt publicly funded political campaigns, the end of racial profiling and police brutality, and so forth; in short all that is necessary to the well-being of the American people. Instead the right has shaped a country that, despite its wealth, ranks the lowest among the developed countries in all the measures of equality.

The patriot would see affirmative action, for example, as not only an issue of justice and reparation for past evils but also as a question of faithful stewardship of the nation's human resources. But the superpatriots have no problem at all with blighted neighborhoods, decaying schools, or despairing populations. For them it is not a sign of societal failure but a token that the mysterious ways of their corporate gods are guiding wealth and prosperity into the hands of the deserving (i.e., themselves) and denying it to the undeserving (i.e., the poor, the working class, the minorities). Nor are superpatriots concerned with Americans' financial security. As pensions disappear for the middle class, the administration's primary concern is to give more tax breaks to the extremely rich. Their view of our pensions is a bit like their view of Middle Eastern oil. Just as they wonder, "How did our oil get buried under their sand?" so they also wonder "How did our investment money get buried in your retirement plan?"

Against the currents of the histories of all of the "advanced" countries, the right wing, after resisting advances such as the New Deal—that is, those measures that ultimately saved a failing capitalism from its own excesses—is currently trying to entirely undo that system. At the same time, the right is trying to undo the postwar consensus on peace and nonintervention. In fact this uncompassionate administration does not even care about future, unborn Americans. Breaking with more than a century of tradition under presidents of both parties, the administration has slashed taxes in wartime. The result has been enormous deficits, part of the "starve the beast" strategy that will make progressive change very difficult for decades to come. Despite the rhetoric about tax cuts, the deficits constitute a kind of "birth tax" in the form of thousands of dollars in debts accrued to every newborn citizen.[16] While the European social model provides free or nearly free medical services, early retirement, and a wide range of social and public services, the right's social model offers very little to the citizen but everything to the wealthy and corporations.

Within the more generous European (or Canadian, Australian, or many other countries') model, health care and education are seen not as privileges but rather as fundamental rights due to all human beings. No one in these countries keeps an oppressive job only to keep its health benefits. In a truly civilized country, citizens' receiving health care does not depend on their keeping a job; it is one's birthright as a human being and as a citizen.[17] Indeed the United States can learn a good deal from our more modest neighbor Canada, where the government, whatever its imperfections, actually takes care of the basic welfare of its citizens. Despite its parallel history as a colonial settler state, Canada has a single-payer national health care system that very few Canadians would trade for our own profit-oriented system. What Canada does not have are blighted neighborhoods, bloated military budgets, massive incarcerations, or police constantly being videotaped beating up black people.

Everyone in a democracy, including most traditional conservatives, is aware of a basic contract between the government and the people—to wit that the government will protect the people, to whatever extent possible, from forces beyond their control. This contract comes to the foreground during natural disasters, but it is always tacitly present. Nor are even natural disasters really "natural"; the broken levees in New Orleans had everything to do with diminished marshlands due to rearranged canals, unfunded levee repairs, social and racial discrimination, unheeded warnings from scientists, and political corruption at all levels. Disasters reveal the limits of rugged can-do individualism. We cannot personally mobilize against terrorism, hurricanes, or pandemics such as avian flu. Only governments, not corporations or "markets," can and should do that.

Conservative British prime minister Margaret Thatcher famously said, "There is no such thing as Society. There are individual men and women, and there are families." But if there is no society, then there is also no Great Britain. Was it the Thatcher family or Great Britain that invaded the Falklands/Malvinas? If the right believes so passionately in privatization, why not go all the way and have Exxon universities, Chevron flood control, Mobil interstate highways, Lockheed space programs, the General Motors Air Force, Pfizer flu-epidemic control, and so forth? And if the right believes so strongly in individualism, why not have each person be their own nation-state: Jimland, Bobland, Peterland, or the United States of Grover Norquist?

Antiterrorist "security" is only one form of the protection for the bodies and minds of the American people. And even there, the new "national security state" has shown precious little concern for the actual security of Americans. The bipartisan 9/11 Commission has repeatedly criticized the administration for "insufficient progress" against terrorism.[18] In the case of the outing of former ambassador Joseph Wilson's wife, Valerie Plame, as a CIA agent, the administration showed more concern with getting revenge against critics—who committed the unforgivable sin of being right—and intimidating future whistle-blowers than with providing national security. If one omits Bush's sub-Churchillian bluster—"he can run, but he can't hide," "we'll smoke him out," "dead or alive"—

what the administration gave us in response to 9/11 was not an allotted war against Osama bin Laden but rather harassment of Arab–Muslim Americans, the shrinking of civil liberties, the increased distribution of political pork, and of course the disastrous Iraq War, which even many generals have called a strategic blunder and a favor to al Qaeda. Although "security" was supposed to prevent our "losing an American city" to terrorists, it now appears that we are well on our way to actually losing an American city—New Orleans—to greed and incompetence.

In fact there is a striking paradox about the administration's claims about watching out for our security. In all areas where we can test and verify administration claims of protecting our security—for example, improving communications, protecting ports and chemical plants, beefing up first responders—its record has been execrable, leading the bipartisan 9/11 Commission to give the administration failing grades. In all the areas shrouded in secrecy and aimed at strengthening the executive, in contrast—spying by the National Security Agency (NSA) on American citizens, black hole prisons, Guantánamo—the administration claims great success. Yet how can we citizens possibly judge, since the secrecy prevents us from really knowing and since the president has placed "enemy combatants" in a legal limbo where no charges need to be brought. Under a regime of secrecy, the administration could conceivably claim that it has arrested dozens of "enemy combatants" about to blow up all the major bridges in the country, and we will have absolutely no way of knowing whether it is true. And we know from the era of Richard Nixon and J. Edgar Hoover that secret spying on Americans easily detours into spying and voyeurism toward political enemies. And given the administration's history of misleading statements, the "trust me" approach is less than reassuring, becoming little more than a blind "follow the leader."

So let us be crystal clear. Despite its bombast (and its bomb blasts), the administration is not protecting us against terrorism. It is fighting against Democrats, but not against terrorists. The administration sees "terrorism" as a political opening, a chance to stoke fears and thus sway elections. The Bush national security state has been more "invested" in both the psychological and financial meanings of that word, in profits for corporations than in actually protecting the populace from political terrorism or natural disasters. Generous with funds for destroying and rebuilding in Iraq, it has been very stingy with funds for rebuilding America's infrastructure; in fact it has done precious little rebuilding even in Iraq. The United States has not beefed up police or protected ports, chemical factories, and nuclear installations. Security, therefore, needs to be redefined so that it has to do not only with armies but also with infrastructure, hospitals, and mass transit. Universal health care, for example, could form an integral part of national security. Can we imagine relying on charities and insurance companies during a major attack on an American city? Can we imagine, during a major health pandemic, having to rely on insurance bureaucrats uniquely worried about our ability to pay? And the Katrina disaster revealed that the very people who promised us security have made us more vulnerable than ever. The various disasters—9/11, the Iraq War, and Katrina—had in common the lack of preparedness (even though much had been fore-seen), the unfulfilled promises, the incompetent management, and the mendacious public relations performed to cover over the incompetence. And in both Baghdad and New Orleans, we find "outsourced" and "no-bid" contracts, where tax-funded "aid" goes not to the locals but to Bechtel and Halliburton, while contracted "security guards" patrol the streets.

Third, one would think that any definition of patriotism or love of country would include the idea of *loving the Constitution*—a love that has been called "civic patriotism." Yet for the administration, the Constitution seems to be nothing but an annoying piece of paper to be ignored or "got around" through clever, lawyerly manipulation of words. Even illegal detention, torture, and military courts are justi-fied in the name of the president as the "commander in chief" clause in the Constitution. Thousands of Arab–Muslim American men have been unjustly corralled and deported—thus alienating the very popula-tion potentially most helpful in the struggle against future attacks—as FBI agents are sent into libraries and bookstores to probe what patrons read. Having been "intimidated by terrorists," free-speech conserva-tive William Safire writes, "we are letting George W. Bush get away with the replacement of the American rule of law with military kanga-roo courts."[19] Various articles in the Bill of Rights, such as the fourth and the sixth, have been virtually suspended in the name of the hastily approved (and largely unread) PATRIOT Act. And in September 2006,

Congress passed an infamous bill largely designed to protect the president from embarrassment or prosecution and to win the 2006 elections, which thoroughly trashes the basic principles of the American Constitution. The bill suspends habeas corpus— the basic right of the accused to challenge their imprisonment, enshrined in Western law ever since the Magna Carta—for detainees in U.S. military prisons. The law gives to the president the ability to determine who is an "enemy combatant" and what abusive investigative techniques or coerced evidence can be used, and what evidence can be kept secret. The president now has the power to lock up anyone he declares an enemy combatant and simply leave him or her in jail without trial. Robin Williams nailed with a quip the contradiction between spreading democracy abroad while subverting it at home: "The Iraqis should take our Constitution; after all we're not using it!"

Against the Constitution the right systematically undercuts the separation of church and state through support for "faith-based initiatives" and undermines the right to privacy through such programs as (the at least provisionally aborted) "Total Information Awareness." The revelations of NSA surveillance of citizens give the lie to all the glorious talk about "small government" and "trusting the people." (An Internet joke suggested that John Ashcroft wanted government so "small that it could fit into your computer.") It was as if, as *Harper's* editor Lewis Lapham put it, "they would like to put the entire country behind a one-way mirror that allows the government to see the people but prevents the people from seeing it."[20] Thus we get official secrecy for the government and surveillance for citizens. In terms of government of, by, and for the people, the superpatriots fail on all counts. Despite their slogans about trusting the people—slogans meant only for political campaigns anyway—they do not actually trust the people with information or power of decision. Real decisions are left to the "decider"—coached of course by Karl Rove and Dick Cheney—the father who knows best.

Fourth, one would think that patriotism or love of country would mean *a readiness to contribute to the general welfare by paying one's fair share of taxes*. The progressive tax system installed by the New Deal was designed to ensure that the wealthy and corporations would help sustain the common goods on which all of us, including corporations, depend. Yet the veritable theology of the right is that all tax

cuts are good tax cuts, and damn the negative consequences for everyone but the superrich. The loudest applause at Republican conventions
invariably goes for promises of even greater tax cuts. The right wing
is so hysterically hyperbolic about taxes that one of its gurus, Grover Norquist (president of Americans for Tax Reform)—in what must
surely qualify as the most outrageous abuse of the Holocaust analogy
ever advanced—likened the progressive tax mentality to "the morality that says the Holocaust is okay."[21] (In the eyes of the right, apparently, only French critics can be guilty of belittling the Holocaust.) In
a grotesque language of false victimization, Norquist equates the racist
murder of powerless millions with the loss of a few tax perks for the
superrich, precisely those who exploit tax shelters, loopholes, and offshore havens while forcing the rest of us to take up the slack. Between
1996 and 2000, already on Clinton's watch, more than three-fifths of
U.S. corporations paid no federal taxes at all, and things have only got
more extreme since then. The oil companies, meanwhile, are offered tax
breaks even at the very height of their profits, while ordinary Americans
suffer at the pump. For rich right-wingers, taxes are for suckers; that
is, the rest of us, who, like the American revolutionaries, suffer from
"taxation without representation."

Fifth, one would think that a definition of patriotism would include
a refusal to profiteer from the country's wars, a misdeed once seen as
literally treasonous but that has recently come to be seen as "normal."
The Bush administration, even while it was claiming to be looking for
a peaceful solution in Iraq, was already doling out more than a billion dollars of taxpayers' money in advance government contracts to
American companies for the reconstruction of the country. The Bechtel
Group, the Fluor Corporation, and Halliburton—all major contribu-
tors to the Republican Party—lined up to reap their rewards. Halliburton, one of the pioneers of military service outsourcing, was reportedly
bleeding off a billion dollars a month for Iraq work in early 2004 and
has been repeatedly accused of overcharging the army. Preying on the
carnage in Iraq, Republican legislators stripped funding bills of any provisions that would hold corporations accountable for profiteering. The
corporate–military eagle, it seems, has become a vulture.

A UN audit, according to the *New York Times* (November 5, 2005),
found that Kellogg, Brown, and Root, a subsidiary of Halliburton, owes

Iraq $208 million for inflated building costs. The division of labor in this profiteering had the Pentagon destroying property through "shock and awe" bombing and American corporations and their subcontracted labor rebuilding the destroyed property in the reconstruction phase, with huge profits at both ends of the process. Millions of Americans' tax dollars slotted for the reconstruction of Iraq simply disappeared, with Iraq still not reconstructed. At one point Halliburton was caught billing the government for $74 million in gasoline that was never delivered. And the well-respected African American Pentagon whistle-blower—Bunnatine Greenhouse—who denounced such fraud was, of course, demoted. While Bush's mediocre cronies "failed upward," the scrupulous whistleblowers "succeeded downward."

Although the Iraqi people have been freed of Saddam and have held elections, one wonders if elections can be called free when they take place under military occupation. The media usually neglect to tell us about the various polls that say that Iraqis want us out of their country (82 percent according to a British Ministry of Defense Poll, and 80 percent according to a Brookings Institution Poll). The Iraqi people still do not have the cheap oil that was promised prewar or even the level of electricity or health care that they enjoyed before the war (and especially before the sanctions). Despite widespread unemployment in Iraq, the Pentagon and its contractors often give reconstruction jobs not to Iraqis but rather to workers from places such as Sierra Leone, paying them the customarily low wages paid in such countries. We have compared these outsourcing corporations to vultures, but the comparison is unfair to vultures, because vultures do not usually create the wars that produce the carrion they feed on.

Sixth, one would think that any definition of patriotism would include the idea of *love for democracy*. But with this administration, secrecy is a byword and democracy is not a concern at all. As columnist Anthony Lewis, formerly of the *New York Times,* puts it, "There has been no more sweeping claim, in living memory, than the Bush Administration's assertion of power to hold any American in detention forever, without a trial and without access to counsel, simply by declaring him an enemy combatant."[22] The administration's fake town hall meetings, along with their possibly illegal campaign practice of denying entrance into the shrine to all but true believers, only reveals their lack of commitment to real town hall democracy. The same right wing that exposed the most lurid details about Clinton's sexual shenanigans, including even titillating information about the shape and bend of the presidential organ, now holds secret the details of government meetings on energy policy, meetings that, unlike Clinton's liaisons, have real impact on the everyday lives of American people. (As a protest poster put it, "When Clinton lied, nobody died.")

The war, conducted (at least retroactively) in the name of "democracy," was not decided on democratically even within the Bush cabinet. What were the common interests that left (selected) President Bush to confer with (unelected) Saudi prince Bandar before conferring with his own secretary of state? (One can imagine the screaming headlines skewering Clinton over a similar lapse: "Clinton Favors Arabs over the American People!" and "Oil Sheiks Now Control American Foreign Policy!") The cabinet apparently never voted on the war, and even cabinet member Paul O'Neill felt that the decision to invade Iraq had already been made before the cabinet meetings. Nor did the American people really have a say either, apart from a kind of coerced charade in Congress, resulting in a congressional approval that President Bush said in advance that he did not need anyway. Bush prodded other states to join in the war despite the opposition of huge majorities among their populations. When all the basic political and economic decisions have been made for us, we wonder what is left of democracy.[23] Democracy also requires an informed populace, yet the government and the media have subjected us to a double whammy. Just as the entertainment- and ratings-driven media cut down on serious political coverage, the right becomes more and more adept at hiding its real policies, whether through misleading slogans or by front-loading benefits and back-loading costs, while planting fiscal time bombs and offering falsely reassuring "sunset clauses," on which, it turns out, the sun is unlikely to ever set.

A number of ideological currents feed into the right's de facto scorn for democracy. For one thing the ideology of free market neoliberalism favors corporations—and their supposed "free speech"—over the free speech of unincorporated ordinary people. For another thing the privatization mania ultimately corrodes democratic governance, as the realm of public debate becomes more and more restricted. The neo-Straussian philosophy of the neocons, meanwhile, authorizes the supposedly farseeing elite to manipulate the putative "mindless masses" through strategic myths. And the religious fanatics of the theocratic right believe that all is justified—including stealing elections—in the struggle against what they choose to define as "evil." All is fair when God is on your side; God, as Jerry Falwell assures us, is "prowar."

The right's antidemocratic attitudes became very clear during the past two elections. Democracy normally means "one person one vote," but the right, so eager to spread freedom and democracy around the world, spent inordinate energy at home on suppressing the vote! Of course here the right continues a certain American tradition, since the Constitution initially "suppressed the vote" by denying it to Native Americans, blacks, women, and unpropertied men. Even after emancipation, parts of the South suppressed the vote through literacy tests, poll taxes, and so forth. In recent elections the Republicans have reached new heights of creativity in this antidemocratic operation. The Conyers Report released on January 5, 2005, described three separate phases of Republican vote suppression in 2004: the run-up to the election, the election itself, and the postelection cover-up. The techniques led to huge statistical anomalies, all of which "happened" to take votes away from John Kerry.[24] The fact is that the American electoral infrastructure, like the material infrastructure, is in disrepair, if not completely broken. Election results give a very false picture because they do not reveal "spoilage"; that is, the votes rejected for one reason or another. Thus a more accurate way of reporting is to specify the proportion of "spoiled" votes and their distribution according to political party, which would reveal that the "spoilage" has been overwhelmingly at the expense of Democrats. In the same vein Mark Crispin Miller points to a whole series of anomalous "upsets," all involving Diebold or ES&S voting machines, where all the anomalies "happened" to favor the Republicans.[25] Here again the superpatriots fail the basic patriotic and democratic tests.

Seventh, one would think that any definition of patriotism would include the idea of *protecting the honor of the country,* out of what those quaint, old-fashioned Founding Fathers called a "decent respect for the opinions of mankind." Yet the Bush administration has shamed all Americans by violating international law. The same administration officials who prattle constantly about "moral values" currently enjoy absolutely no moral standing whatsoever in the world; they are almost universally regarded as dangerous criminals representing a hyperpowerful rogue state. The European Union is now investigating the secret CIA prisons in Eastern Europe, as places where torture can be practiced and as violations of EU law. In the world's eye the Statue of Liberty, as an icon of freedom, has been replaced by the wired statuelike detainees at Abu Ghraib. Monuments of civilization have been replaced by tokens of barbarism. And Bush's pathetic "We do not torture"—rather like Nixon's "I am not a crook"—hardly reassures us.

Eighth, one would think that any definition of patriotism or love of country would have something to do with *a readiness to abandon one's personal priorities to serve the country* in some capacity, whether in the military or in some alternative form of service such as the Peace Corps.[26] The problem arises when different patriotic principles come into conflict, when the willingness to serve in the military conflicts with a recognition that the wars themselves are unconstitutional, for example, and go against the national interest. Although citizens must be ready to "defend one's country," there is a real question if most recent U.S. wars were really meant to defend the country rather than simply to pursue the policy objectives of various administrations. Our critique is addressed not to those who serve but rather to those who have not served and yet promote the wars. The present-day "chicken hawks" preferred not to serve in a war—the Vietnam War—in which they fervently believed. Unlike those who rejected the Vietnam War as immoral and counterproductive and therefore evaded service or became conscientious objectors, the chicken hawks lacked the courage of their convictions. Republican representative Tom DeLay even combined cowardice, mendacity, and racism when he explained to reporters in 1988 that there had been no space in the army for "patriotic folks" such as himself and Dan Quayle during the Vietnam War because too many minority youth had joined the service just to earn money and escape the ghetto.[27] So by DeLay's self-flattering, upside-down illogic, the blacks who served were not really patriotic but he, who did not serve, was patriotic!

Nor does the right shrink from "sliming" any veteran or decorated war hero when it serves its purposes: witness the vicious attacks on Max Cleland, John Kerry, and John Murtha. The Republican Saxby Chambliss ran a TV spot against Max Cleland, who lost his arm and legs in Vietnam, depicting him as virtually in league with Osama bin Laden and Saddam Hussein. The same people who start the wars and exploit our sympathy for the soldiers, furthermore, in many ways do not actually support the soldiers themselves by supplying good armor or veterans' benefits. The superpatriots did not protect soldiers from the effects of Agent Orange, during the Vietnam War, or from the effects of depleted uranium in the two gulf wars (the cause of the notorious Gulf War syndrome). The military budget does not "trickle down" to the grunts on the ground. And thousands of homeless veterans sleep in the streets of America.

Patriotic Fictions

The superpatriots create "patriotic fictions" to mislead American citizens. Apart from using millions of taxpayers' dollars to outsource the selling of the Iraq War to groups such as the Rendon Group, the Pentagon has also staged and managed such events as the toppling of the statue of Hussein and the Jessica Lynch story, both of which turned out to be public-relations spectacles. The most notorious case, however, was that of Pat Tillman, the Arizona Cardinals defensive back who volunteered for the army in the spring after 9/11, giving up a $3.6 million NFL contract. Opposed to the war in Iraq but supportive of the war against al Qaeda in Afghanistan, he was sent first to Iraq and then to Afghanistan on a second tour of duty, where he was killed on April 22, 2004. On April 30, the army announced his Silver Star citation and described his final battle in vivid detail. Tillman was storming a hill to take out the enemy while providing "suppressive fire with an M-249 Squad Automatic Weapon machine gun." During subsequent months investigative reporters revealed that the whole story was a fiction; that higher-ups knew it was a fiction, and that Tillman actually died from "friendly fire."[28]

It is ironic that the right constantly accuses dissenters and critics of treason, when the right in some respects seems to be literally treasonous, at least in terms of its rhetoric. Treason is usually defined as an attempt to subvert or overthrow the government. Yet Grover Norquist, the grand guru of the right-wing surge, speaks giddily of "drowning the government in the bathtub." Were politicians on the left to use such language they would be pilloried in the media as traitors. Pat Robertson, the very model of the piously telegenic superpatriot, calls for nuclear attacks on the State Department and asks God to strike down Supreme Court justices. Representative Tom DeLay denounces the bureaucrats of the

Environmental Protection Agency—actually created by Republicans—as the equivalent of the gestapo. Our form of government calls for government of, for, and by the people, not antigovernment of, for, and by the people, yet the right uses government as a wrecking ball to destroy (certain kinds of) government. Government rolls back government.

Our Pledge of Allegiance, meanwhile, calls for loyalty to the "flag and the Republic for which it stands," not for disloyalty to the republic. Even the name *Republicans* is terribly ironic, since actually existing right-wing Republicans seem so clearly opposed to the classical ideals of the republic itself. The so-called Republicans are actually philosophically anti-Republican in that they are imperialist, since empires are the polar opposite of republics. (To put it simply, *republic* connotes self-rule, while *empire* connotes imposed rule.) But they are also "anti-Republican" in that their whole philosophy contradicts the Latin root etymological meaning of *republic* as *res publica*—that is, the public thing, public matters and issues. The right displays a virulent hostility toward all things public—whether public schools, public radio, public television, and even public national parks—and a converse adoration of all things private—privatization, private enterprise, private savings accounts—even while they dismiss concerns about citizens' "privacy." Since they are not "Republicans" in any true sense of the word, perhaps the Republicans should change their name to something more fitting like "Re-Priva-cons" or "Corporate-neocons."

Over the past decades, the right has taken over most of the levers of power, dominating Congress, the Senate, the executive branch, and the courts. The result has been a disastrous and expensive war, the increasing concentration of wealth, and the atrophy of democratic institutions and civil liberties. Instead of rising tides lifting all boats, we have broken levees sinking all boats. And in the wake of Katrina, the right becomes, to invoke a Southern song, the "hard-hearted Hanna, the vamp of Savanna," so cruel "she pours water on a drowning man." Charity can rescue drowning individuals, but it takes governmental power to construct or repair the broken dam. It is not just that the "country is moving in the wrong direction," it is that the right is driving us over a cliff. And unlike cartoon characters, human beings and social systems do not have the power to defy gravity.

Patriotism and love of country, in the end, have little to do with waving the flag or with grand proclamations such as "I believe that the United States is the greatest country in the world." To think patriotism is reducible to such boasts is like thinking that love for one's children meant constantly calling them "the greatest children in the world." As with parenting, patriotism means not a blind endorsement or grandiose declarations but rather a quiet, ongoing, informed, active, quotidian caring. Love of country means changing the country's diapers, as it were, not just bragging that the baby is cute. German dramatist Bertolt Brecht said, "Happy the Land that Needs no Heroes." But to be a decent citizen in America today requires a kind of heroism. While it requires heroism to go to war, it also requires heroism to oppose a war. It requires heroism to organize a union in a procorporate climate or to be a whistle-blower exposing governmental or corporate lies or corruption, when one is very likely to be punished or demoted. The failed response of the Federal Emergency Management Agency to Katrina meant that ordinary citizens had to become heroes and try to do what government should have done. While the heroic saving of human life is always welcome, especially in disasters, a well-arranged society would not be so dependent on individual heroism.

The whole "greatest country in the world" claptrap, in our view, should be thrown on the trash heap of bombastic clichés. Michael Moore, in his *TV Nation* series, mocked that megalomania with his ironic list of American "number ones": "Yes, we're number one—in pollution! In people incarcerated!" and so forth. Just as in everyday life we dislike individuals who constantly proclaim their fabulousness, so it goes with nations. Saying one country, any country, is the greatest country in the world is like saying that English, or Wolof, is "the greatest language in the world." Every language is the greatest language for its speakers; it is the vehicle for expressing their feelings, their ideas, and their wisdom, just as every country, at least any country not plagued by poverty or war, is the best medium of expression for its native-born citizens. The claim of being the best, in other words, lacks any objective standing; it simply asserts an intimate familiarity that makes one country the best for the speaker.

Patriotism, we have tried to argue, does not always mean supporting official policies; sometimes it means precisely the opposite. When slavery was the law of the land, were the real patriots those who supported slavery and thus the law of the land or those who dared to oppose it? Of whom are we prouder now: the slaveholders or the rebels such as the maroons and the abolitionists such as John Brown? Was Huck Finn a hero when he went along with his father's racism or when he decided to "go to hell" by helping Jim flee from slavery? During the McCarthy period of the blacklists, who were the real patriots—those who jumped on the persecutory bandwagon or those, such as newscaster Edward R. Murrow, the protagonist of the film *Good Night, and Good Luck,* who tried to derail it? When the United States was supporting dictatorships and coups d'état against elected governments in Guatemala, Brazil, Argentina, and Chile, who were the real patriots—those who defended these antidemocratic interventions or those who thought the United States should be true to its official covenant with democratic rule? And in those countries, who were the patriots—those who called for democratic rule or those who made compromises with dictatorship? According to the pseudopatriotic logic that equates love of country with obedience to a specific government, the true German patriots, during the Nazi period, would be those who supported the Nazi regime. But were not the real patriots those who opposed the regime or even those, such as the theologian Dietrich Bonhoffer, who conspired to kill Hitler?

The question of patriotism comes up especially with the endless chain of U.S.-led wars. Everyone recognizes that it was a patriotic duty to support the U.S. government during World War II, since that fight was for survival and against the spread of fascism. But in the case of Vietnam, who were the real patriots? Was it those who pursued the war—then too against a country that had never attacked the United States—that resulted in thousands of Americans and millions of Vietnamese dead and wounded? Or were the patriots those who denounced the war as unjust, unwinnable, and contrary to the interests of the United States? And who were the real patriots during the buildup for the Iraq War—those who naively believed every fanciful administration claim or those who remained skeptical, calling for more information and reflection before rushing off to war and who turned out to be absolutely right in their skepticism?

Patriotism and the Pursuit of Happiness

We began the book by speaking of two crises: one involving what others think of us, and the other involving what we think of others and of ourselves. We asked, "Why do they hate us?" only to discover that the "us" and "them" are not exactly what we assumed. In a sense there is not "them" but only "us" human beings. All wars, as Adlai Stevenson famously put it, are civil wars. Despite some disagreements, there is also a vast zone of overlap between what bothers others about us and what bothers ourselves about us.

Despite the phantasmatic features of some forms of anti-Americanism in France and despite the irrationality of American Francophobia, the United States also needs the critical dialogue with other countries. Americans have much to learn from non-American critiques of the pernicious messianism of U.S. foreign policy, of the public failings of the U.S. social and electoral system, and of the pitfalls of U.S.-led globalization. The social welfare model, whatever its problems, does at least offer a less stressful lifestyle premised on a social safety net and a basic floor of health and security. Although the European social welfare model, and especially the French model, is regularly denounced in the American media and although it is plagued with a certain measure of unemployment (but then U.S. statistics and the prison system hide the true degree of unemployment in the United States), the social welfare model does at least offer its citizens universal health care, virtually free education, unemployment subsidies, disability benefits, shorter work-weeks, and longer summer holidays, while Americans are increasingly moving toward more and more work and stress and fewer and fewer leisure and social benefits and less and less time for friends and family. (Pace the puritan nostrum that "idle hands are the devil's workshop," it is equally true that "overly busy hands are the devil's workshop.") The result is more bottom-line rapaciousness, competitiveness, greed, and anxiety, where panic about downward social mobility becomes an overriding emotion and where stressed-out and burned-out individuals blame themselves or others for systemic failures.

In sum, it is obvious that all is not well in America. Despite the "pursuit of happiness" clause in the Declaration of Independence, the worsening gap between rich and poor and America's aggressive role in the world are making Americans themselves profoundly unhappy. As the

Bush administration crosses more and more formerly sacrosanct lines, many Americans are in a state of mourning. Countless letters to the editors of American newspapers end with phrases such as "I grieve for my country," "I weep for America," "I mourn for the United States," and "Please give us back our country." Who among us can be happy about the prospect of endless wars, continuing as far as the eye can see, where American soldiers kill and are killed abroad and yet with no discernable or even negative effect on the fight against terrorism? What new wars are they even now concocting for us? Are they already discussing how to bypass Congress? Who can be happy about the brutal distribution of wealth to the top and the consequent strangling of the American dream in its cradle?

Alexis de Tocqueville in the 1830s caught a sense of this American unhappiness when he spoke of Americans' "restlessness in the midst of prosperity." Blaming this restlessness on the "competition of all," de Tocqueville spoke of seeing "the freest and best-educated of men ... in the 'happiest' circumstances," yet where a "cloud habitually hung on their brow, and they seemed serious and sad even in their pleasures" because they "never stop thinking of the good things they have not got."[29] Many surveys suggest that Europeans are happier with their lives than Americans are.[30] Of course it would be simplistic to see all French people, for example, as always joyous. (Indeed an old joke says that there are two kinds of French people: "those who complain, and those who complain about the others complaining.") Nor can we see Americans as essentially unhappy or as all unhappy or as all unhappy all the time. De Tocqueville noted many positive features of American life, including an easy capacity to develop "associations," of banding together in informal ways to solve problems. America has also been the site of utopian and communal experimentation. Yet one does recognize a kernel of truth in de Tocqueville's account. But unlike critics such as Samir Amin or Emmanuel Todd, we locate these negative trends not in an inherent cultural trait but rather in a system that encourages envious anxiety as a way of being in the world.

Consumerist capitalism thrives on a feeling of dissatisfaction, a sensation of infinite lack and envy that can never be fulfilled. For comedian George Carlin, the whole system is built on defying one of the Ten Commandments: "Thou shalt not covet thy neighbor's goods." Consumer desire cannot be satisfied. Indeed it is remarkable how many TV commercials are premised on envy and "one ups-personship" between neighbors, colleagues, and even friends. (Remember Carnival Cruise's Kathy Lee Gifford—the same entertainer later revealed to be involved with sweatshops abroad—singing "If my friends could see me now"?)[31] And as it goes with the nation, so it goes with empire. It is no accident that historian Chalmers Johnson spoke in his book of "the sorrows" of empire. The search for total security is as doomed as the search for endless wealth. Could it be that imperial domination and competition make people nervous, that the same forces that place the United States "on the cutting edge" also make Americans "edgy"? Could it be that exacerbated competitive individualism makes people lonely and isolated rather than happy? What are the consequences if every other person's gain is seen as our loss? Does it make us happy to know that we are "on our own" in the "ownership society"? Does it please us to know that if we, or others, fall off the precipice that there is no safety net protecting us from spiraling into the abyss?

Rampant individualism, as we implied earlier, generates a certain level of social unhappiness. We distinguish, however, between *individuality* as a trait and a value and *individualism* as an ideology based on possessiveness and competition. For us it is a question not of the individual versus society but of the individual as inherently social. Individuality is our very birthright; it makes us as personal as our fingerprints, our voiceprint, our DNA. But individuality and sociality are not opposites. A close-knit community characterized by solidarity fosters individuality—in the manner of a collective jazz ensemble that favors the very personal styles of individual players through a larger orchestration and counterpoint. It is no accident that jazz composer and performer Wynton Marsalis speaks of jazz as "musical democracy," combining self- and group expression. What we need now is more jazz and less martial music.

The planet cannot sustain selfish individualism; it does not have room for billions of "individualists," all shouting in unison, like the mindless crowd in Monty Python's *Life of Brian*: "We are all individuals." It is a bit ridiculous to imagine thousands of people singing en masse "I gotta be me! I gotta be me!" Individualists, furthermore, are often more alike than they would like to think. This is especially true of the student followers of right-wing libertarian Ayn Rand, who tend to praise individualism in lockstep identical words—"I believe you have to be your own man" and "follow your own path"—even though their discourse follows a path already well trod by thousands of others.[32] Individuality is a wonderful gift, the reason we prize our friends and our heroes and heroines, but the ideology of individualism undermines solidarity with our fellow citizens. It is a perfect recipe for soul-killing isolation, endless tension, and, ultimately, loneliness—when you play the Lone Ranger, you end up alone. Extreme individualism leads, paradoxically, to a loss of individuality.

Corporate culture appeals to the mystique of individualism to appeal to the little selfish narcissist within all of us. Social Darwinism and lockstep conformity go hand in hand, turning us into an indistinguishable mass of brand consumers, obedient to the commercials that have us purchase products, all in the name of our personal, individual, lifestyle choice, of course. People who define themselves as consumers are looking for happiness in all the wrong places, because happiness, as Jeremy Rifkin puts it, comes from "belonging" and not from "belongings."[33] While individuality lends itself to creative polyphony, individualism lends itself to the strident cacophony of competing interests and individuals.[34] In a winner-take-all society, everyone loses, including the winners, who have always to be afraid of the envy of the angry losers, "afraid somebody's gonna rob 'em," as the song goes, "while they're out getting more."

But a trend is still not an essence. The trend is a social-historical one, that of a country long on the cutting edge of capitalist globalization. American-style capitalism (which is hardly limited to the United States) generates enormous wealth and opportunity for some, but it also generates neurosis, creating what Joel Kovel calls an "isolated, anxiety-ridden self ... a tensely narcissistic state of being ... [a regime of] permanent instability and restlessness."[35] In this world "no matter how much one has, one never really has anything; everything must be proved to exist anew the next day."[36] A certain kind of competition, for example, in games, seems to be a cultural universal and has a very positive role in encouraging excellence. But dog-eat-dog competition leaves all the dogs unhappy. As Wendell Barry puts it, "Rats and roaches live by competition under the law of supply and demand; it is the privilege of human beings to live under the laws of justice and mercy."[37] The right wing offers us, to put it differently, the "family values" of sharks.

The Founding Fathers inscribed "the pursuit of happiness" as a political goal, but today unhappiness has become a political problem. The telltale signs of unhappiness are everywhere. Rich white kids in a suburban school, perched at the very top of the global food chain, vastly entitled and privileged compared to children and adolescents elsewhere, shoot up their fellow students, just because they feel "dissed." (As Chris Rock put it, making fun of the media's psychologizing excuses for the bad behavior of rich white boys: "Whatever happened to craaazeee!") The less well-off occasionally "go postal," and drivers in traffic jams suffer road rage. Meanwhile some people are so hungry they lack basic nutrition, while others are so fat that doctors cannot inject them. (George Carlin wonders how they manage to wipe themselves.)

Or look at the "motiveless malignity" of those right-wing talk show hosts, again among the richest and most pampered people in the world, yet there they are sputtering with rage, railing at immigrants and blacks and those less well off than they are. Why are their fantasies so violent? They run the show yet pretend to be its victims. Look at Bill O' Reilly, that brave defender of the "Christ in Christmas," a man whose speech is so cruel and heartless that he kicks those who are down, to the point of vilifying desperate flood victims waiting on New Orleans roofs for coast guard rescue. Or listen to Ann Coulter, pouring daily poison into the ears of the nation. Or look at the wealthy and powerful, and presumably Christian, Pat Robertson, calling for the assassination of an elected head of a foreign state (Hugo Chavez), one significantly more popular than our own president and who has offered less well-off Americans cheap oil and gas. (Even if the gesture is a publicity stunt meant to needle the U.S. administration, it does remind us that such an offer is not something that would ever occur to our so-called compassionate oilman president.) Unhappiness rears its ugly head as well in the degraded discourse of the political talk shows, where everyone tries to shout down or outmaneuver opponents, where no one ever acknowledges an opposing point or admits to a mistake even after a claim has been proved wrong.[38] Surely Jon Stewart was right to suggest that such shows "harm America."

What fears and aggressions do we read in the faces of the hawks? They are at the very pinnacle of the planetary hierarchy of wealth and power, at the top of the food chain. Yet what do we see in the permanent gangster smirk of Dick Cheney, a man who Maureen Dowd describes as looking like someone "who just swallowed a country,"[39] a man so cold and uncaring, as Ron Reagan pointed out on the *Charlie Rose Show,* that it did not occur to him, even with millions watching, to lend an arm to a frail Nancy Reagan as she walked toward her husband's casket? (One Internet joke had it that Cheney did not actually have all those heart attacks; it was just a Karl Rove trick to suggest that he actually had a heart.) What do we see in the affect-challenged visage of that soft-spoken Strangelove Richard Perle, in the terminally depressed look of Paul Wolfowitz, or in the stern abused-child look of John Ashcroft? Here Donald Rumsfeld seems to be an exception to the rule, but in his case it is exactly his "shit happens" insouciance, his bland capacity to speak of looting, torture, civilian casualties, and possible civil war in a breezy "aw shucks" tone that is so disturbing. The architects of the Iraq War, and especially George W. Bush, Dick Cheney, and Donald Rumsfeld, have unleashed unspeakable carnage, yet it is hard to find even a trace of regret or empathy for victims of the carnage.

What do we make of the look of George W. Bush, scanning the pressroom like a gunslinger in a saloon? His reactions to the war call to mind the very different sensibility of another king. In Shakespeare's play *Henry V,* the king moves in disguise among the soldiers on the battlefield. One of the soldiers muses on the burdens that beset the conscience of a king who sends citizens to war: "If the cause be not good, the king himself hath a heavy reckoning to make, when all those legs and arms and heads, chopped off in a battle, shall join together at the latter day and cry all 'We died at such a place'; some swearing, some crying for a surgeon, some upon their wives left poor behind them. ... Now, if these men do not die well, it will be a black matter for the king that led them to it" (Act IV, Scene I). George W. Bush in this sense has a "heavy reckoning" for all the men and women who did "not die well." Yet does one ever see a shadow of doubt cross his face or the faces of the other architects of the Iraq War? In a press conference Bush speculated, with a shrug, about the probable number of Iraqi civilian dead—for him "about 30,000"—in a nonchalant tone that Jon Stewart compared to "someone guessing at the number of jelly beans in a jar." Bush does not very often show affection or empathy; the emotions registered display an extremely narrow range of affect—from disdain to irritation to righteousness to anger. And it is noteworthy that for the Right Wing Noise Machine, anger in Bush reveals resolve, sincerity, and conviction, while anger in a Howard Dean or a Bill Clinton shows that they have merely "lost it" or are "out of control." Do these partisans of the "culture of life" ever express the slightest remorse not only for the American soldiers who have been killed and wounded but also for all those Iraqi police and soldiers who died to carry out their grand strategic plan?

The architects of our new "national security state" are among the richest and most powerful people in the world, capable of unleashing the shock and awe firepower of the mightiest military machine ever invented, and yet they look at the world with a kind of contempt. Some of the neocons look at the world as a holocaust about to happen. (And thanks to them, it might.) Such, we suggest, are the wages of exceptionalism and of a life dominated by possessive individualism and cutthroat competition. We Americans certainly enjoy some of the rewards of being at the cutting edge of transnational capitalism, but we should not be so deluded as to think that we do not also pay a very heavy price.

The right, for its part, has managed not only to create a good deal of social and economic unhappiness but also to mobilize it to its own political advantage. According to Thomas Frank, "The gravity of discontent pulls in only one in direction: to the right, to the right, farther to the right."[40] The right makes a kind of sense out of the average person's disgruntlement while hiding the deeper social and economic causes of the dissatisfaction. The great failure of the left has been, first, not tying the everyday forms of unhappiness to corporate and systemic causes and, second, not proposing a utopian "pursuit of happiness" in the form of a "critical utopia" that arises out of the dissatisfactions of everyday life—in short that points to that "other world" we all know to be possible.[41]

Corporations create some wonderful inventions and products. We all—at least those of us who can afford them—love our cell phones, iPods, laptops, and DVDs. But that is not the full story. Corporations also abuse us. Why are insurance companies allowed to select their customers on an admittance-to-the-fittest basis, seeking profits at the expense of our health and well-being? Why do the stores on our interstate high-ways offer us an infinite variety of potato chips, with no healthy food beyond moldy nuts and raisins? Why do banks invent new rules that make our accounts poorer and our lives more difficult? Why do oil and gas companies, at a time of windfall profits, create huge service stations with endless rows of self-service pumps but only one immigrant worker cashier, even while falsely claiming that their profits "trickle down" into jobs? Why is it that when corporate profits decline workers are asked to take a pay cut but when profits increase workers are not offered a raise? Why didn't the oil companies help rebuild New Orleans?

There is nothing patriotic about a right wing that wants to play with mininukes, destroy Social Security, invade other countries, end the sep-aration of church and state, and starve the government of all funds not destined for the military and corporations. The everyday frustrations of American life are directly related to right-wing policies and the cold and calculating corporations they support. Envy, dissatisfaction, and fear of downward mobility have become a kind of basic fuel in our society. Individualist logic leads commuters, for example, to condemn transit strikers for the inconvenience the strike has caused rather than to think about how such struggles may fuel a larger protest aimed at protecting Americans' pensions and wages. And is it patriotic to put up with so much abuse from corporations and our government that privileges the corporations? Are we a free people, or are we not?

What we hope to appeal to is a deeper logic of a social desire for more creative and pleasurable forms of work, for collaboration and festivity, even while demystifying the political structures that channel that desire in oppressive directions. Our civic duty is to tap into the more generous and socially minded American traditions while also imagining an alter-ative set of social arrangements that will appeal to deeply rooted but socially frustrated aspirations for democratic dialogue, equality, and community. It seems obvious that human beings want not only power but also self-expression, intimacy, and friendly and gregarious human relations. We are more than ever in need of mobilizing utopias, not in the sense of pie-in-the-sky utopias or scientific blueprint utopias—and here the right is correct in pointing out that such utopias often end badly—but rather in the sense of proposals that arise out of the lived negativities of social existence and that foster the idea that another way of living is possible. It is not a question of Christian charity or sacrifice or of do-gooder service; rather, it is a question of what Frances Moore Lappe calls "relational self-interest," which seeks connection, solidarity, and collective fun, where one is recognized both in one's unmistakable individuality and as an integral part of a group.

At the same time, every social system has some features that might be adopted by others, even if people are ultimately most comfortable in their own cultures. Discovering alternatives is part of the comparative and dialogical approach we have adopted here, which hopefully generates a reciprocal illumination between countries and social systems. The United States has to its credit a farseeing Constitution, democratic mores, a vibrant popular culture, a marvelous university system, and (like Brazil and to a lesser extent France) an elastic ability to absorb immigrant cultures. Other countries can learn from the United States, and the United States can learn from others. Although Brazil's social and economic structures are oppressive, Americans can learn from Brazil in terms of its creative forms of activism, its governing proposals (such as "participatory budgeting"), its innovative approaches to AIDS and laws of copyright, its capacity to survive and thrive with grace and humor, and its gregarious codes of social interaction. Thus we can fantasize, in John Lennon–like terms, about a country that will combine the best of different places. In the case of our three countries, that would be France's health care system, respect for intellectuals, and support for the arts; Brazil's diplomatic vocation for promoting peace, vibrant culture, and ingenious forms of activism; and the United States' democratic mores, popular cultural energy, self-shaping dynamism, and impressive university system (but it would be virtually free, as in France and Brazil).

Conclusion

Narcissistic forms of patriotism, which often amount to little more than infantile and self-centered defensiveness, we have tried to show, actually hurt the country. When legitimate criticism is answered with accusations of treason, then the United States will never change; indeed it can become only more unfair, more unequal, more paranoid, more imperialistic, and more unhappy. Patriotism for us must begin with the assumption that America is not the world but part of the world. Patriotism is not endlessly bragging that our country is the best; rather it is wanting one's country to be the best that it can be and helping it to be that best, which is a very different matter. The arguments begin with the meaning of *best*. Does it mean being the most militarily powerful? The most democratic? The most humane? The most spiritual? The most generous?

We have tried to show that the superpatriots are actually pseudopatriots. They do not love the land or the people. Even when they pay lip service to "homeland security," they do not really take care of our national security, as became obvious not only with the neglect of the pre-9/11 warnings (i.e., the many warnings about bin Laden's attacks in the United States and Condoleezza Rice's shameless evasions about them) but also with the failure to carry out the 9/11 Commission's (fairly cautious) recommendations and with the disastrous response to Hurricane Katrina.

The pseudopatriots, we have demonstrated, despise democracy and disrespect the Constitution. Their patriotism is—the reader may begin a rap rhythm here—bottom-line, offshore, tax-break, blank-check, photo-op, talking-point patriotism. It is environment-defiling, union-busting, neighborhood-blighting, job-outsourcing, country-invading pseudopatriotism. But we hasten to assure you right-wingers that you need not worry. We do not favor deporting you, rendering you, or placing you in a naked guy pile. We would never jail you just to show, to paraphrase one of your gurus (or gurettes) Ann Coulter—gurettes with Tourette's?—that "right-wingers too can go to jail." Despite your various betrayals of the interests of the nation, we will live up to the creed you abused. Apart from the "technicality" that we are not actually in power and you are, it happens that we actually believe in free speech and we oppose the death penalty. We just want you to be divested of your obscene power over the rest of us, after which you can go back to mismanaging sports teams and corporations and petting Arabian horses, but without the benefit of our tax subsidies.

For us it is regrettable that we even have to talk about patriotism, which is not the real issue. In a globalized, interdependent epoch, patriotism must be recast to include global concerns. As the planet seemingly spins toward ecological destruction, it is in a way silly to think of single nations. Global warming and acid rain do not respect state borders, and melting ice raises sea levels everywhere. At the same time, however, it is national governments and their policies that speed the destruction. The tsunami of economic globalization does not respect national boundaries, yet nations still advance the often destructive policies of globalization.

Our purpose here has been to criticize the patriotic cant that has become an obstacle to a more equal and democratic society. At this point we do not need a mild "course correction": we need a complete U-turn. We have not discussed concrete proposals for change, but there are many proposals on the table: real as opposed to merely rhetorical national security, publicly financed political campaigns, restrictions on corporate lobbying, national health care, alternative energy sources, revived infrastructure, inexpensive education, a living wage, retirement security, media ownership reform, equal opportunity, racial justice, the reaffirmation of civil liberties and human rights, a citizens army, polyphonic grassroots democracy, and a national project that goes beyond simply opposing something. Only a terribly diminished and impoverished notion of patriotism would pledge allegiance not to the "flag and the Republic for which it stands" but only to the "war on terror." Misplaced accusations of a lack of patriotism have become a real roadblock to social progress. So we propose a truce and a deal. You right-wingers don't impugn our patriotism, and we won't impugn yours (even though you're destroying the country). So now that that's taken care of, we can go back to debating the real issues: peace, justice, prosperity, democracy, and solidarity both within and outside of our borders.

Patriotism is a form of love, and love of country can take extraordinarily creative forms. Love of country usually begins as love for that slice of humanity closest to us and then spreads outward from self and family to friends and compatriots. But why should love stop at national borders, any more than it should stop at family or neighborhood borders? Can we imagine together a transnational, global patriotism? Within a kind of "polyandrous" patriotism we see patriotism as a question of overlapping affections, a love for country, but without exclusiveness or demonization. We have argued, therefore, for an alert, complex, critical patriotism. Our call is for a multiperspectival patriotism, a love not of specific governments and their policies but rather of the dappled beauty of the raucously engaged nation, a love of the nation's egalitarian rebels, all those who have been "hurt" into activism, much as Ireland "hurt" Yeats into poetry. Our call, therefore, has been for an alternative, ecological, democratic patriotism (reader, begin rap rhythm again): bottom-up, rainbow, whistle-blower, full-throated, call-and-response, many-voiced patriotism. "Glocal" (local and global) planetary patriotism as the only alternative to planetary sadism.

We can close with some old words rich in resonance for present-day debates, evocative of a possible collective dialogue, which would be quite different from the heartless and authoritarian monologue proposed by the right:

> We hold these Truths to be self-evident, that all Men [*sic*] are created equal, that they are endowed by their Creator with certain inalienable rights, that among these are Life, Liberty, and the Pursuit of Happiness.—That to secure these Rights, governments are instituted among Men, deriving their just Powers from the Consent of the Governed.—That whenever any Form of Government becomes destructive of these Ends, it is the right of the People to alter or abolish it, and to institute new Government, laying its foundation on such Principles, and organizing its Powers in such Form, as to them shall seem most likely to effect their Safety and Happiness.

Notes

Authors' note: Except where otherwise noted, all translations are our own.

Preface

1. See, for example, Christophe Marquis, "Study Finds Europeans Distrustful of U.S. Global Leadership," *New York Times*, September 4, 2003, A11.

2. Moncho Tamames, *La Cultura del Mal: Una Guia del Anti-Americanismo* (The Culture of Evil: A Guide to Anti-Americanism) (Madrid: Espejo de Tinta, 2005), 19.

3. Steven Kull, *Expecting More Say* (Washington, DC: Centre on Policy Attitudes, May 10, 1999), 10.

4. *CNN/USATODAY/GALLUP*, February 13, 2002, by polling the nation database.

5. See Heloisa Buarque de Holanda, "Uma Novidade Chamada Brasil," in *Para Entender o Brasil* (São Paulo: Alegro, 2000), 106.

6. See Mark Levine, *Why They Do Not Hate Us* (Oxford: One World Publications, 2005).

7. The Spanish Inquisition pitted Christians against both the Jews and the Muslims, united in their common victimization, but today the right pits the Christians and (at least up to a point) Jews against the Muslims. In the end, we argue, there is no "them," only "themization"; no "others," only "otherization."

8. See, for example, Robert Dreyfuss, *Devil's Game: How the United States Helped Unleash Fundamentalist Islam* (New York: Metropolitan, 2005).

9. Michael Scheur, the CIA official once charged to hunt down Osama bin Laden, writing as "anonymous," provocatively called the United States "bin Laden's only indispensable ally." Quoted in Robert Dreyfuss, *Devil's Game* (New York: Henry Holt, 2005), 338.

10. For a fuller discussion, including the gender dimension of empires, see Zillah Eisenstein, *Against Empire: Feminisms, Racism, and the West* (London: Zed Books, 2004).

11. Well, not routinely, but it does happen. An Iranian American couple told us the following anecdote about a visit to Paris. A Frenchman asked them, "Where are you from?" When they said New York, he answered, "Fuck you." When they explained, "But we are from Iran," he changed his tone: "Then welcome." French friends, meanwhile, told us about unpleasant incidents in the United States, and even of being refused lodging.

12. Paul Hollander, *Anti-Americanism: Critiques at Home and Abroad 1965–1990* (Oxford: Oxford University Press, 1992).

13. David Frum and Richard Perle, *An End to Evil* (New York: Random House, 2003), 9.

14. We contemplated placing all statements meant to be ironic in italics, so as to avoid being quoted out of context but decided that that would be ... unironic.

Chapter 1

1. Cynthia Tucker, "War Doesn't Cost the Moneyed," *Atlanta Journal Constitution,* January 25, 2004.

2. Anatol Lieven, *America Right or Wrong* (New York: Oxford University Press, 2004), 31.

3. See Eric Hobsbawm and Terence Rangers, eds., *The Invention of Tradition* (Cambridge: Cambridge University Press, 1983).

4. See Dinesh D'Souza, *What's So Great about America* (New York: Penguin, 2002).

5. John J. Miller and Mark Molesky, *Our Oldest Enemy: A History of America's Disastrous Relationship with France* (New York: Doubleday, 2004), 45.

6. Moncho Tamames, *La Cultura del Mal: Una Guia del Anti-Americanismo.* Tamames's list of American crimes is predictable and largely accurate, even if highly selective and at times demagogic. At one point he argues that American presidents, taken collectively, have been responsible for more deaths than Hitler and Stalin together. Adding together four million native American victims, four million African and African American victims, six hundred thousand Filipino victims, nine hundred thousand Japanese victims, two million Vietnamese victims, one million Iraqi victims (due to sanctions and invasions), and so forth, Tamames comes up with a total of twenty-nine million deaths. But while some of these figures are roughly accurate, others are misleading. For example, he blames the United States for a million deaths in Rwanda, when France, Belgium, and the Hutu leaders in Rwanda were infinitely more implicated in that genocide. He blames the United States for thirty thousand deaths in Argentina, which is true in the sense that the United States supported the Argentinean dictatorship, but most of the killing was done by Argentineans themselves during the "dirty war." In any case, the crimes are bad enough, without the inflated numbers.

7. Bartolome de las Casas, *The Devastation of the Indies: A Brief Account* (New York: Seabury Press, 1974), 41.

8. Ibid., 43–44.

9. Quoted in Carolyn Boyd, *Historia Patria: Politics, History, and National Identity in Spain, 1875–1975* (Princeton, NJ: Princeton University Press, 1997), 252.

10. See Evo Morales, "I Believe Only in the Power of the People," December 25, 2005, *countercurrents.org*.

11. See Robert Stam, *Tropical Multiculturalism: A Comparative History of Race in Brazilian Cinema and Culture* (Durham, NC: Duke University Press, 1997); and Ella Shohat and Robert Stam, *Unthinking Eurocentrism: Multiculturalism and the Media* (London: Routledge, 1994).

12. See Tony Judt, *Postwar: A History of Europe since 1945* (New York: Penguin, 2005), 278.

13. Tamames makes much of the easy, liberal manners of present-day Spain, with its rejection of old codes of behavior in terms of language, dress, and sexuality, in supposed contrast with the puritanical United States. But this too must be seen in historical context. Under Franco, Spain was one of the most culturally conservative countries in Europe. In the 1960s the United States was a country divided between a militaristic right and a countercultural, experimental "sex, drugs, and rock and roll" left popular culture. Back then it was U.S. culture that favored nude beaches, nude avant-garde performance (à la Living Theatre), and so forth. In the early 1970s, one of the authors—his identity should become obvious through the anecdote—narrowly missed having his beard shaved off by the fascist Spanish border police. We love much about Spanish culture, but Spanish culture, like American culture, is complex, mutating, and contradictory. And the United States, like Spain, is composed of many cultures, some of them bohemian and others rigid and uptight. Unfortunately, it is the culturally conservative right in the United States that wields power today.

14. Judt, *Postwar*, 14.

15. Aime Cesaire, *Discourse on Colonialism* (New York: Monthly Review Press, 1972), 14–15.

16. G.K. Chesterton, *What I Saw in America* (New York: Dodd, Mead, 1922), 7.

17. See Richard Drinnon, *Facing West: The Metaphysics of Indian-Hating and Empire-Building* (New York: Schocken, 1980).

18. Richard Slotkin, *Gunfighter Nation: The Myth of the Frontier in Twentieth-Century America* (New York: Atheneum, 1992), 110.

19. Drinnon, *Facing West*, 221.

20. Francis Fitzgerald, *Fire in the Lake: The Vietnamese and the Americans in Vietnam* (New York: Vintage, 1973), 491–92.

21. Drinnon, *Facing West*, 404.

22. Lawrence F. Kaplan and William Kristol, *The War over Iraq: Saddam's Tyranny and America's Mission* (Washington: Diane Publishing, 2003), 120–21.

23. Richard T. Hughes, *Myths America Lives By* (Urbana: University of Illinois Press, 2004).

24. George Carlin, *When Will Jesus Bring the Pork Chops?* (New York: Hyperion, 2004), 182–83.

25. The ignorance of some American news anchors was brilliantly captured in the Ted Baxter character from the *Mary Tyler Moore Show*.

26. Walter Lippman, "Empire: The Days of Our Nonage Are Over," in *Men of Destiny* (New York: Macmillan, 1927), 215.

27. See Michael Hardt and Antonio Negri, *Multitude: War and Democracy in the Age of Empire* (New York: Penguin, 2004), 8–9.

28. See "Introduction" to Michael Ignatieff, ed., *American Exceptionalism and Human Rights* (Princeton, NJ: Princeton University Press, 2005), 1.

29. Giorgio Agamben, *State of Exception,* trans. Kevin Attell (Chicago: University of Chicago Press, 2005), 3–4.

30. See "Introduction" to Ignatieff, *American Exceptionalism.*

31. Neil Smith, *The Endgame of Globalization* (London: Routledge, 2004), 165.

32. Jürgen Habermas, "The Fall of the Monument," *The Hindu,* June 5, 2003.

33. David Harvey, *A Brief History of Neoliberalism* (New York: Oxford University Press, 2005), 153.

34. See Jan Nederveen Pieterse, "Hyperpower Exceptionalism: Globalization the American Way," *New Political Economy* 8, no. 3 (2003): 299.

35. Alexis de Tocqueville, *The Old Regime and the French Revolution,* trans. Stuart Gilbert (New York: Anchor, 1955), 146.

36. Although French universalism is usually seen as bound up with the revolution of 1789, French revolutionary universalism also had prerevolutionary roots, for example, in the universalism of the Catholic Church. (The word *catholic,* in Latin etymology, means "universal.") In this sense, French universalism forms part of the more general process by which the Enlightenment secularized Christian tropes: the religiously connoted concept of "Providence," for example, was secularized as "Progress," and the Church became the State.

37. Cited in Judt, *Postwar,* 211.

38. Ibid., 760.

39. Alain Duhamel, *Le Désarroi Français* (Paris: Plon, 2003), 36.

40. See T.D. Allman, *Rogue State: America at War with the World* (New York: Nation Books, 2004), 316.

41. Quoted by Tony Judt, "A New Master Narrative? Reflections on Contemporary Anti-Americanism," in *With Us or Against Us: Studies in Global Anti-Americanism,* ed. Tony Judt and Denis Lacorne (New York: Macmillan, 2005), 25.

42. David Beriss, *Black Skins, French Voices* (Boulder, CO: Westview, 2004), 26.

43. These racist "human zoos" that exhibited natives, sometimes caged, were found in most of the colonizing countries. See our own *Unthinking Eurocentrism: Multiculturalism and the Media* (London: Routledge, 1994);

and Nicholas Bancel et al., eds., *Zoos Humains: Au Temps des Exhibitions Humaines* (Paris: La Découverte, 2002).

44. Alain Duhamel, *Les Peurs Françaises* (Paris: Flammarion, 1993), 243.

45. Guy Milliere, *Un Goût de Cendres ... France fin de Parcours?* (Paris: François-Xavier de Guibert, 2002).

46. Ibid., 14.

47. See Sunil Khilnani, *Arguing Revolution: The Intellectual Left in Postwar France* (New Haven, CT: Yale University Press, 1993), 176.

48. Marilena Chaui, *Brasil: Mito Fundadore Sociadade Autoilana* (São Paulo: Pesseu Abamo, 1996), 6.

49. See "85% Dizem Sentir Orgulho de ser Brasileiros," *Folha de São Paulo*, April 13, 2003, A13.

50. Lucia Lippi Oliveira, *Americanos: Representações da Identitdade Nacional no Brasil e nos EUA* (Belo Horizonte: UFMG, 2000), 362.

51. Cited in Eleonora Fabião, "Precarious, Precarious, Precarious: Performance and the Energetic of the Paradox" (PhD diss., New York University, 2006), 134.

52. Luiz Inacio (Lula) da Silva, inaugural address, *Folha de São Paulo*, Caderno Especial "Governo Lula," January 2, 2003.

53. Roberto da Matta, *O Que Faz o Brasil, Brasil?* (Rio de Janeiro: Roccco, 1994), 121–22.

54. Chaui, *Brasil*, 8.

55. Cristovam Buarque, "Titanic Negreiro," *O Globo*, April 3, 2003, 7.

Chapter 2

1. Philippe Roger, *The American Enemy* (Chicago: University of Chicago Press, 2005). All translations are our own, and the citations refer to page numbers in the English edition.

2. Ibid., 113.

3. Ibid., 205.

4. See Andrew Ross and Kristin Ross, eds., "Introduction," in *Anti-Americanism* (New York: NYU Press, 2004), 1.

5. Alexis de Nouailles, cited in Philippe Roger, *The American Enemy*, 211.

6. Émile Boutmy, cited in Philippe Roger, *The American Enemy*, 211.

7. Philippe Roger, *The American Enemy*, 215.

8. Ibid., 361.

9. Tony Judt, "A New Master Narrative? Reflections on Contemporary Anti-Americanism," in *With Us or Against Us: Studies in Global Anti-Americanism*, ed. Tony Judt and Denis Lacorne (New York: Macmillan, 2005), 22.

10. Philippe Roger, *The American Enemy*, 318.

11. See Richard Pells, *Not Like Us: How Europeans Have Loved, Hated, and Transformed American Culture since World War II* (New York: Basic Books, 1997), 57.

12. Judt, *With Us or Against Us,* 278.

13. Philippe Roger, *The American Enemy,* 334

14. The events of October 17, 1961, have become a major or background theme in a number of films, both documentaries (*Une Nuit Porte Disparue*) and fiction films, most notably Michael Haneke's *Caché.*

15. Philippe Roger, *The American Enemy,* 333.

16. Ibid., 374.

17. Jean Baudrillard, "The Spirit of Terrorism," *Le Monde,* November 2, 2001.

18. Philippe Roger, *The American Enemy,* 407.

19. Michael Crozier, "Remarques sur l'antiAmericanisme des Français," in *L'Amérique des Français,* ed. Faure and Bishops, (Paris: François Bourin, 1991) 191.

20. Quoted in Judt, *With Us or Against Us,* 353.

21. Régis Debray, *Vie et mort de l'image: une histoire du regard en Occident* (Paris: Gallimard, 1995).

22. This intra-European racialization forms a lateral version of what was earlier the top-down British racialization of the Irish, or for that matter the Victorian racialization of class, whereby the poor became virtually another "species."

23. J. Hector St. John de Crevecoeur, "Letters from an American Farmer, Describing Certain Provincial Situations, Manners, and Customs ... of the People of North America" (Philadelphia: Mathew Carey, 1793), 46–47. Quoted in Russell Shorto, *The Island at the Center of the World* (New York: Doubleday, 2004), 313.

24. See Russell Shorto, *The Island at the Center of the World.*

25. See ibid., 125.

26. Hipolito da Costa Pereira, *Diario de Minha Viagem para Filadelfia 1798–1799* (Rio de Janeiro: Academia Brasileira de Letras, 1955), 155.

27. Thomas Skidmore, *Brazil: Five Centuries of Change* (Oxford: Oxford University Press, 1999), 32.

28. See Henry M. Brackenridge, *Voyage to South America, Performed by Order of the American Government in the Years 1817 and 1818, in the Frigate Congress,* 2 vols. (London: John Miller, 1820), Vol. 1, 128–29. Cited in Denis Rolland, ed., *Le Brésil et le Monde* (Paris: L'Harmattan, 1998), 25–26.

29. Ibid.

30. See Frank McCann, "Le Brésil et les Etats-Unis: des Relations Complexes a l'épreuve du long terme, XIXe and Xxe Siècles," in *Le Brésil et le Monde,* ed. Rolland, 28.

31. See Thomas Skidmore, *O Brasil Visto de Fora* (São Paulo: Paz e Terra, 2001), 34–35.

32. See Moniz Bandeira, *Presença dos Estados Unidos no Brasil* (Rio: Civilização Brasileira, 1973), 95.

33. Quoted in ibid., 96. Translation ours.

34. Muniz Sodre, drawing on Gilberto Freyre, gives a possible explanation for Prado's anti-American resentment, rooted in a traumatic experience. Freyre

points out that Prado had an unhappy experience in an elegant barber shop in the United States, where the very *moreno* Prado was barred because he was, in Freyre's formulation, "mistakenly taken as Negroid." The incident points to the instability of race in the Americas, where an Anglophile Brazilian aristocrat suffers racism in the United States, where black activists from the United States are told in Latin America that they "do not look black," and where one's racial categorization varies with location, status, and accent.

35. See Antonio Pedro Tota, *O Imperialismo Sedutor: A Americanização do Brasil na Epoca da Segunda Guerra* (São Paulo: Companhia das Letras, 2000).

36. See Frank McCann, cited in *Le Brésil et le Monde,* ed. Rolland, 47.

37. At the same time, Brazil, like the United States, has a different relation to the grand calamities of the European twentieth century. The peoples of the Americas have no world wars or Jewish Holocaust for which they feel responsible or that they are eager to forget, and therefore they have no need to displace guilt for these catastrophes.

38. See Caetano Veloso, *Verdade Tropical* (São Paulo: Companhia das Letras, 1997), 14.

39. The thesis strikes us as somewhat implausible, not because the Bush administration is incapable of spectacular mendacity but rather because it is not clear why the American government could foster an attack on the central symbols of its own power, both military and economic, in a situation where it could not possibly have been clear how such an attack would play out. Furthermore, there is more and more evidence (from Richard Clarke's book and from the bipartisan 9/11 Commission) that the Bush administration was completely uninterested in and unprepared for terrorists attacks within the United States, a fact that has now become an embarrassment for the administration. The attacks might have triggered a revolt against a massively expensive military establishment that had failed to protect American citizens; it was not at all foreordained that the attacks would redound to the favor of George Bush. A massive media campaign was required to channel grief and mourning into feelings of revenge and a desire for war. That said, 9/11 did provide the neocons with the perfect "Pearl Harbor" alibi to go to war.

40. One wonders if Boff applauded all the al Qaeda–inspired bombings—in Bali, Egypt, Saudi Arabia—or only the ones directed against the United States.

41. One index of anti-Americans in Brazil is that sympathetic American lecturers in Brazil are often introduced as words to the effect that "our speaker is American, but he is all right, not pro-Bush, not like the others." Other foreign lecturers, to our knowledge, are not so introduced.

42. McCann in *Le Brésil et le Monde,* ed. Rolland, 51.

43. An Italian Brazilian in Minas Gerais asks us nervously, "Will I be discriminated against in New York as a Latino?" "No one," we reassure him, "looks more normal than you in New York."

44. Here we find a partial parallelism to certain historical moments in the United States, when those who organized against racism were called "un-

American" or "outside agitators," with the difference that in the United States it was the right that made such charges and the so-called agitators were from the same country, while in Brazil both left and right have sometime used the argument that racism in Brazil was an American invention.

45. See Simon Serfaty, *La France Vue par Les Etats-Unis: Réflexions sur la Francophobie a Washington* (Paris: Centre Francaise sur Les Etats-Unis, 2001), 15–16.

46. Dave Barry, "The U.S. and France Must Kiss and Make Up," *International Herald Tribune,* March 15–16, 2003, 19.

47. Centuries later, Bill Clinton notes that because his ancestry goes back to the Louisiana Territories, he is eligible to run as president of France.

48. See William Doyle, *The French Revolution: A Very Short Introduction* (Oxford: Oxford University Press, 2001), 20.

49. See Patrice Higgonet, *Paris: Capital of the World* (Cambridge, MA: Harvard University Press, 2002), 323.

50. Tyler Stovall, *Paris Noir: African Americans in the City of Light* (New York: Houghton Mifflin, 1996), xii.

51. There are a number of possible explanations for this apparent paradox: (1) the U.S. situation was so bad for blacks that even a relatively less racist society was a relief; (2) French people were treating black Americans as Americans rather than as blacks; (3) black intellectuals from the Caribbean were moving from a subtly racist black-majority society to becoming a victimized minority in France, while black Americans were a minority in both the United States and France; (4) French racism (at least in France) was directed less at blacks than at Arabs/Muslims; and (5) as strangers to French culture, black Americans might not always recognize the signs of prejudice.

52. Stovall, *Paris Noir,* 90.

53. Cited in Brent Hayes Edwards, *The Practice of Diaspora: Literature, Translation, and the Rise of Black Internationalism* (Cambridge, MA: Harvard University Press, 2003), 6.

54. Roger Cohen, "France vs. U.S.," *New York Times,* October 20, 1997, A10.

55. Quoted in Thomas Frank, *One Market under God: Extreme Capitalism, Market Populism, and the End of Economic Democracy* (New York: Random House, 2000), 75.

56. If there is any grain of truth in the comparison between anti-Semitism and anti-Americanism, it has to do not with a common victimization—since the United States is definitely not a victim—but rather, perhaps, with common processes of neurotic projection and scapegoating ("they" control everything; it's all a sinister plot, etc.). But otherwise the comparison is obscene and reflects only the extent to which the thinking of some Zionists sees American and Israeli interests as identical.

57. A General Assembly vote (144 to 4) condemned Israel's construction of the wall of separation from the Palestinians, the latter consisting of a microcoalition of the United States, Israel, Micronesia, and Melanesia.

58. See Denis Lacorne, "L'ecartelement de l'homme atlantique," in Christine Faure and Tom Bishop, eds., *L'Amérique des Français*, (Paris: François Bourin, 1992).

59. See Frank Costigliola, *France and the United States: The Cold Alliance since World War II* (New York: Twayne, 1992), 3.

60. Ibid., 40.

61. As cited in "Francophobia.com," www.tfl.fr, February 12, 2003.

62. Dinesh D'Souza, *What's So Great about America* (London: Penguin, 2002), 16.

63. We thank Jessica Scarlatta for pointing out the religious dimension of the Anglo-French rivalry.

64. Costigliola, op. cit., 86.

65. Ibid., 86.

66. Robert Kagan, *Of Paradise and Power: America and Europe in the New World Order* (New York: Knopf, 2003).

67. See Charles A. Kupchan, *The End of the American Era: U.S. Foreign Policy and the Geopolitics of the Twenty-first Century* (New York: Knopf, 2003).

68. It is not only the right-wing press that has been attacking France. Roger Cohen, a onetime *New York Times* correspondent in France, consistently mocked France for not joining the globalization bandwagon, ridiculing them for clinging to their universal health care, their paid vacations, and their unemployment insurances, as if that was the most irrational choice in the world.

69. See Clementine Wallace, "Saying Non to Rupert," *Extra,* July/August 2003.

70. Michael Moore, "Carta a George W. Bush," *O Globo,* March 21, 2003, 9.

Chapter 3

1. See Régis Debray, *La République expliquée a ma Fille* (The Republic Explained to My Daughter) (Paris: Seuil, 1998).

2. Ibid., 8–9.

3. For an excellent study of the relation between the Christian right and the Bush administration, see Esther Kaplan, *With God on Their Side: George W. Bush and the Christian Right* (New York: New Press, 2005).

4. See Blandine Chelini-Pont and Jeremy Gunn, *Dieu en France et aux Etats-Unis: Quand les Mythes Font la Loi* (Paris: Berg, 2005), 33.

5. Ibid., 33.

6. Eric Foner, *The Story of American Freedom* (New York: Norton, 1998), 27.

7. Quoted in Barry Rubin and Judith Colp Rubin, *Hating America* (Oxford: Oxford University Press, 2004), 48.

8. Quoted in Alan Dershowitz, *America Declares Independence* (Hoboken: John Wiley, 2003), 18.

9. Ibid., 59.

10. See Georges Corm, *Orient-Occident, La Fracture Imaginaire* (Paris: La Découverte, 2002), 123.

11. Quoted in Howard Zinn, *Passionate Declarations: Essays on War and Justice* (New York: Harper Collins, 2003), 231.

12. There is a danger here of confusing two order of phenomena; that is, (1) the common situation where free blacks purchased the freedom of enslaved blacks and (2) the less common situation where free blacks bought slaves.

13. See Angela de Castro Gomes, "Venturas e Desventuras de uma Republica de Cidadoas," in *Ensino de Historia: Conceitos, Tematicas, e Metodologia,* ed. Martha Abreu and Rachel Soihet (Rio de Janeiro: Faperj, 1998), 153.

14. It is impossible to mention here all the important Brazilian scholarship on these issues. The following are only a few important works: the eleven-volume study by Boris Fausto, org., *Historia Geral da Civilização Brasileira* (São Paulo: Dife, 1960–84); Francisco Iglesias, *Trajetoria Politica do Brasil* (São Paulo: Companhia das Letras, 1993); Maria Yedda Linhares, org., *Historia Geral do Brasil* (Rio de Janeiro: Campus, 2000); Florestan Fernandes, *A Revolução Burguesa do Brasil* (Rio de Janeiro: Zahar, 1975); Carlos Hasenbalg, *Discriminação e Desigualdades Raciais no Brasil* (Rio de Janeiro: Graal, 1979); Wanderley Guilherme dos Santos, *Cidadania e Justiça* (Rio de Janeiro: Campus, 1979); Jose Eduardo Faria, *Direito e Justiça* (São Paulo: Atica, 1989); Dulce Pandolfi et al., *Cidadania, Justiçã e Violencia* (Rio de Janeiro: Fundação G. Vargas, 1999); and José Murilo de Carvalho, *Cidadania no Brasil: O Longo Caminho* (Rio de Janeiro: Civilização Brasileira, 2002).

15. Maria Celia Paoli and Vera da Silva Telles, "Social Rights: Conflicts and Negotiations in Contemporary Brazil," in *Cultures of Politics, Politics of Culture: Re-visioning Latin American Social Movements,* ed. Sonia E. Alvarez et al. (Boulder, CO: Westview, 1998), 64.

16. Roberto Kant de Lima, "Bureaucratic Rationality in Brazil and the United States," in *The Brazilian Puzzle: Culture on the Borderlands of the Western World,* ed. David J. Hess and Roberto da Matta (New York: Columbia University Press, 1995), 245–46.

17. See George Yudice, *The Expediency of Culture* (Durham, NC: Duke, 2004), 179.

18. See Paul Chevigny, *Edge of the Knife: Police Violence in the Americas* (New York: New Press, 1995).

19. Since "total information awareness" is roughly synonymous with "divine omniscience," one wonders why the Christian right did not denounce the project as blasphemous and idolatrous.

20. William Doyle, *The French Revolution: A Very Short Introduction* (Oxford: Oxford University Press, 2001), 105.

21. Sunil Khilnani, *Arguing Revolution: The Intellectual Left in Postwar France* (New Haven, CT: Yale University Press, 1993), 162.

22. Alain Joxe, *L'Empire du Chaos* (The Empire of Chaos) (Paris: La Découverte, 2004.)

23. Joxe finds republican internationalism in Robespierre's idea that "men of all countries are brothers and that different peoples should aid each other according to their ability in the same way that the members of the same state do." In Robespierre's position, Joxe sees a missed opportunity for the justification of international aid and generosity and the elimination of the debt of the poor nations. Those who oppress any nation, for Robespierre, were the enemy of all nations. This principle can easily be abused, of course, as in the case of "humanitarian interventions," where claims (and often the reality) of oppression and a professed desire to "spread democracy" become a pretext for unilateral actions whose purposes go beyond the humanitarian.

24. From "The Papers of James Madison," quoted in Cass R. Sunstein, *Why Does the American Constitution Lack Social and Economic Guarantees?* in Michael Ignatieff, ed., *American Exceptionalism and Human Rights* (Princeton, NJ: Princeton University Press, 2005), 96.

25. Letter to George Logan, quoted in Frances Moore Lappe, *Democracy's Edge* (San Francisco: John Wiley, 2006), 22.

26. Ibid., 65.

27. From "The Papers of James Madison," quoted in Sunstein, *Why Does the American Constitution Lack Social and Economic Guarantees?* in Ignatieff, ed., *American Exceptionalism*, 96.

28. Ibid., 96.

29. Cited in Charles Derber, *Regime Change Begins at Home: Freeing Americans from Corporate Rule* (San Francisco: Berret-Koehler, 2004), 6.

30. See Foner, *The Story of American Freedom*, 19–20.

31. Ibid., 20.

32. Daniel Lazare, *The Frozen Republic: How the Constitution Is Paralyzing Democracy*, (New York, Harcourt Brace & Company, 1996), 2.

33. Ibid., 213.

34. Nicholas Kristoff, "A Health Care Disaster," *New York Times*, September 25, 2005.

35. See Jean-Benoit Nadeau and Julie Barlow, *Sixty Million Frenchmen Can't Be Wrong* (Naperville, IL: Sourcebooks, 2003), 255.

36. See Jonathon Kozol, *The Shame of the Nation: The Restoration of Apartheid Schooling in America* (New York: Crown, 2005).

37. Cited in Frances Moore Lappe, *Democracy's Edge*, 58.

38. Ibid., 70–81.

39. See Jacob S. Hacker and Paul Pierson, "The Center No Longer Holds," *New York Times Magazine*, November 20, 2005.

40. For an eloquent denunciation of market fundamentalism, see Thomas Frank, *One Market under God: Extreme Capitalism, Market Populism, and the End of Economic Democracy* (New York: Anchor, 2000).

41. See Gary Wills, *A Necessary Evil: A History of American Distrust of Government* (New York: Simon and Schuster, 2002), 21.

42. Timothy B. Smith, *France in Crisis: Welfare, Inequality and Globalization since 1980* (Cambridge: Cambridge University Press, 2004), xi.

Chapter 4

1. Quoted in Neil Smith, *The Endgame of Globalization* (London: Routledge, 2004), 82.

2. Quoted in David Harvey, *A Brief History of NeoLiberalism* (New York: Oxford, 2005), 183.

3. See John Powers, *Sore Winners* (New York: Doubleday, 2004), 154.

4. Todd Gitlin makes this point in relation to both C. Wright Mills and Daniel Bell in his *The Intellectuals and the Flag* (New York: Columbia, 2006), 39.

5. If our experience with students is any guide, it is recent immigrants from Asia and the Caribbean who demonstrate more commitment to the "work ethic" than some Euro-Americans.

6. Samuel P. Huntington, *Who Are We?: The Challenges to America's National Identity* (New York: Simon and Schuster, 2004).

7. Samuel P. Huntington, *The Clash of Civilizations and the Remaking of World Order* (New York: Simon and Schuster, 1996).

8. The so-called expert on Latinos and world cultural clashes seemed to reach for his simultaneous translation headphones whenever the participants spoke French or Spanish. Perhaps we are asking too much, and perhaps Huntington was hiding his intimate knowledge of these languages, but shouldn't experts on Latinos speak Spanish? And shouldn't those who pontificate about worldwide "clashes of cultures" know at least French, historically a key diplomatic language? Could it be that Harvard is lowering its standards in the name of antimulticulturalism?

9. See Seymour Martin Lipset, *American Exceptionalism: A Double-Edged Sword* (New York: W. W. Norton & Company, 1996), 63.

10. See "Christo-fascism": David Neiwert, "Rush, Newspeak, and Fascism," at Orcinus, http://www.cursor.org/stories/fascismintroduction.php (posted August 30, 2003). See also Mark Crispin Miller's invaluable *Cruel and Unusual: Bush/Cheney's New World Order* (New York: Norton, 2004), esp. 251–91.

11. See Thomas Frank, *What's the Matter with Kansas: How Conservatives Won the Heart of America* (New York: Henry Holt, 2004), 16.

12. Cited Esther Kaplan, "Follow the Money," *The Nation,* November 1, 2004, 1–2.

13. See Jim Wallis, *God's Politics: Why the Right Gets It Wrong and the Left Doesn't Get It* (San Francisco: HarperCollins, 2005).

14. See Mahmood Mamdani, *Good Muslim, Bad Muslim* (New York: Pantheon, 2004), 25–26.

15. The situation is analogous, in some ways, to that where some anti-Zionist Arab or Muslim intellectuals begin to reject all Jews as Zionists, thus becoming more Zionist than the Zionists by endorsing the Zionist equation of all Jews with Zionists.

16. See Tony Judt, "A New Master Narrative," in *With Us or Against Us: Studies in Global Anti-Americanism,* ed. Tony Judt and Denis Lacorne (New York: Macmillan, 2005), 24.

17. See Jean Delumeau, *La Peur en Occident* (Paris: Hachette, 2003).

18. Quoted in Thomas Bender, *A Nation among Nations: America's Place in World History* (New York: Hill and Wang, 2006), 189.

19. Ibid., 190–91.

20. See Greg Grandin, *Empire's Workshop: Latin America, the United States, and the Rise of the New Imperialism* (New York: Metropolitan Books, 2006), 20.

21. We use the word *subaltern* here not in the sense of "oppressed" but rather in Gramsci's original sense of intermediate military ranking.

22. See "A L'ONU, La France s'oppose a la création d'une Cour Criminelle Internationale," *Le Monde,* September 6, 1996.

23. See Nicolas Bancel, Pascal Blanchard, and Françoise Verges, *La République coloniale* (Paris: Albin Michel), 11.

24. See François-Xavier Verschave, *Françafrique: le plus long scandale de la république* (Paris: Stock, 1998). Statement from the Franco-African summit of Biarritz in November 1994, cited in Verschave, 333.

25. Ibid., 65.

26. See interview with Jean Carbonare in *Le Nouvel Observateur,* August 4, 1994.

27. See Verschave, *La FrancAfrique,* 26.

28. See Patrick de Saint-Exupéry, *L'inavouable: la France au Rwanda* (Paris: Arènes, 2004), 287–88. At this point there is fairly vast literature on French complicity in the genocide in Rwanda. See, for example, Mehdi Ba, *1994: Un Génocide Français* (Paris : Esprit, 1997); Jean-Paul Goûteux, *Un Génocide Secret d'Etat* (Paris: Editions Sociales, 1998); François-Xavier Verschave, *Complicité de Génocide?* (Paris: La Découverte, 1994); and Dominique Franche, *Généalogie d'un Génocide* (Paris: Mille et Une Nuits, 1997).

29. Patrick de Saint-Exupéry, *L'inavouable,* 287–88.

30. Ibid., 185.

31. See Marie-Monique Robin, *Escadrons de la Mort, Ecole Francaise* (Paris: La Decouverte, 2004).

32. Jan Nederveen Pieterse, "Hyperpower Exceptionalism: Globalization the American Way," *New Political Economy* 8, no. 3 (2003): 140.

33. The parodic equivalent of Duclos's kind of essentialist thinking would be to characterize France as an "essentially cannibal" nation. Here one could cite as "proof" the cave paintings that show evidence of literal cannibalism in the early period, followed by the religious cannibalism of the St. Bartholomew's Day Massacre or the social cannibalism of the French court—here the film *Ridicule* could be marshaled as evidence—moving on to the anti-Semitic

cannibalism of Vichy, to the gastronomic cannibalism of *Delicatessen*. But what, apart from a frisson of narcissistic aggression, is to be gained by such simplistic portraiture?

34. See Allan Gallay, *The Indian Slave Trade: The Rise of the English Empire in the American South, 1670–1717* (New Haven, CT: Yale University Press, 2002).

35. See Amin Maalouf, *In the Name of Identity: Violence and the Need to Belong* (New York: Penguin, 2000), 50.

36. See "Réflexions: Faut-il avais Peur de l'Amérique?" *Le Nouvel Observateur,* July 8, 2004, no. 2070.

37. From the Mark Twain story "The Mysterious Stranger," quoted in Howard Zinn, *Passionate Declarations: Essays on War and Justice* (New York: Harper and Collins, 2003), 74.

38. A. Lieven, "The Push to War," quoted in Alex Callinicos, *The New Mandarins of American Power* (Cambridge, UK: Polity Press, 2003), 54.

39. See Niall Ferguson, "Welcome to the New Imperialism," *The Guardian,* October 21, 2001.

40. Dana Priest, "The Mission," quoted in Callinicos, *The New Mandarins of American Power,* 99–100.

41. See Lewis H. Lapham, *Gag Rule: On the Suppression of Dissent and the Stifling of Democracy* (New York: Penguin, 2004), 141.

42. See Régis Debray, "Confessions d'un Anti-Américain," in *L'Amérique des Français,* ed. Christine Faure and Tom Bishop (Paris: François Bourin, 1992).

43. Pew Research Center for the People and the Press, statistics cited in Gar Alperovitz, *America beyond Capitalism* (Hoboken, NJ: John Wiley, 2005), 192.

Chapter 5

1. See David Brock, *The Republican Noise Machine: Right-wing Media and How It Corrupts Democracy* (New York: Crown Publishers, 2004).

2. See Molly Ivins, "I Will Not Support Hillary Clinton for President," January 29, 2006, www.freepress.org/columns/display/1/2006/1304.com.

3. For a brilliant analysis of this process, see Jacob S. Hacker and Paul Pierson, "The Center No Longer Holds," *New York Times Magazine,* November 20, 2005.

4. Cultural critic Slavoj Žižek points to a historical inversion. While the conservatives used to do the tough jobs for the liberals—the conservatives installed the welfare state to save capitalism—now the social democratic liberals do the tough jobs for the conservatives; that is, they help dismantle the welfare state, push privatization and globalization, and so forth. See Slavoj Žižek, *Iraq: The Borrowed Kettle* (London: Verso, 2004), 70.

5. Take, for example, the chastity debate. Republicans promote chastity among young people, as opposed to sexual education and birth control. The

Democrats' response? They agree that chastity is preferable, but because kids will have sex anyway, they should have condoms available. Does no one have the courage to say that consensual sex is wonderful, that it is a crime to stunt young people's sexuality, that sex is a necessity like eating, and that it is a means of communication like language? Of course sex can be dangerous, just as eating can lead to food poisoning and communication can lead to arguments. But does anyone say that it is better not to eat (because they will eat anyway, they should have food ready anyway) or that it is better not to communicate?

6. See "Urgent Appeal to Save Iraq's Academics," http://new.petitiononline.com/Iraqacad/petiton/html.

7. Taken from Ward Sutton's "Dude, Where's My Party?" *Village Voice*, February 1, 2006, 8.

8. Joel Bakan, *The Corporation: The Pathological Pursuit of Profit and Power* (New York: Free Press, 2004), 134.

9. See Frank Rich, "Truthiness 101: From Frey to Alito," *New York Times*, January 22, 2006.

10. Thomas Frank, *What's the Matter with Kansas: How Conservatives Won the Heart of America* (New York: Henry Holt, 2004), 8.

11. William E. Odom and Robert Dujarric, *America's Inadvertent Empire* (New Haven, CT: Yale University Press, 2004), 213.

12. See Mark Crispin Miller, *Fooled Again* (New York: Basic Books, 2005).

13. Quoted in Richard Leone and Greg Anrig Jr., eds., *The War on Our Freedoms: Civil Liberties in the Age of Terrorism* (New York: Century Foundation, 2003), 72.

14. Quoted in Žižek, *Iraq: The Borrowed Kettle*, 1.

15. Many of these images were easier to see abroad then in the United State. We saw them in the Brazilian journal *Pasquim*.

16. Molly Ivins, we recall, once told the story of two Texas legislators who sponsored and passed a bill forbidding sodomy in Texas. When they celebrated their victory with a high five, another legislator, a critic of the bill, informed them that they had just violated their own law. "What law?" they asked. Answer: "The law that says a prick is not supposed to touch an asshole."

17. "The White House Stages its Daily Show," *New York Times*, February 20, 2005.

18. See Robert Fisk, "The U.S. military and its cult of cruelty," *The Independent*, September 16, 2006.

19. In the 1950s literary critic Leslie Fiedler pointed out in *Love and Death in the American Novel* that while the European novel of initiation centered on sexual initiation (the "sentimental education"), American novels tended to center on an initiation into violence.

20. Justin A. Frank, *Bush on the Couch: Inside the Mind of the President* (New York: HarperCollins, 2004), 118.

21. Examples of right-wing cruelty abound, giving us a glimpse into the creepy right-wing mind-set. Britt Hulme, managing editor of FOX News, for example, responded to the terrorist bombings in London with the following gem of free association: "My first thought—just on a personal basis—when I

heard there had been this attack, and I saw the futures this morning, which were really in the tank, I thought, Hmmm. Time to buy." Another intriguing example was the visit of another FOX anchor, Chris Wallace, to the *Daily Show*. Wallace kept trying to needle Stewart about the fact that one of the former correspondents on the *Daily Show* had made a film that became the number-one box office hit. The assumption was that the only possible reaction on Stewart's part could be envy and irritation, not pleasure in his friend's success. The audience ended up booing Wallace for not getting this point.

22. Michael Rogin, *Ronald Reagan: The Movie* (Berkeley: University of California Press, 1987), xxi.

23. See Joe Conason, *Big Lies* (New York: St. Martin's, 2003), 200.

24. See Nicholas Kristof, "Revolving-Door Master," *New York Times*, October 11, 2002, A33. Commentators have also pointed to earlier Bush links to the Taliban and bin Laden's family and even to the uncanny parallels between George Bush and Osama bin Laden as two rich and spoiled playboys linked to Middle Eastern oil who became religious late in life, who claimed a mandate from God, and who were ready to kill in the name of their fundamentalist beliefs.

25. See T.D. Allman, *Rogue State: America at War with the World* (New York: Nation Books, 2004), 99. See also Antonia Juhasn, *The Bush Agenda: Invading the World, One Economy at a Time* (New York: Harper Collins, 2006).

26. Quoted in Mark Danner, "The Logic of Torture," *New York Review of Books*, June 24, 2004, 71.

27. Carl Bogg's "Introduction" to Carl Boggs, ed., *Masters of War: Militarism and Blowback in the Era of American Empire* (London: Routledge, 2003), 7.

28. Andrew J. Bacevich, *The New American Militarism: How Americans are Seduced by War* (Oxford: Oxford University Press, 2005), 223.

29. Quoted in Chalmers Johnson, *The Sorrows of Empire* (New York: Henry Holt, 2004), 44–45.

30. Bacevich, *The New American Militarism*, 209.

31. Chris Hedges, *What Every Person Should Know about War* (New York: Free Press, 2003), 3.

32. Cited in Harold Bloom, "Reflections in the Evening Land," *Guardian*, December 17, 2005.

33. Quoted in Johnson, *The Sorrows of Empire*, 85–86.

34. See Charles Krauthammer, "The Bush Doctrine," *Time*, March 5, 2001.

35. See Johnson, *The Sorrows of Empire*.

36. Ibid., 58.

37. Michael Parenti, "The Logic of U.S. Intervention," in *Masters of War*, 24–25.

38. See Maureen Dowd, "Vice Axes That 70's Show," *New York Times*, December 28, 2005, A19.

39. Neil Smith, *The Endgame of Globalization* (London: Routledge, 2004), 180.

40. Quoted in Lewis H. Lapham, *Gag Rule: On the Suppression of Dissent and the Stifling of Democracy* (New York: Penguin, 2004), 71–72.

41. See Ralph Peters, "Constant Conflict," *Parameters*, Summer 1997, 4–14: US Army War College, see http://www.informationclearinghouse.info/article3011.htm

42. See William D. Hartung, *How Much Are You Making on the War, Daddy?* (New York: Nation Books, 2003), xxiii.

43. The same racist channeling of empathy operated toward the Vietnamese. Politicians still speak of the fifty-five thousand Americans who died there, yet we seldom hear about the more than two million dead Vietnamese. Even today as the "Swift Boat Veteran" attack ads made clear, it is virtually taboo to say that the Vietnam War was marked by innumerable atrocities. (Fortunately, the film *Winter Soldier*, an account of testimonials by American soldiers concerning the atrocities they committed or witnessed, is now being rereleased.) But the fact is that all imperial wars—the Dutch in Indonesia, the British in Kenya, the French in Algeria, and both the French and the Americans in Vietnam—have entailed atrocities against the "natives." The unleashing of powerful armies on civilians in relatively poor and weak countries does not lead to atrocities; it is by definition an atrocity. But to appreciate that fact, we have to imagine a country invading us that is fifty times more powerful than we are.

44. Quoted in Mark Danner, "Torture and Truth," in the collectively edited *Abu Ghraib: The Politics of Torture* (Berkeley, CA: North Atlantic Books, 2004), 4.

45. See Nina Bernstein, "Once Tortured, Now Tormented by Photos," *New York Times*, May 15, 2004.

46. "Questions for Trent Lott," *New York Times Magazine*, June 20, 2004, 15.

47. From the White House tapes, quoted in Norman Solomon, *War Made Easy: How Presidents and Pundits Keep Spinning Us to Death* (Hoboken, NJ: John Wiley, 2005), 39–40.

48. Cited in Jacob Hacker and Paul Pierson, *Off Center: The Republican Revolution and the Erosion of American Democracy* (New Haven: Yale University Press, 2005), 174.

49. Statistics cited in Frances Moore Lappe, *Democracy's Edge* (San Francisco: John Wiley, 2006), 225.

50. The billionaire Haroldson Lafayette Hunt, founder of the Hunt Oil Company, promoted right wing causes. For further information on Eisenhower's relations with Hunt, see L. Galambos, *Columbia University*, vol. X. See also "Eisenhower, Dwight D. Personal and confidential to Edgar Newton Eisenhower, 8 November 1954," in The Papers of Dwight David Eisenhower, ed. L. Galambos and D. van Ee, doc. 1147 (Baltimore, MD: Johns Hopkins University Press, 1996), http://www.eisenhowermemorial.org/presidential-papers/first-term/documents/1147.cfm (World Wide Web facsimile of the print edition by the Dwight D. Eisenhower Memorial Commission).

51. See James Stimson, *Public Opinion in America: Moods, Cycles, and Swings* (Boulder, CO: Westview, 1998).

52. While the media debate in the United States during the Iraq War was dominated by neocons, partisan hacks, and retired generals, the Brazilian media featured a wide range of academic experts on the Middle East (some of them Americans usually frozen out of the U.S. media).

53. See Mark Crispin Miller, "What's Wrong with this Picture," *Nation*, December 20, 2001.

54. See Paul Krugman, "Pride, Prejudice, Insurance," *New York Times*, November 7, 2005.

55. Jan Nederveen Pieterse, "Neoliberal Empire," *Theory, Culture, and Society* 21, no. 3 (2004).

Chapter 6

1. See editorial "America and Empire—Manifest Destiny Warmed Up?" *Economist*, August 14, 2003.

2. See Vine Deloria Jr. and David E. Wilkins, *Tribes, Treaties, and Constitutional Tribulations* (Austin: University of Texas Press, 1999), 70.

3. See Sean Teuton, "Internationalism and the Native American Scholar," in *Identity Politics Reconsidered*, ed. Linda Martin Alcoff et al. (New York: Palgrave, 2006), 268.

4. Cited in Raymond Williams, *Culture and Society, 1780–1850* (London: Chatto and Windus, 1958), 118.

5. Kenneth O'Reilly, in *Nixon's Piano: Presidents and Racial Politics from Washington to Clinton* (New York: Free Press, 1995), demonstrates that virtually all American presidents either were racist or made enormous concessions to racists.

6. Quoted in Eric Foner, *The Story of American Freedom* (New York: Norton, 1998), 173.

7. Quoted in Richard T. Hughes, *Myths America Lives By* (Urbana: University of Illinois Press, 2004), 120.

8. See Philip S. Foner, ed., *The Life and Writings of Frederick Douglass*, Vol. II (New York: International Publishers, 1950), 188–89.

9. See Mark Crispin Miller, "Preface" to *Cruel and Unusual: Bush/ Cheney's New World Order* (New York and London: Norton, 2005), xiii.

10. Ibid.

11. Cited in article in *New York Times*, November 15, 2005.

12. Joel Kovel, *The Enemy of Nature: The End of Capitalism or the End of the World?* (London: Zed, 2002), 110.

13. Si Kahn, cited in Si Kahn and Elizabeth Minnich, *The Fox and the Henhouse: How Privatization Threatens Democracy* (San Francisco: BK, 2005), 35.

14. Kovel, *The Enemy of Nature*, 21.

15. See Benedict Anderson, *Imagined Communities: Reflections on the Origins and Spread of Nationalism* (London: Verso, 1983).

16. See Ronald Brownstein, "Bush Breaks with 140 Years of History in Plan for Wartime Tax Cut," *Los Angeles Times*, January 13, 2003.

17. The right wing usually talks about health care when it is forced to, usually around election time and then only to undercut or upstage some Democratic proposal through some meaningless band-aid measure such as "slightly less expensive dental care for geriatrics" or "occasional prescription benefits for the sclerotic." When the issue of universal health care does come up, the right wing either changes the subject or demonizes the proposal as "socialist" or as an "antichoice government-run health program," scaring ordinary people by evoking some shadowy bureaucracy, forgetting that these same people are already overshadowed by Kafkaesque HMOs. The truth is that the right wing is terrified of the issue, because if the left managed to introduce universal health care, the popular gratitude would overwhelm the right's electoral possibilities for decades to come.

18. See, for example, *New York Times*, November 15, 2005, A22.

19. William Safire, "Seizing Dictatorial Power," *New York Times*, November 15, 2001, A31.

20. Lewis H. Lapham, *Gag Rule: On the Suppression of Dissent and the Stifling of Democracy* (New York: Penguin, 2004), 88.

21. Ibid., 156–57.

22. Anthony Lewis, "Security and Liberty: Preserving the Values of Freedom," in *The War on Our Freedoms: Civil Liberties in an Age of Terrorism*, ed. Richard C. Leone and Greg Anrig (New York: Century Foundation, 2003), 51.

23. Frances Moore Lappe, *Democracy's Edge* (San Francisco: John Wiley, 2006), 43–46. Parenthetically, we propose that the Democrats follow a new rule for their own public relations strategies: the "what would they have said had it been Clinton rule." The Democrats, in other words, should be as daring, but without lying, as the Republicans have been. For example, what if 9/11 had occurred on Clinton's watch? We all know what the Republicans would have said: "It's his fault!" "The blowjob weakened America!" "They attacked because Clinton opened up to the Arabs and the Palestinians!" "He was so paralyzed by Monicagate that they perceived a breach in security!" (The "rally around the flag effect" seems to work only when Republicans are in office.) What if Clinton had triggered an unnecessary war of choice against a country that was not a threat? We can imagine the cries: "Wag the Dog!" "He did it to distract attention from trouble at home!" What if it had been Clinton who had revealed war plans to an Arab prince before revealing them to his cabinet or Congress or the American people? One can already hear the cries of "Traitor!" "Arab lover!" "Impeachable offense!" "High crimes and misdemeanors!" What would they have said if Clinton had followed up on campaign claims of "trusting the people, not the government" by obsessive secrecy and a massive clamping down on dissent? "Free speech!" "Antidemocratic!" "Dictator!" And if American hostages were kidnapped and murdered under Clinton's watch? We remember the role of the hostage crisis in Jimmy Carter's loss to Ronald Reagan. But with Bush somehow it's all just something happening way

over there; the United States is not dishonored, and the president is not embarrassed, and meanwhile "We are safer in America."

24. For a summary of the report and more information, see Mark Crispin Miller, "None Dare Call It Stolen," *Harper's* 311, no. 1863 (2005).

25. Mark Crispin Miller, *Fooled Again*, 94.

26. Full disclosure: Robert Stam, not believing in the Vietnam War, served for two years in the Peace Corps, in Tunisia.

27. See Joe Conason, *Big Lies* (New York: St. Martin's, 2003), 67.

28. See Frank Rich, "The Mysterious Death of Pat Tillman," *New York Times*, November 6, 2005, WK12.

29. Alexis de Tocqueville, *Democracy in America*, trans. George Lawrence, ed. J.P. Mayer (New York: Doubleday, Anchor Books, 1969), 565, 536, 538.

30. See Katrin Bennhold, "Love of Leisure, and Europe's Reasons," *New York Times*, July 29, 2004, A10.

31. A symptomatic instance of this occurred on the *Daily Show*, when guest Chris Wallace from FOX News premised his humor on the idea that Stewart would automatically be jealous of the success of his former correspondent: "How did you feel, Jon, when you woke up and saw that your former correspondent, with *The Forty-Year-Old Virgin*, has the number one hit movie?" Wallace couldn't imagine that Stewart could be happy about his friend's success, for which Wallace was roundly booed. "We're actually not like you over at FOX," said Stewart.

32. And as teachers, we constantly hear undergraduate students preface the most banal claims with "in my personal opinion," apparently unaware that they are simply mouthing the commonplaces of the day.

33. Jeremy Rifkin, "The European Dream: The New Europe Has Its Own Cultural Vision," *Utne*, September–October, 2004.

34. The paradox of individualism is that the individualist individuals often sound exactly alike. As professors, we occasionally encounter student adherents of the Ayn Rand philosophy. The paradox is that their discourse is usually cookie-cutter identical. They all write that they "personally believe" that one has to "be one's own man," "follow one's own dreams," and so forth.

35. Kovel, *The Enemy of Nature*.

36. Ibid., 42.

37. Quoted in Kahn and Minnich, *The Fox and the Henhouse*, 160.

38. Even before the American Revolution, the Native Americans expressed amazement at how rude and interruptive Europeans were to one another.

39. See Maureen Dowd, "Looking for a Democratic Tough Guy or Girl," *New York Times*, January 18, 2006, A19.

40. Thomas Frank, *What's Wrong with Kansas?* (New York: Henry Holt, 2004), 68.

41. On the concept of critical utopias, see Tom Moylan, *Demand the Impossible: Science Fiction and the Utopian Imagination* (New York: Methuen, 1986).

Index